Communication and Cybernetics 10

Editors: K. S. Fu   W. D. Keidel   W. J. M. Levelt

Communication and Cybernetics

Editors: K. S. Fu, W. D. Keidel, W. J. M. Levelt

Digital Pattern Recognition

Edited by K. S. Fu

With Contributions by
T. M. Cover   E. Diday   K. S. Fu   A. Rosenfeld
J. C. Simon   T. J. Wagner   J. S. Weszka
J. J. Wolf

Second Corrected and Updated Edition

With 59 Figures

Springer-Verlag
Berlin Heidelberg New York 1980

Professor KING SUN FU, PhD

Purdue University, School of Electrical Engineering
West Lafayette, IN 47907, USA

Series Editor:

Professor KING SUN FU, PhD

Purdue University, School of Electrical Engineering
West Lafayette, IN 47907, USA

Professor Dr. WOLF DIETER KEIDEL

I. Physiologisches Institut der Universität Erlangen-Nürnberg
D-8520 Erlangen, Fed. Rep. of Germany

Professor Dr. Willem J. M. Levelt

Max-Planck-Institut für Psycholinguistik, Berg en Dalseweg 79
6522 BC Nijmegen, The Netherlands

ISBN 3-540-10207-8 2. Auflage Springer-Verlag Berlin Heidelberg New York
ISBN 0-387-10207-8 2nd edition Springer-Verlag New York Heidelberg Berlin

ISBN 3-540-07511-9 1. Auflage Springer-Verlag Berlin Heidelberg New York
ISBN 0-387-07511-9 1st edition Springer-Verlag New York Heidelberg Berlin

Library of Congress Cataloging in Publication Data. Main entry under title: Digital pattern recognition. (Communication and cybernetics; 10) Bibliography: p. Includes index. 1. Pattern perception. 2. Automatic speech recognition. I. Fu, King Sun, 1930-Q327.D53 1980 001.53'4 80-20377

Monophoto typesetting, offset printing, and book binding: Brühlsche Universitätsdruckerei, Giessen
2153/3130-543210

Preface to the Second Edition

Since its publication in 1976, the original volume has been warmly received. We have decided to put out this updated paperback edition so that the book can be more accessible to students. This paperback edition is essentially the same as the original hardcover volume except for the addition of a new chapter (Chapter 7) which reviews the recent advances in pattern recognition and image processing. Because of the limitations of length, we can only report the highlights and point the readers to the literature. A few typographical errors in the original edition were corrected.

We are grateful to the National Science Foundation and the Office of Naval Research for supporting the editing of this book as well as the work described in Chapter 4 and a part of Chapter 7.

West Lafayette, Indiana
March 1980   K. S. FU

Preface to the First Edition

During the past fifteen years there has been a considerable growth of interest in problems of pattern recognition. Contributions to the blossom of this area have come from many disciplines, including statistics, psychology, linguistics, computer science, biology, taxonomy, switching theory, communication theory, control theory, and operations research. Many different approaches have been proposed and a number of books have been published. Most books published so far deal with the decision-theoretic (or statistical) approach or the syntactic (or linguistic) approach. Since the area of pattern recognition is still far from its maturity, many new research results, both in theory and in applications, are continuously produced. The purpose of this monograph is to provide a concise summary of the major recent developments in pattern recognition.

The five main chapters (Chapter 2-6) in this book can be divided into two parts. The first three chapters concern primarily with basic techniques in pattern recognition. They include statistical techniques, clustering analysis and syntactic techniques. The last two chapters deal with applications; namely, picture recognition, and speech recognition and understanding. Each chapter is written by one or two distinguished experts on that subject. The editor has not attempted to impose upon the contributors to this volume a uniform notation and terminology, since such notation and terminology does not as yet exist in pattern recognition. Indeed, the diversity of the points of view, notation, and terminology in pattern recognition is a reflection of the fact that this area is in a state of rapid growth and changing orientation. We have not included a chapter on feature (and primitive) extraction and selection, primarily because of the fact that there has been very little major progress made during the last two or three years on this subject. There is no doubt that it is the authors of the individual chapters whose contributions made this volume possible. The editor wishes to express heartfelt thanks to the authors for their cooperation in its rapid completion.

West Lafayette, Indiana
June 1975   K. S. Fu

Contents

4. Syntactic (Linguistic) Pattern Recognition. By K. S. Fu (With 18 Figures)

5. Picture Recognition. By A. Rosenfeld and J. S. Weszka (With 17 Figures)

6. Speech Recognition and Understanding. By J. J. WOLF (With 6 Figures)

7. Recent Developments in Digital Pattern Recognition.
By K. S. FU, A. ROSENFELD, and J. J. WOLF (With 5 Figures)

Contributors

COVER, THOMAS M.
Stanford Electronics Laboratory, Stanford University,
Stanford, CA 94305, USA

DIDAY, EDWIN
Université de Paris IX, Avenue de Pologne,
F-75775 Paris Cedex 16

FU, KING SUN
Purdue University, School of Electrical Engineering,
West Lafayette, IN 47907, USA

ROSENFELD, AZRIEL
Picture Processing Laboratory, Computer Science Center, University of
Maryland, College Park, MD 20742, USA

SIMON, JEAN CLAUDE
Université de Paris VI, Institut de Programmation, Tours 55−56, 4 Place
Jussieu, F-75230 Paris Cedex 05

WAGNER, TERRY J.
University of Texas, Department of Electrical Engineering,
Austin, TX 78712, USA

WESZKA, JOAN S.
Picture Processing Laboratory, Computer Science Center, University of
Maryland, College Park, MD 20742, USA

WOLF, JARED J.
Bolt Beranek and Newman Inc., 50 Moulton Street,
Cambridge, MA 02138, USA

1. Introduction

K. S. Fu

With 2 Figures

1.1 What is Pattern Recognition?

The problem of pattern recognition usually denotes a discrimination or classification of a set of processes or events. The set of processes or events to be classified could be a set of physical objects or a set of mental states. The number of pattern classes is often determined by the particular application in mind. For example, consider the problem of English character recognition; we should have a problem of 26 classes. On the other hand, if we are interested in discriminating English characters from Russian characters, we have only a two-class problem. In some problems, the exact number of classes may not be known initially; and it may have to be determined from the observations of many representative patterns, In this case, we would like to detect the possibility of having new classes of patterns as we observe more and more patterns. Human beings perform the task of pattern recognition in almost every instant of their working lives. Recently, scientists and engineers started to use machines for pattern recognition.

An intuitively appealing approach for pattern recognition is the approach of "template-matching". In this case, a set of templates or prototypes, one for each pattern class, is stored in the machine. The input pattern (with unknown classification) is compared with the template of each class, and the classification is based on a preselected matching criterion or similarity criterion. In other words, if the input pattern matches the template of ith pattern class better than it matches any other templates, then the input is classified as from the ith pattern class. Usually, for the simplicity of the machine, the templates are stored in their raw-data form. This approach has been used for some existing printed-character recognizers and bank-check readers. The disadvantage of the template-matching approach is that it is, sometimes, difficult to select a good template from each pattern class, and to define a proper matching criterion. The difficulty is especially remarkable when large variations and distortions are expected in all the patterns belonging to one class. Recently, the use of flexible template matching or "rubber-mask" techniques has been proposed, see [1.20, 21].

1.2 Approaches to Pattern Recognition

The many different mathematical techniques used to solve pattern recognition problems may be grouped into two general approaches; namely, the *decision-theoretic* (or *statistical*) *approach* and the *syntactic* (or *linguistic*) *approach*. In the decision-theoretic approach, a set of characteristic measurements, called features,

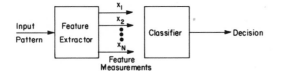

Fig. 1.1. A pattern recognition system

are extracted from the patterns; the recognition of each pattern (assignment to a pattern class) is usually made by partitioning the feature space [1.1]. Most of the developments in pattern recognition research during the past decade deal with the decision-theoretic approach [1.1–18]. Applications include character recognition, crop classification, medical diagnosis, classification of electrocardiograms, etc.

In the decision-theoretic approach, instead of simply matching the input pattern with the templates, the classification is based on a set of selected measurements, extracted from the input pattern. These selected measurements, called "features", are supposed to be invariant or less sensitive with respect to the commonly encountered variations and distortions, and also containing less redundancies. Under this proposition, pattern recognition can be considered as consisting of two subproblems. The first subproblem is what measurements should be taken from the input patterns. Usually, the decision of what to measure is rather subjective and also dependent on the practical situations (for example, the availability of measurements, the cost of measurements, etc.). Unfortunately, at present, there is very little general theory for the selection of feature measurements. However, there are some investigations concerned with the selection of a subset and the ordering of features in a given set of measurements. The criterion of feature selection or ordering is often based on either the importance of the features in characterizing the patterns or the contribution of the features to the performance of recognition (i.e., the accuracy of recognition).

The second subproblem in pattern recognition is the problem of classification (or making a decision on the class assignment to the input patterns) based on the measurements taken from the selected features. The device or machine which extracts the feature measurements from input patterns is called a feature extractor. The device or machine which performs the function of classification is called a classifier. A simplified block diagram of a pattern recognition system is shown in Fig. 1.1 [1]. Thus, in general terms, the template-matching approach may be interpreted as a special case of the second approach—"feature-extraction" approach where the templates are stored in terms of feature measurements and a special classification criterion (matching) is used for the classifier.

In some pattern recognition problems, the structural information which describes each pattern is important, and the recognition process includes not only the capability of assigning the pattern to a particular class (to classify it), but also the capacity to describe aspects of the pattern which make it ineligible for assignment to another class. A typical example of this class of recognition problem is picture recognition or more generally speaking, scene analysis. In this class of recognition problems, the patterns under consideration are usually quite complex

---

[1] The division into two parts is primarily for convenience rather than necessity.

and the number of features required is often very large which makes the idea of describing a complex pattern in terms of a (hierarchical) composition of simpler subpatterns very attractive. Also, when the patterns are complex and the number of possible descriptions is very large, it is impractical to regard each description as defining a class (for example, in fingerprint and face identification problems, recognition of continuous speech, Chinese characters, etc.). Consequently, the requirement of recognition can only be satisfied by a description for each pattern rather than the simple task of classification. In order to represent the hierarchical (tree-like) structural information of each pattern, that is, a pattern described in terms of simpler subpatterns and each simpler subpattern again be described in terms of even simpler subpatterns, etc., the *syntactic* or *structural approach* has been proposed [1.19].

After a very brief summary of some basic pattern recognition methods in this chapter[2] a review of recent progress in both the decision-theoretic approach and the syntactic approach is presented. In the decision-theoretic approach, statistical methods and cluster analysis are discussed. In addition, picture recognition and speech recognition and understanding are included in this volume to demonstrate general applications of pattern recognition methods to the processing of one-dimensional speech signals and two-dimensional pictorial patterns.

1.3 Basic Non-Parametric Decision— Theoretic Classification Methods

The concept of pattern classification may be expressed in terms of the partition of feature space (or a mapping from feature space to decision space). Suppose that N features are to be measured from each input pattern. Each set of N features can be considered as a vector X, called a feature (measurement) vector, or a point in the N-dimensional feature space Ω_X. The problem of classification is to assign each possible vector or point in the feature space to a proper pattern class. This can be interpreted as a partition of the feature space into mutually exclusive regions, and each region will correspond to a particular pattern class. Mathematically, the problem of classification can be formulated in terms of "discriminant functions". Let $\omega_1, \omega_2, \ldots, \omega_m$ be designated as the m possible pattern classes to be recognized, and let

$$X = \begin{bmatrix} x_1 \\ x_2 \\ \vdots \\ x_N \end{bmatrix} \tag{1.1}$$

be the feature (measurement) vector where x_i represents the ith feature measurement. Then the discriminant function $D_j(X)$ associated with pattern class ω_j,

---

[2] For more extensive discussions of existing pattern recognition methods and their applications, refer to [1.1–19 and 1.23–27].

$j=1,\ldots,m$, is such that if the input pattern represented by the feature vector X is in class ω_i, denoted as $X\sim\omega_i$, the value of $D_i(X)$ must be the largest. That is, for all $X\sim\omega_i$,

$$D_i(X)>D_j(X), \quad i,j=1,\ldots,m, \quad i\neq j. \tag{1.2}$$

Thus, in the feature space Ω_X the boundary of partition, called the decision boundary, between regions associated with class ω_i and class ω_j, respectively, is expressed by the following equation.

$$D_i(X)-D_j(X)=0. \tag{1.3}$$

Many different forms satisfying condition (1.2) can be selected for $D_i(X)$. Several important discriminant functions are discussed in the following.

1.3.1 Linear Discriminant Functions

In this case, a linear combination of the feature measurements $x_1, x_2, \ldots, x_N$ is selected for $D_i(X)$, i.e.,

$$D_i(X)=\sum_{k=1}^{N}w_{ik}x_k+w_{i,N+1}, \quad i=1,\ldots,m. \tag{1.4}$$

The decision boundary between regions in Ω_X associated with ω_i and ω_j is in the form of

$$D_i(X)-D_j(X)=\sum_{k=1}^{N}w_kx_k+w_{N+1}=0 \tag{1.5}$$

with $w_k=w_{ik}-w_{jk}$ and $w_{N+1}=w_{i,N+1}-w_{j,N+1}$. Equation (1.5) is the equation of a hyperplane in the feature space Ω_X. If $m=2$, on the basis of (1.5), $i,j=1,2\ (i\neq j)$, a threshold logic device, as shown in Fig. 1.2, can be employed as a linear classifier (a classifier using linear discriminant functions). From Fig. 1.2, let $D(X)=D_1(X)-D_2(X)$, if

$$\text{output} = +1, \quad \text{i.e.,} \quad D(X)>0, \quad X\sim\omega_1$$
$$\text{and if} \quad \text{output} = -1, \quad \text{i.e.,} \quad D(X)<0, \quad X\sim\omega_2. \tag{1.6}$$

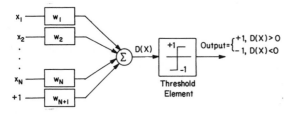

Fig. 1.2. A linear two-class classifier

For the number of pattern classes more than two, $m > 2$, several threshold logic devices can be connected in parallel so that the combinations of the outputs from, say, M threshold logic devices will be sufficient for distinguishing m classes, i.e., $2^M \geqq m$.

1.3.2 Minimum Distance Classifier

An important class of linear classifiers is that of using the distances between the input pattern and a set of reference vectors or prototype points in the feature space as the classification criterion. Suppose that m reference vectors $R_1, R_2, \dots, R_m$, are given with R_j associated with the pattern class ω_j. A minimum-distance classification scheme with respect to $R_1, R_2, \dots, R_m$ is to classify the input X as from class ω_i, i.e.,

$$X \sim \omega_i \quad \text{if} \quad |X - R_i| \text{ is the minimum}, \tag{1.7}$$

where $|X - R_i|$ is the distance defined between X and R_i. For example, $|X - R_i|$ may be defined as

$$|X - R_i| = \sqrt{(X - R_i)^T (X - R_i)}, \tag{1.8}$$

where the superscript T represents the transpose operation to a vector. From (1.8).

$$|X - R_i|^2 = X^T X - X^T R_i - X R_i^T + R_i^T R_i. \tag{1.9}$$

Since $X^T X$ is not a function of i, the corresponding discriminant function for a minimum-distance classifier is essentially

$$D_i(X) = X^T R_i + X R_i^T - R_i^T R_i, \quad i = 1, \dots, m \tag{1.10}$$

which is linear. Hence, a minimum-distance classifier is also a linear classifier. The performance of a minimum-distance classifier is, of course, dependent upon an appropriately selected set of reference vectors.

1.3.3 Piecewise Linear Discriminant Functions (Nearest Neighbor Classification)

The concept adopted in Subsection 1.3.2 can be extended to the case of minimum-distance classification with respect to sets of reference vectors. Let $R_1, R_2, \dots, R_m$ be the m sets of reference vectors associated with classes $\omega_1, \omega_2, \dots, \omega_m$, respectively, and let reference vectors in R_j be denoted as $R_j^{(k)}$, i.e.,

$$R_j^{(k)} \in R_j, \quad k = 1, \dots, u_j,$$

where u_j is the number of reference vectors in set R_j. Define the distance between an input feature vector X and R_j as

$$d(X, R_j) = \min_{k=1, \dots, u_j} |X - R_j^{(k)}|. \tag{1.11}$$

That is, the distance between X and R_j is the smallest of the distances between X and each vector in R_j. The classifier will assign the input to a pattern class which is associated with the closest vector set. If the distance between X and $R_j^{(k)}$, $|X - R_j^{(k)}|$ is defined as (1.8), then the discriminant function used in this case is essentially

$$D_i(X) = \max_{k=1,\ldots,u_i} \{X^T R_i^{(k)} + (R_i^{(k)})^T X - (R_i^{(k)})^T R_i^{(k)}\}, \quad i=1,\ldots,m. \tag{1.12}$$

Let

$$D_i^{(k)} = X^T R_i^{(k)} + (R_i^{(k)})^T X - (R_i^{(k)})^T R_i^{(k)}. \tag{1.13}$$

Then

$$D_i(X) = \max_{k=1,\ldots,u_i} \{D_i^{(k)}(X)\}, \quad i=1,\ldots,m. \tag{1.14}$$

It is noted that $D_i^{(k)}(X)$ is a linear combination of features, hence, the class of classifiers using (1.12) or (1.14) is often called piecewise linear classifiers.

1.3.4 Polynomial Discriminant Functions

An rth-order polynomial discriminant function can be expressed as

$$D_i(X) = w_{i1} f_1(X) + w_{i2} f_2(X) + \ldots + w_{iL} f_L(X) + w_{i,L+1} \tag{1.15}$$

where $f_j(X)$ is of the form

$$x_{k_1}^{n_1} x_{k_2}^{n_2} \ldots x_{k_r}^{n_r} \quad \text{for} \quad \begin{array}{l} k_1, k_2, \ldots, k_r = 1, \ldots, N, \quad \text{and} \\ n_1, n_2, \ldots, n_r = 0 \text{ and } 1. \end{array} \tag{1.16}$$

The decision boundary between any two classes is also in the form of an rth-order polynomial. Particularly, if $r=2$, the discriminant function is called a quadric discriminant function. In this case,

$$f_j(X) = x_{k_1}^{n_1} x_{k_2}^{n_2} \quad \text{for} \quad k_1, k_2 = 1, \ldots, N, \quad \text{and} \quad n_1, n_2 = 0 \text{ and } 1 \tag{1.17}$$

and

$$L = \tfrac{1}{2} N(N+3). \tag{1.18}$$

Typically,

$$D_i(X) = \sum_{k=1}^{N} w_{kk} x_k^2 + \sum_{j=1}^{N-1} \sum_{k=j+1}^{N} w_{jk} x_j x_k + \sum_{j=1}^{N} w_j x_j + w_{L+1}. \tag{1.19}$$

In general, the decision boundary for quadric discriminant functions is a hyper-hyperboloid. Special cases include hypersphere, hyperellipsoid and hyperellipsoidal cylinder.

1.4. Training in Linear Classifiers

The two-class linear classifier discussed in Subsection 1.3.1 is easily to be implemented by a single threshold logic device. If the patterns from different classes are linearly separable (can be separated by a hyperplane in the feature space Ω_X), then, with correct values of the coefficients or weights $w_1, w_2, \ldots, w_{N+1}$ in (1.5), a perfectly correct recognition is possible to be achieved. However, in practice, the proper values of the weights are usually not available. Under such a circumstance, it is proposed that the classifier is designed to have the capability of estimating the best values of the weights from the input patterns. The basic idea is that, by observing patterns with known classifications, the classifier can automatically adjust the weights in order to achieve correct recognitions. The performance of the classifier is supposed to improve as more and more patterns applied. This process is called training or learning, and the patterns used as the inputs are called training patterns. Several simple training rules are briefly introduced in this subsection.

Let Y be an augmented feature vector which is defined as

$$Y = \begin{bmatrix} x_1 \\ x_2 \\ \vdots \\ x_N \\ 1 \end{bmatrix} = \begin{bmatrix} X \\ 1 \end{bmatrix} \tag{1.20}$$

where X is the feature vector of a pattern. Consider two sets of training patterns T_1' and T_2' belonging to two different pattern classes ω_1 and ω_2, respectively. Corresponding to the two training sets there are two sets of augmented vectors T_1 and T_2, each element in T_1 and T_2 is obtained by augmenting the patterns in T_1' and T_2', respectively. That the two training sets are linearly separable means that a weight vector W exists (called the solution weight vector) such that

$$Y^T W > 0 \quad \text{for each} \quad Y \in T_1 \tag{1.21}$$

or

$$Y^T W < 0 \quad \text{for each} \quad Y \in T_2$$

where

$$W = \begin{bmatrix} w_1 \\ w_2 \\ \vdots \\ w_{N+1} \end{bmatrix}. \tag{1.22}$$

The so-called "error-correction" training procedure for a linear classifier can be summarized in the following: For any $Y \in T_1$, the product $Y^T W$ must be positive, i.e., $Y^T W > 0$. If the output of the classifier is erroneous (i.e., $Y^T W < 0$) or undefined (i.e., $Y^T W = 0$), then let the new weight vector be

$$W' = W + \alpha Y \tag{1.23}$$

where $\alpha > 0$ is called the correction increment. On the other hand, for $Y \in T_2$, $Y^T W < 0$. If the output of the device is erroneous (i.e., $Y^T W > 0$) or undefined, then let

$$W' = W - \alpha Y . \tag{1.24}$$

Before training begins, W may be preset to any convenient values.

Three rules for choosing α are suggested:

i) Fixed increment rule — α is any fixed positive number.

ii) Absolute correction rule — α is taken to be the smallest integer which will make the value of $Y^T W$ cross the threshold of zero. That is,

$$\alpha = \text{the smallest integer greater than } \frac{|Y^T W|}{Y^T Y} . \tag{1.25}$$

iii) Fractional correction rule — α is chosen such that

$$|Y^T W - Y^T W'| = \lambda |Y^T W|, \quad 0 < \lambda \leq 2 . \tag{1.26}$$

Or, equivalently,

$$\alpha = \lambda \frac{|Y^T W|}{Y^T Y} . \tag{1.27}$$

The convergence of the three error-correction rules can be proved [1.3]. By convergence, we mean that if the two training sets are linearly separable, the sequence of weight vectors produced by the training rule converges to a solution weight vector in a finite number of training steps or iterations.

1.5. Bayes (Parametric) Classification

Consider that $x_1, x_2, \ldots, x_N$, are random variables where x_i is the noisy measurement of the ith feature. For each pattern class ω_j, $j = 1, \ldots, m$, assume that the multivariate (N-dimensional) probability density (or distribution) function of the feature vector X, $p(X/\omega_j)$, and the probability of occurrences of ω_j, $P(\omega_j)$, are known. On the basis of the *a priori* information $p(X/\omega_j)$ and $P(\omega_j)$, $j = 1, \ldots, m$, the function of a classifier is to perform the classification task for minimizing the probability of misrecognition. The problem of pattern classification can now be formulated as a statistical decision problem (testing of m statistical hypotheses) by defining a decision function $d(X)$, where $d(X) = d_i$ means that the hypothesis $H_i: X \sim \omega_i$ is accepted. Let $L(\omega_i, d_j)$ be the loss incurred by the classifier if the decision d_j is made when the input pattern is actually from ω_i. The conditional loss (or called conditional risk) is

$$r(\omega_i, d) = \int_{\Omega_X} L(\omega_i, d) p(X/\omega_i) dX .\tag{1.28}$$

For a given set of a priori probabilities $P = \{P(\omega_1), P(\omega_2), ..., P(\omega_m)\}$, the average loss (or average risk) is

$$R(P, d) = \sum_{i=1}^{m} P(\omega_i) r(\omega_i, d) .\tag{1.29}$$

Substitute (1.28) into (1.29) and let

$$r_X(P, d) = \frac{\sum_{i=1}^{m} L(\omega_i, d) P(\omega_i) p(X/\omega_i)}{p(X)}\tag{1.30}$$

then (1.29) becomes

$$R(P, d) = \int_{\Omega_X} p(X) r_X(P, d) dX ,\tag{1.31}$$

$r_X(P, d)$ being defined as the *a posteriori* conditional average loss of the decision d for given feature measurements X.

The problem is to choose a proper decision d_j, $j = 1, ..., m$ to minimize the average loss $R(P, d)$, or to minimize the maximum of the conditional average loss $r(\omega_i, d)$ (minimax criterion[3]). The optimal decision rule which minimizes the average loss is called the Bayes' rule. From (1.31) it is sufficient to consider each X separately and to minimize $r_X(P, d)$. If d^* is an optimal decision in the sense of minimizing the average loss, then

$$r_X(P, d^*) \leq r_X(P, d)\tag{1.32}$$

that is,

$$\sum_{i=1}^{m} L(\omega_i, d^*) P(\omega_i) p(X/\omega_i) \leq \sum_{i=1}^{m} L(\omega_i, d) P(\omega_i) p(X/\omega_i) .\tag{1.33}$$

For the (0, 1) loss function, i.e.,

$$L(\omega_i, d_j) = 1 - \delta_{ij} = \begin{cases} 0, & i = j \\ 1, & i \neq j \end{cases}\tag{1.34}$$

the average loss is essentially also the probability of misrecognition. In this case, the Bayes' decision rule is that

$$d^* = d_i, \quad \text{i.e.,} \quad X \sim \omega_i \quad \text{if}$$
$$P(\omega_i) p(X/\omega_i) \geq P(\omega_j) p(X/\omega_j) \quad \text{for all} \quad j = 1, ..., m .\tag{1.35}$$

---

[3] In some classification problems, the information about *a priori* probabilities is not available. The minimax criterion (with respect to the least favorable a priori distribution) is suggested as a classification procedure.

Define the likelihood ratio between class ω_i and class ω_j as

$$\lambda = \frac{p(X/\omega_i)}{p(X/\omega_j)} \tag{1.36}$$

then (1.35) becomes

$$d^* = d_i \quad \text{if} \quad \lambda \gtreqless \frac{P(\omega_j)}{P(\omega_i)} \quad \text{for all} \quad j = 1, \ldots, m. \tag{1.37}$$

The classifier implementing the Bayes' decision rule for classification is called a Bayes classifier.

It is noted from (1.35) that the corresponding discriminant function implemented by a Bayes classifier is essentially

$$D_i(X) = P(\omega_i)p(X/\omega_i), \quad i = 1, \ldots, m \tag{1.38}$$

or equivalently,

$$D_i(X) = \log[P(\omega_i)p(X/\omega_i)], \quad i = 1, \ldots, m. \tag{1.39}$$

The decision boundary between regions in Ω_X associated with ω_i and ω_j is

$$P(\omega_i)p(X/\omega_i) - P(\omega_j)p(X/\omega_j) = 0 \tag{1.40}$$

or

$$\log \frac{P(\omega_i)p(X/\omega_i)}{P(\omega_j)p(X/\omega_j)} = 0. \tag{1.41}$$

As an illustrative example, suppose that $p(X/\omega_i)$, $i = 1, \ldots, m$, is a multivariate Gaussian density function with mean vector M_i and covariance matrix K_i, i.e.,

$$p(X/\omega_i) = \frac{1}{(2\pi)^{N/2}|K_i|^{1/2}} \exp\left[-\tfrac{1}{2}(X - M_i)^{\mathrm{T}}K_i^{-1}(X - M_i)\right], \quad i = 1, \ldots, m. \tag{1.42}$$

Then the decision boundary expressed by (1.41) is

$$\log \frac{P(\omega_i)}{P(\omega_j)} + \log \frac{p(X/\omega_i)}{p(X/\omega_j)}$$

$$= \log \frac{P(\omega_i)}{P(\omega_j)} - \tfrac{1}{2}[(X - M_i)^{\mathrm{T}}K_i^{-1}(X - M_i) - (X - M_j)^{\mathrm{T}}K_j^{-1}(X - M_j)] = 0. \tag{1.43}$$

Equation (1.43) is, in general, a hyperquadrics. If $K_i = K_j = K$, (1.43) reduces to

$$X^{\mathrm{T}}K^{-1}(M_i - M_j) - \tfrac{1}{2}(M_i + M_j)^{\mathrm{T}}K^{-1}(M_i - M_j) + \log \frac{P(\omega_i)}{P(\omega_j)} = 0 \tag{1.44}$$

which is a hyperplane.

It is noted that from (1.35) the Bayes' decision rule with $(0, 1)$ loss function is also the unconditional maximum-likelihood decision rule. Furthermore the (conditional) maximum-likelihood decision may be regarded as the Bayes' decision rule (1.35) with equal *a priori* probabilities, i.e., $P(\omega_i) = 1/m$, $i = 1, \ldots, m$.

1.6 Sequential Decision Model for Pattern Classification

In the statistical classification systems described in Section 1.5, all the N features are observed by the classifier at one stage. As a matter of fact, the cost of feature measurements has not been taken into consideration. It is evident that an insufficient number of feature measurements will not be able to give satisfactory results in correct classification. On the other hand, an arbitrarily large number of features to be measured is impractical. If the cost of taking feature measurements is to be considered or if the features extracted from input patterns are sequential in nature, one is led to apply sequential decision procedures to this class of pattern recognition problems [1.1].

The problem is especially pertinent when the cost of taking a feature measurement is high. For example, if the feature to be measured is in an industrial process and the measurement requires that the process be interrupted or completely stopped, or if elaborate equipment, excessive time, or a complicated and risky operation (in biomedical applications) is required to perform the measurement, then these factors may prohibit its use. Thus, there is a balance between the information provided by the feature measurement and the cost of taking it. A trade-off between the error (misrecognition) and the number of features to be measured can be obtained by taking feature measurements sequentially and terminating the sequential process (making a decision) when a sufficient or desirable accuracy of classification has been achieved.

Since the feature measurements are to be taken sequentially the order of the features to be measured is important. It is expected that the features should be ordered such that measurements taken in such an order will cause the terminal decision earlier. The problem of feature ordering is a rather special problem in sequential recognition systems.

Application of sequential decision procedures to pattern classification was proposed by Fu. If there are two pattern classes to be recognized, Wald's sequential probability ratio test (SPRT) can be applied. At nth stage of the sequential process, that is, after the nth feature measurement is taken, the classifier computes the sequential probability ratio

$$\lambda_n = \frac{p_n(X/\omega_1)}{p_n(X/\omega_2)} \tag{1.45}$$

where $p_n(X/\omega_i)$, $i = 1, 2$, is the (multivariate) conditional probability density function of X for pattern class ω_i. The λ_n computed by (1.45) is then compared with two stopping boundaries A and B. If

$$\lambda_n \geq A, \quad \text{then the decision is that } X \sim \omega_1, \tag{1.46}$$

and if

$$\lambda_n \leq B, \quad \text{then the decision is that } X \sim \omega_2 . \tag{1.47}$$

If $B < \lambda_n < A$, then an additional feature measurement will be taken and the process is proceeding to the $(n+1)$th stage. The two stopping boundaries are related to the error (misrecognition) probabilities by following expressions

$$A = \frac{1 - e_{21}}{e_{12}}$$

and

$$B = \frac{e_{21}}{1 - e_{12}}$$

(1.48)

where e_{ij} = probability of deciding $X \sim \omega_i$ when actually $X \sim \omega_j$ is true, $i, j = 1, 2$. Following Wald's sequential analysis, it has been shown that a classifier, using the SPRT, has an optimal property for the case of two pattern classes, that is, for given e_{12} and e_{21}, there is no other procedure with at least as low error probabilities or expected risk and with shorter length of average number of feature measurements than the sequential classification procedure.

Equations (1.46) and (1.47) with equality signs represent the decision boundaries which partition the feature space into three regions; namely, the region associated with ω_1, the region associated with ω_2, and the region of indifference (or null region). The region between the two boundaries is the region of indifference, in which no terminal decision is made. It can be seen that the decision boundaries in a sequential classification process vary with the number of feature measurements n.

For more than two pattern classes, $m > 2$, the generalized sequential probability ratio test (GSPRT) can be used. At nth stage, the generalized sequential probability ratios for each pattern class are computed as

$$U_n(X/\omega_i) = \frac{p_n(X/\omega_i)}{[\prod_{q=1}^{m} p_n(X/\omega_q)]}, \quad i = 1, 2, \ldots, m . \tag{1.49}$$

The $U_n(X/\omega_i)$ is then compared with the stopping boundary of ith pattern class, $A(\omega_i)$, and the decision procedure is to reject the pattern class ω_i from further consideration, that is, X is not in the class ω_i if

$$U_n(X/\omega_i) < A_n(\omega_i), \quad i = 1, 2, \ldots, m . \tag{1.50}$$

The stopping boundary is determined by the following relationship

$$A_n(\omega_i) = \frac{1 - e_{ii}}{[\prod_{q=1}^{m} (1 - e_{iq})]^{1/m}}, \quad i = 1, 2, \ldots, m . \tag{1.51}$$

After the rejection of pattern class ω_i from consideration, the total number of pattern classes is reduced by one and a new set of generalized sequential probability ratios is formed. The pattern classes are rejected sequentially until only one is left which is accepted as the recognized class. The rejection criterion suggested, though somewhat conservative, will usually lead to a high percentage of correct recognition because of the fact that only the pattern classes which are the most unlikely to be true are rejected.

For two pattern classes, $m = 2$, the classification procedure (1.50) is equivalent to Wald's SPRT and the optimality of SPRT holds. For $m > 2$, whether the optimal property is still valid remains to be justified. However, the classification procedure is close to optimal in that the average number of feature measurements required to reject a pattern class from further consideration is nearly minimum when two hypotheses (the hypothesis of a pattern class to be rejected and the hypothesis of a class not rejected) are considered.

1.7 Bibliographical Remarks

References [1.1–5, 12] represent earlier publications in book form on decision-theoretic pattern recognition. Most of them are dealing with one or several special subjects or methods. References [1.6–11] provide more complete presentations on statistical pattern recognition. Reference [1.9] contains also a systematic presentation on scene analysis. References [1.16, 17] discuss primarily various methods related to character recognition. Reference [1.19] deals exclusively with syntactic pattern recognition. Reference [1.18] discusses primarily statistical pattern recognition with, however, one introductory chapter for syntactic pattern recognition. There have been many conferences and symposiums on pattern recognition during the last ten years. Some of the proceedings of the conferences and symposiums have been published in book form [1.22–27]. The proceedings of the First (1973) and Second (1974) International Joint Conference on Pattern Recognition also contains many good quality papers on this subject.

References

1.1   K. S. FU: *Sequential Methods in Pattern Recognition and Machine Learning* (Academic Press, New York 1968)
1.2   G. S. SEBESTYEN: *Decision in Pattern Recognition* (Macmillan, New York, 1962)
1.3   M. J. NILSSON: *Learning Machines-Foundations of Trainable Pattern—Classifying Systems* (McGraw-Hill, New York 1965)
1.4   J. M. MENDEL, K. S. FU (eds.): *Adaptive, Learning and Pattern Recognition Systems: Theory and Applications* (Academic Press, New York 1970)
1.5   W. MEISEL: *Computer-Oriented Approaches to Pattern Recognition* (Academic Press, New York 1972)
1.6   K. FUKUNAGA: *Introduction to Statistical Pattern Recognition* (Academic Press, New York 1972)
1.7   E. A. PATRICK: *Fundamentals of Pattern Recognition* (Prentice-Hall, Princeton 1972)
1.8   H. C. ANDREWS: *Introduction to Mathematical Techniques in Pattern Recognition* (Wiley, New York 1972)
1.9   R. O. DUDA, P. E. HART: *Pattern Classification and Scene Analysis* (Wiley, New York 1973)
1.10 C. H. CHEN: *Statistical Pattern Recognition* (Hayden Book Co., Washington, D.C., 1973)
1.11 T. Y. YOUNG, T. W. CALVERT: *Classification, Estimation, and Pattern Recognition* (American Elsevier, New York 1974)

1.12 P. W. BECKER: *Recognition of Patterns* (Polyteknisk Forlag, Copenhagen 1968)
1.13 M. M. BONGARD: *Pattern Recognition* (Nanka, Moscow 1967; Spartan Books, Washington, D.C. 1970)
1.14 A. G. ARKADEV, E. M. BRAVERMAN: *Learning in Pattern Classification Machines* (Nanka, Moscow 1971)
1.15 N. G. ZAGORUYKO: *Recognition Methods and Their Applications* (Radio Sovetskoe, Moscow 1972)
1.16 V. A. KOVALEVSKY: *Character Readers and Pattern Recognition* (Spartan Books, Washington, D.C. 1968)
1.17 J. R. ULLMAN: *Pattern Recognition Techniques* (Butterworth & Co., London 1973)
1.18 J. T. TOU, R. C. GONZALEZ: *Pattern Recognition Principles* (Addison-Wesley, 1974)
1.19 K. S. FU: *Syntactic Methods in Pattern Recognition* (Academic Press, New York 1974)
1.20 B. WIDROW: The 'Rubber-Mask' Technique; Part I and Part II, in *Learning Systems and Intelligent Robots*, ed. by K. S. FU and J. T. TOU (Plenum Press, New York 1974)
1.21 Y. P. CHIEN, K. S. FU: "A Flexible-Template Technique for Boundary Detection," Tech. Rept. TR-EE 75-4, School of Electrical Engineering, Purdue University, West Lafayette, Indiana 47907, April 1975
1.22 G. C. CHENG, R. S. LEDLEY, D. K. POLLOK, A. ROSENFELD (eds.): *Pictorial Pattern Recognition* (Thompson Book Co., Boston 1968)
1.23 A. GRASSELLI (ed.): *Automatic Interpretation and Classification of Images* (Academic Press, New York 1969)
1.24 L. N. KANAL (ed.): *Pattern Recognition* (Thompson Book Co., Boston 1968)
1.25 S. WATANABE (ed.): *Methodologies of Pattern Recognition* (Academic Press, New York 1969)
1.26 S. WATANABE (ed.): *Frontiers of Pattern Recognition* (Academic Press, New York 1972)
1.27 K. S. FU (ed.): *Pattern Recognition and Machine Learning* (Plenum Press, New York 1971)

2. Topics in Statistical Pattern Recognition

T. M. COVER and T. J. WAGNER

Pattern recognition, from the broadest viewpoint, is the study of how one puts abstract objects or patterns into categories in a simple reliable way. We have chosen three areas to review: Nonparametric Discrimination, Finite Memory Learning, and Pattern Complexity. We feel that these statistical areas will ultimately play a role in any global pattern recognition theory which evolves.

2.1 Nonparametric Discrimination

2.1.1 Introduction

A statistician observes a random vector X with values in $\mathbb{R}^d$ and wishes to estimate its *state* $\theta \in \{1, ..., M\}$. For this purpose he collects *data* $(X_1, \theta_1), ..., (X_n, \theta_n)$ where two possible assumptions, representing extremes in viewpoints, will be considered.

(A) $(X_1, \theta_1), ..., (X_n, \theta_n)$ is a sequence of independent, identically distributed random vectors with the distribution of (X, θ) which is given by

$$P\{\theta = j\} = \pi_j, \quad 1 \le j \le M, \tag{2.1a}$$

$$P\{X \le x | \theta = j\} \text{ has a probability density } f_j, \quad 1 \le j \le M. \tag{2.1b}$$

(B) $(X_1, \theta_1), ..., (X_n, \theta_n)$ is a sequence of independent random vectors where, for each $1 \le i \le n$, X_i has a probability density f_{θ_i}.

Assumption (A), the Bayesian viewpoint, models θ as a random variable with a probability distribution (2.1a) while (B), the deterministic viewpoint, treats $\theta_1, ..., \theta_n$ as a deterministic sequence selected by nature. If (X, θ) is independent of the data, the nonparametric discrimination problem is to determine how the statistician should use X and the data to estimate θ when he assumes only (A) or (B) and that $f_1, ..., f_M$ are almost everywhere continuous on $\mathbb{R}^d$ [1].

A *discrimination rule*, or, simply, *rule* or *procedure*, is a sequence $\{\delta_n\}$ where, for each n, the decision $\hat{\theta}$ of the rule, is determined by

$$\delta_n : \mathbb{R}^d \times (\mathbb{R}^d \times \{1, ..., M\})^n \to [0, 1]^M,$$

$$\delta_n = (\delta_{n1}, ..., \delta_{nM}), \quad \sum_{j=1}^{M} \delta_{nj} = 1, \tag{2.2}$$

$$P\{\hat{\theta} = j | X, (X_1, \theta_1), ..., (X_n, \theta_n)\} = \delta_{nj}, \quad 1 \le j \le M.$$

---

[1] This last assumption essentially restricts the statistician to not only dealing with measures which are absolutely continuous with respect to Lebesgue measure but ones which also have Riemann integrable densities. This restriction is sometimes relaxed or replaced by the assumption that $f_1, ..., f_M$ are discrete densities.

Thus $\hat{\theta}$ is a randomized decision drawn according to a distribution δ_n which is allowed to depend on the past observations. For each n, there are M conditional probabilities of error for the rule $\{\delta_n\}$ given the data, namely,

$$L_n^j = P\{\hat{\theta} \neq j | (X_1, \theta_1), \ldots, (X_n, \theta_n), \theta = j\}, \quad 1 \leq j \leq M .$$

L_n^j is a random variable whose value is the limiting frequency of errors made when a large number of observations, all with state j, have their states estimated with δ_n and the given data. For the Bayesian problem

$$L_n = P\{\hat{\theta} \neq \theta | (X_1, \theta_1), \ldots, (X_n, \theta_n)\}$$
$$= \sum_{j=1}^{M} \pi_j L_n^j$$

is the probability of error for δ_n given the data. Its value is the limiting frequency of errors made when a large number of independent observations, whose states now occur independently with the distribution (2.1a), have their states estimated with δ_n and the given data. The L_n^j's (and L_n, when one can use the Bayesian assumption) measure the performance that the statistician will get when he applies the rule to his data.

It is also convenient to have rules which can make no decision, or "reject" the observation. Here

$$\delta_n : \mathbb{R}^d \times (\mathbb{R}^d \times \{1, \ldots, M\})^n \rightarrow [0, 1]^{M+1}$$
$$\delta_n = (\delta_{n0}, \ldots, \delta_{nM}); \quad \sum_{j=0}^{M} \delta_{nj} = 1$$
$$P\{\hat{\theta} = j | X, (X_1, \theta_1), \ldots, (X_n, \theta_n)\} = \delta_{nj}, \quad 0 \leq j \leq M$$

describes a rule where $\hat{\theta} = 0$ means "reject" or make no decision. One now has $2M$ random variables

$$L_n^j = P\{\hat{\theta} \neq j, 0 | (X_1, \theta_1), \ldots, (X_n, \theta_n), \theta = j\}, \quad 1 \leq j \leq M$$
$$R_n^j = P\{\hat{\theta} = 0 | (X_1, \theta_1), \ldots, (X_n, \theta_n), \theta = j\}, \quad 1 \leq j \leq M$$

representing, respectively, the probability of error for the rule given the data and $\theta = j$, and the probability of reject for the rule given the data and $\theta = j$. With the Bayesian assumption

$$L_n = \sum_1^M \pi_j L_n^j$$
$$R_n = \sum_1^M \pi_j R_n^j$$

become, respectively, the probability of error and the probability of reject for the rule, given the data, with the analogous frequency interpretations to those used earlier.

One obvious rule that might be employed in the Bayesian problem is to estimate $\pi = (\pi_1, \ldots, \pi_M)$, $f = (f_1, \ldots, f_M)$ from the data and then use these estimates in the Bayes procedure as though they were correct. The class of such rules that

one obtains by using different estimates of $f_1, ..., f_M$ from the data are called
"two-step" procedures. A similar designation is also used in the deterministic
problem.

A rule $\{\delta_n\}$ is termed *symmetric* if the order of the data $(X_1, \theta_1), ..., (X_n, \theta_n)$ is
immaterial to the value of δ_n (e.g., a permutation of $(X_1, \theta_1), ..., (X_n, \theta_n)$ leaves δ_n
unchanged). A rule is termed *local* if there is an integer r such that, with proba-
bility one, δ_n depends on X and at most its r nearest neighbors and their states.
Local rules are, of course, symmetric. A local rule is called *consistent* if, whenever
an observation is deleted from the data, $\hat{\theta}$ remains unchanged as long as that
observation is not one of the r_0 nearest neighbors of X where r_0 is the smallest
integer r for which the rule satisfies the definition of being local.

Examples:

1) The Bayes rule for (2.1) does not depend on the data and is therefore a
consistent local rule with $r_0 = 0$.

2) Let h be a positive number and let $\hat{\theta}$ be the state which has the most number
of observations within a distance h of X. Ties are broken at random. This rule
is a two-step rule which is symmetric but not local.

3) The k-nearest neighbor rule (k-NNR) takes $\hat{\theta}$ to be the state which occurs
most often among the k nearest neighbors of X. Two types of ties can occur, ties
in voting and ties in distance. In the first case, say with $k=5$ and $M=3$, the votes
of the nearest neighbors of X may be $1, 1, 2, 2, 3$. In this situation the k-NNR
breaks the tie at random between states 1 and 2. Ties in distance occur with
probability 0 when the conditional probability measures have probability densities as we have assumed. The k-NNR is a consistent local rule with $r_0 = k$.

4) Suppose $d=1$ and $M=2$. One looks at the data and finds a threshold t
such that one of the two decision procedures

$$\hat{\theta} = \begin{cases} 2, & x \geq t \\ 1, & x < t \end{cases}$$

$$\hat{\theta} = \begin{cases} 1, & x \geq t \\ 2, & x < t \end{cases}$$

minimizes the frequency of state 2 errors given that the frequency of state 1 errors
is less than or equal to α, $0 < \alpha < 1$. This rule is symmetric but neither two-step
nor local.

One of the questions that statisticians, or at least researchers, always ask
about a rule is how well it performs in the large sample case. In fact, the bulk
of investigation for the nonparametric descrimination problem so far has been
devoted to demonstrating asymptotic properties of various rules.

For the Bayesian problem, rules of the form (2.2) are called asymptotically
optimal if

$$L_n \xrightarrow{n} L^* \text{ in probability}$$

where $L^* = L^*(\pi, f)$, the Bayes probability of error, is the smallest probability of
error possible when the distribution (2.1) is known. Rules which allow rejects are

called asymptotically optimal if

$$L_n \xrightarrow{n} L \text{ in probability}$$

$$R_n \xrightarrow{n} R \text{ in probability}$$

where, when (2.1) is known, R is the smallest probability of reject possible among all rules which have a probability of error less than or equal to L.

For the deterministic problem, asymptotic optimality is difficult to describe except in the case $M = 2$. For this case rules of the form (2.2) are asymptotically optimal if

$$L_n^1 \xrightarrow{n} L_1 \text{ in probability}$$

$$L_n^2 \xrightarrow{n} L_2 \text{ in probability}$$

where, assuming f_1, f_2 are known, L_1 is the smallest probability of error possible given $\theta = 1$ for all rules with a probability of error, given $\theta = 2$, less than or equal to L_2.

Other notions of asymptotic optimality are possible in the deterministic case. One can think of the data unfolding, one observation at a time, yielding a frequency of errors after n observations equal to

$$\frac{1}{n-1} \sum_1^{n-1} I_{[\hat{\theta}_{j+1} \neq \theta_{j+1}]}$$

where $\hat{\theta}_{j+1}$ is the estimate of θ_{j+1} from X_{j+1} and $(X_1, \theta_1), \ldots, (X_j, \theta_j)$ using δ_j. If $L^*(\hat{\pi}, f)$ represents the Bayes probability of error computed with the empirical probabilities $\hat{\pi}_1, \ldots, \hat{\pi}_M$ (from n observations), one can now consider rules asymptotically optimal if

$$\frac{1}{n-1} \sum_1^{n-1} I_{[\hat{\theta}_{j+1} \neq \theta_{j+1}]} - L^*(\hat{\pi}, f) \xrightarrow{n} 0 \text{ in probability}$$

uniformly in the sequences $\{\theta_i\}$. Such a rule has a robust character in that it drives the difference between the observed frequency of errors and its expected empirical counterpart to zero regardless of the sequence $\{\theta_i\}$. Nevertheless, the quantity $L^*(\hat{\pi}, f)$ which is being tracked is irrevocably linked to the past in that it tells us nothing about future performance unless the future empirical distribution of the sequence $\{\theta_i\}$ is the same as that in the past.

In the following two subsections we review recent work on the Bayesian problem and all of the work of which we are aware for the deterministic problem. The emphasis in these subsections is on describing rules and their asymptotic properties, if any. The next subsection is devoted to error rate estimation. That is, given the data and a particular rule, how does the statistician estimate the current performance of his rule? The final subsection is devoted to recent results in nonparametric density estimation.

2.1.2 The Deterministic Problem

In this subsection we review the known results for the deterministic problem where, for simplicity, we consider only $M=2$. The standard asymptotic result for two-step procedures is due to FIX and HODGES [2.1]. In particular, if $\hat{f}_i$ is a consistent estimate of f_i from the data [2] for each i and if $\{x:f_1(x)=tf_2(x)\}$ has zero probability with each density, then

$$\hat{\theta}=\begin{cases}1, & \hat{f}_1(X)/\hat{f}_2(X)\geq t\\2, & \hat{f}_1(X)/\hat{f}_2(X)<t\end{cases}$$

yields [3]

$$L_n^i\to P\{\theta'\neq i|\theta=i\}\overset{\Delta}{=}L_i\ \text{in probability}\ i=1,2$$

where

$$\theta'=\begin{cases}1, & f_1(X)/f_2(X)\geq t\\2, & f_1(X)/f_2(X)<t\end{cases}$$

and $0<t<\infty$ is fixed but arbitrary. The Neyman-Pearson lemma guarantees that L_1 is the smallest possible probability of error, given $\theta=1$, for any rule which has a probability of error, given $\theta=2$, less than or equal to L_2. Thus if the set $\{x:f_1(x)=tf_2(x)\}$ has zero probability with each density, then two-step procedures using consistent estimates are asymptotically optimal. The convergence of the L_n^i can be strengthened to convergence with probability one if the requirement for consistent estimates is replaced by strongly consistent estimates. While the above two-step rules are asymptotically optimal, it is nevertheless assumed that one has picked a suitable t for the given application. For example, one has to be satisfied with the value of L_2 obtained. Finally, if $\hat{f}_i$ is any one of the usual density estimates from the observations having state i we need only have an infinite number of observations from each state in order to satisfy the given consistency requirements.

The rule suggested by FIX and HODGES was the forerunner of the k-nearest neighbor rule of COVER and HART [2.2] (see Ex. 3). In the context of the density estimation approach here, their rule is obtained by setting $\hat{f}_i(x)=M_i/n_iV$ where

a) n_i is the number of observations in the data with state i,

b) V is the volume of the smallest sphere S about x containing at least k observations from the data,

c) M_i is the number of observations having state i which are contained in S, and

d) $k=k(n_1,n_2)\to\infty$, $k(n_1,n_2)/n_i\to0$, $i=1,2$, when $n_1,n_2\to\infty$ with n_1/n_2 bounded away from 0 and ∞.

The metric used in proving consistency of these densities was the ordinary Euclidean metric although the result holds for other metrics. There is, of course,

---

[2] $\hat{f}_i$ is a consistent estimate of f_i if $\hat{f}_i(x)\overset{n}{\to}f_i(x)$ in probability for each x at which f_i is continuous. The estimate is called strongly consistent if the convergence is with probability one.

[3] The result in [2.1] is somewhat stronger than stated here.

a very slight additional restriction put on the sequences $\{\theta_i\}$ in order to obtain the consistent density estimates of the above rule.

FIX and HODGES [2.3], assuming simple cases for normal densities, computed the average probability of error of each type for $n_1 = n_2$ and $k = 1$, $k = 3$. For the univariate case these probabilities were compared with the corresponding ones obtained by estimating the parameters in the optimal linear discriminant function. Their conclusion was

"If the populations to be discriminated are well known, and have been investigated to establish that the normal distribution gives a good fit and that the variances and correlations do not change much when the means are changed, and if the classification to be made warrants the labor of matrix inversion, then the linear discriminant function should certainly be used. If on the other hand, the populations are either not well known, or are known not to be approximately normal, or to have very different covariance matrices; or if the discrimination is one in which small decreases in probability of error are not worth extensive computations, then the simple nonparametric rule, perhaps with $k \geq 3$, seems to have the edge."

KENDALL [2.4] discussed two procedures, the first one called the convex-hull method. Here

$$\hat{\theta} = \begin{cases} 1 & \text{if} \quad X \in A_1 \bar{A}_2 \\ 2 & \text{if} \quad X \in A_2 \bar{A}_1 \\ 0 & \text{otherwise}, \end{cases}$$

where A_i is the convex-hull of the observations with state i. Despite the simplicity of this procedure the statistician will, with probability one, be making no decision as $n_1, n_2 \rightarrow \infty$ for typical densities f_1, f_2 which have a common support. KENDALL also described a procedure termed the order-statistic method. Here one looks at the coordinate with the best discrimination (e.g., most decisions) using the convex-hull method. The remaining observations which are not discriminated are used with another coordinate in the same manner and so on. At the end of the process one has a sequence of tests on each coordinate which are applied until X is discriminated or until one exhausts the coordinates and makes no decision. This rule, while also simple, has the same difficulty as the convex-hull method.

QUESENBERRY and GESSAMAN [2.5] introduced a procedure using the theory of coverages which, for the $M = 2$ case, can be described as follows. Let $P_i(\cdot)$ denote the probability measure on Borel subsets of $\mathbb{R}^d$ corresponding to the density f_i. If the data contains n_i observations with state i, then, given α_1, α_2 with $0 \leq \alpha_1, \alpha_2 \leq 1$, and using any ordering function which satisfies mild conditions, sets A_1, A_2 can be found for which $P_j(A_j)$ is a random variable with a Beta distribution Beta$[a_j, n_j - a_j + 1]$, a_j being the integer part of $\alpha_j(n_j + 1)$. Letting

$$\hat{\theta} = \begin{cases} 1 & \text{on} \quad \bar{A}_1 A_2 \\ 2 & \text{on} \quad \bar{A}_2 A_1 \\ 0 & \text{on} \quad \bar{A}_1 \bar{A}_2 \cup A_1 A_2 \end{cases}$$

then yields the inequalities

$$L_n^1 \leq P_1(A_1)$$
$$L_n^2 \leq P_2(A_2)$$

where, in addition, $P_i(A_i) \xrightarrow{n_i} \alpha_i$ in probability, $i = 1, 2$. Thus one can control the two types of error probabilities asymptotically to be less than or equal to α_1, α_2, respectively. The difficulty with this procedure is that one cannot be sure that the reject region has minimum probability for each state value and no procedure for constructing A_1, A_2 was given which guaranteed this unless f_1, f_2 were known to belong to special parametrically described families of densities. Even if one were willing to make one of these parametric assumptions the rejection rates may still be too high for the given application. Finally, the method given, when extended to $M > 2$ states, requires regions of partial decisions, that is, if X falls in a set $S_{i_1,\ldots,i_k}$, then one merely asserts that X has one of the states $i_1, \ldots, i_k$.

In [2.5] the regions A_1 and A_2 are not specified even though one has already picked the $n_i + 1$ blocks of each type. ANDERSON and BENNING [2.6] described a method for picking the ordering functions and A_1, A_2 such that the region of no decision tends to have a small probability for each state value while, at the same time, keeping the properties of [2.5] for controlling the individual error probabilities.

BEAKLEY and TUTEUR [2.7] eliminated the no decision region altogether. Methods for determining a sequence of statistically equivalent blocks $B_1, \ldots, B_{n_1+1}$ for state 1 were given with the property that *all* n_2 observations from state 2 were contained in B_1. Thus if

$$\hat{\theta} = \begin{cases} 2, & X \in \bigcup_1^m B_i \\ 1, & X \in \bigcup_{m+1}^{n_1+1} B_i \end{cases}$$

then $L_n^1 = P_1(\bigcup_1^m B_1)$ is a random variable with Beta $[n, n-m+1]$ distribution, and L_n^1 can be controlled as in the QUESENBERY and GESSAMAN case. $L_n^2 = P_2(\bigcup_{m+1}^{n_1+1} B_i) = 1 - P_2(\bigcup_1^m B_i)$ intuitively is being minimized since all of the state 2 observations are in B_1. The conditions needed to insure the asymptotic optimality of this procedure are unknown, however.

HENRICHON and FU [2.8, 9] and ANDERSON [2.10] have also discussed various discrimination rules but little is known analytically about their proposed procedures. OWEN et al. [2.11], for the two-state univariate case, described a scheme which asymptotically locates the extrema of $F_2(x) - tF_1(x)$ where F_i is the distribution function corresponding to f_i. The procedure requires that (a) the set of extrema is finite and (b) the smallest distance between the extrema is known. Thus the regions $\{x : f_1(x)/f_2(x) \geq t\}$ and $\{x : f_1(x)/f_2(x) < t\}$ can asymptotically be found for these assumptions and, in fact, the procedure is asymptotically optimal in this case. GESSAMAN and GESSAMAN [2.12] experimentally compared various rules for three different sample sizes and three different choices of bivariate normals for f_1, f_2.

In [2.13] VAN RYZIN, using kernel estimates for the densities and empirical frequencies for the states in Bayes rule, showed that estimating θ_{n+1} from X_{n+1} and $(X_1, \theta_1), \ldots, (X_n, \theta_n)$ yields

$$\frac{1}{n} \sum_1^n I_{[\hat{\theta}_{i+1} \neq \theta_{i+1}]} - L^*(\hat{\pi}, f) \xrightarrow{n} 0 \text{ in probability}$$

uniformly in all sequences $\{\theta_i\}$.

2.1.3 The Bayesian Problem

In this subsection we review the recent work on the Bayesian problem where, for the most part, we use the review paper of COVER [2.14] as our starting point.

Two-step rules are asymptotically optimal if one uses reasonable estimates of $\pi_1, ..., \pi_M, f_1, ..., f_M$. In particular, if

$$\hat{\theta} = \begin{cases} j, \hat{\pi}_j \hat{f}_j(X) \geq \hat{\pi}_i \hat{f}_i(X), & 1 \leq i \leq M \\ \text{ties are broken arbitrarily} \end{cases}$$

then

$$L_n \xrightarrow{n} L^* \text{ in probability}$$

when $\hat{\pi}_1, ..., \hat{\pi}_M, \hat{f}_1, ..., \hat{f}_M$ are consistent estimates of $\pi_1, ..., \pi_M, f_1, ..., f_M$ from the data. In fact,

$$L_n \xrightarrow{n} L^* \text{ with probability one}$$

if the estimates are strongly consistent. This Bayesian analogue of the FIX-HODGES result for the deterministic problem does not appear specifically in the literature (see, however, ROBBINS [2.15], VAN RYZIN [2.16], SCHWARTZ [2.17] and GLICK [2.18] for similar versions).

If $\{\delta_n\}$ is a symmetric rule then L_n, and R_n, if rejects are allowed, are symmetric functions of the data. The HEWITT-SAVAGE 0–1 law [2.19, 20] implies that such sequences of random variables converge with probability one to a constant or diverge with probability one. This appealing all-or-nothing behavior for symmetric rules appears to be difficult to take advantage of, however, in analyzing any particular rule.

In some situations the statistician wants to estimate the state of a specific X where it is demanded that a decision be made after each new observation in the data. If he uses a two-step procedure, then he wants one which, in some sense, can be recursively updatable for each value of X as the data unfolds, one observation at a time. For $M = 2$, VAN RYZIN [2.21] demonstrated the asymptotic optimality of a two-step procedure which essentially uses recursive versions of kernel density estimates for f_1, f_2. For a similar procedure, WOLVERTON and WAGNER [2.22] showed that $L_n \xrightarrow{n} L^*$ with probability one and that

$$P[\bigcup_{k=n}^{\infty} \{L_k - L^* \geq \varepsilon\}] \leq A/n^{(2d+1)}$$

for a particular choice of window width in the density estimates. REJTÖ and RÉVÉSZ [2.23], with additional assumptions on the derivatives of f_1, f_2, have shown that

$$P[L_n - L^* \geq \varepsilon] \leq e^{-An^{(d+1)/2d+1}}$$

for a scheme similar to [2.22]. In each of the above procedures symmetry has been sacrificed to obtain a recursive procedure.

One of the difficulties in applying the rule of example 2) in Subsection 2.1.1 is that the statistician does not know how to choose the value of h^4. A nice idea was investigated by PELTO [2.24] who, for $M=2$ and known π_1, π_2, examined different ways of choosing h from the data. One method consists of choosing an h which minimizes

$$\pi_1 \hat{L}_n^1 + \pi_2 \hat{L}_n^2$$

where $\hat{L}_n^1, \hat{L}_n^2$ are the deleted estimates of L_n^1, L_n^2 from the data (see Subsection 2.1.4). An argument was given which indicates that this method yields an asymptotically optimal rule. Unfortunately the argument is incomplete since it does not take into consideration the fact that the h chosen is now a random variable. Also discussed was a second method for choosing h, which heuristically has a smaller bias in estimating $\pi_1 L_n^1 + \pi_2 L_n^2$.

The k-nearest neighbor rule [see example 3) of Subsection 2.1.1] was initially investigated by COVER and HART [2.2] who, among other things, showed that the single nearest neighbor rule asymptotically "plays nature against itself". For example, for $M=2$,

$$EL_n \rightarrow \int_{\mathbb{R}^d} \frac{2\pi_1 f_1 \pi_2 f_2}{\pi_1 f_1 + \pi_2 f_2}\, dx \triangleq L(1)$$

which is the same probability of error obtained using the rule

$$\delta(X)=j \text{ with probability } \pi_j f_j(X)/(\pi_1 f_1(X) + \pi_2 f_2(X)), \quad j=1, 2,$$

that is, the rule that chooses state j with its *a posteriori* probability given X. However, for a finite amount of data, the single nearest neighbor rule is a deterministic rule (with probability one) which achieves its effective randomization in the large sample case by partitioning each small neighborhood of x into many small subregions where, on each subregion, the decision for a given state is constant and where the total fraction of subregion areas for state j is approximately $\pi_j f_j(x)/\sum_1^M \pi_j f_j(x)$. What, of course, makes the rule interesting is the tight inequality [2.2]

$$L^* \leqq L(1) \leqq 2L^*(1-L^*).$$

Beyond this COVER and HART showed, for the k-nearest neighbor rule, that

$$EL_n \xrightarrow{n} L(k)$$

and gave tight bounds for $L(k)$ in terms of L^*, WAGNER [2.25] demonstrated that

$$L_n \xrightarrow{n} L(k) \text{ in probability}$$

---

[4] This rule is the two-step rule obtained by using the empirical estimates of $\pi_1, ..., \pi_M$ and kernel estimates of $f_1, ..., f_M$ with a kernel width h and a kernel which is uniform over the unit sphere centered at the origin (see Subsection 2.1.5).

with convergence being with probability one if all components of X have a finite first moment with the density $\sum_1^M \pi_i f_i$. FRITZ [2.26] has shown that the above convergence for the single nearest neighbor rule is always with probability one and that $P\{|L_n - L(1)| \geq \varepsilon\}$ is asymptotically dominated by $A \exp(-B\sqrt{n})$ where A and B are functions of ε and d but not of the distribution of (X, θ).

Suppose the statistician is looking at a large amount of data with $\pi_1 = \pi_2 = 1/2$ and $f_1 = N(-1, 1)$, $f_2 = N(1, 1)$. For positive values of x, state 2 observations will be denser than state 1 observations, while for negative x the reverse will be true. For example, for x greater than 0, one will tend to see each state 1 observation surrounded by strings of state 2 observations. One reasonable thing to try to do is "edit out" the weaker class. WILSON [2.27] took this approach by first editing the data with the k-nearest neighbor rule and then using the nearest neighbor rule on the edited data set. For example,

1) let $\hat{\theta}_j$ be the k-NNR estimate of θ_j from X_j and the data with (X_j, θ_j) *deleted*, $1 \leq j \leq N$, and
2) edit (X_j, θ_j) from the data if $\hat{\theta}_j \neq \theta_j$.

The single nearest neighbor rule is now used with the edited data set to estimate the state θ of an unclassfied observation X. WILSON showed that

$$EL_n \xrightarrow{n} L^E(k)$$

where $L^E(k) \leq L(k)$ for all k and, for the first 3 odd values of k,

$$L^* \leq L^E(1) \leq 1.2L^*$$
$$L^* \leq L^E(3) \leq 1.149L^*$$
$$L^* \leq L^E(5) \leq 1.10L^* \ ^5 .$$

where, for comparison, the k-nearest neighbor rule has

$$L^* \leq L(1) \leq 2L^*$$
$$L^* \leq L(3) \leq 1.31L^*$$
$$L^* \leq L(5) \leq 1.2L^* .$$

Thus, by editing out the less dense observations with the k-NNR, one not only reduces the storage requirements for future classification but improves the asymptotic performance over the k nearest-neighbor rule as well. This rule is symmetric but not local since, for example, an arbitrary number of nearest neighbors of X can be deleted in the editing process. Also it is not known if $L_n \xrightarrow{n} L^E(k)$ in any sense.

Other rules have been suggested whose primary purpose is to reduce the data before the nearest neighbor rule is applied, for example, the condensed nearest neighbor rule and the reduced nearest neighbor rule [2.28–31]. CHANG [2.32] has considered reducing the data by merging two nearest vectors of the same

---

[5] There is a flaw in WILSON's argument which may make these bounds only approximate.

state into a weighted average of the two as long as the recognition rate on the data is not lowered. All three rules are nonsymmetric and nothing is known analytically about their finite or asymptotic performance.

HELLMAN [2.33] considered modifying the k-nearest-neighbor rule to allow rejects. The modified rule makes the decision of the k-nearest-neighbor rule only if all k nearest neighbors agree; otherwise it makes no decision. It was shown that

$$EL_n \xrightarrow{n} L$$
$$ER_n \xrightarrow{n} R$$

where, for the given asymptotic reject rate R, the corresponding probability of error L satisfies

$$L \leqq (1 + k/2) L_R^* .$$

Here L_R^* is the smallest possible probability of error for all rules with a given probability of reject less than or equal to R and the constant $(1 + k/2)$ is the smallest possible. Thus, when $k = 2$ and when errors are twice as costly as rejects, the above rule always performs better than the single nearest-neighbor rule. The modified rule is symmetric, local and consistent.

CHOW [2.35], in one of the earliest applications of decision theory to pattern recognition, modified the Bayes rule to allow rejects. In particular, if

$$r(x) = 1 - \max_{1 \leqq i \leqq M} \{ \pi_i f_i(x) / f(x) \}$$
$$f(x) = \sum_1^M \pi_i f_i(x)$$

then the rule

$$\hat{\theta} = \begin{cases} j \text{ when } 1 - (\pi_j f_j(X) / f(X)) = r(X) \leqq t \\ 0 \text{ when } r(X) > t \end{cases}$$

yields a probability of error L and a probability of reject R which are functions of t, $0 \leqq t \leqq 1$, and, furthermore, for each t, $R(t)$ is the smallest reject probability of any rule with an error probability less than or equal to $L(t)$. In [2.34] CHOW exhibited a simple relationship between L and R, namely,

$$L(t) = - \int_0^t t' \, dR(t') = \int_0^t R(t') \, dt' - t R(t) .$$

2.1.4 Probability of Error Estimation

Estimating the probability of error that a statistician has with a particular rule and his data, sometimes called error estimation in the literature, is the topic of this subsection. The emphasis is on the existence of distribution-free bounds for these estimates and, because such bounds occur infrequently in statistical problems, we first describe a distribution-free bound for estimating distribution functions which will be used later for probability of error estimates with a particular class of rules.

Let $X_1, X_2, \ldots$ be a sequence of independent identically distributed random variables with a common distribution function F. Suppose F is unknown to us and we wish to estimate it from $X_1, \ldots, X_n$. If F_n is the empirical distribution function for $X_1, \ldots, X_n$ [e.g., $F_n(x)$ is the frequency of the first n observations less than or equal to x] then the Glivenko-Cantelli theorem asserts that

$$D_n \overset{\Delta}{=} \sup_x |F_n(x) - F(x)| \xrightarrow{n} 0 \text{ with probability one}.$$

While this reassures the statistician that, for large n, F_n should be a good estimate of F in the sense of making D_n small, he cannot infer, say, how large n should be in order to insure that

$$P[D_n \geq \varepsilon] \leq \delta,$$

where ε, δ are two pre-assigned arbitrary positive numbers. What is being sought here is very similar to finding confidence intervals for estimating an unknown parameter, the main difference being that this problem is nonparametric and we want an n here which will work for all F. A nice result of Dvoretsky et al. [2.36] is that

$$P[D_n \geq \varepsilon] \leq C_0 e^{-2\varepsilon^2 n},$$

where C_0 is a universal constant which does not depend on F. Choosing the smallest n such that

$$C_0 e^{-2\varepsilon^2 n} \leq \delta$$

satisfies our requirements. The bound above, which works for all F, is called *distribution free* because it does not depend on F.

Probability of error estimation is the problem of how the statistician estimates the *current* performance of his rule, that is, the performance he will get when he applies the rule to his data. In particular, in the Bayesian problem, the statistician would like to estimate L_n from the given data while in the deterministic problem he would like to estimate L_n^j, $1 \leq j \leq M$, from the data, and, indeed, he may wish to estimate these latter quantities in the Bayesian problem as well. In addition, the statistician may wish to estimate the ultimate performance of the rule, if any, with the data. In the Bayesian problem, for example, suppose he has a rule for which

$$L_n \xrightarrow{n} L \text{ in probability},$$

where L is not necessarily equal to L^*. L then is the performance of the rule with an infinite amount of data. In those situations where there is the possibility of gathering more data, the statistician would be interested in L if only because a large value of L would indicate that the proposed discrimination is unfeasible.

Generally, though, the interest is in L_n since the data is always finite. We will comment on another aspect of these two different problems later in this subsection.

TOUSSAINT [2.37] has recently published an extensive bibliography on the estimation of error probabilities to which we refer the reader for an historical perspective and a complete survey, while we concentrate here on distribution-free aspects of the error estimation problem. The recent review by KANAL [2.38], particularly the section on error estimation, is also highly recommended. The estimates[6] which have been considered extensively are as follows.

(A) *Resubstitution Estimate:* $\hat{L}_n \triangleq \frac{1}{n} \sum_1^n I_{[\hat{\theta}_j \neq \theta_j]}$ where $\hat{\theta}_j$ is the estimate of θ_j using δ_n with X_j and all of the data.

(B) *Holdout Estimate:* $\hat{L}_n \triangleq \frac{1}{n\alpha} \sum_{n-n\alpha+1}^n I_{[\hat{\theta}_j \neq \theta_j]}$ where $\hat{\theta}_j$ is the estimate of θ_j using $\delta_{n-n\alpha}$ with X_j and $(X_1, \theta_1), \ldots, (X_{n(1-\alpha)}, \theta_{n(1-\alpha)})$, $n-n\alpha < j \leq n$. The fraction of the data "held out" is α and we have assumed that αn is an integer.

(C) *Deleted Estimate:* $\hat{L}_n \triangleq \frac{1}{n} \sum_1^n I_{[\hat{\theta}_j \neq \theta_j]}$ where $\hat{\theta}_j$ is the estimate of θ_j using δ_{n-1} with X_j and the data with (X_j, θ_j) deleted.

(D) *Rotation Estimate:* $\hat{L}_n \triangleq \frac{1}{n} \sum_1^n I_{[\hat{\theta}_j \neq \theta_j]}$ where $\hat{\theta}_j$ is the estimate of θ_j using δ_{n-l} with X_j and the data where the l-block that contains (X_j, θ_j) is deleted. Here, l is an integer which divides n (e.g., $n=ml$) and the data is partitioned into m consecutive l-blocks: $(X_{(i-1)l+1}, \theta_{(i-1)l+1}), \ldots, (X_{il}, \theta_{il})$, $1 \leq i \leq m$.

Obviously the deleted estimate is a special case of the rotation estimate with $l=1$. The rotation estimate and the holdout estimate are, in general, not symmetric since they depend on the order of the observations. With $l=n/2$ the rotation estimate is just the average of two holdout estimates, the regular one and the one with the data reversed. The re-substitution estimate is frequently an optimistic estimate of L_n, but has been shown by FRALICK and SCOTT [2.39] to be a consistent estimate of L^* for a wide class of asymptotically optimal two-step procedures. With the nearest neighbor rule, for example, (A) always yields an estimate of 0 for L_n. The deleted estimate can require considerable computation but, with local rules, the computation is reasonable and its intuitive appeal can be taken advantage of.

The aspect which interests us here is whether these estimates have distribution-free performance bounds for any types of rules. In [2.40], for the Bayesian problem, it is shown that for any consistant local rule using k nearest neighbors

$$E(L_n - \hat{L}_n)^2 \leq \frac{(2k+\frac{1}{4})}{n} + \frac{2k(2k+\frac{1}{4})^{\frac{1}{2}}}{n^{3/2}} + \frac{k^2}{n}, \tag{2.3}$$

where $\hat{L}_n$ is the deleted estimate of L_n. Thus, for a given ε, $\delta > 0$, an n can be specified using (2.3) and Chebychev's inequality to insure that

$$P[|\hat{L}_n - L_n| \geq \varepsilon] \leq \delta$$

---

[6] For simplicity we consider these estimates for the Bayesian problem. Their counterparts for the deterministic problem are usually obvious.

regardless of the nonparametric discrimination problem considered. The n obtained through the use of (2.3), however, is probably far from the smallest possible.

Several comments are appropriate. First, the variance of $\hat{L}_n$, usually a focus of study in the literature, is more or less irrelevant since the pertinent mean-square quantity is $E(\hat{L}_n - L_n)^2$. Second, the result (2.3) seems surprising since it does not depend on d! Thus, if the statistician uses a local rule he does not need to be concerned about extraneous or irrelevant components affecting the accuracy of the deleted estimate. Finally (2.3) is valid for arbitrary conditional measures, which may include atoms, provided ties are broken in a satisfactory way. For example, suppose $Z_1, Z_2, \ldots$ is a sequence of independent random numbers from $[0, 1]$ where Z_i is "attached" to (X_i, θ_i) for each $i = 1, 2, \ldots$. If ties in distance are broken by choosing the observations with the smallest attached numbers then the ordering of the neighbors of X is specified with probability one and (2.3) holds for local rules using this ordering.

This result can also be used to select the best set of l out of d components for use with a local rule. For example, if one has m different subsets of the d components and picks that subset with the smallest deleted risk estimate, then the probability that he has picked a subset whose L_n is within 2ε of that of the best subset of those tested is $\geq 1 - (mA/\varepsilon^2)$ where A is given by the right-hand-side of (2.3). Putting $m = \binom{d}{l}$ then allows the selection of the best set of l components, although the n required in the bound, to be useful, will probably be quite large. While it seems to be true that deleted estimates work well for local rules, one should not conclude that they will necessarily work well for all rules or that any other estimate will work well for local rules. One might wonder why it is that local rules, using k-nearest neighbors, have a performance bound which does not depend on d but only on k. Intuitively it seems that local rules exchange k for d; for example, the nearest neighbor rule essentially reduces the discrimination procedure to one dimension since only distances from the observations to x are factors in the decision.

The re-substitution estimate, often criticized in the literature, also yields a distribution-free performance bound on linear rules. First consider the deterministic problem for $M = 2$ and $d = 1$ with rules of the form

$$\hat{\theta} = \begin{cases} 2, & X > t \\ 1, & X \leq t \end{cases}$$

where t is some function of the data. If n_i observations have state i, and if $\hat{F}_i$ represents the empirical distribution function for the observations with state i, then $\hat{F}_2(t)$ is the re-substitution estimate of $P\{\hat{\theta} \neq 2 | \theta = 2\} = F_2(t) = L_n^2$ while $1 - \hat{F}_1(t)$ is the re-substitution estimate of $P\{\hat{\theta} \neq 1 | \theta = 1\} = 1 - F_1(t) = L_n^1$. Thus, for *all* functions t,

$$P[|\hat{L}_n^1 - L_n^1| \geq \varepsilon] \leq C_0 e^{-2n_1 \varepsilon^2}$$
$$P[|\hat{L}_n^2 - L_n^2| \geq \varepsilon] \leq C_0 e^{-2n_2 \varepsilon^2} .$$

This result may generalize to higher dimensions but, for the present, remains an open question. For example, let $Z, Z_1, Z_2, \ldots$ be a sequence of independent, identically random vectors with values in $\mathbb{R}^m$ and suppose that we can extend the KIEFER and WOLFOWITZ [2.41] result from semi-infinite rectangles to half planes, namely, to

$$P\left\{\sup_a \left|\frac{1}{n}\sum_1^n I_{[a^T Z_i \leq 0]} - P[a^T Z \leq 0]\right| \geq \varepsilon\right\} \leq C_0 e^{-Cn\varepsilon^2} \tag{2.4}$$

where C_0, C depend on m but not on the distribution of Z. Consider rules of the form

$$\hat{\theta} = \begin{cases} 2, & a^T \Phi(X) \geq 0 \\ 1, & a^T \Phi(X) < 0 \end{cases}$$

where

$$a = \begin{pmatrix} a_1 \\ \vdots \\ a_m \end{pmatrix}, \quad \Phi(X) = \begin{pmatrix} \varphi_1(X) \\ \vdots \\ \varphi_m(X) \end{pmatrix}$$

and X takes values in $\mathbb{R}^d$. The "φ-functions" are fixed and the vector a is a function of the data. (See COVER [2.42] for the development of the φ-function approach and related capacity theorems.) By taking $m = 2$, $d = 1$ and $\varphi_1(x) = x$, $\varphi_2(x) = -1$ we obtain the previous rules with $a_1 = 1$ and $a_2 = t$. As before, we recognize that the first term on the left-hand side of (2.4) corresponds to the re-substitution estimate of L_n^i so that for all vectors a

$$P[|\hat{L}_n^i - L_n^i| \geq \varepsilon] \leq C_0 e^{-Cn_i\varepsilon^2} \quad i = 1, 2.$$

The actual dependence of C and C_0 on m in [2.41] is unknown although it is known that C decreases with m. The performance bound which might be obtained here, while distribution-free, requires that the amount of data needed per state depend on m, the number of features selected. This has been observed before using linear discriminant functions with Gaussian data, the latest analysis being FOLEY [2.43].

Returning to an earlier discussion suppose that the statistician wishes to estimate the ultimate performance of his rule from the data where, for simplicity, we will assume that the ultimate performance is L^*. We now give an example that shows that no reasonable estimate of L^* will have a distribution-free performance. If $\hat{L}_n^*$ is any function of the data used to estimate L^* then its performance is distribution-free if, for each $\varepsilon > 0$,

$$\sup_{\pi, f} P[|\hat{L}_n^* - L^*| \geq \varepsilon] \xrightarrow{n} 0$$

where the supremum is taken over all distributions for which $f_1, \ldots, f_M$ are almost everywhere continuous. It is easy to see that this is equivalent to

$$\sup_{\pi, f} (E|\hat{L}_n^* - L^*|) \xrightarrow{n} 0. \tag{2.5}$$

Taking $M=2$, $\pi_1=\pi_2=1/2$ and

$$f_1=\begin{cases} 2, & \dfrac{2j-2}{2k} \leq x < \dfrac{2j-1}{2k}, & j=1,\ldots,k \\ 0 \text{ elsewhere} \end{cases}$$

$$f_2=\begin{cases} 2, & \dfrac{2j-1}{2k} \leq x < \dfrac{2j}{2k}, & j=1,\ldots,k \\ 0 \text{ elsewhere} \end{cases}$$

we have $L^*=0$. Furthermore, we see that if, for each fixed $\theta_1,\ldots,\theta_n$, $\hat{L}_n^*$ is an almost everywhere continuous function of $x_1,\ldots,x_n$, then

$$E\hat{L}_n^*=\textstyle\sum_{\theta_1,\ldots,\theta_n}(\tfrac{1}{2})^n \int\ldots\int \hat{L}_n^*((x_1,\theta_1),\ldots,(x_n,\theta_n)) f_{\theta_1}(x_1)\ldots$$
$$\ldots f_{\theta_n}(x_n)dx_1\ldots dx_n$$
$$\xrightarrow{k} \textstyle\sum_{\theta_1,\ldots,\theta_n}(\tfrac{1}{2})^n \int_0^1\ldots\int_0^1 \hat{L}_n^*((x_1,\theta_1),\ldots,(x_n,\theta_n))dx_1\ldots dx_n.$$

Thus, as $k\to\infty$, $E\hat{L}_n^*$ tends to its average estimate of L^* for the "no information" experiment (e.g., $\pi_1=\pi_2=1/2$ and f_1,f_2 both uniform on $[0,1]$). For reasonable estimates of L^* (for example, consistent estimates of L^*) this last quantity does not tend to 0 with n. Thus (2.5) is violated. Bounds on performance of estimates of L^* thus necessarily involve quantities which require more *a-priori* information than is available for the nonparametric discrimination problem.

Estimating L^* from the data can be done in many ways. For example, one could take any two-step procedure and use the estimates considered earlier for L_n. For $M=2$ and assuming that

$$\int_{\{x:\pi_1 f_1(x)=\pi_2 f_2(x)\}} [\pi_1 f_1(x)+\pi_2 f_2(x)]dx=0$$

all of these estimates are consistent estimates of L^* when consistent estimates of π_2,π_1,f_2,f_1 are used [2, 39, 44]. Also, GLICK [2.18] has shown that if one uses consistent estimates $\hat{\pi}_1,\ldots,\hat{\pi}_M,\hat{f}_1,\ldots,\hat{f}_M$ then

$$\hat{L}^*=1-\int \max(\hat{\pi}_1\hat{f}_1,\ldots,\hat{\pi}_M\hat{f}_M)dx$$

is a consistent estimate of L^*. Other techniques for estimating L^* have utilized unlabeled observations, an idea first proposed by CHOW [2.34]. For example, $L^*=1-Er(X)$ where, as in Subsection 2.1.3,

$$r(x)= \max\{\pi_1 f_1(x),\ldots,\pi_M f_M(x)\}/f(x),$$
$$f(x)= \textstyle\sum_1^M \pi_i f_i(x).$$

Thus one can estimate $r(x)$ from the labeled observations with, say, $\hat{r}(x)$ and then estimate $Er(X)$ by

$$\frac{1}{T}\textstyle\sum_1^T \hat{r}(Y_i)$$

where $Y_1, \ldots, Y_T$ are the unlabeled observations. Various techniques for estimating $r(\cdot)$ from the labeled observations have been considered by FUKUNAGA and KESSELL [2.45], and FUKUNAGA and HOSTETLER [2.46].

Finally one may be interested in recursive estimates of L^*. One possibility is the estimate used earlier by VAN RYZIN [2.13], namely,

$$\frac{1}{n-1} \sum_1^{n-1} I_{[\hat{\theta}_{j+1} \neq \theta_{j+1}]}$$

where $\hat{\theta}_{j+1}$ is the estimate of θ_{j+1} using δ_j with X_{j+1} and $(X_1, \theta_1), \ldots, (X_j, \theta_j)$. Straightforward arguments (e.g., WOLVERTON [2.47] show that if

$$L_n \xrightarrow{n} L \text{ in probability (or with probability one)}$$

then

$$\frac{1}{n-1} \sum_1^{n-1} I_{[\hat{\theta}_{j+1} \neq \theta_{j+1}]} \xrightarrow{n} L \text{ in probability (or with probability one)}.$$

2.1.5 Density Estimation

Nonparametric density estimation has its raison d'etre rooted in applications like the two-step rules for nonparametric discrimination. After looking at density estimation from a more basic point of view we discuss the results which have been presented since the two paper review of WEGMAN [2.48, 49] and the paper of COVER [2.50].

Density estimation can be viewed as a special case of learning the law of a sequence. This rather basic viewpoint, though certainly not original, singles out a natural error criterion from the seemingly many ad hoc ones which have been considered [2.48]. Suppose $X_1, X_2, \ldots$ is a sequence of independent, identically distributed random vectors with values in $\mathbb{R}^d$ and a common probability measure μ on the Borel σ-algebra β^d of $\mathbb{R}^d$. Estimating the law of the sequence is the problem of finding an estimate μ_n of μ from $X_1, \ldots, X_n$. If the Borel set is *fixed* then

$$\mu_n(B) \triangleq \frac{1}{n} \sum_1^n I_{[X_i \in B]}$$

is the obvious choice as an estimate for the value $\mu(B)$ since it is the minimum variance unbiased estimate of $\mu(B)$. As a function on β^d, μ_n is called the empirical probability measure for $X_1, \ldots, X_n$. The Glivenko-Cantelli theorem states that it is a uniformly good estimate of intervals $(-\infty, x]$, that is,

$$\sup_{\{B: B = (-\infty, x], x \in \mathbb{R}^d\}} |\mu_n(B) - \mu(B)| \to 0 \text{ with probability one}.$$

While it is true that the supremum above can be extended to a larger class of subsets of β^d it nevertheless cannot be extended in general to all Borel sets, see RAO [2.51].

Now, however, assume that we know that μ is absolutely continuous with respect to Lebesgue measure with an almost everywhere continuous probability density f. The empirical probability measure seems inappropriate as an approximation to μ since it is atomic with mass $1/n$ at $X_1, \ldots, X_n$ and, necessarily,

$$\sup_{B \in \beta^d} |\mu_n(B) - \mu(B)| = 1 .$$

Is there then an estimate μ_n in the absolutely continuous case for which

$$\sup_{B \in \beta^d} |\mu_n(B) - \mu(B)| \xrightarrow{n} 0 \text{ with probability one} . \tag{2.6}$$

Suppose we choose some estimate μ_n which is absolutely continuous with a Radon-Nikodym derivative f_n so that we may think of f_n as an estimate of f from $X_1, \ldots, X_n$. Because

$$|\mu_n(B) - \mu(B)| = |\int_B f_n(x)dx - \int_B f(x)dx|$$
$$\leq \int_B |f_n - f| dx \leq \int_{\mathbb{R}^d} |f_n(x) - f(x)| dx$$

we conclude that (2.6) follows whenever

$$\int |f_n(x) - f(x)| dx \xrightarrow{n} 0 \text{ with probability one} . \tag{2.7}$$

From the viewpoint of estimating the law of a sequence the natural distance between f and its estimate f_n thus appears to be $\int |f_n(x) - f(x)| dx$. GLICK [2.52], extending SCHEFFÉ's theorem [2.53], showed that (2.7) follows whenever f_n is an appropriately measurable probability density for all n which is strongly consistent. In addition, he shows that if f_n is a probability density for all n which is just consistent, then

$$\int |f_n(x) - f(x)| dx \to 0 \text{ in probability} . \tag{2.8}$$

If f_n is not a probability density for each n it is also possible to give conditions which insure (2.7) or (2.8), although they are not always easy to apply (see GLICK's corollary B).

The kernel estimate of f from $X_1, \ldots, X_n$ is given by

$$f_n(x) = \sum_1^n K((x - X_i)/r_n)/nr_n^d$$

where K, the kernel, is an arbitrary probability density and $\{r_n\}$ is a sequence of positive numbers. The kernel estimate is a probability density for each n and always satisfies the measurability requirements of GLICK referred to above. Depending on the conditions put on K and $\{r_n\}$ [2.54–57] the kernel estimate is consistent or strongly consistent and (2.7) or (2.8) then follow.

One of the disadvantages of the kernel estimate of f is that the sequence $\{r_n\}$ is chosen without regard to the data. Since r_n controls the degree of smoothing of the kernel estimate f_n about the observations $X_1, \dots, X_n$ it seems desirable to have the data itself play a role in the amount of smoothing. If, in the deterministic discrimination problem, one lets $f_1 = f_2 = f$ then the FIX-HODGES estimate of f_1 and f_2 can be combined to yield

$$\hat{f} = \hat{f}_1 + \hat{f}_2 = \frac{k(n_1, n_2)}{nV} = \frac{k(n)}{nV} \text{ where } n_1 = [n/2], n_2 = n - n_1$$

and V is the volume of the smallest sphere, centered at x, which contains at least k of the n observations. In particular $\hat{f}$ is a consistent estimate of f whenever

$$k(n) \xrightarrow{n} \infty$$
$$k(n)/n \to 0 .$$

This result has usually been attributed to LOFTSGAARDEN and QUESENBERRY [2.58]. Additional conditions on k insure strong consistency [2.59]. The nice feature of the FIX-HODGES estimate is that the data does play a part in the smoothing of the estimate about $X_1, \dots, X_n$. However,

$$\int_{\mathbb{R}^d} \hat{f}(x)dx = \infty$$

for all n so that (2.6) is not possible for this estimate. WAGNER [2.60] has considered letting r_n be a function of the data in the kernel estimate of f [e.g., $r_n = r_n(X_1, \dots, X_n)$] and has, for $d = 1$, given general conditions for consistency. One particular example of these conditions combines the features of the FIX-HODGES estimate by letting r_n be the average of the distances of X_j to its $k(n)$ nearest neighbor from $X_1, \dots, X_n$.

Recently, spline methods have been investigated for density estimation [2.61–63]. Here, for $d = 1$, one fits a spline, usually a cubic spline, to the empirical distribution function of $X_1, \dots, X_n$ with the derivative of the spline being the resulting density estimate. How one chooses the degree of the spline, the points for the knots and the boundary conditions are part of the investigations mentioned.

In [2.64] WAHBA establishes the best possible convergence rate for

$$E[f(x) - \hat{f}_n(x)]^2$$

where $\hat{f}_n(x)$ is any estimate of $f(x)$ and where f is assumed to belong to the Sobolev space of functions $W_p^{(m)}$. In addition, conditions are given for the various types of density estimates to achieve this rate.

2.2 Learning with Finite Memory

There was great emphasis in the early 1960's on recursive or adaptive methods for learning. The work of ABRAMSON and BRAVERMAN [2.65] initiated interest in recursive learning algorithms that were computationally simple. For example, if

$X_1, X_2, \ldots$ are i.i.d. normal random variables $N(\theta, 1)$, with unknown mean θ, and if θ has a normal prior distribution, then $p(\theta | X_1, X_2, \ldots, X_n)$ is also normal with a mean given by a simple recursive function of the sufficient statistic $\bar{X}_n = \frac{1}{n} \sum X_i$. This work was generalized by FRALICK [2.66] and imbedded in the structure of conjugate prior distributions (RAIFFA and SCHLAIFER [2.67]) by SPRAGINS [2.68]. Subsequently, however, this work was misinterpreted because of the emphasis on the interpretation that distributions $f(x | \theta)$ with finite dimensional sufficient statistics require less memory than those that do not. However, when investigated closely, this interpretation is difficult to support. While it is true, for the example, that $\bar{X}_n$ is a sufficient summary of $X_1, X_2, \ldots, X_n$, it is also true that the interleaved decimal expansion $\tilde{X}$ of $X_1, X_2, \ldots, X_n$ represents all the information in the sample, and $\bar{X}$ and $\tilde{X}_n$ are both single real numbers.

One way to make sense out of what is meant by less memory of the past is to restrict the memory to be finite and pursue the question of which problems are easiest under this constraint. But how are we to know which of our real valued statistics are well behaved when quantized, and how should these quantizations be updated? These questions led COVER [2.69] to investigate learning algorithms of the form $T_{n+1} = f(T_n, X_{n+1}, n)$, where $T_n \in \{1, 2, \ldots, m\}$ is the current state of memory. If f is independent of n, the algorithm is said to be *time-invariant*, otherwise the algorithm is *time-varying*. The *memory size* is m, and T_n is the *state of memory* at time n. It was found that ease of learning has nothing to do with the existence of sufficient statistics.

In this section we shall survey past work on these questions and present some of the current difficulties and open problems.

We are given a sequence of independent, identically distributed observations $\{X_n\}_{n=1}^{\infty}$ where each observation X_n is drawn according to the probability measure P. There are two hypotheses H_0 and H_1 with a priori probabilities π_0 and $\pi_1 = 1 - \pi_0$, where under H_t, $P = P_t$ for $t = 0, 1$. We assume that π_0, π_1, P_0 and P_1 are known, and that $P_0 \neq P_1$.

Let $d_n \in \{H_0, H_1\}$ denote the decision made at time n. If d_n is allowed to depend on $X_1, X_2, \ldots, X_n$ then a standard likelihood ratio test yields a probability of error tending exponentially to zero in the sample size n. However, the likelihood ratio is real valued. It requires infinite memory to store it exactly. We could try to estimate the degradation introduced in this method by the use of finite memory, but we prefer to take the more fundamental viewpoint discussed below.

We shall consider algorithms $\mathscr{A}$ of the form

$$
\begin{aligned}
&T_n = f(T_{n-1}, X_n, n), \\
&d_n = d(T_n), \\
&T_n \in \{1, 2, \ldots, m\}, \\
&d_n \in \{H_0, H_1\}, \forall n.
\end{aligned}
\tag{2.9}
$$

If f is a single valued mapping, then $\mathscr{A}$ is said to be a *deterministic* rule, if f is a randomized mapping, then $\mathscr{A}$ is called a *randomized* or stochastic rule.

Elementary decision theoretic considerations show that the error probability cannot be lowered by randomization in d or T_0.

The probability of error at time n is defined by

$$P(m, n) = Pr\{d(T_n) \neq H\}, \tag{2.10}$$

where H is the true hypothesis, $d(T_n)$ is the decision at time n, and m is the memory size. We shall denote by a star the optimal probability of error

$$P^*(m, n) = \inf_{\mathscr{A}} P(m, n), \tag{2.11}$$

where the class of automata $\mathscr{A}$ (e.g., time-invariant, time-varying) will be clear from the context. Finally, consider the limit for an infinite number of samples

$$P(m, \infty) = \lim_{n \to \infty} \sup P(m, n); \quad P^*(m, \infty) = \inf_{\mathscr{A}} P(m, \infty). \tag{2.12}$$

The objective is, for given $m, n, P_0, P_1, \pi_0, \pi_1$ to find the algorithm (f, d, T_0) which minimizes the probability of error $P(m, n)$ or $P(m, \infty)$.

Parts of the following review of the finite memory literature have been contributed by M. HELLMAN.

2.2.1 Time-Varying Finite Memory

In the infinite sample, time-varying, two hypothesis problem, COVER [2.69] has shown that a four-state memory (two bits) is sufficient to insure that the probability of error tends to zero. Basically, one bit is used to remember the current favorite hypothesis and one bit to keep track of the success or failure of test blocks which become increasingly larger. KOPLOWITZ [2.70] has recently shown that COVER's rule can be reduced to a 3-state form. He also demonstrated that an m-state, time-varying memory has an asymptotic error probability of zero for any $(m-1)$-hypothesis problem. Further, KOPLOWITZ proved that, in general, m-states are necessary for this behavior. HIRSCHLER and COVER [2.71] showed that eight states are sufficient to determine the rationality or irrationality of the parameter of a coin, given independent coin flips.

MULLIS and ROBERTS [2.72] investigated a sequential decision problem with time-varying finite memory. The cost for an observation and the cost for each type of error are variable. They find necessary conditions for an optimal design and used an iterative technique to find an approximation to the optimal rule.

WAGNER [2.73] applied time-varying rules for estimating the mean of a distribution. For Bernoulli observations WAGNER's scheme is very close to optimal since its maximum absolute error is at most $1/m$ with $2m$ states in memory.

For the finite sample problem MUISE and BOORSTYN [2.74] establish that the optimal time-varying rule essentially stores a quantized version of the likelihood ratio, although the quantization is not of any simple form. Using detectors of the form given by MUISE and BOORSTYN will result in the fastest decay of error probability with increasing sample size. The result that 4 states allows the error probability to decay to zero cannot be (or at least to date has not been) inferred from their work.

ROBERTS and TOOLEY [2.75] attacked the problem of estimating a parameter with a time-varying finite memory. They restrict their rules to be of a special form which, although not optimal in general, does make sense (and is probably optimal) for many problems of interest.

KOPLOWITZ and ROBERTS [2.76] unified and extended this work. In particular, their demonstration of necessary and sufficient conditions for the optimal state transition function should prove valuable.

TOOLEY and ROBERTS [2.77] extended these ideas to estimating random processes with finite memory. BAXA and NOLTE [2.78] used rules similar to those of ROBERTS and TOOLEY for the detection problem. Their rules, while suboptimal, show good performance for even three bits of memory.

COVER et al. [2.79] established the existence of an optimal rule for the finite sample problem. This work also demonstrates that knowledge of the sample size can be of use in lowering the error probability. In particular, there is a problem (testing whether the bias of a coin is 10^{-10} vs. 10^{-20} with a two state memory) for which the ε-optimal infinite sample solution has $P^*(2, \infty) = 10^{-5}$, while the optimal finite sample solution has $P^*(2, n) < 2 \times 10^{-9}$ for sample sizes $n \approx 2 \times 10^{11}$. This paper then goes on to examine the structure of optimal time-varying algorithms for finite n. First it shows that the optimal rule is deterministic. The proof notes that a randomized rule can be thought of as a collection of deterministic rules indexed by a random variable ω. The error probability of the randomized rule $P_n(e)$ equals $EP_n(e|\omega)$ where the expectation is over ω. There then must be at least one value ω_0 such that $P_n(e|\omega_0) \leq P_n(e)$. By using the deterministic time-varying rule induced by ω_0 we thus suffer no greater loss.

This reasoning fails to go through for time-invariant rules because the deterministic rule induced by ω_0 need not be time-invariant, even though the original randomized rule was. Even so, it indicates that the source of randomization need not be a true random number generator.

Still considering the time-varying problem, this paper then shows that the optimal rule is likelihood ratio in form. That is, under an appropriate renumbering of the states of memory, higher likelihood ratio observations cause transitions to higher numbered states. This result simplifies the earlier proof established by MUISE and BOORSTYN [2.74].

ROBBINS [2.80], SAMUELS [2.81], COVER [2.82], TANAKA [2.83–91] and TARUMI [2.92] have proved similar results [such as $P^*(m, \infty) = 0$, for $m \geq 4$] for the two-armed bandit problem with a time-varying finite memory constraint.

2.2.2 Time-Invariant Finite Memory

In [2.93] HELLMAN and COVER demonstrated that

$$P^*(m, \infty) = \min \left\{ \frac{2\sqrt{\pi_0 \pi_1 \gamma^{m-1}} - 1}{\gamma^{m-1} - 1}, \pi_0, \pi_1 \right\} \tag{2.13}$$

where γ is a measure of the distance between H_0 and H_1. When $\pi_0 = \pi_1 = 1/2$ we have

$$P^*(m, \infty) = \frac{1}{\gamma^{(m-1)/2} + 1} . \tag{2.14}$$

The parameter γ is defined by

$$\gamma = \bar{l}/\underline{l} > 1 \tag{2.15}$$

where $\bar{l}$ is the essential supremum on the likelihood ratio $l(x)$ and $\underline{l}$ is the essential infimum. Clearly $P_0 \neq P_1$ implies $\bar{l} > 1$, $\underline{l} < 1$ and $\gamma > 1$. Since $\gamma > 1$, we see that $P^*(m, \infty)$ goes to zero exponentially in m.

The form of the optimal machine was derived in [2.93]. Here we will merely examine its structure. Let

$$\mathcal{K}_\varepsilon = \{x : l(x) \geq [(1/\bar{l}) + \varepsilon]^{-1}\} \tag{2.16}$$

and

$$\mathcal{T}_\varepsilon = \{x : l(x) \leq \underline{l} + \varepsilon\} . \tag{2.17}$$

Thus for small ε, $\mathcal{K}_\varepsilon$ and $\mathcal{T}_\varepsilon$ have likelihood ratios close to $\bar{l}$ and $\underline{l}$, respectively. Furthermore $P_0(\mathcal{K}_\varepsilon) > 0$ and $P_1(\mathcal{T}_\varepsilon) > 0$ by the definitions of $\bar{l}$ and $\underline{l}$.

Consider the machine which transits from state i to $i+1$ if $X \in \mathcal{K}_\varepsilon$ and $i \leq m-1$; from i to $i-1$ if $X \in \mathcal{T}_\varepsilon$ and $i \geq 2$; and stays in the same state otherwise. This machine changes state only on a subsequence of high information observations, thereby making maximal use of its limited memory to store information. However, it is seen that states 1 and m are the states in which we are most certain of our decisions. Therefore once in an end state we would like the machine to stay there for a long time before leaving. Randomization achieves this.

If in state 1 and $X \in \mathcal{K}_\varepsilon$, move to state 2 with small probability δ (and stay in state 1 with probability $1 - \delta$). If in state m and $X \in \mathcal{T}_\varepsilon$, move to state $m-1$ with probability $k\delta$ (and stay in state m with probability $1 - k\delta$). Leave all other transitions as they were.

The purpose of not fixing $k = 1$ is to allow asymmetries in the structure of the machine to compensate for asymmetries in the statistics (e.g., $\pi_0 \neq \pi_1$, etc.). For symmetric problems the optimal value is $k = 1$.

In [2.93] it is shown that with k properly chosen, as ε, $\delta \to 0$, the probability of error tends to $P^*(m, \infty)$, so that this is an optimal class of algorithms. The simple structure of this class is pleasing, and somewhat unexpected, since no constraints were placed on the "complexity" of the mapping f.

Randomization is generally required to ε-achieve $P^*(m, \infty)$ [2.93]. In fact, for discrete distributions, HELLMAN and COVER [2.94] showed that there can be arbitrarily large discrepancies between the performance of randomized and deterministic rules for a fixed memory size. On the other hand, HELLMAN [2.95] demonstrated that deterministic rules are asymptotically optimal for large memories, if memory size is measured in bits.

FLOWER and HELLMAN [2.96] examined the finite sample problem for Bernoulli observations. They found that most properties of the infinite sample solution carry over. For optimal designs, transitions are made only between adjacent states, and randomization is needed. However, in the finite sample problem randomization is needed on all transitions toward the center state (i.e., on transitions from states of low uncertainty to states with higher uncertainty). SAMANIEGO [2.97] proved that this structure is optimal for $m=3$ when attention is restricted to symmetric machines and problems.

LYNN and BOORSTYN [2.98] examined the finite sample problem for observations with continuous symmetric distributions. They calculated the probability of error for algorithms of a particular form which they call finite memory linear detectors. For this type of detector a transition occurs from state i to $i-1$ if $i \leq m-1$ and $X_n > D$; a transition occurs from state i to $i-1$ if $i \geq 2$ and $X_n < -D$; and the transition is from state i to itself in all other cases. The threshold D is optimized over the non-negative real line. The authors noted that this form of machine is somewhat restrictive, but that its simplicity makes it attractive. It resembles the ε-optimal solution to the infinite sample problem in many respects.

SHUBERT and ANDERSON [2.99] studied a form of generalized saturable counter and found performance to be close to optimal. The simplicity of this class of rules makes it attractive for implementation on binary data. SHUBERT [2.100] also studied a variant of the Bernoulli hypothesis testing problem in which the machine observes not only $\{X_n\}$, but also two reference sequences $\{Y_n\}$ and $\{Z_n\}$ with biases p_1 and p_2 respectively. He showed that if memory is increased by one bit then a deterministic machine can perform better than the optimal randomized machine.

SAMANIEGO [2.101] investigated the problem of estimating the parameter of a Bernoulli distribution and, restricting attention to a certain form of machine, finds minimax solutions using a variant of the mean-square-error loss criterion. If p is the true value of the parameter and $\hat{p}$ is the estimate, his loss function is $(p-\hat{p})^2/(p(1-p))$. The machine is restricted to make transitions only between adjacent states, and to move up on heads and down on tails.

HELLMAN [2.102] examined the infinite sample, Gaussian estimation problem and showed that the problem can be reduced to a quantization problem. This result also applies to a larger class of infinite sample estimation problems.

SHUBERT [2.103] has recently established some interesting results on the structure of optimal finite memory algorithms for testing k hypotheses, for $k \geq 3$. This problem remains unsolved, but SHUBERT was able to exhibit a counterexample to the natural conjecture that the optimal algorithm has a tree structure for its transition rule. Other relevant references in finite memory include [2.14, 104–111].

The outstanding open problems in this area are
   i) k-hypothesis testing with finite memory
  ii) estimation with finite memory
 iii) establishing optimality of likelihood ratio transition rules for finite-sample time-invariant rules.

2.3 Two-Dimensional Patterns and Their Complexity

Human visual pattern recognition deals with two- and three-dimensional scenes. What we need for a systematic investigation of statistical pattern recognition applied to two- and three-dimensional scenes are the following:

1) A systematic description of two-dimensional scenes. This description should allow for degrees of resolution. It is very clear in practice that many scenes that differ point to point may in fact be perceived by a visual system as the same scene. Thus a suitable metric on the set of all two-dimensional scenes must be developed.

2) A sequence of sequentially more refined partitions of the pattern space. For example, one standard scheme of representing a two-dimensional image is to quantize it into small squares, each square of which has associated a brightness level belonging to some finite set. Alternatively, one might have a metric defined on the pattern space and describe the scene to ε-accuracy by finitely describing some pattern that lies within ε of the true perceived pattern. Thus the representation of a pattern would consist of a canonical pattern P and a real number $\varepsilon > 0$.

3) There should be an algebra on the pattern space corresponding to the usual manipulations—union, intersection, obscuring of images, complementations, rotations, translations, etc. Some notions on developing an algebra on the space of man's senses are discussed in COVER [2.14].

4) There should be a notion of a universal intrinsic complexity of patterns. At first the idea seems absurd that a Martian, a Human, and a member of some far away galaxy would all perceive the image of a cabin by a lake with smoke coming out of the chimney as having the same intrinsic complexity. While it is certainly true that there are certain familiar stored scenes which facilitate an efficient description of the image, it turns out that this cultural bias manifests itself as an additive constant which is washed out by scenes of sufficient complexity. Indeed, using a modified notion of KOLMOGOROV-SOLOMONOFF-CHAITIN [2.112–114] complexity, in which the complexity of an image is defined to be the length of the shortest binary computer program that will cause a computer to print out the image to the desired degree of accuracy, we can prove that the intrinsic complexity of an image is universal. We shall develop some of the properties of the complexity notion for patterns.

The intrinsic complexity of patterns sits by itself as the most efficient description of the pattern, but we wish to invest this notion with further operational significance. For example, of what use is this information in allowing one to infer the classification of new, as yet unseen patterns? We find that by putting this problem into a gambling context in which one's degree of belief is immediately reflected in the amount of money gambled, that there is an absolute duality between the amount of money which can be won in sequential gambling schemes on a pattern and the number of bits of compression that can be achieved in the pattern by taking it from its raw form to its shortest program.

Furthermore, in addition to being able to make an exponential amount of money on the inference of patterns exhibited bit by bit, we find that we can also infer the classification of new patterns. We show here that the amount of money that can be made corresponds to the complexity of the classification function which classifies each pattern into its appropriate category. So although the underlying classification function is not known, sequential inferences can be made in a universal way about this unknown classification function in such a manner that the amount of money S_n achieved after n patterns have been presented is given by $2^{n-K(f)}$, where $K(f)$ is the length in bits of the shortest binary program describing the classification function f. As a particular application, we shall show that the standard linearly separable, quadratically separable, and spherically separable pattern sets yield an inference procedure generating an amount which is given by $S_n \approx 2^{n[1-H(d/n)]}$, where d is the number of degrees of freedom of the classification surface, n is the number of points being classified, and $H(p) = -p \log p - q \log q$ is Shannon's entropy function.

Technically, the approach given in this section is not statistical in that we make deterministic statements about the intrinsic complexity of a sequence and the amount of money that a gambling scheme will surely have earned on this sequence. However, the universal gambling schemes have the property that they contain all known finitely describable statistical inference procedures as a special case. In addition, they have an optimality property which guarantees that the amount of money earned is earned at a rate which is the maximum possible, given known statistics.

2.3.1 Pattern Complexity

In this section we shall consider the intrinsic complexity of patterns and the extent to which this notion is well defined. Past work in the computer science and artificial intelligence literature on the decomposition of pictures into their basic building blocks is consistent with our motivation, but we shall look at the simplest description over all possible descriptions. Also, work on computational geometry and Perceptron complexity by MINSKY and PAPERT [2.115] is an attempt to measure picture complexity with respect to Perceptrons. We shall consider picture complexity with respect to so-called universal computers.

Kolmogorov Complexity

Let N denote the natural numbers $\{0, 1, 2, ...\}$. Let $\{0, 1\}^*$ denote all binary sequences of finite length. Let $x \in \{0, 1\}^*$ denote a finite binary sequence and let $x(n) = (x_1, x_2, ..., x_n)$ denote the first n terms. Let A be a partial recursive function $A: \{0, 1\}^* \times N \rightarrow \{0, 1\}^*$. Let $l(x)$ denote the length of the sequence x. Then $K_A(x(n)|n) = \min_{A(p,n)=x(n)} l(p)$ is the program complexity of KOLMOGOROV et al. [2.112–114]. We know that

i) $K(x(n)|n) \leq K_B(x(n)|n) + C_B$
      for all $n \in N$, $\forall x$, $\forall B$

$$\text{(2.18)}$$

ii) $|\{x \in \{0, 1\}^* : K(x) = k\}| \leq 2^k$,
       $\forall k \in N$.

Now we define a complexity measure for functions $f:D\to\{0,1\}$, where the domain D is some finite set. Let A be a universal partial recursive function.

Definition. $K_A(f|D) = \min\limits_{\substack{A(p,x)=f(x) \\ x\in D}} l(p)\,.$ (2.19)

We assume throughout that the inputs (p, n) and (p, x) for A are suitably presented to the computer (partial recursive function) A. Thus the complexity of f given the domain D is the minimum length program p such that a Turing machine A, or equivalently a mechanical algorithm A, can compute $f(x)$ in finite time, for each $x\in D$.

Example 1. Let $D=\{0,1\}^d$.

Let $f(x) = \begin{cases} 1, & \sum x_i = \text{odd} \\ 0, & \sum x_i = \text{even}\,. \end{cases}$

Then $K(f|D)=c$, where c is some small constant independent of d. The parity function above is easy to describe and thus has essentially zero complexity.

Pattern Complexity

Let $D=\{1,2,\dots,m\}\times\{1,2,\dots,m\}$ denote a *retina* and x denote a *pattern*, $x:D\to\{0,1\}$. The interpretation is that the cell (i,j) of the retina has brightness level $x(i,j)$. Let A be a universal partial recursive function. We shall consider A fixed and henceforth drop the subscript in K_A.

Definition: The *pattern complexity* of the pattern x is given by

$$K(x) = \min\limits_{\substack{A(p,(i,j))=x(i,j) \\ \forall(i,j)\in D}} l(p)$$

We have the following properties:

i) $K(x)\le K_B(x)+c, \quad \forall x, \quad \forall B,$
ii) $K(x)\le m^2+c, \quad \forall x.$

Here are some examples without proof:

i) The blank pattern $x_0\equiv 0$ has $K(x_0)=0(1)$, where $0(1)$ denotes a (small) constant independent of the retina size m.

ii) The single spot pattern

$$x(i,j) = \begin{cases} 1, & (i,j)=(i_0,j_0) \\ 0, & \text{otherwise} \end{cases}$$

has

$$K(x)\le 2\log m+0(1)\,.$$

iii) If x is the pattern corresponding to a rectangular subset of D, then $K(x)\le 6\log m+0(1)$.

iv) Let C be a circle thrown down on the retina, and let $x(i,j)=1$ if and only if $(i,j)\in C$. Then $K(x)\le 6\log m+0(1)$.

2.3.2 Inference of Classification Functions

This section follows the presentation in COVER [2.116]. Given a domain D of patterns $D = \{x_1, x_2, \ldots, x_n\}$ and an unknown classification function $f : D \rightarrow \{0, 1\}$ assigning the patterns to two classes, we ask for an intelligent way to learn f as the correctly classified elements in D are presented one by one. We ask this question in a gambling context in which a gambler, starting with one unit, sequentially bets a portion of his current capital on the classification of the new pattern. We find the optimal gambling system when f is known a priori to belong to some family F. We also exhibit a universal optimal learning scheme achieving $\exp_2 [n - K(f|D) - \log(n+1)]$ units for each f, where $K(f|D)$ is the length of the shortest binary computer program which calculates f on its domain D. In particular it can be shown that a gambler can double his money approximately $n[1 - H(d/n)]$ times, if f is a linear threshold function on n patterns in d-space.

Let F denote a set of (classification) functions $f : D \rightarrow \{0, 1\}$. For example, F might be the set of all linear threshold functions. Let $|F|$ denote the number of elements in F. The interpretation will be that D is the set of patterns, and $f(x)$ is the classification of the pattern x in D.

Consider the following gambling situation. The elements of D are presented in any order. A gambler starts with one dollar. The first pattern $x_1 \in D$ is exhibited. The gambler then announces amounts b_1 and b_0 that he bets on the true class being $f(x_1) = 1$ and $f(x_1) = 0$, respectively. Without loss of generality we can set $b_1 + b_0 = 1$. The true value $f(x_1)$ is then announced, and the gambler loses the incorrect bet and is paid even money on the correct bet. Thus his new capital is

$$S_1 = \begin{cases} 2b_1, & f(x_1) = 1 \\ 2b_0, & f(x_1) = 0. \end{cases}$$

Now a new pattern element $x_2 \in D$ is exhibited. Again the gambler announces proportions b_1 and b_0 of his current capital that he bets on $f(x_2) = 1$ and $f(x_2) = 0$, respectively. Without loss of generality let $b_0 + b_1 = 1$. Thus the bet sizes are $b_1 S_1$ and $b_0 S_1$. Then $f(x)$ is announced and the gambler's new capital is

$$S_2 = \begin{cases} 2b_1 S_1, & f(x_2) = 1 \\ 2b_0 S_2, & f(x_2) = 0. \end{cases} \tag{2.20}$$

Continuing in this fashion, we define

$$b_1^{(k)} \{x_k | \{x_1, f(x_1)\}, \ldots, \{x_{k-1}, f(x_{k-1})\}\}, \ x_k \in D$$

and $b_0^{(k)} = 1 - b_1^{(k)}$, $b_0^{(k)} \geq 0$, $b_1^{(k)} \geq 0$ as a gambling scheme that depends only on the previously observed properly classified (training) set.

The accrued capital is

$$S_k = \begin{cases} 2b_1^{(k)} S_{k-1}, & f(x_k) = 1 \\ 2b_0^{(k)} S_{k-1}, & f(x_k) = 0 \end{cases} \tag{2.21}$$

for $k=1, 2, ..., n$ and $S_0 = 1$. Let

$$b = \{\{b_0^{(1)}, b_1^{(1)}\}, \{b_0^{(2)}, b_1^{(2)}\}, ..., \{b_0^{(n)}, b_1^{(n)}\}\}$$

denote a sequence of gambling functions.

Theorem 1. For any $F \subseteq D^{\{0, 1\}}$, there exists a gambling scheme b^* achieving $S_n(f) = S^* = 2^{n - \log|F|}$ units, for all f in F and for all orders of presentation of the elements $x \in D$. Moreover, there exists no b that dominates b^* $\forall f$; thus b^* is minimax. This gambling scheme is given by the expression

$$b_1^{(k)*}(x) = \frac{|\{g \in F : g(x_i) = f(x_i), i = 1, 2, ..., k-1, \text{ and } g(x) = 1\}|}{|\{g \in F : g(x_i) = f(x_i), i = 1, 2, ..., k-1\}|}. \tag{2.22}$$

Remark. This gambling scheme simply asserts at time k, "Bet all of the current capital on the hypotheses $f(x_k) = 1$ and $f(x_k) = 0$ in proportion to the number of functions g in F that *agree* on the training set and assign the new pattern x_k to classes $g(x_k) = 1$ and $g(x_k) = 0$, respectively".

Example: Let D denote a set of n vectors in Euclidean d-space $\mathbb{R}^d$. Let us also assume that $\{x_1, x_2, ..., x_n\} = D$ is in *general position* in the sense that every d-element subset of D is linearly independent. Let F be the set of all linear threshold functions on D; i.e., $f \in F$ implies there exists $w \in \mathbb{R}^d$, such that

$$f(x) = \text{sgn}(w^t x - T), \quad \forall x \in D,$$

where

$$\text{sgn}(t) = \begin{cases} 1, & t \geq 0 \\ 0, & t < 0. \end{cases}$$

Then from COVER [2.42], we have $|F| = 2 \sum_{k=0}^{d} \binom{n-1}{k}$, $\forall d, n$. Using bounds derived from Stirling's approximation, it can be shown that

$$\log\left(2 \sum_{k=0}^{d} \binom{n-1}{k}\right) \approx nH\left(\frac{d}{n}\right), \quad \text{for} \quad n \geq 2d. \tag{2.23}$$

Thus we conclude, for $n \geq 2d$, that an amount $S_n = 2^{n[1 - H(d/n)]}$ can be won if in fact the n patterns are linearly separable in $\mathbb{R}^d$. Note also that $H(d/n)$ is the Kolmogorov complexity of most of the linear threshold functions $f \in F$. Finally, we observe that S_n is not much greater than 1 until $n \geq 2d$, at which point S_n grows exponentially. This is yet more evidence that $n = 2d$ is a natural definition of the capacity of a linear threshold pattern recognition device with d variable weights [2.42]. This result is a special case of the following theorem:

Theorem 2: There exists a betting scheme b^* such that the total accumulated capital satisfies $S(f) \geq 2^{n - K(f|D) - \log(n+1)}$.

Other aspects of complexity and inference can be found in COVER [2.117].

References

2.1   E. Fix, J. L. Hodges: "Discriminatory Analysis. Nonparametric Discrimination: Consistency Properties", Rep. 4, Project no. 21-49-004, USAF School of Aviation Medicine, Randolph Field, Texas (1951)

2.2   T. Cover, P. Hart: IEEE Trans. Information Theory IT-**13**, 21 (1967)

2.3   E. Fix, J. L. Hodges: "Discriminatory Analysis. Nonparametric Discrimination: Small Sample Performance", Rep. 11, Project no. 21-49-004, USAF School of Aviation Medicine, Randolph Field, Texas (1952)

2.4   M. G. Kendall: Discrimination and Classification, in *Proc. Intern. Symp. Multivariate Analysis*, ed. by P. R. Krishnaiah (Academic Press, New York 1966)

2.5   C. P. Quesenberry, M. P. Gessaman: Ann. Math. Statist. **39**, 664 (1968)

2.6   M. W. Anderson, R. D. Benning: IEEE Trans. Information Theory IT-**16**, 541 (1970)

2.7   G. W. Beakley, F. B. Tuteur: IEEE Trans. Computers C-**21**, 1337 (1972)

2.8   E. G. Henrichon, K. S. Fu: IEEE Trans. Computers C-**19**, 362 (1970)

2.9   E. G. Henrichon, K. S. Fu: IEEE Trans. Computers C-**18**, 614 (1969)

2.10   T. W. Anderson: Some Nonparametric Multivariate Procedures Based on Statistically Equivalent Blocks, in *Proc. Intern. Symp. Multivariate Analysis,* ed. by P. R. Krishnaiah (Academic Press, New York 1966)

2.11   J. Owen, D. B. Brick, E. A. Henrichon: Pattern Recognition **2**, 227 (1970)

2.12   M. P. Gessaman, P. H. Gessaman: J. Am. Stat. Assoc. **67**, 468 (1972)

2.13   J. Van Ryzin: Ann. Math. Statist. **37**, 976 (1966)

2.14   T. Cover: Learning in Pattern Recognition, in *Methodologies of Pattern Recognition,* ed. by S. Watanabe (Academic Press, New York 1969)

2.15   H. Robbins: Ann. Math. Statist. **35**, 1 (1964)

2.16   J. Van Ryzin: Sankhya Ser. A **28**, 261 (1966)

2.17   S. C. Schwartz: Convergence of Risk in Adaptive Pattern Recognition Procedures, in Proc. 5th Allerton Conf. Circuit and System Theory, (1967) pp. 800–807

2.18   N. Glick: J. Am. Stat. Assoc. **67**, 116 (1972)

2.19   E. Hewitt, J. L. Savage: Trans. Am. Math. Soc. **80**, 470 (1955)

2.20   L. Breiman: *Probability* (Addison-Wesley, Reading, Mass. 1968)

2.21   J. Van Ryzin: J. Math. Anal. Appl. **20**, 359 (1967)

2.22   C. T. Wolverton, T. J. Wagner: IEEE Trans. Information Theory IT-**15**, 258 (1969)

2.23   L. Rejtö, P. Révész: Problems of Control and Information Theory **2**, 67 (1973)

2.24   C. R. Pelto: Technometrics **11**, 775 (1969)

2.25   T. J. Wagner: IEEE Trans. Information Theory IT-**17**, 566 (1971)

2.26   J. Fritz: IEEE Trans. Information Theory IT-**21**, 552 (1975)

2.27   D. L. Wilson: IEEE Trans. Systems Man Cybernetic SMC-**2**, 408 (1972)

2.28   P. Hart: IEEE Trans. Information Theory IT-**14**, 515 (1968)

2.29   G. W. Gates: IEEE Trans. Information Theory IT-**18**, 431 (1972)

2.30   J. R. Ullman: IEEE Trans. Information Theory IT-**20**, 541 (1974)

2.31   C. W. Swonger: Sample Set Condensation for a Condensed Nearest Rule for Pattern Recognition, in *Frontiers of Pattern Recognition,* ed. by S. Watanabe (Academic Press, New York 1972)

2.32   C. L. Chang: IEEE Trans. Computers C-**23**, 1179 (1974)

2.33   M. E. Hellman: IEEE Trans. Systems Science Cybernetic SSC-**6**, 179 (1970)

2.34   C. K. Chow: IEEE Trans. Information Theory IT-**16**, 41 (1970)

2.35   C. K. Chow: IRE Trans. Electronic Computers EC-**6**, 247 (1957)

2.36   A. Dvoretzky, J. Kiefer, J. Wolfowitz: Ann. Math. Statist **27**, 642 (1956)

2.37   G. T. Toussaint: IEEE Trans. Information Theory IT-**20**, 472 (1974)

2.38   L. Kanal: IEEE Trans. Information Theory IT-**20**, 697 (1974)

2.39   S. C. Fralick, R. W. Scott: IEEE Trans. Information Theory IT-**17**, 440 (1971)

2.40   W. H. Rogers, T. J. Wagner: Ann. Statist. **6**, 506 (1978)

2.41   J. Kiefer, J. Wolfowitz: Trans. Am. Math. Soc. **87**, 173 (1958)

2.42   T. Cover: IEEE Trans. Electronic Computers IT-**10**, 618 (1965)

2.43   D. H. Foley: IEEE Trans. Information Theory IT-**18**, 618 (1972)

2.44   T. J. Wagner: Ann. Statist **1**, 359 (1973)

2.45   K. Fukunaga, D. Kessell: IEEE Trans. Information Theory IT-**19**, 434 (1973)

2.46 K. FUKUNAGA, L. HOSTETLER: IEEE Trans. Information Theory, IT-**21**, 285 (1975)

2.47 C. T. WOLVERTON: IEEE Trans. Information Theory IT-**18**, 119 (1972)

2.48 E. J. WEGMAN: Technometrics **14**, 533 (1972)

2.49 E. J. WEGMAN: J. Statist. Comp. Simulation **1**, 225 (1972)

2.50 T. COVER: A Hierarchy of Probability Density Function Estimates, in *Frontiers of Pattern Recognition*, ed. by S. WATANABE (Academic Press, New York 1972)

2.51 R. R. RAO: Ann. Math. Statist. **33**, 659 (1962)

2.52 N. GLICK: Utilitas Math. **6**, 61 (1974)

2.53 H. SCHEFFÉ: Ann. Math. Statist. **18**, 434 (1947)

2.54 E. PARZEN: Ann. Math. Statist. **33**, 1065 (1947)

2.55 T. CACOULLOS: Ann. Instit. Statist. Math. **18**, 178 (1966)

2.56 E. A. NADARAYA: Theory Prob. Appl. **10**, 186 (1965)

2.57 J. VAN RYZIN: Ann. Math. Statist **40**, 1765 (1969)

2.58 D. O. LOFTSGAARDEN, C. P. QUESENBERRY: Ann. Math. Statist. **38**, 1261 (1965)

2.59 T. J. WAGNER: IEEE Trans. Systems Man Cybernetic SMC-**3**, 289 (1973)

2.60 T. J. WAGNER: IEEE Trans. Information Theory IT-**21**, 438 (1974)

2.61 L. BONEVA, D. KENDALL, I. STEFANOV: J. Roy. Statist. Soc. **33**, 1 (1971)

2.62 G. WAHBA: "Interpolating Spline Methods for Density Estimation II. Variable Knots", Tech. Rep. # 337, Dept. of Statistics, University of Wisconsin, Madison, Wisconsin (1973)

2.63 G. WAHBA: Ann. Statist. **3**, 15 (1975)

2.64 G. WAHBA: Ann. Statist. **3**, 30 (1975)

2.65 N. ABRAMSON, D. BRAVERMAN: IRE Trans, Information Theory IT-**8**, 58 (1962)

2.66 S. C. FRALICK: "The Synthesis of Machines Which Learn Without a Teacher", Techn. Rep. no. 6103-8, Stanford Electronics Labs., Stanford, California (1964)

2.67 H. RAIFFA, R. SCHLAIFER: *Applied Statistical Decision Theory* (Harvard University Press, Boston, Mass. 1961)

2.68 J. SPRAGINS: IEEE Trans. Information Theory IT-**12**, 223 (1966)

2.69 T. M. COVER: Ann. Math. Statist. **40**, 828 (1969)

2.70 J. KOPLOWITZ: IEEE Trans. Information Theory IT-**21**, 44 (1975)

2.71 T. M. COVER, P. HIRSCHLER: Ann. Statist **3**, 939 (1975)

2.72 C. T. MULLIS, R. A. ROBERTS: IEEE Trans. Information Theory IT-**20**, 440 (1974)

2.73 T. J. WAGNER: IEEE Trans. Information Theory IT-**18**, 523 (1972)

2.74 R. W. MUISE, R. R. BOORSTYN: "Detection with Time-Varying Finite-Memory Receivers", Abstracts of papers, 1972 IEEE Intern. Symp. Information Theory, (1972)

2.75 R. A. ROBERTS, J. R. TOOLEY: IEEE Trans. Information Theory IT-**16**, 685 (1970)

2.76 J. KOPLOWITZ, R. ROBERTS: IEEE Trans. Information Theory IT-**19**, 631 (1973)

2.77 J. R. TOOLEY, R. ROBERTS: IEEE Trans. Systems Man Cybernetic SMC-**3**, 294 (1973)

2.78 E. G. BAXA, L. W. NOLTE: IEEE Trans. Systems Man Cybernetics SMC-**2**, 42 (1972)

2.79 T. COVER, M. FREEDMAN, M. HELLMAN: Information and Control **30**, 49–85 (1976)

2.80 H. ROBBINS: Proc. Nat. Acad. Sci. **42**, 920 (1956)

2.81 S. M. SAMUELS: Ann. Math. Statist. **39**, 2103 (1968)

2.82 T. M. COVER: Information and Control **12**, 371 (1968)

2.83 K. TANAKA: Bull. Math. Statist. **14**, 31 (1970)

2.84 K. TANAKA: Bull. Math. Statist. **14**, 61 (1970)

2.85 K. TANAKA: Mathematics **24**, 249 (1970)

2.86 K. TANAKA: Bull. Math. Statist. **14**, 13 (1971)

2.87 K. TANAKA, E. ISOGAI: Tamkang J. Math.

2.88 K. TANAKA, K. INADA, S. IWASE: Tamkang J. Math. **5**, 85–101 (1974)

2.89 K. TANAKA, K. INADA: "Some Extension of the Two-Armed Bandit Problem with Finite Memory", Sci. Rep. Niigata Univ., Series A, **10**, 5 (1973)

2.90 K. TANAKA, K. INADA: "Some Statistical Method with Finite Memory", Sci. Rep. Niigata Univ., Series A, **10**, 27 (1973)

2.91 K. TANAKA, E. ISOGAI, S. IWASE: "On a Sequential Procedure with Finite Memory for Testing Statistical Hypotheses", Sci. Rep. Niigata University, Series A, **11**, 31 (1974)

2.92 T. TARUMI: "Estimation of the Direction of a Bivariate Normal Mean with Finite Memory", Memoirs of the Faculty of Science, Kyushu University, Series A, Mathematics **26**, 351 (1972)

2.93 T. COVER, M. HELLMAN: Ann. Math. Statist. **41**, 765 (1970)

2.94   T. Cover, M. Hellman: Ann. Math. Statist. **42**, 1075 (1971)
2.95   M. E. Hellman: IEEE Trans. Information Theory IT-**18**, 499 (1972)
2.96   R. A. Flower, M. E. Hellman: IEEE Trans. Information Theory IT-**18**, 429 (1972)
2.97   F. Samaniego: IEEE Trans. Information Theory IT-**20**, 387 (1974)
2.98   P. F. Lynn, R. Boorstyn: Bounds on Finite Detectors, presented at 1972 IEEE Intern. Symp. Information Theory, Asilomar, California (1972)
2.99   B. Shubert, C. Anderson: IEEE Trans. Information Theory IT-**19**, 644 (1973)
2.100 B. Shubert: IEEE Trans. Information Theory IT-**2**, 384 (1974)
2.101 F. Samaniego: IEEE Trans. Information Theory IT-**19**, 636 (1973)
2.102 M. E. Hellman: IEEE Trans. Information Theory IT-**20**, 382 (1974)
2.103 B. Shubert: "Some Remarks on the Finite-Memory K-Hypotheses Problems", Techn. Rep. NPS55Sy74101, Naval Postgraduate School, Monterey, California (1974)
2.104 M. L. Tsetlin: Avtomat. i Telemeh. **22**, 1345 (1961) (Available in English translation)
2.105 V. Y. Krylov: Avtomat. i Telemeh. **24**, 1226 (1963) (Available in English translation)
2.106 V. I. Varshavskii, I. P. Vorontsova: Avtomat. i Telemeh. **24**, 327 (1963) (Available in English translation)
2.107 K. S. Fu, T. J. Li: "On the Behavior of Learning Automato and its Applications", Purdue University Techn. Rep. no. TR-EE 68-20 (1968)
2.108 B. Chandrasekaran, D. W. S. Shen: IEEE Trans. Systems Science Cybernetic SSC-**4** (1968)
2.109 T. Cover, M. Hellman: IEEE Trans. Information Theory IT-**16**, 185 (1970)
2.110 P. F. Lynn: Finite Memeory Detectors; Ph. D. Thesis, Dept. of Electr. Engg., Polytechnic Inst. of Brooklyn (1971)
2.111 C. T. Mullis: A Class of Finite Memory Decision Processes; M. S. Thesis, Dept. Electr. Engg., Univ. of Colorado (1968)
2.112 A. N. Kolmogorov: Problemy Peredaci Informaccii **1**, 3 (1965)
2.113 R. J. Solomonoff: Information and Control **7**, 1, 224 (1964)
2.114 G. J. Chaitin: J. Assoc. Comput. Mach. **13**, 547 (1966)
2.115 M. Minsky, S. Papert: *Perceptrons* (MIT Press, Cambridge, Mass 1969)
2.116 T. Cover: "Generalization on Patterns Using Kolmogorov Complexity", Proc. 1st Intern. Joint Conf. Pattern Recognition, Washington, C. D. (1973)
2.117 T. Cover: "Universal Gambling Schemes and Kolomogorov Complexity", Standford Statistics Department Technical Report # 12 (1974)

3. Clustering Analysis

E. Diday and J. C. Simon

With 11 Figures

Cluster analysis is one of the Pattern Recognition techniques and should be appreciated as such. It may be characterized by the use of resemblance or dissemblance measures between the objects to be identified.

An evaluation of the significations of such measures is made; examples are given.

After presenting a general model of clustering techniques, the general properties of a cluster, of a clustering operator and of a clustering model are examined.

The goal of a clustering analysis is usually to obtain a symbolic description of the problem and from this an identification procedure. The main clustering algorithms are presented according to the symbolic descriptions: hierarchies, minimum spanning trees, partitions and their representations.

Special attention is given to the dynamic cluster method, which handles adaptively a partition in clusters and a set of symbolic representations of the clusters. Examples are given of this method when the symbolic representation is either a kernel, a probability law or a linear manifold.

Results are given of the dynamic cluster algorithm when the distance measures may also be modified among a class of distances.

Some general conclusions and a proposal for research are finally given.

3.1 Introduction

3.1.1 Relations Between Clustering and Pattern Recognition

The Pattern Recognition (P.R.) field has developed mostly as statistical classification techniques. Though it is clear that human P.R. is a lot more than classification, great difficulties have limited the results obtained by more ambitious methods such as "scene analysis".

Thus at the present time P.R. and classification are for the most part equivalent terms.

Definition of Classification and Identification

Let X be a variable object defined by n variables $(x_1, x_2, ..., x_n)$. Let X be an object defined by n parameters $(x_1, x_2, ..., x_n)$.

Let $\mathbf{X}$ be the "space" of these variables X and of these objects or points X.

Let $E = \{X_1, ..., X_m\}$ be the set of m of these objects.

A *representation* is any material sign which designates an object.

The usual *interpretations* of these representations can be found either in a natural language or in an abstract machine language.

i) In natural language, X is a variable object; $x_1,...,x_n$ are the variable measures on the objects. X is the name of an object; $x_1,...,x_n$ are the results of measures on this object. Usually a measure has the properties of a "*quantitative value*"; length, weight, amplitude, age, etc. But sometimes no such interpretation can be found: state, color, name, illness, etc. Then it is said that the value is "*qualitative*".

ii) In an abstract machine language, the interpretation of X is a set of variable input data; $x_1, ..., x_n$ are the atomic variable input data. X is the name of a datum; $x_1,...,x_n$ are the states of the data of global name X.

Let Ω be the set of p names ω_i

$$\Omega = \{\omega_1,...,\omega_p\}.$$

An *identification* is a mapping $\mathscr{E}$, which may be not defined on all the ranges of **X**

$$\mathscr{E}:\mathbf{X}\to\Omega$$

or

$$\mathscr{E}:(x_1,...,x_n)\to\omega_i.$$

Of course this definition is *not constructive*. One has to exhibit an algorithm or procedure or program which will allow a machine implementation. On the other hand this mapping must have a *proper semantic interpretation:* if X is the result of a measurement on an object, the image ω_i of the mapping should be the name of the object.

This mapping defines equivalence classes C_i on the space **X**

$$C_i = \{X|\mathscr{E}:X\to\omega_i\}.$$

All the objects of the same C_i having the same name ω_i are usually interpreted as different occurrences of the same object, for example, a phoneme, a letter or an image feature, etc.

In the context of "clustering", it is customary to call a class a "cluster" and the set of classes the "partition".

The practical problem of *classification* is to find a constructive *identification function* (or program or operator) which will perform the above mapping.

Most of the time, the experimenter provides a "*training set*" T, which is a finite number of examples of the mapping $\mathscr{E}$

$$T = \{(X, \omega)\}.$$

The classification specialist then selects a "good" function and adjusts it on the training set. If this function is defined on all of the ranges of X, a *generalization* of the experimental examples is obtained in the space **X**.

It is clear that this "function" must obey very special properties to be satisfactory for a given P.R. problem. The recognition function has to satisfy the *semantics* of the problem.

Unfortunately the choice is made under many other considerations. Often, simplicity guides the P.R. specialists: for example, he adjusts some linear discriminant functions (hyperplanes) to the training set. Disappointing results are then obtained outside of the training set. The generalizing properties of the function are not satisfactory. This is not surprising: the semantic of the P.R. problem has not been taken into account! Why should we expect that the frontier between classes would be hyperplanes in $\mathbb{R}^n$?

The main difficulties of P.R. are then

i) to define the semantics of P.R., in other words to define what properties the P.R. function must have.

ii) To find a constructive function which will satisfy the above semantics.

Remark

The identification of an object is the act of giving the name of a class to an object of E.

The identification operator is also called identifier or classification operator or classifier or categorizer or decision machine.

The term classification and later clustering is given to the overall process and, in particular, to the determination of an identification operator.

A Definition of Clustering

Clustering is a classification technique for which

i) The semantic of the classification problem is given by similarities between the objects X.

ii) Usually all the objects X to be classified are known by their measurements.

iii) Usually no training set is given a priori.

iv) The set of names Ω has to be determined by the process.

As the number m of objects X_i to be classified is manageable, the identification function can be implemented by links in a memory. This differs somewhat of a P.R. problem such as a voice or an image recognition for which the number of possible measured objects would be immense. Then an algorithm or program has to be looked for.

3.1.2 A General Model of Clustering

Three basic functions h, g, $\mathscr{E}$ and their results may be described in a clustering process.

i) h and the Initial Description

From a universe $\mathscr{U}$ a function h allows us to abstract an initial description of an object X of a space $\mathbf{X}$. This description is represented:

— by some initial structured data (i.s.d.),

— by similarity measures between objects computed from the i.s.d.,

— eventually by some names or labels given to the i.s.d.

The domain of h is the space $\mathbf{X}$ of objects of a universe $\mathscr{U}$.

ii) g and the Symbolic Description

From the i.s.d. and the other information of the initial description, g gives a "symbolic" or "general" description which reduces or rather abstracts the information. Abstraction must be taken here in the sense of suppressing the details that are not essential but keeping, if possible, the important properties. For instance, all the objects X of a cluster or class will be described or represented by the same symbolic representation, which may reduce to a name, the same for a cluster.

iii) & and the Identification

From the i.s.d. and the symbolic description, an identification or labelling is obtained. This means that all the objects X of the domain of h have a name ω from a finite set of names Ω. An effective procedure performs the mapping $\mathscr{E}: X \rightarrow \omega$. In this context, this procedure (or algorithm, or program) is called a *clustering identification operator* or simply an identification operator. The classes P_i, determined by $\mathscr{E}$ on E, are called *clusters*. The set of P_i is called a *partition P*

$$P = \{P_1, P_2, \ldots, P_i, \ldots, P_k\} .$$

By convention the effective procedure which interactively determines h, g, $\mathscr{E}$ is called a *clustering process* or simply a clustering.

3.2 The Initial Description

As has been said, the measures from a universe $\mathscr{U}$ allow us to establish for an object X an initial structured datum (i.s.d.)

The properties of $\mathscr{U}$ allow us to compute from the different i.s.d. a resemblance measure between objects X.

3.2.1 Interpretation of the Initial Structured Data

The result of n measurements on an object X is a list of parameters $(x_1, x_2, \ldots, x_n)$.

Each of these parameters has an interpretation in the universe $\mathscr{U}$. They may be:

i) *Quantitative:* x is isomorphic to a real number or rather to a number as it is represented on a computer, which is closer to the mathematical concept of rational numbers.

ii) *Qualitative:* Then x may materialize as one of the elements of a finite set $\{x\}$. The interpretation in $\mathscr{U}$ is usually a name or a qualifier, for instance, a colour, an illness name, a nationality, a profession.

A complete or partial order may exist on the set $\{x\}$, for instance, small, medium, large; or young, middle-age, old.

If no order exists on the set, x is said to be a *nominal qualitative* variable, otherwise an *ordinal qualitative* variable. For more details see SNEATH and SOKAL [3.1, 62].

iii) *Binary:* The variable may take two states, usually called 0 or 1. If arithmetic operations are legal on x, they are called *binary quantitative*, otherwise *binary qualitative*.

3.2.2 Resemblance and Dissemblance Measures

Let us specify our notation.

Let X be a variable object, and $x_1, x_2, ..., x_n$ the n variable measures which characterize X (boldface italic letters).

Let X_i be an object, indexed by i, and $x_{i1}, x_{i2}, ..., x_{in}$ the i.s.d. which inform us on X_i (lightface italic letters).

The measurements may be performed on m objects X_i $(1 \leq i \leq m)$. It is often useful to consider the list of realizations of the variable x_p, when measuring these m objects.

Let Y be the corresponding variable. It is the cartesian product of m elementary variables x_j. Y_j the value of Y_j is a list of realizations, i.e., a list of the same measurement on the m objects

$$Y_j = (x_{1j}, x_{2j}, ..., x_{mj})$$

	Y_1	Y_2	Y_j	Y_n
X_1	x_{11}	$x_{12} ... x_{1j} ... x_{1n}$		
X_2	x_{21}	x_{22}		
$\vdots$	$\vdots$			
X_i	x_{i1}	.... x_{ij} ... x_{in}		
$\vdots$	$\vdots$			
X_m	x_{m1}	.... $x_{mj} ... x_{mn}$.		

The table gives the complete results of n measurements on m objects. Each elementary variable x_j $(1 \leq j \leq n)$ may take a value in a set of possible values. If this set is finite, the total number of realizations of a variable x_j is equal to r_j.

Definition of a Similarity Measure and of a Dissimilarity Measure

Resemblance and dissemblance are terms equivalent to similarity and dissimilarity.

A similarity measure τ (or dissimilarity measure λ) gives a numerical value to the notion of closeness (or farness) between two objects X_i, X_q from the i.s.d. of their observations. $\tau(X_i, X_q)$ [or $\lambda(X_i X_q)$] is a real valued, symmetric function, whose domain is the set of possible $X \times X$. Usually a high value of τ (or λ) indicates high similarity or closeness (or dissimilarity and farness).

A distance d is a real valued, symmetric function, obeying three axioms, whose domain is again $\mathbf{X} \times \mathbf{X}$. Let $d(X_i, X_q)$ be such a function, which we may write

$d(i, q)$ if no confusion is possible. This function satisfies three axioms.

reflexivity $\qquad\qquad d(i,\ i)=0\ ,$ (3.1)

symmetry $\qquad\qquad d(i,\ q)=d(q,\ i)\ ,$ (3.2)

triangle inequality $\quad d(i,\ q)\leq d(i,\ p)+d(p,\ q)\ .$ (3.3)

A distance is a particular dissimilarity function.
An *ultrametric distance* δ satisfies the first two axioms and

$$\delta(i,\ q)\leq \mathrm{Sup}\ [\delta(i,\ p),\ \delta(p,\ q)]\ .$$ (3.4)

A value of d close to 0 implies a high similarity or closeness.
Similarity and distance measure may be normalized, by dividing the numerical function by the maximum value. Then the range of variation is $[0, 1]$.

Remark

The fundamental purpose of a distance or similarity measure is to *induce an order* on the set of couples (X_i, X_q) for any i or q. An infinity of distances or similarities may induce the same order. In fact simplicity and calculability is the guide of the specialist in classification. He tries to choose a function which seems to be reasonable, *according to what he knows of the properties of* $\mathcal{U}$.
  It is easy to understand that many such choices can be made, as the following paragraphs will show.

Quantitative Dissemblance Measures

The measurements x_i may be interpreted in $\mathcal{U}$ as numbers. Many dissemblance measures have been proposed between two objects X_i and X_q

Minkowsky metric $\quad d_1(X_i, X_q)=\left[\sum_{j=1}^{n}|x_{ij}-x_{qj}|^{\frac{1}{\lambda}}\right]^{\lambda}\ ,$ (3.5)

Camberra metric $\quad d_2(X_i, X_q)=\sum_{j=1}^{n}\dfrac{|x_{ij}-x_{qj}|}{|x_{ij}+x_{qj}|}\ ,$ (3.6)

Chebychev metric $\quad d_3(X_i, X_q)=\max_{j}|x_{ij}-x_{qj}|\ ,$ (3.7)

Quadratic metric $\quad d_4(X_i, X_q)=(X_i-X_q)^{\mathrm{T}}Q(X_i-X_q)\ ,$ (3.8)

where Q is a $n\times n$ positive definite matrix,

Mahalanobis metric $\quad d_5(X_i, X_q)=(\det W)^{\frac{1}{p}}(X_i-X_q)^{\mathrm{T}}W^{-1}(X_i-X_q)\ ,$ (3.9) where W is the covariance matrix of $(Y_1, \ldots, Y_m)$,

Correlation
$$d_6(X_i, X_q) = \frac{\sum_{j=1}^{n} (x_{ij} - \bar{x}_j)(x_{qj} - \bar{x}_j)}{[\sum_{j=1}^{n} (x_{ij} - \bar{x}_j)^2 \sum_{j=1}^{n} (x_{qj} - \bar{x}_j)^2]^{\frac{1}{2}}}, \tag{3.10}$$

"City block" metric $d_7(X_i, X_q) = \sum_{j=1}^{n} w_j |x_{ij} - x_{qj}|$, $\tag{3.11}$

"Chi-square" metric $d_8(X_i, X_q) = \sum_{j=1}^{n} \frac{1}{x_{\cdot j}} \left[\frac{x_{ij}}{x_{i\cdot}} - \frac{x_{qj}}{x_{q\cdot}} \right]^2$, $\tag{3.12}$
(Benzecri)

where $x_{\cdot j} = \sum_{i=1}^{m} x_{ij}$ and $x_{i\cdot} = \sum_{j=1}^{n} x_{ij}$.

Qualitative Resemblance Measure

The interpretation or meaning in $\mathcal{U}$ of a similarity measure has to be carefully criticized if the measurements are qualitative.

For example, how can two names, or two colors be added or multiplied?

The representation of the measurements has to reflect the properties in $\mathcal{U}$. For instance, some transformations in $\mathcal{U}$ should not change the similarity measure.

As an example, instead of coding colors by integers, let us code them by a list of 0, with the occurrence of a 1. Arithmetic operations on such vectors will give results invariant with a permutation of the code. Then most of the distance formulas of the preceding paragraph can be used, without absurd results.

Other representations may take into account an order in the set of the elementary measurements.

Qualitative Ordinal Coding

Let us examine the solutions currently taken for the qualitative ordinal measurements. Each of the measurements is an ordered value.

i) Kendall's Rank Correlation

Let X_i and X_q be two measured objects

$$X_i = (x_{i1}, \ldots, x_{ij}, \ldots, x_{ik}, \ldots, x_{in})$$
$$X_q = (x_{q1}, \ldots, x_{qj}, \ldots, x_{qk}, \ldots, x_{qn}).$$

Let

$$\Delta_{jk}^i = \begin{cases} 1 & \text{if } x_{ij} > x_{ik} \\ -1 & \text{if } x_{ij} < x_{ik} \\ 0 & \text{if } x_{ij} = x_{ik}. \end{cases}$$

The distance measure is

$$d(X_i, X_q) = 1 - \frac{2}{n(n-1)} \sum_{j<k} \Delta_{jk}^q \Delta_{jk}^i = 1 - \tau. \tag{3.13}$$

ii) x_{ij} is a Sequence of States

Let as an example

$$x_{ij} = (a, b, c, d, e)$$
$$x_{qj} = (b, c, a, d).$$

A minimum number of operations are necessary to identify the first 4 characters of the second sequence with the first 4 characters of the first. This number may be taken as $|x_{ij} - x_{qj}|$. These operations may be permutations or deletions; see, e.g., Sellers [3.60].

Binary Distance Measures

X_i and X_q are binary lists (or vectors, if one prefers this term). Let a, b, c, e be integers such that

a is equal to the number of occurrence of $x_{ij} = 1$ and $x_{qj} = 1$,
b is equal to the number of occurrence of $x_{ij} = 0$ and $x_{qj} = 1$,
c is equal to the number of occurrence of $x_{ij} = 1$ and $x_{qj} = 0$,
e is equal to the number of occurrence of $x_{ij} = 0$ and $x_{qj} = 0$.

These definitions are symbolically described by Table T.

Table T

X_q \\ X_i	1	0
1	a	b
0	c	e

Various distance measures have been employed, mainly in the field of biology, where the binary variable indicates the absence or presence of a character.

Russel and Rao
$$d_1(X_i, X_q) = \frac{a}{a+b+c+e}, \tag{3.14}$$

Jaccard and Needham
$$d_2(X_i, X_q) = \frac{a}{a+b+c}, \tag{3.15}$$

Dice
$$d_3(X_i, X_q) = \frac{a}{2a+b+c}, \tag{3.16}$$

Sokal and Sneath
$$d_4(X_i, X_q) = \frac{a}{a+2(b+c)}, \tag{3.17}$$

SOKAL and MICHENER $$d_5(X_i, X_q) = \frac{a+e}{a+b+c+e},$$ (3.18)

(simple matching coefficient)

KULZINSKY $$d_6(X_i, X_q) = \frac{a}{b+c},$$ (3.19)

ROGERS and TANIMOTO $$d_7(X_i, X_q) = \frac{a+e}{a+e+2(b+c)},$$ (3.20)

YULE $$d_8(X_i, X_q) = \frac{ae-bc}{ae+bc},$$ (3.21)

Correlation $$d_9(X_i, X_q) = \frac{ae+bc}{[(a+b)(c+e)(a+c)(b+e)]^{\frac{1}{2}}}.$$ (3.22)

Resemblance Measures Between Elementary Variables

Up to now we have treated resemblance measures *between objects*. It is interesting also to consider resemblance measures *between measurements* themselves. Let us recall that the result of the measurements on an object X_i is a list of *elementary measurements*.

$$X_i = (x_{i1}, x_{i2}, \ldots, x_{ie}, \ldots, x_{ik}, \ldots, x_{in});$$

x_{ie} and x_{ik} are the realizations of the variables x_e and x_k. Let us assume that these realizations are finite in number, r_e for x_e and r_k for x_k. Such variables have been called *qualitative nominal*, and, if a significant order exists on the realizations, *qualitative ordinal*.

We have previously defined Y_e and Y_k as the lists of elementary measurements on the *m* objects of the variables x_e and x_k, respectively.

A "contingency table" is set up from Y_e and Y_k; let n_{ij} be the number of objects such that the variables x_e and x_k had, respectively, the realization indexed by i and j, among the respective possible r_e and r_j realizations.

Such a contingency table allows us to define a distance between Y_e and Y_k, the lists of the measurements of rank e and k.

$$d(Y_e, Y_k) = \sum_{i=1}^{p} n_i \cdot \sum_{j=1}^{r} \left| \frac{n_{ij}}{n_{i\cdot}} - \frac{n_{\cdot j}}{n_{\cdot\cdot}} \right|,$$ (3.23)

and a resemblance measure

$$d(Y_e, Y_k) = \frac{1}{n_{\cdot\cdot}} \sum_{i=1}^{p} \max_{j} n_{ij}.$$ (3.24)

Chi-square with $(p-1)(r-1)$ degrees of freedom under the hypothesis of bivariate normality and independence

$$d(Y_e, Y_k) = n_{\cdot\cdot} \sum_{i=1}^{p} \sum_{j=1}^{r} \left[n_{ij} - \frac{n_{i\cdot} n_{\cdot j}}{n_{\cdot\cdot}} \right]^2 \frac{1}{n_{i\cdot} n_{\cdot j}}.$$ (3.25)

Table 3.1

Y_k \ Y_e	1	2	...	j	...	r	Totals
1	n_{11}	n_{12}		n_{1j}		n_{1r}	$n_1.$
2	n_{21}	n_{22}		n_{2j}		n_{2r}	$n_2.$
$\vdots$							
i	n_{i1}			n_{ij}			$n_i.$
$\vdots$							
p	n_{p1}					n_{pr}	
Totals	$n._1$	$n._2$		$n._j$		$n._r$	$n..$

Similarity measures based on the information

$$d_I(Y_e, Y_k) = I(Y_e) + I(Y_k) - I(Y_e \cap Y_k),\qquad(3.26)$$

where

$$I(Y_e) = -\sum_i p_i.\ \log_2 p_i.\quad \text{where}\quad p_i. = \frac{n_i.}{n..},\qquad(3.27)$$

$$I(Y_k) = -\sum_j p._j \log_2 p._j\quad \text{where}\quad p._j = \frac{n._j}{n..},\qquad(3.28)$$

$$I(Y_e \cap Y_k) = \sum_{i,j} p_{ij} \log_2 p_{ij}.\qquad(3.29)$$

Under the independence hypothesis between Y_i and Y_j, one shows that

$$d_I(Y_e, Y_k) \simeq \frac{1}{\log 2} \sum_i \sum_j \frac{(p_{ij} - p_i.\, p._j)^2}{p_i.\, p._j} \simeq \frac{\chi^2}{\log 2}.\qquad(3.30)$$

Resemblance Measures Between Groups of Objects

It is also useful to define distances between some subsets A of the set of the m measured objects.

Let μ be a function of the set of all subsets of E in $\mathbb{R}^+$ such that

$$\mu(A) = \sum_{a \in A} \mu(a)\ \forall A \in E.$$

μ is a "measure" on the set of points of E.

Let us give

$$D(X, A) = \frac{1}{\mu(A)} \sum_{a \in A} d(x, a), \tag{3.31}$$

$$G(A) = \frac{1}{\mu(A)} \sum_{a \in A} \mu(a)a, \tag{3.32}$$

$$\operatorname{var} A = \frac{1}{\mu(A)} \sum_{a \in A} \mu(A)d(a, G(A)), \tag{3.33}$$

where d is given by a quadratic metric; the Koenig-Huygens theorem can be used and one deduces the following formulas $(A_1, \ldots, A_k)$; is a partition of E:

$$D(x, A) = \mu(A)\left[d(x, G(A)) + \operatorname{var} A\right], \tag{3.34}$$

$$\operatorname{var}\left(\bigcup_{i=1}^{k} A_i\right) = \sum_{i=1}^{k} (A_i) \operatorname{var} A_i + D(A_1, \ldots, A_k), \tag{3.35}$$

where

$$D(A_1, \ldots, A_k) = \sum_{i=1}^{k} \mu(A_i)d(G(A_i), G(\bigcup_{j=1}^{k} A_j)). \tag{3.36}$$

In the case of a partition in two classes we have

$$D(A, B) = \frac{\mu(A)\mu(B)}{\mu(A) + \mu(B)} d(G(A), G(B)). \tag{3.37}$$

Table 3.2

Y_e	A_1	A_2	
1	n_{11}	n_{12}	$n_1.$
2			
$\vdots$			
k	n_{k1}	n_{k2}	$n_k.$
	$n._1$	$n._2$	

3.3 Properties of a Cluster, a Clustering Operator and a Clustering Process

The purpose of a "*clustering*" is to obtain a partition P of a set E of m objects X_i, by the use of a resemblance or dissemblance measure, most often a distance d.

A *partition P* is a set of disjoint subsets of E; an element P_s of P is called here a *cluster*.

At the start, the m objects X_i are known by their measures, more generally by what we called the initial description.

The goal of a "*clustering process*" is to define a mapping $\mathscr{E}$, the identification

$$\forall i, \quad \mathscr{E}: X_i \to P_s. \tag{3.38}$$

$\mathscr{E}$ has to have a constructive representation, which is called a "*clustering identification operator*"; in other words, the procedure or program which will classify X_i in the cluster P_s. The index s has the interpretation of a name.

It seems essential to distinguish a clustering identification operator from the way to build it, which, by convention, we called a clustering process.

The identification operator $\mathscr{E}$ can be defined through two types of implementation.

i) A program: Given X_i, the index s of P_s can be computed for all i.

ii) Links in memory: Each X_i is labelled by an s; this information is kept in a computer memory. This implementation is possible because of the cardinality m of the set E, which is small compared to the usual classification object set cardinality.

The specialist expects the clusters and thus the identification operator $\mathscr{E}$ to have some definite properties relevant to the semantic of his problem.

3.3.1 Properties of Clusters and Partitions

Homogeneity

A cluster P_s is said to be *homogeneous*

$$\text{iff} \quad X_i, X_j \in P_s \quad \text{and} \quad X_k \notin P_s$$
$$d(X_i, X_j) \leq d(X_i, X_k) \quad \text{and} \quad d(X_i, X_j) \leq d(X_j, X_k).$$

A partition P is said *homogeneous* if the above property is true for all $P_s \in P$.

The interpretation of this property means that two elements of the same cluster are more similar than to any other element of E outside of the cluster.

Usually this desirable property is not verified with the initial d given by the experimenter.

It is customary to define an ultradistance δ for which a cluster and the partition will be homogeneous.

Let a "chain" c_{jk} between X_j and X_k be a list of objects beginning with X_j, ending with X_k. Let $\mathscr{C}_{jk}$ be the set of possible chains between X_j and X_k.

$$c_{jk} = X_j, \dots, X_q, X_{q+1}, \dots, X_k.$$

Let

$$\lambda(c_{jk}) = \text{Sup}[d(X_q, X_{q+1})] \quad \text{for all} \quad q$$
$$\delta(X_i, X_k) = \text{Inf}[\lambda(c_{jk})] \quad \text{for} \quad c_{jk} \in \mathscr{C}_{jk}. \tag{3.39}$$

It is easy to see that δ satisfies the three properties of ultrametric distances

$$\delta(X_i, X_i) = 0 , \tag{3.1}$$

$$\delta(X_i, X_j) = \delta(X_j, X_i) , \tag{3.2}$$

$$\delta(X_i, X_j) \leq \mathrm{Sup}\,[\delta(X_i, X_k), \delta(X_j, X_k)] . \tag{3.4}$$

This distance δ may be called a "chain distance". We will say that a cluster or a partition is called *chain-homogeneous* if it is homogeneous for δ.

Typical examples of chain homogeneity are found in two dimensional situations, for which d is the euclidian distance. Then a "good" cluster or partition is chain homogeneous (or δ-homogeneous) and not homogeneous (or d-homogeneous).

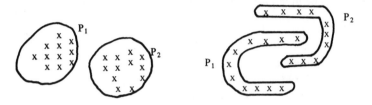

Fig. 3.1   Fig. 3.2

In Figs. 3.1 and 3.2, P_1 and P_2 are δ-homogeneous but not d-homogeneous.

Stability of a Cluster or of a Partition

Usually a good partition minimizes some evaluation function W, which, in a sense, plays the role of the energy of a potential theory.

As *an example*, let us take

$$\mathrm{Sup}\,P_s = \max\,[d(X_i, X_j)] \qquad X_i, X_j \in P_s .$$

Let P_s' be a cluster obtained from P_s by eliminating some objects and taking new ones, but having the same number of objects.

If $\mathrm{Sup}\,P_s > \mathrm{Sup}\,P_s'$, P_s will be said to be better than P_s' in the sense of that criterion. If no other P_s' better than P_s can be found, P_s will be said to be stable.

3.3.2 Properties of a Clustering Identification Operator $\mathcal{E}$ or of a Clustering Process

An identification operator $\mathcal{E}$ is the result of a clustering process $\mathcal{O}$. Each of these algorithms may have desirable properties, related to the semantic of the problem. Two classes $\mathcal{T}$ and $\mathcal{P}$ of such properties are current. We will say following FISHER and VAN NESS [3.26] that these algorithms are $\mathcal{T}$-admissible or $\mathcal{P}$-admissible, if they have the property $\mathcal{T}$ of $\mathcal{P}$.

𝒯 Admissibility

𝓔 or 𝒪 is 𝒯-admissible if from E the same partition P in "cluster" P_s is obtained when *either* X_i is transformed in TX_i, *or* d is transformed in d', *or* both at the same time.

It would be unrealistic to consider any transformation T, or any change of d. An example of a realistic T is the change of cartesian frame in a two dimensional problem.

Many transformations on d are invariant on the result P, for example, those which do not change the order of the set of couples (X_i, X_j) are frequently of that nature for specific 𝓔 or 𝒪.

𝒫 Admissibility

Let the ideal partition P_{id} be given at the start. The mapping

$$𝓔_{id}: E \to P_{id}$$

can be considered as a "training set".

The problem is then to build 𝒪, which from X and d will give 𝓔 isomorphic to $𝓔_{id}$. Then 𝒪 and 𝓔 are said to be 𝒫-admissible.

Important Remark

It must be clear to the reader that no universal ideal algorithm exists, which possesses all the above properties. Some of them are incompatible.

Usually the game is played in the other way. A clustering algorithm is proposed and tested on practical situations; if it is found "satisfactory", then the properties are examined.

We will then describe the most currently used clustering algorithms and give some of their properties.

3.4 The Main Clustering Algorithms

In this section the main clustering algorithms are described. To give some kind of order to a theme with so many variations, the choice is made to classify the methods according to their "symbolic description".

All of them start from an "initial description":

1) A set E of elements X_i, each X_i being a list of measures x_{ij}. We have called this an i.s.d.

2) A triangular measure table (called also a matrix), each measure being a resemblance or dissemblance between X_i and X_j of E.

From this initial description, a clustering algorithm gives a "symbolic description", which usually is not the final result looked for (see Subsection 3.1.2). Recall that this final result is a satisfactory identification of all the elements of E by the name of a cluster and a common description of the elements under that name.

Four symbolic descriptions are distinguished:
  i) A *hierarchy* on the set E.
  ii) The *minimum spanning tree* (m.s.t.) on E.
  iii) A *partition* of E and the symbolic representations of each cluster.
  iv) A *cross partition* of E and the corresponding representations.

The descriptions i) and ii) are obtained from the triangular matrix. The corresponding algorithms are said to be *agglomerative* (also inductive or bottom up).
  Descriptions iii) and iv) are obtained directly from the i.s.d. The corresponding algorithms are said to be *divisive* (also deductive or top down).

Definitions and Remarks

The definitions of a hierarchy and of a minimum spanning tree are given in the next subsections.
  Let us recall the definition of a *partition* (see Subsection 3.1.1).
  Let E be a set of m elements. A partition P is a set of subsets of E.

$$P = \{P_1, P_2, \ldots, P_k\}$$

such that

$$P_i \cap P_j = \emptyset, \forall i, j, \tag{3.40}$$

and

$$\bigcup_{j=1\ldots k} P_j = E. \tag{3.41}$$

In set theory the P_j are called equivalence classes or simply classes. In this context we call usually them clusters. A k-partition has k classes.
  A *cross partition* is obtained by repeated intersection of k-partitions. $P^1, P^2, \ldots, P^q$.

$$\Pi = P^1 \cap P^2 \cap \ldots \cap P^q.$$

Π is a set of disjoint subsets of E, for which (3.40) and (3.41) are true. We shall see in Subsection 3.4.7 that a cross-partition allows us to define the "strong patterns".
  The object of a clustering analysis is sometimes only a symbolic description. For instance, the taxonomists of natural science are satisfied with classification trees or hierarchies between species.
  But most of the time the objective is to separate the objects of E in disjoint classes or clusters (the identification) and besides the name of the cluster to give *some properties common to the elements of a cluster*. The usual means for this is to present a *symbolic representation* for each cluster, for instance, a "typical" element or a "skeleton" or a kernel made of a few elements. As an example, medical doctors would describe an illness by the name and a few typical patients.
  Thus if k is the number of clusters of a partition P or of a cross partition Π, we will speak of the k representations of the clusters and call them $A_1 A_2 \ldots A_k$. Their interpretation may reduce to a name, but usually they are a lot more complex.

3.4.1 Hierarchies

Ultrametric distances, or briefly ultrametrics, have been mentioned. They induce on the power set of a set E a structure called a hierarchy. Inversely a hierarchy is a partial order on the power set of a set E. It implies ultrametric distances between the elements of E. In this subsection, the elements of E are called the atoms of the hierarchy.

Definition of a Hierarchy

Let E be the set of objects $\{X_1 \ldots X_m\}$. Let $\mathscr{P}(E)$ be the power set of E and $H \subset \mathscr{P}(E)$. H is a hierarchy if
   i) $E \in H$.
   ii) $\forall X_i \in E$ then $\{X_i\} \in H$.
   iii) $\forall h, h' \in H$, if $h \cap h' \neq \emptyset$ then either $h \subset h'$, or $h' \subset h$.

Example

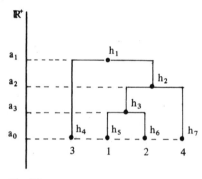

$E = \{1, 2, 3, 4\}$
$H = \{h_1 \ldots h_7\}$

$h_1 = E$
$h_2 = \{1, 2, 3\}$
$h_3 = \{1, 2\}$
$h_4 = \{3\}, \quad h_5 = \{1\}, \quad h_6 = \{2\}, \quad h_7 = \{4\}$

$h_1 \ldots h_7$ are the elements of the hierarchy.
$h_4 \ldots h_7$ may be called the atoms.
h_1, h_2, h_3, may be called the clusters.

Fig. 3.3

Definition and Properties of an Ultrametric

A distance δ is called an ultrametric, if it satisfies the first two axioms of a distance, see (3.1) and (3.2), the third being (3.4)

$$\delta(i, k) \leq \text{Sup}[\delta(i, j), \delta(j, k)] .$$

i, j, k designate any of three elements of a set E.

Then any triangle (i, j, k) is isosceles.

Let $\delta(i, j) \leq \delta(j, k)$; then from (3.4) $\delta(i, k) \leq \delta(j, k)$. As $\delta(j, k) \leq \text{sup}[\delta(i, j), \delta(i, k)]$ the relation $\delta(j, k) \leq \delta(i, j)$ is true.

Thus $\delta(j, k) = \delta(i, k)$.

Finally $\delta(i, j) \leq \delta(j, k) = \delta(i, k)$.

The triangle is isosceles or equilateral; the base of the triangle is less than or equal to the two sides.

Figure 3.3 is a current representation of a hierarchy H. From this representation it is easy to define an ultrametric on H. Let us project the tree on $[0, 1]$, a segment of $\mathbb{R}^+$, according to Fig. 3.3. Let the distance between two atoms be the value of the segment $a_0 a_j$ $(j=1, 2, 3)$, a_j being the projection of h_j, root of the smallest subtree having the two atoms as leaves. In the example of Fig. 3.3, $\delta(1, 4) = |a_0 a_2|$, h_2 is the root of the smallest subtree having the leaves 1 and 4. It is clear that this distance is an ultrametric. By varying the shape of the tree an infinity of other ultrametrics can be defined.

3.4.2 Construction of a Hierarchy

Most often distances or more generally dissemblance measures are given between the elements of a set E. From that information, how can we find a reasonable hierarchy.

Let i, j be two elements of E, $d(i, j)$ a distance between i and j. Let $d_r(i, j)$ the distances such that

$$d_r(i, j) \geq d(i, j) . \tag{3.42}$$

If for all r and i, j, there exists an upper bound $b(i, j)$,

$$d_r(i, j) \leq b(i, j) , \forall r . \tag{3.43}$$

The family of d_r is said to be a "bounded metric". A *least upper bound* (l.u.b.) can be found for the family of d_r. Let it be $\underset{r}{\mathrm{Sup}}\, d_r(i, j)$.

Similarly if a family of bounded ultrametric is defined, there exists an l.u.b. ultrametric.

Let us come back now to a set E, on which a distance $d(i, j)$ is given between any two elements i, j. Let $d(i, j)$ be a bound for a family of ultrametrics. It may be a dissemblance measure. The l.u.b. ultrametric of this family will be called δ, the *subdominant ultrametric of d*. ROUX [3.55] has shown that δ is unique and has given an algorithm to build it.

Roux Algorithm

The idea is to make every triangle isosceles with the base inferior or equal to the two equal sides. Let $d(i, j)$ be the dissemblance or distance between two atoms i, j, $\Delta(i, j)$ be a variable, $\delta(i, j)$ the ultrametric.

Step 1 $\forall i, j \in E$ *do* $\Delta(i, j) \leftarrow d(i, j)$.

Step 2 $\forall (i, j, k)$ *do*
  if $\Delta(j, k) = \mathrm{Sup}\,[\Delta(j, k), \Delta(k, i), \Delta(j, i)]$ *then*
    $\Delta(j, k) \leftarrow \mathrm{Sup}\,[\Delta(k, i), \Delta(j, i)]$ *else*
  if $\Delta(k, i) = \mathrm{Sup}\,[\Delta(j, k), \Delta(k, i), \Delta(j, i)]$ *then*
    $\Delta(k, i) \leftarrow \mathrm{Sup}\,[\Delta(j, k), \Delta(j, i)]$ *else*
    $\Delta(j, i) \leftarrow \mathrm{Sup}\,[\Delta(j, k), \Delta(k, i)]$.

Step 3   If for all (i, j) no modification has been observed in Step 2 *then* $\delta(i, j) \leftarrow \Delta(i, j)$, *else go to* Step 2.

Roux has shown that δ thus obtained is the ultrametric subdominant of d. From δ it is easy to build the hierarchy.

Lance and William General Algorithm [3.41]

Let E be a set of objects, designated by numbers $1, 2 \ldots m$.

Step 0   Compute the triangular table of distances $d(i, j)$.

Step 1   Let p, q be the pair of objects such that $d(p, q)$ is the smallest of all the table.
Then
— suppress q from the table,
— replace p by r,
— compute all $d(r, i)$.

Step 2   If the number of rows and columns of the table is greater than one *go to* Step 1, *else* stop.

An element such as r may be called a cluster. It is made at least of two atomic objects of E. The clusters r will play the role of a non-atomic h of a hierarchy.

The general formula to compute $d(i, r)$ is

$$d(i, r) = a_p d(i, p) + a_q d(i, q) + bd(p, q) + c|d(i, p) - d(i, q)| . \tag{3.44}$$

where $d(p, q) = \sum_{i \in p} d(i, q)$.

Different results are obtained according to the values of the parameters a_p, b_q, b, c; see Anderberg [3.1].

N.B. G. Gaillat has proposed a way to speed up this algorithm. Instead of merging the objects one by one into one of the clusters, find all the objects the distances of which are smaller than $k\varepsilon$. Reiterate until no object can be merged. By choosing a proper ε and taking $k = 1, 2, 3, \ldots$, a hierarchy is obtained which approaches the hierarchy of the former algorithm.

Single Linkage

$a_p = a_q = \frac{1}{2}$, $b = 0$, $c = -\frac{1}{2}$. Johnson [3.71] has shown that the different d obtained define the subdominant ultrametric. Sokal and Sneath (Ref. [3.62], p. 256) have demonstrated that this algorithm gives also the *minimum spanning tree*. From (3.44), if $d(i, p) > d(i, q)$, then $|d(i, p) - d(i, q)| = d(i, p) - d(i, q)$ and $d(i, r) = d(i, q)$.

The distance to r is the distance to the closest point. The final result shows the "chain effect".

Complete Linkage

$$a_p = a_q = \frac{1}{2}, \quad b = 0, \quad c = \frac{1}{2} . \tag{3.45}$$

Then

$$d(i, r) = d(i, p).$$

The distance to r is the distance to the most distant element.

Average Linkage

Let $|r|$ be the number of atoms in r.

$$a_p = |p|/|r|, \quad a_q = |q|/|r|, \quad b = c = 0. \tag{3.46}$$

Centroid Method

$$a_p = |p|/|r|, \quad a_q = |q|/|k|, \quad b = -a_p \cdot a_q, \quad c = 0. \tag{3.47}$$

The distance is computed from the "centroid" of a cluster; see (Ref. [3.1], p. 148).

Ward Technique

$$a_p = \frac{|i| + |p|}{|i| + |r|}, \quad a_q = \frac{|i| + |q|}{|i| + |r|}, \quad b = \frac{-|i|}{|i| - |r|}, \quad c = 0. \tag{3.48}$$

WISHART [3.67] has shown that the technique proposed by WARD [3.66] is a special case of LANCE and WILLIAM's with the above coefficients.

In fact at each step the two clusters which minimize the error sum of squares are merged,

$$D(p, q) = \frac{|p| \, |q|}{|p| + |q|} d[G(p), G(q)]; \tag{3.49}$$

see (3.37).

The Chain Effect

The definition of a "chain" has been given in Subsection 3.3.1. Between two elements X_i, X_j of E, an ultrametric $\delta(i, j)$ has been defined, considering all the possible chains between X_i, X_j. ROUX [3.55] has shown that this ultrametric is the subdominant of d. Thus $\delta(i, j)$ is the length of the shortest chain between X_i and X_j.

Example

Thus the use of an ultrametric (hierarchies based on the subdominant, m.s.t.) will give a result showing the "chain effect": two elements will be determined as close if a short chain exists between them. They may be put in the same cluster, even if they are far apart.

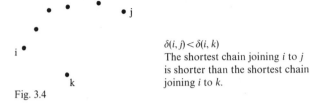

$\delta(i, j) < \delta(i, k)$
The shortest chain joining i to j
is shorter than the shortest chain
joining i to k.

Fig. 3.4

3.4.3 The Minimum Spanning Tree

A graph Γ is a couple (E, A), E being a set of m elements $i, j, \ldots$ called *nodes*, A being a set of couples of nodes, for instance (i, j). An element of A such as (i, j) is called an *arc*. It may have a *value*, for example $d(i, j)$.

Usually "$(i, j) \in A$ imply $(j, i) \in A$" is false. In this context, we will assume that this last relation is *true*, the graph is "non oriented".

A *path* (p, q) is a chain of arcs starting from the node p, and ending in the node q

$$(p, i_1), (i_1, i_2) \ldots (i_k, q).$$

Following the property of a "non-oriented" graph, we assume that a path cannot use (j, i) if (i, j) is already in the chain of arcs.

A *circuit* is a path starting and ending at the same node.

A *connected graph* will be here a graph such that every two nodes are connected by a path.

A *tree* is a connected graph with no circuit.

Definition

The "minimum spanning tree" is the tree on E, for which $\sum d(i, j)$ is minimum.

It is clear that, if all $d(i, j)$ are different, the m.s.t. is unique. An evident property is the following one: let i, j be two nodes. They are connected by a path; let it be different from arc (i, j). Suppose that (i, j) is added to the tree, then a circuit exists. To suppress it we have to disconnect one of the arcs of the path i to j, for instance (p, q). In the sum of distances, $d(i, j)$ replaces $d(p, q)$ and we can assume

$$d(i, j) > d(p, q).$$

This property means that any arc of the path connecting two nodes i, j of a minimum spanning tree is smaller than the arc i, j. From this property result the following algorithms.

Prim Algorithm or nearest neighbour [3.50].

Let $i, p, q \in E$.

  Step 1   Start from any node i; let i be in the set T.

  Step 2   *While $T \neq E$ do*:

  $\forall p \notin T$ and $\forall q \in T, d(p, q)$ is the minimum distance; then put p in T and (p, q) in A.

Kruskal Algorithm [3.40]

Step 1 List all arcs (i, j) in the order of increasing $d(i, j)$.

Step 2 Put the first arc (p, q) on the list into A.

Step 3 Put the next arc on the list into A, except if a circuit can be formed with the arcs already in A.

Step 4 *If* all nodes are connected Stop, *else* go to Step 3.

Example

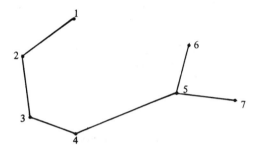

Fig. 3.5

	List	A	Circuit
KRUSKAL on Fig. 3.5	5 6	5 6	
	3 4	3 4	
	5 7	5 7	
	2 3	2 3	
	6 7		5 6 7
	1 2	1 2	
	1 4		1 2 3 4
	4 5	4 5	
	1 6		
	1 5		
	4 7		
PRIM on Fig. 3.5	5		A
	5 6		56
	5 6 7		57
	4 5 6 7		45
	3 4 5 6 7		34
	2 3 4 5 6 7		23
	1 2 3 4 5 6 7		12

N.B. The minimum spanning tree is in fact a concept closely related to the hierarchy obtained from the subdominant, or the single linkage; see JOHNSON [3.71] and SOKAL and SNEATH [3.62].

3.4.4 Identification from a Hierarchy or a Minimum Spanning Tree

Hierarchies and the minimum spanning tree are symbolic descriptions of the situation. The final step has yet to be taken: find the clusters, i.e., the partition in classes into which to put the objects (the identification). Many methods have been proposed: SOKAL and SNEATH [3.62], LERMAN [3.42], and ZAHN [3.70]. The problem of partitioning the m.s.t. has been specially studied in the U.S.S.R., YOLINKA, ZAGORUIKO [3.72].

Three drawbacks are obvious:

— The first is to require thresholds of somewhat arbitrary nature.

— The second is to require frequently a large amount of memory in computation: tables of $m(m-1)/2$ elements if E has m objects. The prim algorithm asks only for m memory elements. This becomes unmanageable if m is say above a few thousand.

— The third is the "chain effect".

This is the reason why, since 1965, some other techniques have been proposed. They seem more important for the specialist of Pattern Recognition. We will examine them now.

3.4.5 A Partition and the Corresponding Symbolic Representations

The aim of a clustering process is to be able to identify the objects of the set X in k clusters.

The general idea is to have some representation of each of these k clusters, and from the knowledge of these, to identify the objects. Let us give the principle of two algorithms α and β.

Algorithm α

Step 1   (initialization)
Let k elements X_q of E, chosen at random, be the "representation" of the k clusters. Let us call them $A_1, A_2, ..., A_j, ..., A_k$.

Step 2   (clustering)
For all i, any element X_i of E is assigned to cluster j, iff $d(X_i, A_j)$ is minimum.

Step 3   (is the representation correct)
For all j, a new mean A_j is computed.
A_j is the new representation of cluster j.

Step 4   (stability)
If no A_j has changed, Stop, *else go to* Step 2.

Algorithm β

Step 1   Same as α.

Step 2   One element X_i of E is assigned to cluster j, iff $d(X_i, A_j)$ is minimum.

Step 3   A new representation A_j is computed; it is the mean of the elements of cluster j, including the last element.

Step 4   *If* all elements X_i of E have been put in a cluster, Stop, *else go to* Step 2.

In algorithm α, the representations A_j change when *all* the elements have been assigned to the clusters. Then the new means A_j are computed. The set $\{A_1,...,A_k\}$ is the new symbolic description of the clusters [3.27, 32, 36].

In algorithm β, the representation of a cluster j moves after the assignation of an element X_i to this cluster. A new mean is then computed on the cluster with the new element [3.4, 5, 44, 65, 67].

Many refinements have been introduced in these algorithms (ANDERBERG[3.1], Chapter 7). For instance, the ISODATA method of HALL and BALL introduces seven threshold parameters to control the clustering: split and union thresholds of the "cluster centers" techniques. Nevertheless, without going into technicalities, the general idea is to modify iteratively a symbolic description of the clusters, given by the A_j and the identification of the X_i, given by the assignment of X_i to a cluster.

3.4.6 Optimization of a Criterion

In mathematical terms, the problem of finding a "good partition" of E may be stated as follow:

Let W be a given criterion on E.

  i) Find the partition P which optimizes W.

 ii) Find the partition P which optimizes W, among all the partitions in k classes.

Some authors such as FORTIER and SALOMON [3.28], and JENSEN [3.38] undertook i) but did not obtain realistic results for large arrays.

It may be shown that the methods of the "cluster centers" described by algorithm α or β belong to ii), BEALE [3.5], ANDERBERG [3.1].

In fact all the working techniques minimize a criterion W, but without any guarantee of attaining the best possible minimum.

Many *different partitions* can be obtained:

— From the hierarchy or m.s.t., by changing the thresholds leading to the final identification.

— From the algorithms α or β, by changing the random drawings of the X_i either initially or during the execution of the algorithms.

— From the "cluster centers" methods by changing the thresholds of split and union.

A general study of these partitions may be quite informative on the nature of the data. We will consider it in the next section.

3.4.7 Cross-Partitions

Let $P^1,...,P^q$ be q k-partitions and let P_j^i be the cluster j of the partition P^i. Thus

$$P^i = (P_1^i, P_2^i, ..., P_j^i, ..., P_k^i), \quad i = 1, 2, ..., q.$$

An element $X \in E$ has been in cluster α_1 in the first partition P^1, in cluster α_2 in P^2..., in cluster α_q in P^q. To E we can associate a mapping $H:E \rightarrow \mathbb{N}^q$ such that with each $X \in E$ is associated a q-vector.

Let X and X' be two elements of E and $H(X)=(\alpha_1, \alpha_2, ..., \alpha_q)$, $H(X')= (\beta_1, \beta_2, ..., \beta_q)$. Let us define $\delta(X, X')$ as the number of index for which $\alpha_i = \beta_i$. It is easy to see that δ is an ultrametric distance.

Let

$$F_q(X) = \{X' \in E | \delta(X, X') = q\} ,$$

and

$$F_p(X) = \{X' \in E | \delta(X, X') \geq p\} .$$

Definition of the Strong Patterns

The following properties are equivalent and define a *cross-partition* Π, for which each class is a "*strong pattern*"; see Simon and Diday [3.73].

 i) $\Pi = P^1 \cap P^2 ... \cap P^q$, cf. Section 3.4.

 ii) Π is the partition defined by the quotient space E/H.

 iii) Π is the partition defined by the connected part of the graph $\Gamma_q = (E, F_q)$.

Intuitively a class of Π is made up with elements X, which are always in the same clusters in the q k-partitions P^j.

More generally, let us consider the set γ_p of connected parts of the nodes of the graph $\Gamma_p = (E, F_p)$. The list $\gamma_1, ..., \gamma_p, ..., \gamma_q$ defines a hierarchy on E, δ being the ultrametric (of course $\Pi = \gamma_q$).

It may be useful to consider γ_1, called the set of *weak patterns*.

Fuzzy Sets

The introduction of Zadeh's concept of fuzzy sets is interesting now. It allows us
— To obtain news patterns (or clusters, or classes) from set operations on the strong patterns.
— To obtain these new patterns, without having to represent them, for instance by computing their mean, or by knowing their elements.
— To extract as much information as possible from the knowledge of strong patterns.

Each strong pattern $\pi \in \Pi$ can be considered as a fuzzy set; the "fuzzy characteristic function" of $X \in E \subset X$ is

$$\lambda_\pi(X) = \delta(X, Y)/q \quad \text{with} \quad Y \in \pi .$$

It is clear that $\lambda_\pi(X) = 1$ if $X \in \pi$ and λ_π is the same for all $Y \in \pi$.
λ_π indicates the degree of similarity between two strong patterns.

Presentation of the Table of the "Strong Patterns"

A program is written to give a table called the table of strong patterns. It represents the different types of patterns: the first column of the Table 3.3 gives the name of each element of E in an order such that each element X is followed by

Table 3.3. Table of strong patterns for RUSPINI's data

Number of points	1st	2nd	3rd	4th	5th	δ_{ij}		
1	1	3	3	1	4	0		
2	1	3	3	1	4	0		
3	1	3	3	1	4	0		
5	1	3	3	1	4	0	A_1	
6	1	3	3	1	4	0		
9	1	3	3	1	4	0		
10	1	3	3	1	4	0		
8	1	3	3	1	6	1		
4	1	3	3	1	6	0		
7	1	3	3	1	6	0	A_2	B_1
11	1	3	3	1	6	0		
12	1	3	3	1	6	0		
13	1	3	3	1	6	0		
14	1	3	3	1	5	1		
15	1	3	3	1	5	0		
16	1	3	3	1	5	0		
17	1	3	3	1	5	0	A_3	
18	1	3	3	1	5	0		
19	1	3	3	1	5	0		
20	1	3	3	1	5	0		
21	2	2	1	2	2	5		
22	2	2	1	2	2	0		
23	2	2	1	2	2	0		
24	2	2	1	2	2	0		
25	2	2	1	2	2	0		
26	2	2	1	2	2	0		
27	2	2	1	2	2	0		
28	2	2	1	2	2	0		
29	2	2	1	2	2	0	A_4	B_2
30	2	2	1	2	2	0		
31	2	2	1	2	2	0		
32	2	2	1	2	2	0		
33	2	2	1	2	2	0		
34	2	2	1	2	2	0		
35	2	2	1	2	2	0		
36	2	2	1	2	2	0		
37	2	2	1	2	2	0		

Number of points	1st	2nd	3rd	4th	5th	δ_{ij}		
38	2	2	1	2	2	0		
39	2	2	1	2	2	0		
40	2	2	1	2	2	0	A_4	
41	2	2	1	2	2	0		
42	2	2	1	2	2	0		
43	2	2	1	2	2	0		
44	3	4	1	4	1	4		
45	3	4	1	4	1	0		
46	3	4	1	4	1	0		
47	3	4	1	4	1	0		B_2
48	3	4	1	4	1	0		
49	3	4	1	4	1	0		
50	3	4	1	4	1	0		
51	3	4	1	4	1	0		
52	3	4	1	4	1	0	A_5	
53	3	4	1	4	1	0		
54	3	4	1	4	1	0		
55	3	4	1	4	1	0		
56	3	4	1	4	1	0		
57	3	4	1	4	1	0		
58	3	4	1	4	1	0		
59	3	4	1	4	1	0		
60	3	4	1	4	1	0		
61	4	1	2	3	3	5		
62	4	1	2	3	3	0		
63	4	1	2	3	3	0		
64	4	1	2	3	3	0		
65	4	1	2	3	3	0		
66	4	1	2	3	3	0		
67	4	1	2	3	3	0		
68	4	1	2	3	3	0	A_6	B_3
69	4	1	2	3	3	0		
70	4	1	2	3	3	0		
71	4	1	2	3	3	0		
72	4	1	2	3	3	0		
73	4	1	2	3	3	0		
74	4	1	2	3	3	0		
75	4	1	2	3	3	0		

the element X' such that $\delta(X, X')$ is minimum. One finds on each line the name of the element X followed by $\alpha_1,\dots,\alpha_k$ which describe the vector $H(X)$. The value $\Delta(X, X') = k - \delta(X, X')$ corresponding to two consecutive elements x, y is given in the last column and easily permits the detection of the strong and weak patterns. If $\Delta(X, X') = k$, this means that X is the last element of a weak pattern. If $\Delta(X, X') = 0$, this means that X and X' belong to the same strong pattern; the sequences of 0 in this last column therefore characterize the strong patterns.

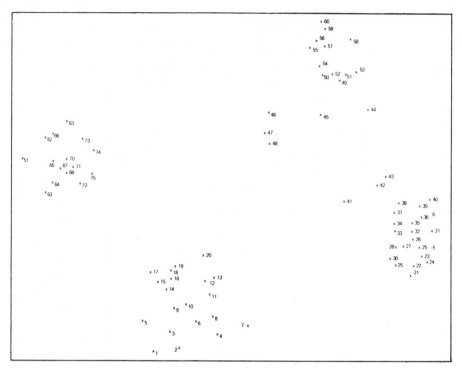

Fig. 3.6

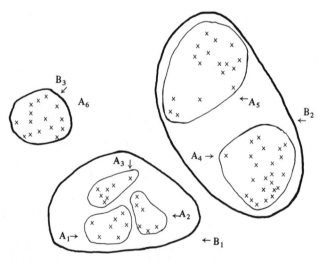

Fig. 3.7

The table has been set for data given by Fig. 3.6 with data from RUSPINI [3.56]. Figure 3.7 gives the strong patterns $A_1, ..., A_6$ and weaker patterns B_1, B_2, B_3.

3.5 The Dynamic Clusters Method

This method is based upon the choice and use of the three functions, h, g, $\mathscr{E}$ defined in Subsection 3.1.2. We will recall how these functions are introduced in hierarchical clustering and in partitioning. Four examples of the choice of g will be given.

3.5.1 An Example of h, g, $\mathscr{E}$ in Hierarchies

The building up of a hierarchy, already described in Subsection 3.4.2, can be done by using the general formalism of Subsection 3.1.2.

To build the hierarchy we start from the set E and work step by step with an "agglomerative" technique.

At step i, let g_i be the symbolic description function and let $\mathscr{E}_i$ be the identification function.

i) The "initial description" is given by h. It is represented by some initial structured data and a resemblance measure between objects. The "symbolic description" g_0 gives each object as a class consisting of one element only.

ii) The two classes p, q which are "nearest" are merged. The new symbolic description given by g_i is the set of previous classes, minus p and q, replaced by a new class (p, q).

iii) The distance of each class to the new one is computed. The distance of each object to a class is computed. $\mathscr{E}_i$ identifies each object to the nearest class.

iv) The procedures ii) and iii) are executed $|E| - 1$ times.

At the completion, the symbolic description is given by $g = \cup g_i$. It is made of the nested classes of the hierarchy. The identification function $\mathscr{E} = \cup \mathscr{E}_i$ permits the mapping of each object into the classes of the hierarchy.

3.5.2 Construction of h, g, $\mathscr{E}$ in Partitioning

i) h is defined as usual.

ii) Let $\mathbb{L}$ be the space of possible symbolic descriptions. $\mathbb{L}$ cannot be completely defined; it includes any type of representation of a cluster considered as useful or satisfactory.

Let $\mathbb{P}_k$ be the set of partitions of $\mathbf{X}$ in a number of classes smaller than or equal to k. Remember the distinction between E and $\mathbf{X}$ (see Subsection 3.1.1): $E \subset \mathbf{X}$.

Let $\mathbb{L}_k$ be the set of $L = (A_1, A_2, \ldots, A_k)$ such that $A_i \in \mathbb{L}$. A_i is a *representation* of the class or cluster i. It may be an element, the mean, a kernel, a skeleton, a feature, etc.

Let us define a measure R

$$R : \mathbf{A} \times \,]k] \times \mathbb{P}_k \to \mathbb{R}^+ \quad \text{with} \quad]k] = \{1, 2, \ldots, k\} \,.$$

$\mathbf{A}$ is a space, which depends on the algorithm, for instance $\mathbf{X}$ or $\mathbb{L}$.

If $A = X$ the function R will be noted $R(X, i, P)$. Then $g(P)$ is a mapping from $\mathbb{P}_k$ into $\mathbb{L}_k$ such that

$$\forall P \in \mathbb{P}_k, \quad g(P) = L = (A_1, A_2, ..., A_k)$$

with $A_i = \{X_j \in E | j = j_1, j_2, ..., j_{n_i}$ and R minimum$\}$.

iii) $\mathscr{E}$ is a mapping of $\mathbb{L}_k$ in $\mathbb{P}_k$ which gives the identification of the objects. Let D be a dissemblance measure

$$D: \mathbf{X} \times \mathbb{L} \to \mathbb{R}^+ .$$

Then $\mathscr{E}(L) = P$ with the classes P_i given by

$$P_i = \{X \in E | D(X, A_i) \leq D(X, A_j), \quad \forall j \neq i\} .$$

3.5.3 The Dynamic Clusters Algorithm

The basic idea is to use successively the g and $\mathscr{E}$ defined in the preceding sub-section, until a stable state is obtained.

Intuitively, starting from a set L of kernels A_i, each object X of E is assigned to the nearest kernel. A first partition of E is obtained. From this partition a new set L is given by the measure R. The new L is a better description of the partition. Again a new partition is obtained and so on, up to a stable situation.

With a reasonable choice of g and $\mathscr{E}$, the algorithm decreases a criterion $W(L, P)$. This criterion expresses the fitness of L to P. Let us be more specific.

The algorithm generates two sequences

$$\{v_p\} \text{ in } \mathbb{L}_k \times \mathbb{P}_k \quad \text{such that} \quad v_p = (L^{(p)}, P^{(p)}),$$

$$\{u_p\} \text{ in } \mathbb{R} \quad\quad\quad \text{such that} \quad u_p = W(v_p).$$

Let $P^{(0)}$ be an initial k-partition. $P^{(0)}$ can be drawn at random or better "guessed".

$$L^{(0)} = g(P^{(0)}) \quad \text{and} \quad v_0 = (L^{(0)}, P^{(0)}) .$$

Having v_p, $v_{p+1} = (L^{(p+1)}, P^{(p+1)})$ is such that $P^{(p+1)} = \mathscr{E}(L^{(p)})$ and $L^{(p+1)} = L^{(p+1)} = g(P^{(p+1)})$.

Definitions

i) The criterion $W: \mathbb{L}_k \times \mathbb{P}_k \to \mathbb{R}^+$ is given by

$$W(L, P) = \sum_{i=1}^{k} \sum_{X \in A_i} R(X, i, P) . \tag{3.50}$$

ii) The measure $R: A \times]k] \times \mathbb{P}_k \to \mathbb{R}^+$ is said to be *square*,

if $W(L, \mathscr{E}(M)) \leq W(M, \mathscr{E}(M))$ implies

$\quad\quad W(L, \mathscr{E}(L)) \leq W(L, \mathscr{E}(M))$ for all $L, M \in \mathbb{L}_k$.

iii) An element $v=(L,P)\in \mathbb{L}_k \times \mathbb{P}_k$ is called *unbiased* for the functions $\mathscr{E}$ and g, iff $P=\mathscr{E}\circ g(P)$ and $L=g\circ\mathscr{E}(L)$.

The following theorem may be demonstrated.

Theorem

If R is square, the sequence u_p is decreasing and monotonous.

If $\forall P\in\mathbb{P}_k$ and $\forall i$, $R(X,i,P)$ has a unique minimum, the sequence v_n converges toward an unbiased v.

We will now give four different g, which will give symbolic descriptions as:
— a part of E,
— a probability distribution,
— a factorial axis,
— an object and a distance.

N.B. The techniques described in Subsection 3.4.5 (ISODATA, k-means) are special cases of the more general algorithm described here, for which the symbolic description of a class is the center of gravity or mean.

3.5.4 The Symbolic Description is a Part of X or $\mathbb{R}^n$

Non-Sequential Techniques

If $\mathbf{A}=\mathbb{R}^n$, n being the number of parameters x_i of an object X, a possible symbolic description of a class is the center of gravity. Then we recover the techniques described in Subsection 3.4.5.

According to the choice of D, R, and $\mathbf{A}$, the criterion W has the following interpretation, cf. DIDAY [3.19].

Let d be a quadratic distance; thus

$$d(X,X')=(X-X')^t Q(X-X'),\tag{3.51}$$

Q being a definite positive, symmetric matrix.

Let μ be a measure such that,

$$\mu(A)=\sum_{Z\in A}\mu(Z),$$

and

$$\mathrm{var}(B)=\frac{1}{\mu(B)}\sum_{X\in B}\mu(X)d(X,G(B)),$$

$$G(B)=\frac{1}{\mu(B)}\sum_{X\in B}X\mu(X).$$

a) Constant Ponderation
$$\begin{cases}D(X,A)=\dfrac{1}{\mathrm{Card}(A)}\sum_{Z\in A}d(X,Z)\\[2mm] R(X,i,P)=D(X,P_i)\dfrac{\mathrm{Card}(P_i)}{\mathrm{Card}(A_i)}\end{cases}$$

$$W(L,P)=\sum_{i=1}^{k}\mathrm{Card}(P_i)\left[\mathrm{var}(P_i)\,\mathrm{var}(P_i)+\mathrm{var}(L_i)+d(G(P_i),G(A_i))\right].\tag{3.52}$$

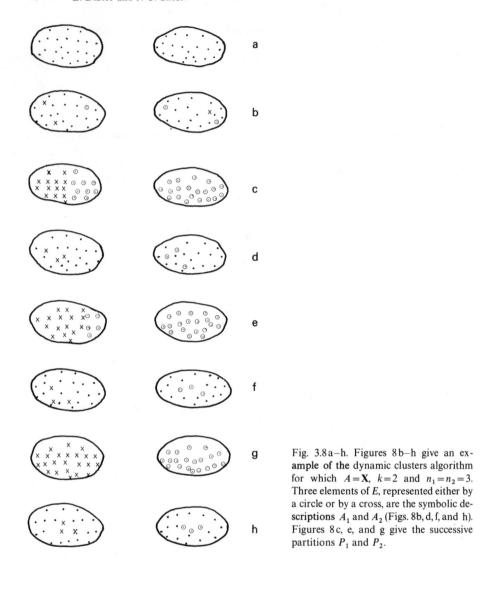

Fig. 3.8a–h. Figures 8b–h give an example of the dynamic clusters algorithm for which $A = \mathbf{X}$, $k = 2$ and $n_1 = n_2 = 3$. Three elements of E, represented either by a circle or by a cross, are the symbolic descriptions A_1 and A_2 (Figs. 8b, d, f, and h). Figures 8c, e, and g give the successive partitions P_1 and P_2.

b) Variable Ponderation
$$\begin{cases} D(X, A) = \sum_{Z \in A} \mu(\dot{Z}) \cdot d(X, Z) \\ R(X, i, P) = \mu(X) \cdot D(X), P_i) \end{cases}$$

$$W(L, P) = \sum_{i=1}^{k} \mu(P_i) \mu(A_i) \left[\text{var}(P_i) + \text{var}(A_i) + d(G(A_i), G(P_i)) \right]. \qquad (3.53)$$

c) Center of Gravity Method
$$\begin{cases} D(X, A) = d(X, G(A)) \\ R(X, i, P) = d(X, G(P_i)) \end{cases}$$

$$W(L, P) = \sum_{i=1}^{k} \mu(P_i) \text{var}(P_i). \qquad (3.54)$$

Sequential Techniques

It may happen that $|E|$ is quite large, say 10^4. It would be impractical to treat the whole set in one process. The set is divided in N subsets; let us call them "packs".

The elements of a pack are introduced by assigning its objects to the nearest A_i of L. When the pack is empty, the set L is readjusted according to the adopted algorithm.

It may be shown that the non-sequential and sequential techniques converge towards the same solutions, decreasing the same criteria.

On a practical basis the sequential techniques enables less memory to be used, but the non-sequential techniques are faster; they require less adjustment of the symbolic representation, DIDAY [3.20].

Remark

From *now to the end of this Section* 3.5, it will be supposed that $\mathbf{A}=\mathbb{L}$ and $n_i=1$ for all i.

This means only that R is a measure of the form

$$R:\mathbb{L}\times]k]\times \mathbb{P}_k\rightarrow\mathbb{R}^+$$

and

$$g(P)=L=(A_1, A_2,...,A_k)$$

is such that A_i is the element of $\mathbb{L}$ which minimizes R.

Let us recall that $\mathbb{L}$ was described as the space of possible representations of a class or cluster.

3.5.5 Partitions and Mixed Distributions

This subsection describes the use of the dynamic clusters approach to solve the problem of "mixed distributions", familiar to the statistical P.R. specialists.

Let us assume that the distribution probability function f can be written

$$f(X)=\sum_{j=1}^k P_j f_j(X) \tag{3.55}$$

— p_j is the a priori probability of the jth distribution,
— f_j is a probability distribution function, belonging to a known family.

The problem is well known under the name of "resolution of mixture": a probability distribution (for instance an histogram) being given, try to find if it is the result of several stochastic phenomena, occurring with various distributions.

A number of techniques have been proposed for that goal. They are of two types:

i) In (3.55), k and the type of the f_j are known. An estimation is made of the p_i and of the f_j, which are assumed of the form

$$f_j(X)=\varphi(X, \theta_j) \tag{3.56}$$

θ_j unknown, but φ known.

ii) In (3.55), k, the p_j and the forms of the f_j are estimated.

The i) category techniques are estimation techniques, the ii) category includes Bayesian methods, supervised or unsupervised learning, stochastic approximation, etc.

The first category techniques differ in the type of estimators they use: method of moments — maximum likelihood (RAO [3.52], DAY [3.14]), minimum χ^2, etc. Most of them require Gaussian distributions in the univariate case. RAO [3.52] needs two classes only.

BHATTACHARYA [3.4] gave a graphical method to determine the number of classes, but needs a great number of observations to be collected and the different distributions to be adequately separated, DOROFEYUK [3.24].

DAY [3.14] dealt with two components, which may be multivariate.

Another approach to the estimation problem of model (3.55) is COOPER and COOPER's [3.12]: the unknown parameters are deduced from the moments of the overall observed distribution.

Many hypotheses must be made when studying the general cases such as: when is the number of components greater than two, or for multivariate Gaussian distribution, etc. (e.g., DAY assumed that the covariance matrices are equal; from a practical point of view COOPER and COOPER studied only the case of two distributions differing only by their means).

The algorithms of the approximation type are very different. Many of them attempt a Bayesian approach, PATRICK and HANCOCK [3.47], PATRICK and COSTELLO [3.48], PATRICK [3.49], AGRAWALA [3.2], though through various techniques. The hypotheses to be made differ from one method to another, but are usually very restrictive.

This sort of approach permits one to formalize the mixed distributions detection problem in terms of unsupervised learning [3.2, 25, 49].

An information criterion can also be used for a stochastic approximation algorithm, YOUNG and CORALUPPI [3.68]. Though restricted to a one-dimensional Gaussian distribution, it is very interesting, because it does not require the knowledge of the actual number of components in the mixture.

The Dynamic Cluster Approach

This approach is not based on formula (3.55). The idea is only to find in the population the possible existence of samples of known distribution, but no assumption has to be made on the global distribution.

However, if the user is entitled to make the assumption of (3.55), then a "mixture type" solution will be obtained.

The algorithm is presented without restrictions on the form of the distribution functions, the dimension of the samples, or the number of components, DIDAY and SCHROEDER [3.21].

Let E be a set of m observations (the objects) on which n measures (the parameters) have been made.

Let $\lambda \in \mathbb{L} \subset \mathbb{R}^s$ and f_λ be a family of distribution functions.

If $n = 1$, this family could be the univariate Gaussian distributions: $\lambda = (\mu, \sigma)$, $s = 2$.

The result of the algorithm is a couple (L, P) with $L = (\lambda_1, \ldots, \lambda_k)$ and $P = (P_1, \ldots, P_k) \cdot P$ is a k-partition of E such that, for all $i \in [1, 2, \ldots, k]$, P_i may be considered as a "likely" sample of the distribution f_{λ_i}.

For this we maximize the likelihoods of the k "samples" P_i for the distributions f_{λ_i},

$$\max \prod_i V_{\lambda_i}(P_i) \tag{3.57}$$

with

$$V_{\lambda_i}(P_i) = \prod_{X \in P_i} f_{\lambda_i}(X). \tag{3.58}$$

Let us define D and R (see Subsection 3.5.2)

$$D(X, \lambda) = \log \frac{\tilde{f}}{f_\lambda(X)} \tag{3.59}$$

with $\tilde{f} \geq \max f_\lambda(X)$, for all λ and $X \in E$. If D is small, f_λ is large

$$R(\lambda, i, P) = \sum_{X \in P_i} D(X, \lambda) = \sum_{X \in P_i} \log \frac{\tilde{f}}{f_\lambda(X)},$$

with $|P_i| = \text{card}(P_i)$, and according to (3.57),

$$R(\lambda, i, P) = \log \frac{\tilde{f}^{|P_i|}}{V_{\lambda_i}(P_i)}. \tag{3.60}$$

The criterion $W(L, P)$ becomes

$$W(L, P) = \sum_{i=1}^k R(\lambda_i, i, P), \tag{3.61}$$

$$W(L, P) = \sum_{i=1}^k \log \frac{\tilde{f}^{|P_i|}}{V_{\lambda_i}(P_i)}, \tag{3.62}$$

or

$$W(L, P) = K - \sum_{i=1}^k \log V_{\lambda_i}(P_i), \tag{3.63}$$

with $K = m \log \tilde{f}$.

W expresses the maximization of the product of the likelihoods of the "samples" P_i.

N.B. A slightly different R could be taken in (3.59), which would introduce an "information" measure,

$$R(\lambda, i, P) = \sum_{X \in P_i} f_\lambda(X) \log \frac{\tilde{f}}{f_\lambda(X)}. \tag{3.64}$$

Then $\mathscr{E}$ and g become

$$\mathscr{E} = \mathbb{L}_k \rightarrow \mathbb{P}_k \quad \text{or} \quad \mathscr{E}(L) = P$$

with P

$$P_i = \{X \in E | D(X, \lambda_i) \leq D(X, \lambda_j), \quad \forall j \neq i\}.$$

This is equivalent to

$$P_i = \{X \in E | f_{\lambda_i}(X) \geq f_{\lambda_j}(X), \forall j \neq i\}.$$

The objects of E are assigned to the class to which they most likely belong

$$g: \mathbb{P}_k \to \mathbb{L}_k \quad \text{or} \quad g(P) = L,$$

where λ_i is such that $R(\lambda_i, i, P) = \min_{\lambda \in \mathbb{L}} R(\lambda, i, P).$

This according to (3.60) is equivalent to the determination of λ_i by the

$$\max_{\lambda \in \mathbb{L}} V_\lambda(P_i).$$

λ_i is the maximum likelihood estimator of λ, deduced from the sample cluster P_i.

$g(P)$ is uniquely determined, since generally there exists only one maximum likelihood estimator for λ, FOURGEAUD and FUCHS [3.29].

Theorem

The dynamic clusters algorithm applied to mixed distributions will result in the monotonous increase and convergence of the sequence

$$u_p = \sum_{i \in]k]} \log V_{\lambda_i}(p) \, [P_i^{(p)}].$$

Moreover the sequence $v_p = (L^{(p)}, P^{(p)})$ converges towards an unbiased element.

If E may be supposed to be a sample of a distribution relevant to (3.44) then the overall distribution on $\mathbb{R}^n$ can be deduced from E and (L, P)

$$\forall X \in \mathbb{R}^n, \quad f(X) = \sum_{i=1}^k \Pr[X \in P_i] f_{\lambda_i}(X).$$

The probabilities $\Pr[X \in P_i]$ are estimated by the frequencies $|P_i|/m$.

This algorithm may thus give a general solution to the "mixture resolution" problem. Of course, the result has to be verified with adequate tests.

Gaussian Distributions

Now let the family of probability distributions f_λ, with $\lambda \in \mathbb{L}$, be the Gaussian family, i.e.,

$$\forall x \in \mathbb{R}^n, \quad f(x) = \frac{1}{(2\pi)^{n/2} \sqrt{\det V}} \exp\left[-\tfrac{1}{2}(x-\mu)^\mathrm{T} V^{-1}(x-\mu)\right], \quad (3.65)$$

where $\lambda = (\mu, V)$ with

$$\begin{cases} \mu \in \mathbb{R}^n \text{ the mean-vector of the distribution} \\ V \in \mathbf{M} \text{ the } n^2 \text{ covariance matrix .} \end{cases}$$

Here, $\mathbb{L} = \mathbb{R}^n \times \mathbf{M}$ (if $\mathbf{M}$ is the space of all n^2 symmetric, positive definite matrices) and we have $\mathbb{L} \subset \mathbb{R}^s$ with $s = n(n+3)/2$.
Now, we can define D, R, W, f, and g

$$D(x, \lambda) = cst + \tfrac{1}{2} [\log (\det V) + (x - \mu)^T V^{-1} (x - \mu)] . \tag{3.66}$$

Since V^{-1} is a positive definite and symmetric matrix, it can be considered as a metric tensor and we shall denote by $d_{V^{-1}}$ the distance it defines.

$$\forall x, y \in \mathbb{R}^n : d_{V^{-1}}^2 (x, y) = (x - y)^T V^{-1} (x - y)$$

$$D(x, \lambda) = cst + \tfrac{1}{2} [\log (\det V) + d_{V^{-1}}^2 (x, \mu)]$$

$$R(\lambda, i, P) = \sum_{x \in P_i} D(x, \lambda) \tag{3.67}$$

$$R(\lambda, i, P) = cst + \tfrac{1}{2} \sum_{x \in P_i} [\log (\det V) + d_{V^{-1}}^2 (x, \mu)] .$$

$\sum_{x \in P_i} d_{V^{-1}}^2 (x, \mu)$ is the quadratic dispersion of the set P_i around the point μ for the metric V^{-1}.

$$W(L, P) = cst + \sum_{i=1}^{k} R(\lambda_i, i, P), \quad \text{where} \quad \lambda_i = (\mu_i, V_i)$$

$$W(L, P) = cst + \tfrac{1}{2} \sum_{i=1}^{k} \sum_{x \in P_i} [\log (\det V_i) + d_{V^{-1}}^2 (x, \mu_i)] . \tag{3.68}$$

$$\mathscr{E} : \mathbb{L}_k \to \mathbb{P}_k \text{ with } P_i = \{ x \in E / D(x, \lambda_i) \leq D(x, \lambda_j) \; \forall j \in \,]k] \}$$

x being assigned to the lower index class in case of equality.

$$\forall i \in \,]k] : P_i = \{ x \in E / \log (\det V_i) + d_{V_i^{-1}}^2 (x, \mu_i) \leqq \log (\det V_j) + d_{V_i^{-1}}^2 (x, \mu_j), \; \forall j \in \,]k] \} .$$

$g : P_k \to \mathbb{L}_k$.
$P \to L$, where, for all $i \in \,]k]$, μ_i and V_i are the maximum likelihood estimates of the mean-vector and of the covariance matrix of the sample P_i.

We know that these estimates are given by

$$\mu_i = \frac{1}{|P_i|} \sum_{x \in P_i} x \quad \text{and} \quad V_i = \frac{1}{|P_i|} \sum_{x \in P_i} (x - \mu_i)(x - \mu_i)^T .$$

In this particular case we see that the function f reclassifies the element of E in the following way.
The "distance" between an $x \in E$ and the ith kernel $\lambda_i = (\mu_i, V_i)$ is expressed as the sum of two quantities:

$d_{V_i^{-1}}^2(x, \mu_i) = $ distance from x to μ_i for the metric V_i and $\log(\det V_i)$, which does not depend on x but only on V_i and is a characteristic feature of the dispersion of the ith distribution. Therefore the k kernels define k local metrics on $\mathbb{R}^n$.

The unbiased element obtained at the point of convergence gives a system of k local metrics Δ_i around k different points μ_i (the mean-vectors) such that

— Δ_i is entirely defined by μ_i and a positive definite, symmetric matrix V_i, with:

The distance between $x \in \mathbb{R}^n$ and μ_i in terms of Δ_i: $\log(\det V_i) + d_{V_i^{-1}}^2(x, \mu_i)$ and

— if $P = (P_1, \ldots, P_k)$ is the k-partition of E which is determined by the λ_i, $(i = 1, \ldots, k)$, i.e.:

$P_i = \{x \in E \mid x$ is nearer in terms of Δ_i to μ_i than to any μ_j in terms of $\Delta_j\}$.

— Then, $\mu_i = $ mean-vector of P_i, and $V_i = $ covariance matrix of P_i.

We can consider that our algorithm has given a solution to the following problem: find local metrics in $\mathbb{R}^n$ that express in some way the features of E. In fact, the contour-lines of the points that are equidistant from μ_i in terms of Δ_i are the ellipsoids of inertia of the Gaussian distribution with parameters (μ_i, V_i); in this case the algorithm is therefore able to detect ellipsoidal clusters.

Let us give some information on the existing I.R.I.A. (Institut de Recherche d'Informatique et d'Automatisme) program and its experimental results.

Input

The data array, the number k of classes, the family of probability distribution functions; the initial partition is drawn at random.

Output

The partition obtained at the point of convergence, the values of the criterion function for each step during the convergence, and, for each class, the estimated parameters of the distributions and the likelihoods.

The two following experiments use the algorithm to detect Gaussian distributions.

i) *The data*: an artificial sample proposed by DUDA and HART [3.25]: 25 observations drawn from the one-dimensional two component Gaussian mixture

$$P_1 = 1/3 \quad \mu_1 = -2 \quad \sigma_1 = 1$$
$$P_2 = 2/3 \quad \mu_2 = +2 \quad \sigma_2 = 1.$$

— Using the dynamic cluster algorithm, in the particular case of Gaussian distributions

Input: $k = 2$.

Output: $P_1 = 8/25, \quad \mu_1 = -2.2, \quad \sigma_1 = 0.8$
$\quad\quad\quad\quad\ P_2 = 17/25, \quad \mu_2 = 1.8 \quad\quad \sigma_2 = 1.2$.

(The convergence is achieved in 2 iterations; we obtained exactly the two drawn samples, associated with their maximum-likelihood parameters.)

— Using the DUDA and HART method (which necessarily requires Gaussian distributions)

Input : $k=2,$ $\sigma_1=\sigma_2=1,$ $P_1=1/3,$ $P_2=2/3$.

Output : $\mu_1=-2.1,$ $\mu_2=1.7$.

ii) 150 points in $\mathbb{R}^2$ have been drawn from three two-dimensional Gaussian populations:

$$\mu_1=(0;0), \Sigma_1=\begin{pmatrix} 4 & -2\sqrt{\frac{3}{2}} \\ 2\sqrt{\frac{3}{2}} & 1 \end{pmatrix}.$$

— The principal axis of the equiprobable ellipsoids of this distribution makes an angle of $\pi/3$ with the first coordinate axis.

$$\mu_2=(0;3), \Sigma_2=\begin{pmatrix} \frac{1}{4} & 0 \\ 0 & \frac{1}{4} \end{pmatrix}$$

$$\mu_3=(4;3), \Sigma_3=\begin{pmatrix} 4 & -2\sqrt{\frac{3}{2}} \\ -2\sqrt{\frac{3}{2}} & 1 \end{pmatrix} \text{(gives an angle of } \frac{5}{3}\pi\text{)}.$$

Asking for 3 classes, the algorithm has been used starting from different initial partitions and the results achieved with the best criterion value are, see Fig. 3.9,

$$\mu_1=(-0.1;-0.1), \Sigma_1=\begin{pmatrix} 2.8 & 1.4 \\ 1.4 & 1.0 \end{pmatrix}$$

$$\mu_2=(-0.1;2.9), \Sigma_2=\begin{pmatrix} 0.22 & -0.03 \\ -0.03 & 0.26 \end{pmatrix}$$

$$\mu_3=(3.9;3.0), \Sigma_3=\begin{pmatrix} 3.2 & -1.8 \\ -1.8 & 1.4 \end{pmatrix}.$$

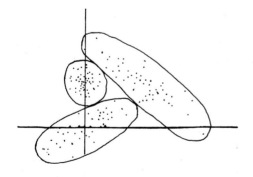

Fig. 3.9. Clusters have been detected by the algorithm after eight iterations, three classes being requested

3.5.6 Partitions and Factor Analysis

The following method generalizes factor analysis. On that last topic see HARMAN [3.33] or BENZECRI [3.8]. The idea replaces looking for a manifold of minimum inertia by a simultaneous search for a number of such manifolds.

The dynamic clusters algorithm will use the manifolds as symbolic representations or kernels of the clusters. It does converge towards a solution, which minimizes the inertia of each cluster versus its kernel, see Diday and Schroeder [3.21].

Let E be the set of objects X to be classified. Each object is defined by n parameters x. Let us consider it as a point of $\mathbb{R}^n$. Thus $\mathbf{X} = \mathbb{R}^n$.

A finite system of weight $\mu(X) \geq 0$ is assigned to each $X \in E$.

The space of kernels is $\mathbb{L} = R^n \times \mathscr{V}_q(\mathbb{R}^n)$ where $\mathscr{V}_q(\mathbb{R}^n)$ is the set of q-dimensional vector subspaces (or affine subspaces) of $\mathbb{R}^n$ ($q \leq n$).

Let $\mathbb{L} = (A, V)$ be the linear manifold of $\mathbb{R}^n$ with origin A and the direction of which is given by the subspace V. Intuitively, L is the manifold parallel to V which contains A.

Let $\mathbb{L}_k$ be the space of all k-tuples of q-dimensional linear manifolds ($q \leq n$) of $\mathbb{R}^n$ and $\mathbb{P}_k$ be defined as in Subsection 3.5.3. Finally, on $\mathbb{R}^n$ we have a positive definite quadratic form M which determines a distance between points in $\mathbb{L}^n$ as well as a norm on $\mathbb{R}^n$

$$\forall X, X' \in \mathbb{R}^n, \quad d(X, X')^2 = M(X - X', X - X') = \| X - X' \|_M^2 . \tag{3.69}$$

Let us define the D, $\mathscr{E}$, R, g W of dynamic clusters.

D and $\mathscr{E}$: $D : \mathbb{R}^n \times \mathbb{L} \to \mathbb{R}^+$ is a "distance" between the elements of E and the linear manifolds of $\mathbb{R}^n$ such that

$$\forall X \in E, \quad \forall \lambda = (A, V) \in X$$
$$D(X, \lambda) = \mu(X) \| (X - A) - \Pi^v(X - A) \|_M^2 , \tag{3.70}$$

where $(X - A) \in \mathbb{R}^n$ and $\Pi^v(X - A)$ is the nearest element of V to $(X - A)$ in $\mathbb{R}^n$.

Such an element is known to exist uniquely (cf. Riesz and Nagy [3.53]). It is the orthogonal projection of $(X - A)$ on V.

$D(X, \lambda)$ may be intuitively interpreted as the moment of inertia of x with respect to the affine subspace.

The corresponding identification function $\mathscr{E} : \mathbb{L}_k \to \mathbb{P}_k$ is the same as above; cf. Subsections 3.5.2 and 3.5.5.

The new class P_i consists of the points that are "nearer" to L_i than any other manifold L_j, i.e., the moment of inertia of which in respect to L_i is lower than L_j, $\forall j$.

R and g: $R : \mathbb{L} \times]k] \times \mathbb{P}_k \to \mathbb{R}^+$ is a similarity measure between classes and linear manifolds such that

$$R(\lambda, i, P) = \sum_{x \in P_i} D(X, \lambda) .$$

To simplify the notation $\tilde{R}$ will also be used for the following transformations

$$\tilde{R} : \mathbb{L}_k \times]k] \times \mathbb{P}_k \to \mathbb{R}^+$$

with

$$\tilde{R}(L, i, P) = \sum_{x \in P_i} D(X, \lambda_i') = R(\lambda_i, i, P) .$$

The corresponding function that allows one to get new kernels is

$$g : \mathbb{P}_k \rightarrow \mathbb{L}_k \quad \text{with} \quad g(P_1 \ldots P_k) = (\lambda_1 \ldots \lambda_k),$$

where λ_i is such that for all i

$$\forall \lambda \in \mathbb{L}, \quad \tilde{R}(L, i, P) = R(\lambda_i, i, P) \leq R(\lambda, i, P).$$

Since $R(\lambda, i, P)$ may be interpreted as the moment of inertia of the class P_i for λ, L_i is the q-dimensional linear manifold of $\mathbb{R}^n$ with respect to which the moment of inertia of P_i is minimum.

This is the problem of least-squares linear adjustment reduced to find the principal inertia axis.

The classical results in factor analysis let us say that such a manifold contains the center of gravity G_i of P_i and is directed along the subspace V_i which is generated by the q first principal axis of inertia of the class P_i (see, for instance, [3.8]).

Let $W : \mathbb{L}_k \times \mathbb{P}_k \rightarrow \mathbb{R}^+$ be such that

$$(L, P) \in \mathbb{L}_k \times P_k \quad W(L, P) = \sum_{i=1}^{k} \tilde{R}(L, i, P).$$

One can interpret $W(L, P)$ as the sum of the dispersions of the classes P_i around the manifolds L_i.

The Dynamic Clusters Algorithm

The algorithm is defined as in Subsection 3.5.3 by using the $\mathscr{E}$ and g functions. The algorithm is based on the aggregation of clusters of points around affine manifolds, behaving like centers and iteratively improved, to which the nearest observations are assigned.

The algorithm starts from k axes or n-dimensional affine subspaces that are either estimated or computed from a random partition.

Let us note that the initial sampling may be improved by a technique that avoids hollow classes during the first iterations [3.19]. The criterion is computed for all couples $(L^{(p)}, P^{(p)})$ where $P^{(p)}$ is the partition obtained at the pth iteration and $L^{(p)} = g(P^{(p)})$, the corresponding affine manifolds.

The sequence u_p which allows one to study the convergence of the algorithm is defined as in Subsection 3.5.3 by $u_p = W(L^{(p)}, P^{(p)})$.

It can be proved that R is square and the previous theorem therefore implies that u_p decreases and converges.

Let us give some information on the existing I.R.I.A. program.

Input

The data array, the maximum number of classes: k, the dimension of the manifolds: $q = 1, 2, 3, \ldots$ (straight lines, planes, etc.). The initial partition is drawn at random.

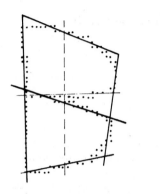

Fig. 3.10   Fig. 3.11

Output

The partition obtained at the point of convergence for each class: the q axes of
the corresponding manifolds and the inertia explained by these q axes, a measure
of the quality of the obtained partition (the criterion and a graphical representation of the results).

An Experiment: Find Features on Letters

The algorithm has been applied in the following way: E is a set of 141 points in
$\mathbb{R}^2$ which represents the letter B in the plane, Fig. 3.10. A uniform system of
weights is assigned to E,

$$\forall x \in E \quad \mu(x) = 1/\text{card}(E).$$

The metric M is the usual euclidean metric and $\mathbb{L}$ is the set of all affine straight
lines in the plane

$$\mathbb{L} = \mathbb{R}^2 \times \vec{\mathscr{V}}_1(\mathbb{R}^2).$$

The number of classes is $k=6$. The eliminating technique has been used for hollow
classes.

The graphic representation of the results consists in a projection on the first
principal plane of inertia of the global analysis of the 141 points, of the centers
of gravity and of the axis of each class.

The random initial drawings have given six axes, see Fig. 3.10, that correctly
reconstitute the skeleton of a B (according to the fact that this representation only
uses straight lines). The convergence has been achieved after 12 iterations in both
cases.

The results are given in Table 3.4.

Table 3.4

% of inertia explained by the first principal axis		
	1st drawing	2nd drawing
Global analysis	66.6	66.6
Class 1	98.6	99.77
Class 2	98.79	98.13
Class 3	99.21	99.81
Class 4	99.31	98.2
Class 5	99.86	99.05
Class 6	98.67	98.99
Criterion value (∗) at the point of convergence	0.302	0.461

(∗) The criterion helps to estimate the quality of the results of different drawings and therefore to make a choice among the results.

The same experiment was performed on a set of points representing the letter A. Three classes were requested, $k=3$. The result is displayed by Fig. 3.11.

Of course, it is not assumed that this method, somewhat heavy, is the best to find the features of an image. But the example seems illustrative of the possibilities of the technique.

3.6 Adaptive Distances in Clustering

3.6.1 Descriptions and Results of the Adaptive Distance Dynamic Cluster Method

The set E to be classified is a finite set of $\mathbb{R}^n$.

Let $\mathbb{L}=\mathbb{R}^n \times \mathscr{D}$ where $\mathscr{D}$ is the set of all Euclidian distances on $\mathbb{R}^n$, the associated matrices of which have their determinants equal to 1.

A resemblance measure D between an element X of E and an element $\lambda=(a,d)$ of $\mathbb{L}$ is defined as

$$D(X, \lambda)=d(X, a).$$

A resemblance measure I between any finite subset B of $\mathbb{R}^n$ and an element $\lambda=(a,d)$ of $\mathbb{L}$ is defined as

$$I(B, \lambda)=\sum_{Z\in B}d(a, Z).$$

$I(B, \lambda)$ therefore is the moment of inertia of B with respect to the point a for the distance d.

Let $\mathbb{P}_k$ be the set of all partitions of E in k classes and $\mathbb{L}_k$ the set of all k-tuples $(\lambda_1,...,\lambda_k)$ where $\lambda_i\in\mathbb{L}=\mathbb{R}^n \times \mathscr{D}$, k is assumed given a priori.

The Criterion

The criterion which we try to optimize is the application of $V_k = \mathbb{L}_k \times \mathbb{P}_k$ in $\mathbb{R}^+$ defined as

$$W(v) = W(L, P) = \sum_{i=1}^{k} I(P_i, \lambda_i) = \sum_{i=1}^{k} \sum_{Z \in P_i} d(a_i, Z), \qquad (3.71)$$

where

$v = (L, P),$

$L = (\lambda_1, \ldots, \lambda_k)$ with $\lambda_i = (a_i, d_i),$

$P = (P_1, \ldots, P_k).$

To minimize W is equivalent to searching among all couples for the one which minimizes the sum of the moments of inertia of the classes P_i with respect to the point a_i for the distance d_i.

One can see that the distance is not determined once for all and moreover is different from one class to another.

The Method

The aim of the algorithm is to find an element v of V_k which minimizes $W(v)$. It consists in starting from an element $v \in V_k$ of building a sequence v_p such that the associated value of the criterion $W(v_p)$ is decreasing. To build this sequence two functions are used:

— $f : \mathbb{L}_k \to P_k$ the function which associates a partition of E in k classes with k point-distance couples.

— $g : \mathbb{P}_k \to \mathbb{L}_k$ the function which associates k point-distance couples with a partition of E in k classes.

The sequence (v_p) is then defined by $v_0 = (L^{(0)}, P^{(0)})$ any couple in V_k, and $v_{p+1} = (g \circ f(L^{(p)}), f(L^{(p)}))$ if $v_p = (L^{(p)}, P^{(p)})$.

Let us now define f and g more precisely.

The Identification Function $\mathscr{E} : \mathbb{L}_k \to \mathbb{P}_k$

If $L \in \mathbb{L}_k$ with $L = (\lambda_1, \ldots, \lambda_k)$ and $\lambda_i = (a_i, d_i),$ $f(L)$ is the partition $P = (P_1, \ldots, P_k),$ where

$$P_i = \{X \in D | D(X, \lambda_i) < D(X, \lambda_j), \ \forall j \neq i\},$$

since

$D(X, a_i) = d_i(a, X_i),$

$P_i = \{X \in E | d_i(X, a_i) < d_i(X, a_j), \ \forall j \neq i\}.$

Therefore the class P_i is made of the elements of E which are nearer to a_i in terms of d_i than to any a_j in terms of d_j for $j \neq i$.

The Symbolic Description Function $g: \mathbb{P}_k \to \mathbb{L}_k$

If $P=(P_1,\ldots,P_k)$ is a partition of E into k class, $g(P)$ is the k-tuple $L=(\lambda_1,\ldots,\lambda_k)$ where $\lambda_i=(a_i, d_i)$ such that

$$I(P_i, (a_i, d_i)) = \min I(P_i, (a, d)), \quad \text{for} \quad (a, d) \in \mathbb{R}^n \times \mathcal{D}. \tag{3.72}$$

If B is a finite subset of $\mathbb{R}^n$, d an euclidian distance on $\mathbb{R}^n$, and a^* defined as

$$I[B, (a^*, d)] = \min_{a \in \mathbb{R}^n} I[B, (a, d)], \tag{3.73}$$

one can prove that a^* is the center of gravity of B (a^* does not depend on d). If B is still a finite set of $\mathbb{R}^n$, and if a couple (a^*, d^*) defined as

$$I[B, (a^*, d^*)] = \min I[B, (a, d)], \quad \text{for} \quad (a, d) \in \mathbb{R}^n \times \mathcal{D} \tag{3.74}$$

is searched, then one can prove the following proposition by using the above property and the results of SEBESTYEN [3.59] and ROMEDER [3.54].

Proposition

— a^* is the center of gravity of B,
— d^* is the distance defined by the matrix $N=|Q|^{1/n} \cdot Q^{-1}$ where Q is the covariance matrix of B (i.e. d^* is the Mahalanobis distance associated with B).
Consequently the function g will associate a partition $(P_1,\ldots,P_k)$ the k-tuple $(\lambda_1,\ldots,\lambda_k)$ where λ_i is the couple: *center of gravity of P_i-Mahalanobis distance of P_i.*

Convergence Properties

The sequence (v_p) is said to be convergent if and only if $\exists N,\ \forall p > N,\ v_p = V_N$. Let us note

$$v_p = (L^{(p)}, P^{(p)})$$
$$L^{(p)} = (\lambda_1^{(p)},\ldots,\lambda_k^{(p)})$$
$$\lambda_i^{(p)} = (a_i^{(p)}, d_i^{(p)})$$

$Q_i^{(p)}$ is the covariance matrix of $P_i^{(p)}$.

By using the results of ROMEDER [3.54] one can prove the following result.

Theorem

The sequence v_p converges and the following criterion decreases

$$W(v_p) = \sum_{i=1}^{k} \sum_{X \in P_i^{(p)}} d_i^{(p)}(a_i^{(p)}, X). \tag{3.75}$$

This criterion can also be written as

$$W(v_n) = n \sum_{i=1}^{k} \operatorname{card}(P_i^{(p)}) \cdot |Q_i^{(p)}|^{1/n}. \tag{3.76}$$

Interpretation

It can be proved that this algorithm tends to give classes such that the product of the variances of each class on all inertia axis of this same class is the least possible.

Moreover the solution which is obtained is invariant for any change of basis on the vector space $\mathbb{R}^n$, which contains the space E of the objects to be classified. For instance, the multiplication of any variable by a constant does not modify the final result of the algorithm.

This is an example of $\mathscr{T}$ admissibility; cf. Subsection 3.3.2.

3.6.2 A Generalization of the Adaptive Distance Algorithm

In the above algorithm, we were seeking simultaneously an element $a \in \mathbb{R}^n$ and a distance d, which optimize a given function. This will be done now in two steps, DIDAY and GOVAERT [3.22, 30].

The Criterion

It is the function $W: \mathbb{P}_k \times L_k \times \varDelta_k \to \mathbb{R}^+$ defined by

$$W(P, L, \varDelta) = \sum_{i=1}^{k} I(P_i, \lambda_i, d_i)$$

where

$$P = (P_1, \ldots, P_k) \in \mathbb{P}_k$$
$$L = (\lambda_1, \ldots, \lambda_k) \in \mathbb{L}_k$$
$$\varDelta = (d_1, \ldots, d_k) \in \varDelta_k .$$

The goal is to find the triple $(P, L, \varDelta)$ which minimizes W.

The Algorithm

It may be represented by the diagram of Fig. 3.12. It is built from three functions f, g, e.

$$\mathbb{P}_k \xrightarrow{g} \mathbb{L}_k$$
$$\nwarrow_{f} \quad \swarrow_{e}$$
$$\varDelta_k$$

If $L = (\lambda_1, \ldots, \lambda_k) \in \mathbb{L}_k$ and $\varDelta = (d_1, \ldots, d_k) \in \varDelta_k$. $P = (P_1, \ldots, P_k) = f(L, \varDelta)$ is defined by

$$P_i = \{X \in E | D(X, \lambda_i, d_i) \leq D(X, \lambda_j, d_j), \ \forall j \neq i\} . \tag{3.77}$$

— $g: \varDelta_k \times \mathbb{P}_k \to \mathbb{L}_k$.

If $\varDelta = (d_1, \ldots, d_k) \in \varDelta_k$ and $P = (P_1, \ldots, P_k) \in \mathbb{P}_k$. $g(P, \varDelta)$ is the k-uple $L = (\lambda_1, \ldots, \lambda_k) \in \mathbb{L}_k$, where λ_i is such that

$$I(P_i, \lambda_i, d_i) = \min_{\lambda \in A} I(P_i, \lambda, d_i) . \tag{3.78}$$

— $e: \mathbb{P}_k \times \mathbb{L}_k \to \varDelta_k$.

If $P=(P_1,...,P_k)\in\mathbb{P}_k$ and $L=(\lambda_1,...,\lambda_k)\in\mathbb{L}_k$. $e(P,L)$ is the k-uple $\varDelta=(d_1,...,d_k)\in\varDelta_k$, where d_i is such that

$$I(P_i, \lambda_i, d_i) = \min_{d\in\mathcal{D}} I(P_i, \lambda_i, d). \qquad (3.79)$$

From an initial element $v_0=(P_0, L_0, \varDelta_0)$ a sequence $v_p=(P_p, L_p, \varDelta_p)$ is built with the three functions f, g, e.

$$v_{p+1}=(P_{p+1}, L_{p+1}, \varDelta_{p+1})$$

with

$$P_{p+1}=f(L_p, P_p)$$
$$L_{p+1}=g(L_p, f(L_p, P_p))$$
$$\varDelta_{p+1}=e\{f(L_p, P_p), g[\varDelta_p, f(L_p, P_p)]\}.$$

Convergence of the Algorithm

By *definition* I is said *square*, cf. Subsection 3.5.3, if

$$W(P, L, \varDelta) \geqq W(P, g(P, \varDelta), \varDelta),$$

and

$$W(P, L, \varDelta) \geqq W(P, L, e(P, L)).$$

An example of a square I

$$I = \sum_{X\in B} D(X, \lambda, d),$$

where B is a finite part of E.

It may be shown that if I is square, if A and $\mathcal{D}$ are finite sets, and if W is defined everywhere, then v_p converges and W decreases.

Since f and g are constructive functions, the algorithm may be implemented if one is able to obtain the element of $\mathcal{D}$ which minimizes I.

This is true if $\mathcal{D}$ is finite or has special properties such as, for instance, being the space of quadratic distances. Otherwise one may minimize without optimizing, which is enough to insure convergence.

3.7 Conclusion and Future Prospects

The general idea of all these methods is to build an identification function (clustering) or a symbolic description from two types of information.
— on one hand, the experimental results,
— on the other, the a priori representation of a class or cluster.

In fact, these representations rely heavily on the *concept of potential or inertia functions*.

The "classifier specialist" selects this representation from the knowledge of the properties of his experimental universe.

The clustering algorithms maximize the adequacy of the representations of a partition in classes or clusters.

The prospect of research is quite open. We cite some topics:

— Study and use of new representations.

— Convergence conditions of the dynamic cluster algorithm according to the properties of the resemblance or dissemblance function of the representation of a class.

— Introduction of fuzziness and of overlapping subsets.

— Learning concept on the resemblance or dissemblance functions of a representation.

— Study of the properties of the operators; cf. Subsections 3.3.1 and 3.3.2.

Recent advances on these topics may be found in a book [3.74] in which it is shown that many problems of clustering may be settled as mathematical optimization problems. New problems are also considered, for instance, adaptive encoding, multi-criteria clustering, adaptive ultrametrics, typological discrimination, clustering with constraint, etc.

References

3.1   M. R. ANDERBERG: *Cluster Analysis for Applications* (Academic Press, New York 1973)
3.2   A. K. AGRAWALA: IEEE Trans. IT-**16**, 373 (1970)
3.3   J. M. BALL: "Classification Analysis"; Tech. Note. Stanford Res. Inst., Menlo Park, California (1970)
3.4   G. G. BATTACHARYA: "A Simple Method of Resolution of a Distribution into Gaussian Components"; Biometrics (1967)
3.5   BEALE: Bull. I.S.E. (London) **43**, Bk. 2, 92 (1969)
3.6   J. P. BENZECRI: "Construction ascendante d'une classification hiérachique"; L.S.M. I.S.U.P. (1969)
3.7   J. P. BENZECRI: "Algorithmes rapides d'agrégation" (Sup. class.); L.S.M. I.S.U.P. (1970)
3.8   J. P. BENZECRI: *Analyse des données*, I. La taxinomie (Dunod, Paris 1973) (ISBN-2-04-007153-9)
3.9   J. P. BRIANNE: "L'algorithme d'échange", Thèse de 3ème cycle, L.S.M. I.S.U.P. (1972)
3.10 M. CHERNOFF: Metric considerations in cluster analysis. In: Proc. 6th Berkeley Symposium on Math. Stat. and Prob. (1970)
3.11 R. M. CORMACK: J. Royal Statist. Soc. Serie A, **134**, 321 (1971)
3.12 D. B. COOPER, P. W. COOPER: Information and Control **7**, 416 (1964)
3.13 P. W. COOPER: Computer and Information Sci. **2**, 123 (1964)
3.14 N. E. DAY: Biometrika **56**, 463 (1969)
3.15 E. DIDAY: Revue statistique appliquée **19**, 19 (1971)
3.16 E. DIDAY: "Optimisation en classification automatique et reconnaissance des formes"; Revue francaise d'Automatique, Informatique et Recherche Opérationnelle (RAIRO) **3**, 61 (1972)
3.17 E. DIDAY: Thèse d'Etat, Université de Paris VI (1972)
3.18 E. DIDAY: "Analyse factorielle typologique"; Rapport Laboria, n 27, IRIA, Rocquencourt (78) (1973)
3.19 E. DIDAY: The dynamic clusters and optimization in non-hierarchical clustering. 5th IFIP (Rome 1973)
3.20 E. DIDAY: The dynamic clusters method and sequentialization in non-hierarchical clustering. In: Intern. Joint Conf. Pattern Recognition, Washington (1973)

3.21 E. DIDAY, A. SCHROEDER, Y. OK: The dynamic clusters method in pattern recognition. In: Information Processing 74; IFIP, 691 (1974)

3.22 E. DIDAY, G. GOVAERT: "Adaptative resemblance measure in pattern recognition"; Computer oriented learning process-NATO, ASI Bonas. (1974)

3.23 E. DIDAY: "Classification automatique séquentielle pour grands tableaux"; B-1 RAIRO Série bleue (1975)

3.24 A. A. DOROFEYUK: Rev. Automation, Remote Control **32**, 1928 (1971)

3.25 R. O. DUDA, P. E. HART: *Pattern Classification and Scene Analysis* (Wiley, New York 1973)

3.26 L. FISHER, J. VAN NESS: Biometrika **58**, 91 (1971)

3.27 E. W. FORGEY: "Cluster analysis of multivariate data"; AAAS Biometric Society (WNAR) Riverside, California, USA

3.28 J. FORTIER, H. SOLOMON: Clustering procedures, in: *Multivariate Analysis*, ed. by P. R. KRISHNAIAH (Academic Press, New York 1966)

3.29 C. FOURGAUD, A. FUCHS: *Statistique* (Dunod, Paris 1971)

3.30 G. GOVAERT: "Classification automatique et distances adaptatives"; Thèse de 3ème cycle. Institut de Programmation (1975)

3.31 J. C. GOWER, G. J. S. ROSS: Appl. Stat. **18**, 54 (1969)

3.32 D. HALL, G. BALL: A clustering technique for summerizing multivariate data. Behavorial Science **12** (1967)

3.33 H. H. HARMAN: *Modern Factor Analysis* (University of Chicago Press, Chicago 1968)

3.34 Y. C. YO, A. K. AGRAWALA: Proc. IEEE **56**, 2101 (1968)

3.35 M. JAMBU: "Techniques de classification automatique"; Thèse de 3ème cycle (L.S.M. I.S.U.P.) (1972)

3.36 R. J. JANCEY: Aust. J. Bot. **14**, 127 (1966)

3.37 N. JARDINE, R. SIBSON: *Mathematical Taxonomy* (Wiley, New York 1971)

3.38 R. E. JENSEN: Operation Research **12**, 1034 (1969)

3.39 W. KÖHLER: *La psychologie de la forme* (Gallimard 1964)

3.40 J. B. KRUSKAL, JR.: Proc. Am. Math. Soc. **7**, 48 (1956)

3.41 G. N. LANCE, W. T. WILLIAMS: Comp. J. **9**, 373 (1967)

3.42 I. C. LERMAN: *Les bases de la classification automatique* (Gauthier, Villars 1970)

3.43 I. C. LERMAN: Rev. Stat. Appl. **21**, 23 (1973)

3.44 J. MAC QUEEN: Some methods for classification and analysis of Multivariate observations. The 5th Berkeley Symp. Mathematics, Statistics and Probability **1** (1967)

3.45 J. N. MORGAN, R. C. MESSENGER: *Thaid* (Thomson-Shore, Ann-Arbor, Michigan 1973)

3.46 R. A. NORTHOUSE, F. R. FROM: Proc. First Intern. Joint Conf. Pattern Recognition, Washington (1973)

3.47 E. A. PATRICK, J. C. HANCOCK: IEEE Trans. IT-**12**, 362 (1966)

3.48 E. A. PATRICK, J. P. COSTELLO: IEEE Trans. IT-**16**, 556 (1970)

3.49 E. A. PATRICK: *Fundamentals of Pattern Recognition* (Prentice Hall, Englewood Cliffs, New Jersey 1972)

3.50 R. C. PRIM: Bell Syst. Tech. J. **36**, 1389 (1957)

3.52 C. R. RAO: J. Roy. Stat. Soc., Series B **10**, 159 (1948)

3.53 F. RIESZ, NAGY: *Leçons d'analyse fonctionelle* (Gauthier Villars, Paris 1968)

3.54 J. M. ROMEDER: "Méthodes de discrimination"; Thèse de 3ème cycle, Statistique Mathématique, Faculté des Sciences de Paris VI (1969)

3.55 M. ROUX: "Un algorithme pour construire une hierarchie particulière"; Thèse de 3ème cycle (L.S.M. I.S.U.P.) (1968)

3.56 H. R. RUSPINI: Inf. Sci. **2**, 319 (1970)

3.57 G. SANDOR, E. DIDAY, Y. LECHEVALLIER: "Résultats récents concernant la méthode des nuées dynamiques et application à la recherche de profils biologiques"; European Chapter of ACM, Davos (1973)

3.58 A. J. SCOTT, M. J. SYMONS: Biometrics **27**, 387 (1971)

3.59 G. S. SEBESTYEN: Decision Making Processes in Pattern Recognition; in: *ACM Monograph Series* (The Macmillan Company, New York 1962)

3.60 P. SELLERS: J. Combinatorial Theory (A) **16**, 253 (1974)

3.61 J. C. SIMON: "A Formal Aspect of Pattern Recognition and Scene Analysis"; I.J.C.P.R. II. Copenhagen (1974)

3.62 P. Sneath, R. Sokal: *Numerical Taxonomy* (W. M. Freeman, San Francisco 1973)
3.63 J. S. Spragins: IEEE Trans. IT-**12**, 223 (1966)
3.64 M. Tenenhaus, J. Bouroche: Metra **9**, 407 (1970)
3.65 R. L. Thorndike: Psychometrica **18**, 267 (1953)
3.66 J. H. Ward: Am. Stat. Assoc. J. **58**, 236 (1963)
3.67 D. Wishart: "Some Problems in the Theory and Application of the Methods of Numerical Taxonomy"; Ph.D. Thesis, University of St. Andrews (1971)
3.68 T. Y. Young, G. Coraluppi: IEEE Trans. IT-**16**, 258 (1970)
3.69 L. A. Zadeh: Inf. Control **8**, 338 (1965)
3.70 C. T. Zahn: IEEE Trans. C-**20**, 68 (1971)
3.71 S. G. Johnson: Psychometrika **32**, 241 (1967)
3.72 V. N. Yolkina, N. G. Zagoruiko: "Quantitative Criteria of Taxonomy Quality and Use in the Process of Decision Making"; Vychislitel'nye Systemy, issue 36 Computer Systems Institute of Mathematics, Novosibirsk (Russian)
3.73 J. C. Simon, E. Diday: Compt. Rend. Acad. Sci. (Paris) **275**, serie A, 1003 (1972)
3.74 E. Diday et al.: "Optimisation on classification automatique", INRIA Edit (1979). Available at INRIA, Rocquencourt, 78150 France

4. Syntactic (Linguistic) Pattern Recognition

K. S. Fu

With 18 Figures

This chapter provides an overview, illustrated by a great number of examples, of the syntactic (linguistic) pattern recognition. Languages are used to describe patterns, and syntax analysis procedures are employed as recognition procedures. Methods for the selection of pattern primitives are presented. Both one-dimensional (string) and high-dimensional grammars are discussed and their applications to one-dimensional and high-dimensional patterns demonstrated. Problems for further research are suggested.

4.1 Syntactic (Structural) Approach to Pattern Recognition

As it was pointed out in Chapter 1, most of the developments in pattern recognition research during the past decade deal with the decision-theoretic approach [4.1–11] and its applications. In some pattern recognition problems, the structural information which describes each pattern is important, and the recognition process includes not only the capability of assigning the pattern to a particular class (to classify it), but also the capacity to describe aspects of the pattern which make it ineligible for assignment to another class. A typical example of this class of recognition problem is picture recognition or more generally speaking, scene analysis. In this class of recognition problems, the patterns under consideration are usually quite complex and the number of features required is often very large which make the idea of describing a complex pattern in terms of a (hierarchical) composition of simpler subpatterns very attractive. Also, when the patterns are complex and the number of possible descriptions is very large it is impractical to regard each description as defining a class (for example, in fingerprint and face-identification problems, recognition of continuous speech, Chinese characters, etc.). Consequently, the requirement of recognition can only be satisfied by a description for each pattern rather than the simple task of classification.

Example 4.1. The pictorial patterns shown in Fig. 4.1 can be described in terms of the hierarchical structures shown in Fig. 4.2.

In order to represent the hierarchical (tree-like) structural information of each pattern, that is, a pattern described in terms of simpler subpatterns, and each simpler subpattern again described in terms of even simpler subpatterns, etc., the linguistic or structural approach has been proposed [4.12–16]. This approach draws an analogy between the (hierarchical, tree-like) structure of patterns and the syntax of languages. Patterns are specified as building up out of subpatterns in various ways of composition just as phrases and sentences are built up by

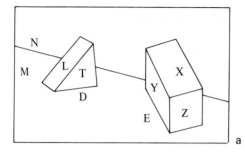

Fig. 4.1a and b. The pictorial patterns for Example 4.1. a) Scene A, b) Aerial photograph F
Color code:

Magenta	Commercial
Red	High density housing
Light brown, tan, sand	Low density housing, roads, suburban
Blue	Water
Light green	Rural
Dark green	Forest

a

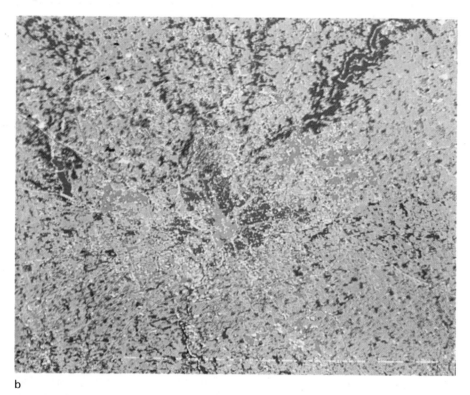

b

concatenating words and words are built up by concatenating characters. Evidently, for this approach to be advantageous, the simplest subpatterns selected, called "pattern primitives", should be much easier to recognize than the patterns themselves. The "language" which provides the structural description of patterns in terms of a set of pattern primitives and their composition operations, is sometimes called "pattern description language". The rules governing the composition of primitives into patterns are usually specified by the so-called "grammar" of the pattern description language. After each primitive within the pattern is identified, the recognition process is accomplished by performing a syntax analysis or parsing of the "sentence" describing the given pattern to determine whether or not it is syntactically (or grammatically) correct with respect to the specified

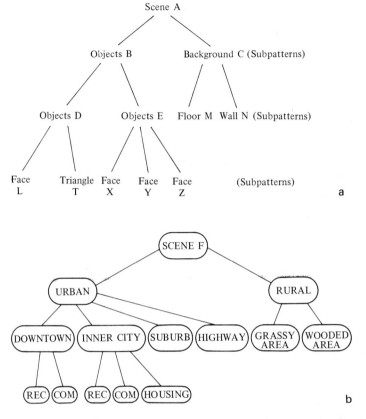

Fig. 4.2a and b. Hierarchial structural descriptions of a) Scene A and b) an aerial photograph F

grammar. In the meantime, the syntax analysis also produces a structural description of the sentence representing the given pattern (usually in the form of a tree structure).

The linguistic approach to pattern recognition provides a capability for describing a large set of complex patterns using small sets of simple pattern primitives and of grammatical rules. As can be seen later, one of the most attractive aspects of this capability is the use of the recursive nature of a grammar. A grammar (re-writing) rule can be applied any number of times, so it is possible to express in a very compact way some basic structural characteristics of an infinite set of sentences. Of course, the practical utility of such an approach depends upon our ability to recognize the simple pattern primitives and their relationships represented by the composition operations.

The various relations or composition operations defined among subpatterns can usually be expressed in terms of logical and/or mathematical operations. For example, if we choose "concatenation" as the only relation (composition operation) used in describing patterns, then for the pattern primitives shown in Fig. 4.3a the rectangle in Fig. 4.3b would be represented by the string *aaabbcccdd*.

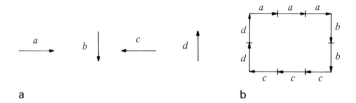

Fig. 4.3a and b. A rectangle and its pattern primitives

More explicitly, if we use "+" for the "head-to-tail concatenation" operation, the rectangle in Fig. 4.3b would be represented by the string $a+a+a+b+b+c+c+c+d+d$, and its corresponding tree-like structure would be

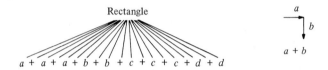

Similarly, a slightly more complex example is given in Fig. 4.4 using the pattern primitives in Fig. 4.3a. It is noted that, in this case, both the primitives and the relation between them are represented by the symbols in the string.

An alternative representation of the structural information of a pattern is to use a "relational graph". For example, a relational graph of Picture F in Fig. 4.1b is shown in Fig. 4.5. Since there is a one-to-one corresponding relation between a linear graph and a matrix, a relational graph can certainly also be expressed as a "relational matrix". In using the relational graph for pattern description, we can broaden the class of allowed relations to include any relation that can be conveniently determined from the pattern. [Notice that (i) the concentenation is the only natural operation for one-dimensional languages, and (ii) a graph, in general, contains closed loops whereas a tree does not.] With this generalization, we may possibly express richer descriptions than we can with tree structures. However, the use of tree structures does provide us a direct channel to adapt the techniques of formal language theory to the problem of compactly representing and analyzing patterns containing a significant structural content.

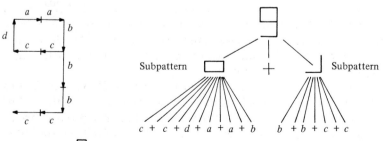

Fig. 4.4. Pattern ⊐ and its structural description

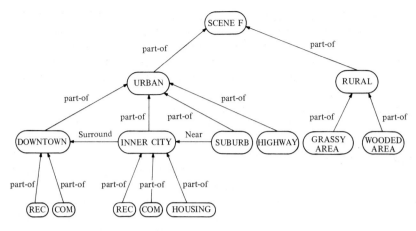

Fig. 4.5. A relational graph of scene *F*

4.2 Linguistic Pattern Recognition System

A linguistic pattern recognition system can be considered as consisting of three major parts; namely, preprocessing, pattern description or representation, and syntax analysis[1]. A simple block diagram of the system is shown in Fig. 4.6. The functions of preprocessing include (i) pattern encoding and approximation, and (ii) filtering, restoration and enhancement. An input pattern is first coded or approximated by some convenient form for further processing. For example, a black-and-white picture can be coded in terms of a grid (or a matrix) of 0's and 1's, or a waveform can be approximated by its time samples or a truncated Fourier series expansion. In order to make the processing in the later stages of the system more efficient, some sort of "data compression" is often applied at this stage. Then, techniques of filtering, restoration and/or enhancement will be used to clean the noise, to restore the degradation, and/or to improve the quality of the coded (or approximated) patterns. At the output of the preprocessor, presumably, we have patterns with reasonably "good quality". Each preprocessed pattern is then represented by a language-like structure (for example, a string or a graph).

---

[1] The division of three parts is for convenience rather than necessity. Usually, the term "linguistic pattern recognition" refers primarily to the pattern representation (or description) and the syntax analysis.

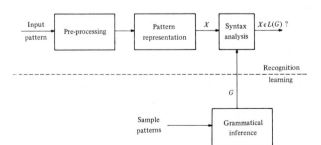

Fig. 4.6. Block diagram of a linguistic pattern recognition system

The operation of this pattern-representation process consists of (i) pattern segmentation, and (ii) primitive (feature) extraction. In order to represent a pattern in terms of its subpatterns, we must segmentize the pattern and, in the meantime, identify (or extract) the primitives and relations in it. In other words, each preporcessed pattern is segmentized into subpatterns and pattern primitives based on prespecified syntactic or composition operations; and, in turn, each subpattern is identified with a given set of pattern primitives. Each pattern is now represented by a set of primitives with specified syntactic operations. For example, in terms of "concatenation" operation, each pattern is represented by a string of (concatenated) primitives. More sophisticated systems should also be able to detect various syntatic relations within the pattern. The decision on whether or not the representation (pattern) is syntactically correct (i.e., belongs to the class of patterns described by the given syntax or grammar) will be performed by the "syntax analyzer" or "parser". When performing the syntax analysis or parsing, the analyzer can usually produce a complete syntactic description, in terms of a parse or parsing-tree, of the pattern provided it is syntactically correct. Otherwise, the pattern is either rejected or analyzed on the basis of other given grammars, which presumably describe other possible classes of patterns under consideration.

Conceptually, the simplest form of recognition is probably "template-matching". The string of primitives representing an input pattern is matched against strings of primitives representing each prototype or reference pattern. Based on a selected "matching" or "similarity" criterion, the input pattern is classified in the same class as the prototype pattern which is the "best" to match the input. The hierarchical structural information is essentially ignored. A complete parsing of the string representing an input pattern, on the other hand, explores the complete hierarchical structural description of the pattern. In between, there are a number of intermediate approaches. For examples, a series of tests can be designed to test the occurrences or non-occurrence of certain subpatterns (or primitives) or certain combinations of subpatterns or primitives. The result of the tests (for example, through a table look-up, a decision tree, or a logical operation) is used for a classification decision. Notice that each test may be a template-matching scheme or a parsing for a subtree representing a sub-pattern. The selection of an appropriate approach for recognition usually depends upon the problem requirement. If a complete pattern description is required for recognition, parsing is necessary. Otherwise, a complete parsing could be avoided by using other simpler approaches to improve the efficiency of the recognition process.

In order to have a grammar describing the structural information about the class of patterns under study, a grammatical inference machine is required which can infer a grammar from a given set of training patterns in language-like representations[2]. This is analogous to the "learning" process in a decision-theoretic pattern recognition system [4.1–11, 17–20]. The structural description of the class of patterns under study is learned from the actual sample patterns from that class. The learned description, in the form of a grammar, is then used for pattern description and syntax analysis (see Fig. 4.6). A more general form of

---

[2] At present, this part is performed primarily by the designer.

learning might include the capability of learning the best set of primitives and the corresponding structural description for the class of patterns concerned.

Practical applications of linguistic pattern recognition include the recognition of English and Chinese characters, spoken digits, and mathematical expressions, the classification of bubble-chamber and spark-chamber photographs, chromosomes and fingerprint images, and the identification of machine parts [4.21–37].

4.3 Selection of Pattern Primitives

As was discussed in Section 4.1, the first step in formulating a linguistic model for pattern description is the determination of a set of primitives in terms of which the patterns of interest may be described. This will be largely influenced by the nature of the data, the specific application in question, and the technology available for implementing the system. There is no general solution for the primitive selection problem at this time. The following requirements usually serve as a guideline for selecting pattern primitives.

(i) The primitives should serve as basic pattern elements to provide a compact but adequate description of the data in terms of the specified structural relations (e.g., the concatenation relation).

(ii) The primitives should be easily extracted or recognized by existing non-linguistic methods, since they are considered to be simple and compact patterns and their structural information not important.

For example, for speech patterns, phonemes are naturally considered as a "good" set of primitives with the concatenation relation[3]. Similarly, strokes have been suggested as primitives in describing handwriting. However, for general pictorial patterns, there is no such "universal picture element" analogous to phonemes in speech or strokes in handwriting[4]. Sometimes, in order to provide an adequate description of the patterns, the primitives should contain the information which is important to the specific application in question. For example, if the size (or shape or location) is important in the recognition problem, then the primitives should contain information relating to size (or shape or location) so that patterns from different classes are distinguishable by whatever method is to be applied to analyze the descriptions. This requirement often results in a need for semantic information in describing primitives [4.12].

The following simple example is used to illustrate that, for the same data, different problem specifications would result in different selections of primitives.

Example 4.2. Suppose that the problem is to discriminate rectangles (of different sizes) from non-rectangles. The following set of primitives is selected:

$a' -$ $0°$ horizontal line segment

$b' -$ $90°$ vertical line segment

$c' - 180°$ horizontal line segment

$d' - 270°$ vertical line segment .

---

[3] The view of continuous speech as composed of one sound segment for each successive phoneme is, of course, a simplification of facts.

[4] It is also interesting to see that the extraction of phonemes in continuous speech and that of strokes in handwriting are not a very easy task with respect to the requirement (ii) specified above.

The set of all rectangles (of different sizes) is represented by a single sentence or string $a'b'c'd'$:

If, in addition, the problem is also to discriminante rectangles of different sizes, the above description would be inadequate. An alternative is to use unit-length line segments as primitives:

The set of rectangles of different sizes can then be described by the language

$$L = \{a^n b^m c^n d^m | n, m = 1, 2, ...\} . \tag{4.1}$$

Requirement (ii) may sometimes conflict with requirement (i) due to the fact that the primitives selected according to requirement (i) may not be easy to recognize using existing techniques. On the other hand, requirement (ii) could allow the selection of quite complex primitives as long as they can be recognized. With more complex primitives, simpler structural descriptions (e.g., simple grammars) of the patterns could be used. This trade-off may become quite important in the implementation of the recognition system. An example is the recognition of two-dimensional mathematical expressions in which characters and mathematical notations are primitives [4.25, 26]. However, if we consider the characters as subpatterns and describe them in terms of simpler primitives (e.g., strokes or line segments), the structural descriptions of mathematical expressions would be more complex than the case of using characters directly as primitives.

Another example is the recognition of Chinese characters [4.22–24]. From the knowledge about the structure of Chinese characters, a small number of simple segmentation operations such as

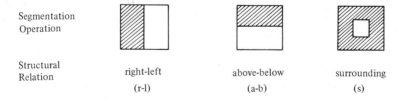

can be used. Each operation also generates a particular structural relation between the two neighboring subpatterns or primitives. Applying these operations recursively, that is, segmentizing each subpattern again by any one of the three

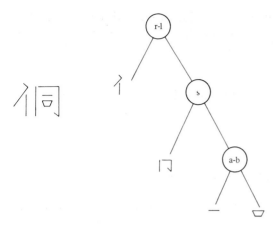

Fig. 4.7. A structural description of Chinese character "伺"

operations, we can segmentize a Chinese character into its subpatterns and primitives. If the primitives can be extracted or recognized by existing techniques, a Chinese character can be described syntactically with the given set of structural relations. An illustrative example is given in Fig. 4.7. It is anticipated that the resulting structural descriptions will be much more complex if we choose basic strokes as the primitives.

One of the earliest papers describing the decomposition of pictorial patterns into primitives [4.38] presented a conceptually appealing method which allows the recognition system to (heuristically) determine the primitives by inspection of training samples. A pattern is first examined by a programmed scan. The result of the scan is to produce descriptions of segments of the picture (subpictures) which are divisions conveniently produced by the scanning process, and not necessarily true divisions. The scanning process also includes preprocessing routines for noise-cleaning, gap-filling, and curve-following. The subpictures obtained in the scan are analyzed and connected, when appropriate, into true picture parts; a description is given in terms of the length and slope of straight-line segments and the length and curvature of curved segments. The structural relations among various segments (primitives) of a picture is expressed in terms of a connection table (Table of Joins). The assembly program produces a "statement" which gives a complete description of the pattern. The description is independent of the orientation and the size of the picture, the lengths of the various parts being given relative to one another. It is, in effect, a coded representation of the pattern and may be regarded as a one-dimensional string consisting of symbols chosen from a specified alphabet. The coded representation gives the length, slope and curvature of each primitive, together with details of the ends and joins to other primitives. No explicit consideration is given to formalizing the pattern syntax.

A formal model for the abstract description of English cursive script has been proposed by EDEN and HALLE [4.39]. The primitives are four distinct line segments in the form of a triplet

$$\sigma_j = [(x_{j_1}, y_{j_1}), (x_{j_2}, y_{j_2}), \theta_j] \qquad (4.2)$$

where (x_j, y_j)'s represent the approximate location of the end points of the line segment, and θ_j refers to the sense of rotation from the first to the second end point. θ_j is positive if the sense of rotation is clockwise and negative if counterclockwise. The four primitives are:

$$\sigma_1 = [(1, 0), (0, 0), +]$$ "bar"

$$\sigma_2 = [(1, 1), (0, 0), +]$$ "hook"

$$\sigma_3 = [(0, 0), (0, 1), +]$$ "arch"

$$\sigma_4 = [(1, \varepsilon), (0, 0), +], \quad 0 < \varepsilon < 1,$$ "loop"

They can be transformed by changing the sign of θ or by reflection about the horizontal or vertical axis. These transformations generate 28 strokes (because of symmetry, the arch generates only four strokes), but only nine of them are of interest in the English script commonly used.

A word is completely specified by the stroke sequence comprising its letters. A word is represented by the image of a mapping of a finite sequence of strokes into the set of continuous functions, the mapping being specified by concatenation and tracing rules applied in specific order. Only two concatenation rules are required. The first specifies stroke locations within a letter. The rule prescribes that two consecutive strokes are concatenated by identifying the abscissa of the terminal end-point of the first stroke with that of the initial end-point of the second stroke. The second rule states that across a letter boundary, the leftmost end-point of the stroke following the boundary is placed so as to be to the right of the rightmost end-point of the penultimate stroke before the letter boundary. The simple cursive strokes of the word "globe" are shown in Fig. 4.8 and their concatenation in Fig. 4.9. These concatenation rules are not sufficient to specify all sequences of English letters unambiguously. Nevertheless, the ambiguities are intrinsic to the writing system, even in careful handwriting.

No formal syntax was attempted for the description of handwriting. Interesting experimental results on the recognition of cursive writing were obtained

Fig. 4.8. Cursive strokes of "globe"

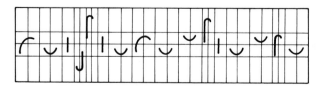

Fig. 4.9. Stroke sequence representation of the word "globe"

by EARNEST [4.40] and MERMELSTEIN [4.41] using a dictionary and rather heuristic recognition criteria. In addition, the dynamics of the trajectory (in space and time) that the point of the pen traces out as it moves across the paper has also been studied [4.42]. The motion of the pen is assumed to be controlled by a pair of orthogonal forces, as if one pair of muscles controls the vertical displacement and another the horizontal.

More general methods for primitive selection may be grouped roughly into methods emphasizing boundaries and methods emphasizing regions. These methods are discussed in the following.

4.3.1 Primitive Selection Emphasizing Boundaries or Skeletons

A set of primitives commonly used to describe boundaries or skeletons is the chain code given by FREEMAN [4.43, 44]. Under this scheme, a rectangular grid is overlaid on the two-dimensional pattern, and straight line segments are used to connect the grid points falling closest to the pattern. Each line segment is assigned an octal digit according to its slope. The pattern is thus represented by a chain (or string) or chains of octal digits. Figure 4.10 illustrates the primitives and the coded string describing a curve. This descriptive scheme has some useful properties. For example, patterns coded in this way can be rotated through multiples of 45° simply by adding an octal digit (modulo 8) to every digit in the string (however, only rotations by multiples of 90° can be accomplished without some distortion of the pattern). Other simple manipulations such as expansion, measurement of curve length, and determination of pattern self-intersections are easily carried out. Any desired degree of resolution can be obtained by adjusting the fineness of the grid imposed on the patterns. This method is, of course, not limited to simply-connected closed boundaries; it can be used for describing arbitrary two-dimensional figures composed of straight or curved lines and line segments.

Notable work using FREEMAN's chain code include efforts by KNOKE and WILEY [4.45] and by FEDER [4.46]. KNOKE and WILEY attempted to demonstrate

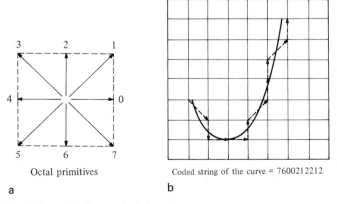

Octal primitives   Coded string of the curve = 7600212212

a   b

Fig. 4.10a and b. Freeman's chain code

that linguistic approaches can usually be applied to describe structural relation-ships within patterns (hand-printed characters, in this case). FEDER's work con-sidered only patterns which can be encoded as strings of primitives. Several bases for developing pattern languages are discussed, including equations in two vari-ables (straight lines, circles and circular arcs, etc.), pattern properties (self-inter-sections, convexity, etc.), and various measures of curve similarity. The computa-tional power (automaton complexity) required to detect the elements of these pattern languages is studied. However, this problem is complicated considerably by the fact that (i) these languages are mostly context-sensitive and not context-free, (ii) the chain code yields only a piecewise linear approximation of the original pattern, and (iii) the coding of a typical curve is not unique, depending to a degree on its location and orientation with respect to the coding grid.

Other applications of the chain code include description of contour maps [4.47], "shape matching" [4.48], and identification of high energy particle tracks in bubble chamber photographs [4.49]. Contour lines can be encoded as chains. Contour map problems may involve finding the terrain to be flooded by a dam placed at a particular location, the water shed area for a river basin, the terrain visible from a particular mountain-top location, or the determination of optimum highway routes through mountainous terrain. In shape matching, two or more two-dimensional objects having irregular contours are to be matched for all or part of their exterior boundary. For some such problems the relative orientation and scale of the objects to be matched may be known and only translation is required. The problem of matching aerial photographs to each other as well as to terrain maps falls into this category. For other problems either orientation, or scale, or both may be unknown and may have to be determined as part of the problem. An example of problems in which relative orientation has to be deter-mined is that of the computer assembly of potsherds and jigsaw puzzles [4.50].

Other syntatic pattern recognition systems using primitives with the emphasis on boundary, skeleton or contour information include systems for hand-printed character recognition [4.51–53], bubble chamber and spark chamber photo-graph classification [4.27, 28, 54, 55], chromosome analysis [4.29, 56, 57], finger-print identification [4.30–32, 58, 59], face recognition [4.60, 61], and scene analysis [4.62–64].

4.3.2 Pattern Primitives in Terms of Regions

A set of primitives for encoding geometric patterns in terms of regions has been proposed by PAVLIDIS [4.65]. In this case, the basic primitives are halfplanes in the pattern space[5] (or the field of observation). It can be shown that any figure (or arbitrary polygon) may be expressed as the union of a finite number of con-vex polygons. Each convex polygon can, in turn, be represented as the inter-section of a finite number of halfplanes. By defining a suitable ordering (a sequence) of the convex polygons composing the arbitrary polygon, it is possible to deter-mine a unique minimal set of maximal (in an appropriate sense) polygons, called primary subsets, the union of which is the given polygon. In linguistic analogy,

---

[5] This could be generalized to halfspaces of the pattern space.

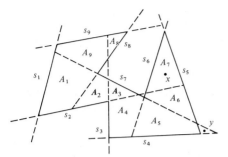

Fig. 4.11. Polygon A of Example 4.3

a figure can be thought of as a "sentence", the convex polygons composing it as "words" and the halfplanes as "letter". This process is summarized in this subsection.

Let A be a bounded polygon and let $s_1, s_2, \ldots, s_n$ be its sides. A point x in the plane will be said to be positive with respect to one side if it lies on the same side of the extension of a side as the polygon does with respect to the side itself. Otherwise, it will be said to be negative with respect to that side.

Example 4.3. For the polygon A given in Fig. 3.11, the point x is positive with respect to the sides s_5 and s_6, but negative with respect to s_7. Similarly, y is positive with respect to s_4 and s_7, but negative with respect to s_5. Extending all the sides of A on both directions, A is intersected by some of these extensions, and it is subdivided into $A_1, A_2, \ldots, A_9$ convex polygons.

Obviously, the points which are positive with respect to a side form a half-plane whose boundary is the extension of the side. Let h_i denote the halfplane corresponding to the side s_i, and let Q denote the intersection of all the halfplanes $h_1, h_2, \ldots, h_n$ in A. If A is convex, then $A = Q$. If A is not convex, then Q may be empty or simply different from A. Let Q_I represent the intersection of all the half-planes except $s_{i_1}, \ldots, s_{i_k}$ where $I = \{i_1, \ldots, i_k\}$, the index set. Then we can define a sequence of Q_I as follows

$$Q = \bigcap_{i=1}^{n} h_i$$

$$Q_j = \bigcap_{\substack{i=1 \\ i \neq j}}^{n} h_i \tag{4.3}$$

$$Q_{jk} = \bigcap_{\substack{i=1 \\ i \neq j, i \neq k}}^{n} h_i .$$

This is an increasing sequence since $Q \subset Q_j \subset Q_{jk} \ldots$. The last element of the sequence will be the whole plane, and it is obtained for $I = \{1, \ldots, n\}$. If a sequence of the above form has a maximal element, then that set is called a primary (convex) subset of A. A non-empty member of such a Q-sequence which is also a subset of A is called a nucleus of A if all the previous elements of the sequence are empty. Consequently, it can be shown that the union of the primary subsets of A precisely equals A.

For a given polygon the primary subsets can be found by forming all the sequences $Q, Q_j, Q_{jk}, \ldots$ and searching for their maximal elements. This is a well-defined procedure and, hence, the primary subsets of A are unique.

If the original figure (polygon) has not been approximated by an arbitrary polygon but by one whose sides were parallel to certain prespecified directions $\phi_1, \phi_2, \ldots, \phi_k$, then the figure can be represented by a finite number of convex polygons. Any one of the halfplanes determined by the sides of the polygon will actually be a parallel translation of the halfplanes H_i determined by the chosen directions. These halfplanes play the role of primitives. If G denotes the group of parallel translations, then each primary subset R_j can be expressed as

$$R_j = \bigcap_{i=1}^{2k} g_i^j H_i, \qquad g_i^j \in G, \tag{4.4}$$

where the intersection goes over $2k$ because each direction defines two halfplanes. If a halfplane does not actually appear in the formation of R_j, it will still be included in the above expression with an arbitrary transformation g which will be required only to place its boundary outside the field of observation. The original polygon A can then be represented as

$$A = \bigcup_{j=1}^{l} R_j = \bigcup_{j=1}^{l} \bigcap_{i=1}^{2k} g_i^j H_i. \tag{4.5}$$

If a similarity measure between two convex polygons A and B, denoted by $S(A, B)$, can be appropriately defined, we may be able to find a finite set B of convex polygons $B_1, \ldots, B_N$ such that for every convex polygon A of interest there will exist a member of B and a member of G to satisfy

$$S(A, gB) < \delta$$

for a prespecified δ. The members of B will be referred to as the basic components, and, consequently, we can write

$$A = \bigcup_{i=1}^{l} g_i B_{k(i)}. \tag{4.6}$$

It should be noted that this approach provides a formalism for describing the syntax of polygonal figures and more general figures which can be approximated reasonably well by polygonal figures. The analysis or recognition procedure requires the definition of suitable measures of similarity between polygons. The similarity measures considered so far are quite sensitive to noise in the patterns and/or are difficult to implement practically on a digital computer. A somewhat more general selection procedure of pattern primitives based on regions has been recently proposed by ROSENFELD and STRONG [4.66].

Another form of representing polygonal figures is the use of primary graphs [4.67, 68]. The primary graph of a polygon A is one whose nodes correspond to the nuclei and the primary subsets of A, and its branches connect each nucleus to all the primary subsets containing it. An example is given in Fig. 4.12. Primary

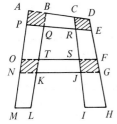

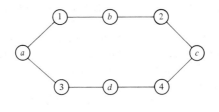

Primary Subset or Nucleus	Label
ABLM	a
ADEP	b
CDHI	c
OFGN	d
ABQP	1
CDER	2
OTKN	3
SFGJ	4

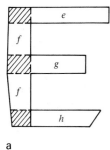

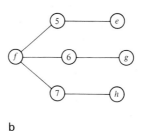

a   b

Fig. 4.12. a) Polygonal figures and b) corresponding primary graphs

subsets and nuclei of polygons approximating the figures are shown in Fig. 4.12a (shaded areas are nuclei). Primary graphs for the corresponding polygons in a) are given in Fig. 4.12b. This form of representation may not characterize a figure uniquely; however, it does provide information describing it, and, in particular, about its topology. Also, as will be seen later in this chapter, patterns represented by graphs can be formally described by graph grammars.

Another approach to the analysis of geometric patterns using regions is encountered primarily in the problem of scene analysis [4.9, 63]. MINSKY and PAPERT [4.69] have considered the direct transformation of a gray scale picture to regions, bypassing the edge-finding, line-fitting procedures. Regions are constructed as the union of squares whose corners have the same or nearly the same gray scale. The method proposed by GUZMAN [4.70] assumes that a picture can be reduced by preprocessing to a list of vertices, lines and surfaces. Various heuristics, based on the analysis of types of intersection of lines and surfaces, are applied to this list to compose its elements into two- or three-dimensional regions. Some candidate pattern recognition schemes have been investigated, all of which involve methods for matching the reduced pattern descriptions against a proto-type dictionary. The procedure studied by BRICE and FENNEMA [4.71] decomposes a picture into atomic regions of uniform gray scale. A pair of heuristics is used to join these regions in such a way as to obtain regions whose boundaries are determined more by the natural lines of the scene than by the artificial ones introduced by quantization and noise. Then a simple line-fitting technique is used to approximate the region boundaries by straight lines and finally, the scene analyzer interprets the picture using some simple tests on object groups generated by a GUZMAN-like procedure.

4.4 Pattern Grammar

Assume that a satisfactory solution of the "primitive selection" problem is avail-able for a given application. The next step is the construction of a grammar (or grammars) which will generate a language (or languages) to describe the pat-terns under study. Ideally, it would be nice to have a grammatical inference ma-chine which would infer a grammar from a given set of strings describing the patterns under study. Unfortunately, such a machine has not been available ex-cept for some very special cases [4.72]. In most cases so far, the designer con-structs the grammar based on the *a priori* knowledge available and his experience. It is known that increased descriptive power of a language is paid for in terms of increased complexity of the analysis system (recognizer or acceptor). Finite-state automata are capable of recognizing or accepting finite-state languages although the descriptive power of finite-state languages is also known to be weaker than that of context-free and context-sensitive languages. On the other hand, non-finite, non-deterministic devices are required, in general, to accept the languages generated by context-free and context-sensitive grammars. Except for the class of deterministic languages, non-deterministic parsing procedures are usually needed for the analysis of context-free languages. The trade-off between the descriptive power and the analysis efficiency of a grammar for a given appli-cation is, at present, almost completely justified by the designer. (For example, a precedence language may be used for pattern description in order to obtain good analysis efficiency; or, on the other hand, a context-free programmed gram-mar generating a context-sensitive language may be selected in order to describe the patterns effectively.) The effect of the theoretical difficulty may not be serious in practice, as long as some care is exercised in developing the required grammars. This is especially true when the languages of interest are actually finite-state, even though the form of the grammars may be context-sensitive, or when the languages may be approximated by finite-state languages. The following simple examples illustrate some of the points discussed above, particularly the increased power of the productions of the more general classes of grammars.

Example 4.4. It is desired to construct a grammar to generate the finite-state language $L = \{a^n b^n c^n | 1 \leqq n \leqq 3\}$. This might be the language describing, say, the set of equilateral triangles of side length one, two, or three units. In order for the grammar to be compatible with a top-down goal-oriented analysis procedure, the grammar must produce terminals in a strictly left-to-right order, and, at most, one terminal may be produced by a single application of any production. Non-terminals may not appear to the left of terminal symbols, but the generation of nonterminals is otherwise unrestricted.

1) A finite-state grammar

$$G_1 = (V_N, V_T, P, S)$$

where

$$V_N = \{S, A_1, A_2, B_{10}, B_{20}, B_{30}, B_{21}, B_{31}, B_{32}, C_1, C_2, C_3\},$$

$$V_T = \{a, b, c\}$$

P:
$$\begin{array}{ll} S \to aA_1 & B_{21} \to bC_2 \\ S \to aB_{10} & B_{30} \to bB_{31} \\ A_1 \to aA_2 & B_{31} \to bB_{32} \\ A_1 \to aB_{20} & B_{32} \to bC_3 \\ A_2 \to aB_{30} & C_1 \to c \\ B_{10} \to bC_1 & C_2 \to cC_1 \\ B_{20} \to bB_{21} & C_3 \to cC_2 \,. \end{array}$$

2) A context-free grammar (in Greibach Normal Form)

$$G_2 = (V_N, V_T, P, S)$$

where

$$V_N = \{S, A_1, A_2, B_1, B_2, B_3, C\}$$

$$V_T = \{a, b, c\}$$

P:
$$\begin{array}{ll} S \to aA_1C & B_3 \to bB_2 \\ A_1 \to b & B_2 \to bB_1 \\ A_1 \to aB_2C & B_1 \to b \\ A_1 \to aA_2C & C \to c \\ A_2 \to aB_3C \,. \end{array}$$

3) A context-free programmed grammar

$$G_3 = (V_N, V_T, J, P, S)$$

where

$$V_N = \{S, B, C\}$$

$$V_T = \{a, b, c\}$$

$$J = \{1, 2, 3, 4, 5\}$$

P:	Label	Core	Success field	Failure field
	1	$S \rightarrow aB$	{2, 3}	{∅}
	2	$B \rightarrow aBB$	{2, 3}	{∅}
	3	$B \rightarrow C$	{4}	{5}
	4	$C \rightarrow bC$	{3}	{∅}
	5	$C \rightarrow c$	{5}	{∅}

Even for this simple case, the context-free grammar is considerably more compact than the finite-state grammar. For this example, a context-sensitive grammar would not be much different from the context-free grammar and, hence, has not been given. However, the context-free programmed grammar is still more compact than the context-free grammar.

Example 4.5. The language

$$L = \{a^n b^n c^n d^n | n \geq 1\}$$

could be interpreted as the language describing squares of side length $n = 1, 2, \ldots$

L is known as a context-sensitive language, and can be generated in the following two ways.

1) A context-sensitive grammar

$$G_1 = (V_N, V_T, P, S)$$

where

$$V_N = \{S, A, B, C, D, E, F, G\}$$
$$V_T = \{a, b, c, d\}$$

P:		
	$S \rightarrow aAb$	$dG \rightarrow Gd$
	$A \rightarrow aAC$	$aG \rightarrow abcD$
	$A \rightarrow D$	$bG \rightarrow bbcD$
	$Dc \rightarrow cD$	$dFB \rightarrow dFd$
	$Dd \rightarrow dD$	$dFd \rightarrow Fdd$
	$DC \rightarrow EC$	$cF \rightarrow Fc$
	$EC \rightarrow Ed$	$bF \rightarrow bbc$
	$DB \rightarrow FB$	$aF \rightarrow ab$
	$Ed \rightarrow Gd$	$bB \rightarrow bcd$
	$cG \rightarrow Gc$.	

2) A context-free programmed grammar

$$G_2 = (V_N, V_T, P, S, J)$$

where

$$V_N = \{S, A, B, C, D\}$$

$$V_T = \{a, b, c, d\}$$

$$J = \{1, 2, 3, 4, 5, 6, 7\}$$

P: Label	Core	Success field	Failure field
1	$S \rightarrow aAB$	$\{2, 3\}$	$\{\emptyset\}$
2	$A \rightarrow aAC$	$\{2, 3\}$	$\{\emptyset\}$
3	$A \rightarrow D$	$\{4\}$	$\{\emptyset\}$
4	$C \rightarrow d$	$\{5\}$	$\{6\}$
5	$D \rightarrow bDc$	$\{4\}$	$\{\emptyset\}$
6	$B \rightarrow d$	$\{7\}$	$\{\emptyset\}$
7	$D \rightarrow bc$	$\{\emptyset\}$	$\{\emptyset\}$

It is noted that if n is finite, then $L = \{a^n b^n c^n d^n | n = 1, \ldots, N\}$ can certainly also be generated by a finite-state or context-free grammar.

It should be remarked that a grammar is most appropriate for description when the pattern of interest is built up from a small set of primitives by recursive application of a small set of production rules. Also, the "primitive selection" and the "grammar construction" should probably be treated simultaneously rather than in two different stages. There is no doubt that a different selection of pattern primitives will result in a different grammar for the description of a given set of patterns. Sometimes, a compromise is necessary in order to develop a suitable grammar. Example 4.2 may also be used to illustrate this point. Referring to the example, it is evident that the grammar which generates $L = \{a^n b^m c^n d^m | n, m = 1, 2, \ldots\}$ will be much more complex than the grammar generating $a' b' c' d'$.

Although many classes of patterns appear to be intuitively context-sensitive, context-sensitive (but not context-free) grammars have rarely been used for pattern description simply because of their complexity. Context-free languages have been used to describe patterns such as English characters [4.21], chromosome images [4.29], spark-chamber pictures [4.27], chemical structures [4.73], fingerprint patters [4.30], and spoken digits [4.33].

Example 4.6. The following is a context-free grammar describing the chromosome images shown in Fig. 4.13 [4.29].

$$G = (V_N, V_T, P, \{\langle \text{submedian chromosome} \rangle, \langle \text{telocentric chromosome} \rangle\})$$

where

$$V_N = \{\langle\text{submedian chromosome}\rangle, \langle\text{telocentric chromosome}\rangle, \langle\text{arm pair}\rangle,$$
$$\langle\text{left part}\rangle, \langle\text{right part}\rangle, \langle\text{arm}\rangle, \langle\text{side}\rangle, \langle\text{bottom}\rangle\}$$

$$V_T = \left\{ \underset{a}{\cap} \quad \underset{b}{|} \quad \underset{c}{\cup} \quad \underset{d}{\}} \quad \underset{e}{\smile} \right\}$$

and

P: $\langle\text{submedian chromosome}\rangle \rightarrow \langle\text{arm pair}\rangle \langle\text{arm pair}\rangle$
      $\langle\text{telocentric chromosome}\rangle \rightarrow \langle\text{bottom}\rangle \langle\text{arm pair}\rangle$
      $\langle\text{arm pair}\rangle \rightarrow \langle\text{side}\rangle \langle\text{arm pair}\rangle$
      $\langle\text{arm pair}\rangle \rightarrow \langle\text{arm pair}\rangle \langle\text{side}\rangle$
      $\langle\text{arm pair}\rangle \rightarrow \langle\text{arm}\rangle \langle\text{right part}\rangle$
      $\langle\text{arm pair}\rangle \rightarrow \langle\text{left part}\rangle \langle\text{arm}\rangle$
      $\langle\text{left part}\rangle \rightarrow \langle\text{arm}\rangle c$
      $\langle\text{right part}\rangle \rightarrow c \langle\text{arm}\rangle$
      $\langle\text{bottom}\rangle \rightarrow b \langle\text{bottom}\rangle$
      $\langle\text{bottom}\rangle \rightarrow \langle\text{bottom}\rangle b$
      $\langle\text{bottom}\rangle \rightarrow e$
      $\langle\text{side}\rangle \rightarrow b \langle\text{side}\rangle$
      $\langle\text{side}\rangle \rightarrow \langle\text{side}\rangle b$
      $\langle\text{side}\rangle \rightarrow b$
      $\langle\text{side}\rangle \rightarrow d$
      $\langle\text{arm}\rangle \rightarrow b \langle\text{arm}\rangle$
      $\langle\text{arm}\rangle \rightarrow \langle\text{arm}\rangle b$
      $\langle\text{arm}\rangle \rightarrow a$

In addition to (i) the trade-off between the language descriptive power and the analysis efficiency, and (ii) the compromise sometimes necessary between the primitives selected and the grammar constructed, the designer should also be aware of the need to control the excessive strings generated by the constructed grammar. The number of pattern strings available in practice is always limited. However, in most cases, the grammar constructed would generate a large or infinite number of strings[6]. It is hoped that the excessive strings generated are similar to the available pattern strings. Unfortunately, this may not be true since the grammar, in many cases, is constructed heuristically. The problem may become very serious when the excessive strings include some pattern strings which should belong to other classes. In this case, adjustments should be made to exclude these strings from the language generated by the constructed grammar.

---

[6] It may be argued that, in practice, a pattern grammar can always be finite-state since it is constructed from a finite number of pattern strings. However, the finite-state grammar so constructed may require a large number of productions. In such a case, a context-free or a context-free programmed pattern grammar may be constructed for the purpose of significantly reducing the number of productions.

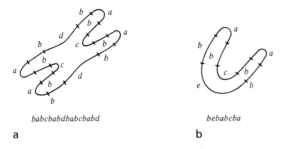

babcbabdbabcbabd   bebabcba

a   b

Fig. 4.13. a) Submedian chromosome and b) telocentric chromosome

Recently, probably due to their relative effectiveness in describing natural language structures, transformational grammars have been proposed for pattern description [4.74–77]. Transformational grammars would allow the possibility of determining from the pattern generative mechanism a simple base grammar (deep structure) which generates a certain set of patterns and a problem-oriented set of transformations. Through the base grammar and the transformations, the original set of patterns can be described.

From the above discussion, it might be concluded that, before efficient grammatical inference procedures are available, a man-machine interactive system would be suitable for the problem of grammar construction. The basic grammar and the various trade-offs and compromises have to be determined by the designer. The results of any adjustment on the grammar constructed can be easily checked and displayed through a computer system.

4.5 High-Dimensional Pattern Grammars

4.5.1 General Discussion

In describing patterns using a string grammar, the only relation between subpatterns and/or primitives is the concatenation; that is, each subpattern or primitive can be connected only at the left or right. This one-dimensional relation has not been very effective in describing two- or three-dimensional patterns. A natural generalization is to use a more general formalism including other useful relations [4.21, 76–81]. Let R be a set of n-ary relations ($n \geq 1$). A relation $r \in R$ satisfied by the subpatterns and/or primitives $X_1, \ldots, X_n$ is denoted $r(X_1, \ldots, X_n)$. For example, TRIANGLE (a, b, c) means that the ternary relation TRIANGLE is satisfied by the line segments a, b, and c, and ABOVE (X, Y) means that X is above Y. The following examples illustrate pattern descriptions using this formalism of relations.

Example 4.7. The mathematical expression

$$\frac{a+b}{c}$$

can be described by

$$\text{ABOVE}(\text{ABOVE}(\text{LEFT}(a, \text{LEFT}(+, b)), -), c)$$

where $\text{LEFT}(X, Y)$ means that X is to the left of Y.

Example 4.8. The following grammar will generate sentences describing houses [4.122].

$$G = (V_N, V_T, P, S)$$

where

$V_N = \{\langle\text{house}\rangle, \langle\text{side view}\rangle, \langle\text{front view}\rangle, \langle\text{roof}\rangle, \langle\text{gable}\rangle,$
$\quad \langle\text{wall}\rangle, \langle\text{chimney}\rangle, \langle\text{windows}\rangle, \langle\text{door}\rangle\}$

$$V_T = \left\{ \begin{array}{l} \square\,,\ \square\,,\ \blacksquare\,,\ \boxplus\,,\ \triangle\,,\ \square\,,\ \diagdown\,,\ \rightarrow\,,\ (,)\,, \\ \odot\,,\ \bigcirc\,,\ \uparrow\,,\ \longmapsto \end{array} \right\}$$

$S = \langle\text{house}\rangle$

P: $\langle\text{door}\rangle \rightarrow \blacksquare$

$\quad \langle\text{window}\rangle \rightarrow \boxplus,\ \langle\text{windows}\rangle \rightarrow \rightarrow (\langle\text{windows}\rangle, \boxplus)$

$\quad \langle\text{chimney}\rangle \rightarrow \square,\ \langle\text{chimney}\rangle \rightarrow \square$

$\quad \langle\text{wall}\rangle \rightarrow \square,\ \langle\text{wall}\rangle \rightarrow \bigcirc (\langle\text{door}\rangle, \square)$

$\quad \langle\text{wall}\rangle \rightarrow \odot (\langle\text{windows}\rangle, \square)$

$\quad \langle\text{gable}\rangle \rightarrow \triangle,\ \langle\text{gable}\rangle \rightarrow \uparrow (\langle\text{chimney}\rangle, \triangle)$

$\quad \langle\text{roof}\rangle \rightarrow \diagdown,\ \langle\text{roof}\rangle \rightarrow \uparrow (\langle\text{chimney}\rangle, \diagdown)$

$\quad \langle\text{front view}\rangle \rightarrow \uparrow (\langle\text{gable}\rangle, \langle\text{wall}\rangle)$

$\quad \langle\text{side view}\rangle \rightarrow \uparrow (\langle\text{roof}\rangle, \langle\text{wall}\rangle)$

$\quad \langle\text{house}\rangle \rightarrow \langle\text{front view}\rangle$

$\quad \langle\text{house}\rangle \rightarrow \longmapsto (\langle\text{house}\rangle, \langle\text{side view}\rangle)$.

The notation

$\quad \rightarrow (X, Y)$ means that X is to the right of Y,

$\quad \odot (X, Y)$ means that X is inside of Y,

$\quad \bigcirc (X, Y)$ means that X is inside on the bottom of Y,

$\quad \uparrow (X, Y)$ means that X rests on top of Y,

$\quad \longmapsto (X, Y)$ means that X rests to the right of Y.

House	Description
⌂	$\uparrow (\triangle, \square)$
⌂	$\uparrow \left(\uparrow (\square, \triangle), \bigcirc (\square, \square) \right)$
⌂	$\mapsto \left(\uparrow (\uparrow (\square, \diagdown), \odot (\boxplus, \square)), \uparrow (\triangle, \bigcirc (\square, \square)) \right)$

A simple two-dimensional generalization of string grammars is to extend grammars for one-dimensional strings to two-dimensional arrays [4.84, 85]. The primitives are the array elements and the relation between primitives is the two-dimensional concatenation. Each production rewrites one subarray by another, rather than one substring by another. Relationships between array grammars and array automata (automata with two-dimensional tapes) have been studied recently [4.85].

4.5.2 Special Grammars

SHAW, by attaching a "head" (hd) and a "tail" (tl) to each primitive, has used the four binary operators $+$, $\times$, $-$, and $*$ for defining binary concatenation relations between primitives [4.86, 87].

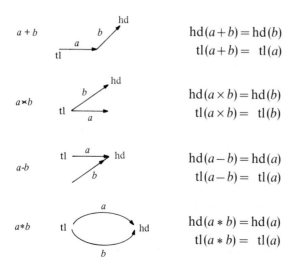

$$\begin{aligned} \text{hd}(a+b) &= \text{hd}(b) \\ \text{tl}(a+b) &= \text{tl}(a) \end{aligned}$$

$$\begin{aligned} \text{hd}(a \times b) &= \text{hd}(b) \\ \text{tl}(a \times b) &= \text{tl}(b) \end{aligned}$$

$$\begin{aligned} \text{hd}(a-b) &= \text{hd}(a) \\ \text{tl}(a-b) &= \text{tl}(a) \end{aligned}$$

$$\begin{aligned} \text{hd}(a * b) &= \text{hd}(a) \\ \text{tl}(a * b) &= \text{tl}(a) \end{aligned}$$

For string languages, only the operator + is used. In addition, the unary operator ~ acting as a tail/head reverser is also defined; i.e.,

$$\text{hd}(\sim a) = \text{tl}(a)$$
$$\text{tl}(\sim a) = \text{hd}(a).$$

In the case of describing patterns consisting of disconnected subpatterns, the "blank" or "don't care" primitive is introduced. Each pictorial pattern is represented by a "labelled branch-oriented graph" where branches represent primitives.

The grammar which generates sentences (PDL expressions) in PDL (Picture Description Language) is a context-free grammar

$$G = (V_N, V_T, P, S)$$

where

$$V_N = \{S, SL\}$$
$$V_T = \{b\} \cup \{+, \times, -, /, (,)\} \cup \{l\}, \quad b \text{ may be any primitive (including the "null point primitive" } \lambda \text{ which has identical tail and head)}$$

and

$$S \to b, \, S \to (S\phi_b S), \, S \to (\sim S), \, S \to SL, \, S \to (/SL),$$
$$SL \to S^l, \, SL \to (SL\phi_b SL), \, SL \to (\sim SL), \, SL \to (/SL),$$
$$\phi_b \to +, \, \phi_b \to \times, \, \phi_b \to -, \, \phi_b \to *$$

l is a label designator which is used to allow cross-reference to the expressions S within a description. The $/$ operator is used to enable the tail and head of an expression to be arbitrarily located.

Example 4.9. The following grammar illustrates the operations of PDL for pattern structural description.

$$G = (V_N, V_T, P, S)$$

where

$$V_N = \{S, A, \text{House}, \text{Triangle}\}$$
$$V_T = \{\xrightarrow{a}, \nearrow^b, \searrow^c, \downarrow e, (,), +, \times, -, *, \sim\}$$

and P:

$$S \to A, \, S \to \text{House}$$
$$A \to (b + (\text{Triangle} + c))$$
$$\text{House} \to ((e + (a + (\sim e))) * \text{Triangle})$$
$$\text{Triangle} \to ((b + c) * a)$$
$$L(G) = \{(b + (((b + c) * a) + c)), ((e + (a + (\sim e))) * ((b + c) * a))\}.$$

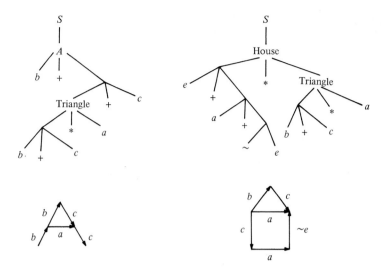

Fig. 4.14. PDL structural description of "A" and "House"

The structural description in terms of a parse tree of the patterns "A" and "House" is shown in Fig. 4.14. A top-down parsing procedure (see Sect. 4.6) was used for the recognition of PDL expressions describing pictorial patterns [4.87].

Once we include relations more than just concatenations, the description of a pattern may be more conveniently represented by a relational graph, where nodes represent subpatterns or primitives and branches denote (binary) relations [7]. (Refer to Sect. 4.1.) When n-ary relations are involved, a graph-representable description can be obtained by transforming all relations into binary ones. A unary relation $r(X)$ can be changed to a binary one $r'(X, \lambda)$ where λ denotes the "null" primitive. $r(X_1, \ldots, X_n)$ $(n > 2)$ can be transformed into a composition of binary relations, such as

$$r_1(X_1, r_2(X_2, \ldots, r_{n-1}(X_{n-1}, X_n)),$$

or into a conjunction of binary relations

$$r_1(X_{11}, X_{12}) \wedge r_2(X_{21}, X_{22}) \wedge \ldots \wedge r_k(X_{k1}, X_{k2}),$$

or into a combination of these. For example, the ternary relation TRIANGLE (a, b, c) could be transformed into either one of the following equivalent binary relations:

$$\mathrm{CAT}(a, b) \wedge \mathrm{CAT}(b, c) \wedge \mathrm{CAT}(c, a)$$

or

$$\Delta(b, \mathrm{CAT}(a, c))$$

---

[7] This straightforward representation is called a "labelled node-oriented directed graph".

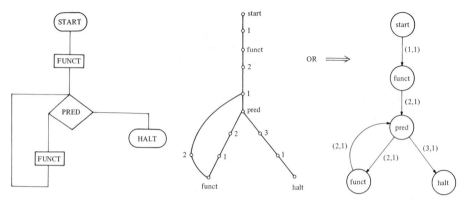

Fig. 4.15. Transformation from plex structure to graphs

where CAT(X, Y) means that hd(X) is concatenated to tl(Y), i.e., CAT$(X, Y)=$ $X + Y$, and $\Delta(X, Y)$ means that the line X is connected to form a triangle with the object Y consisting of two concatenated segments. In general, replacement of an n-ary relation with binary ones using composition requires the addition of more levels in the description.

Based on an idea in [4.51], FEDER has formalized a "plex" grammar which generates languages with terminals having an arbitrary number of attaching points for connecting to other primitives or subpatterns [4.73]. The primitives of the plex grammar are called N-Attaching Point Entity (NAPE). Each production of the plex grammar is in context-free form in which the connectivity of primitives or subpatterns is described by using explicit lists of labelled concatenation points (called joint lists). While the sentences generated by a plex grammar are not directed graphs, they can be transformed by either assigning labelled nodes to both primitives and concatenation points as suggested by PFALTZ and ROSENFELD [4.88] or by transforming primitives to nodes and concatenations to labelled branches. Figure 4.15 gives an example to illustrate such transformations [4.89].

PFALTZ and ROSENFELD have extended the concept of string grammars to grammars for labelled graphs called webs. Labelled node-oriented graphs are explicitly used in the productions. Each production describes the rewriting of a graph α into another graph β and also contains an "embedding" rule E which specifies the connection of β to its surrounding graph (host web) when α is rewritten. A web grammar G is a 4-tuple

$$G = (V_N, V_T, P, S)$$

where V_N is a set of nonterminals; V_T is a set of terminals; S is a set of "initial" webs; and P is a set of web productions. A web production is defined as [8]

$$\alpha \rightarrow \beta, E$$

---

[8] In a most general formulation, the contextual condition of the production is added.

where α and β are webs, and E is an embedding of β. If we want to replace the subweb α of the web ω by another subweb β, it is necesseray to specify how to "embed" β in ω in place of α. The definition of an embedding must not depend on the host web ω since we want to be able to replace α by β in any web containing α as a subweb. Usually E consists of a set of logical functions which specify whether or not each vertex of $\omega - \alpha$ is connected to each vertex of β.

Example 4.10. Consider the web grammar

$$G = (V_N, V_T, P, S)$$

where

$$V_N = \{\dot{A}\}, \quad V_T = \{a, b, c\}, \quad S = \{\dot{A}\}$$

and

$$P: 1) \quad \dot{A} \rightarrow a \quad \qquad E = \{(p, a)|(p, A) \text{ an edge in the host web}\}$$

$$2) \quad \dot{A} \rightarrow a \quad \qquad E \text{ is the same as in (1).}$$

The language of this grammar is the set of all webs of the form

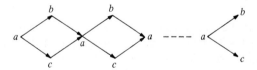

It is noted that web grammars are vertex—or node-oriented compared with the branch—or edge-oriented grammars (e.g., PDL, Plex grammars, etc.). That is, terminals or primitives are represented as vertices in the graph rather than as branches. Some applications of web grammars for picture description can be found in [4.90, 91].

An important special case of a web grammar is that in which the terminal set V_T consists of only a single symbol. In this case, every point of every web in the language has the same label, so that we can ignore the labels and identify the webs with their underlying graphs. This type of web grammar is called a "graph grammar", and its language is called graph language [4.92]. The formalism of web grammars has been rather extensively analyzed [4.88, 90]. The relations among PDL grammars, plex grammars and web grammars have been discussed by SHAW [4.89] and ROSENFELD [4.93].

PAVLIDIS [4.92, 94] has generalized string grammars to graph grammars by including nonterminal symbols which are not simple branches or nodes. An mth-order nonterminal structure is defined as an entity which is connected to

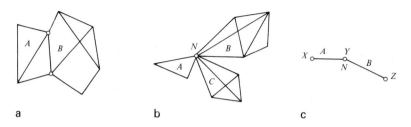

Fig. 4.16a–c. Illustration of a) $A*B$, b) $N(A+B+C)$ and c) ANB

the rest of the graph by m nodes. In particular, a second-order structure is called a branch structure and a first-order structure a node structure. Then an mth-order context-free graph grammar G_g is a quadruple

$$G_g = (V_N, V_T, P, S)$$

where

> V_N is a set of mth-order nonterminal structures: nodes, branches, triangles,..., polygons with m vertices;
> V_T is a set of terminals: nodes and branches;
> P is a finite set of productions of the form $A \to \alpha$, where A is a nonterminal structure and α a graph containing possibly both terminals and nonterminals. α is connected to the rest of the graph through exactly the same nodes as A;
> S is a set of initial graphs.

The expression $A*B$ denotes that the two graphs A and B are connected by a pair of nodes (Fig. 4.16a), and $N(A+B+C)$ denotes that the graphs A, B and C are connected through a common node N (Fig. 4.16b). Thus the production $A \to B*C$ where A, B and C are branch structures should be interpreted as: replace branch structure A by branch structures B and C connected to the graph through the same nodes as A. No other connection exists between B and C. Similarly, the production $N \to M(A+B)$ should be interpreted as: replace node structure N by a node structure M and two other structures A and B connected to the rest of the graph by the same node as N. When no ambiguity occurs, we can use simple concatenations, e.g., ANB to denote a nonterminal subgraph consisting of a branch structure A with nodes X and Y connected to the node structure N through Y and a branch structure B with nodes Y and Z connected to N through Y (Fig. 4.16c). The subgraph is connected to the rest of the graph through the nodes X and Z.

The following examples illustrate the use of graph grammars for pattern description:

Example 4.11. The following grammar describes graphs representing two terminal series-parallel networks (TTSPN)

$$G_g = (V_N, V_T, P, S)$$

where

$$V_N = \{S, B\}, \qquad V_T = \{\tfrac{b}{\cdot}, \tfrac{n}{\cdot}\}, \qquad S = \{nBn\}$$

and P: (1) $B \rightarrow B\dot{n}B$
          (2) $B \rightarrow B * B$
          (3) $B \rightarrow b$.

A typical generation would be

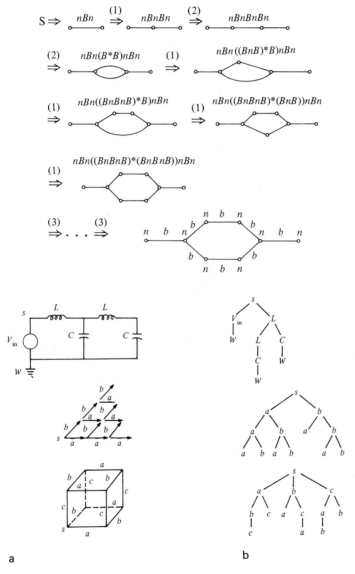

Fig. 4.17. a) Patterns and b) corresponding tree representations

By extending one-dimensional concatenation to multi-dimensional concatenation, strings are generalized to trees. Tree grammars and the corresponding recognizers, tree automata, have been studied recently by a number of authors [4.95, 96]. Naturally, if a pattern can be conveniently described by a tree, it will easily be generated by a tree grammar. For example, in Fig. 4.17, patterns and their corresponding tree representations are listed in (a) and (b), respectively [4.97, 98].

4.6 Syntax Analysis as Recognition Procedure

As it was pointed out in Section 4.2, a parsing or syntax analysis is necessary if a complete description of the input pattern is required for recognition. This requirement may be necessary due to the fact that the number of pattern classes is very large such as in a fingerprint recognition problem. It may also be necessary in the case that the complete description of each pattern will be stored for data retrieval purpose. In this section, syntax analysis for finite-state and context-free (string) languages will be briefly reviewed [4.99, 100]. Parsing of context-sensitive languages and web (and graph) languages is still an important topic for investigation. Regular tree languages are accepted by tree automata. The procedure of constructing a tree automaton to accept the language generated by a tree grammar is available [4.95–97].

4.6.1 Recognition of Finite-State Languages

Finite-state automata are known to recognize or accept finite-state languages [4.100]. If a class of patterns can be described by a finite-state language, a finite-state automaton can then be constructed to recognize the strings or sentences describing this class of patterns.

Definition 4.1. A non-deterministic finite-state automaton is a quintuple $(\Sigma, Q, \delta, q_0, F)$, where Σ is a finite set of input symbols (alphabet), Q is a finite set of states, δ is a mapping of $Q \times \Sigma$ into subsets of Q, $q_0 \in Q$ is the initial state, and $F \subseteq Q$ is the set of final states.

The interpretation of $\delta(q, a) = \{q_1, q_2, \ldots, q_l\}$ is that the automaton A, in state q, scanning a on its input tape, chooses any one of $q_1, \ldots, q_l$ as the next state and moves its input head one square to the right. The mapping δ can be extended from an input symbol to a string of input symbols by defining

$$\delta(q, \lambda) = \{q\}$$
$$\delta(q, xa) = \bigcup_{q_i \in \delta(q,x)} \delta(q_i, a), \quad x \in \Sigma^* \quad \text{and} \quad a \in \Sigma.$$

Furthermore, we can define

$$\delta(\{q_1, q_2, \ldots, q_l\}, x) = \bigcup_{i=1}^{l} \delta(q_i, x).$$

When $\delta(q, a)$ consists of only a single state, the automaton is called a deterministic finite-state automaton.

A string x is accepted by A if there is a state p such that

$$p \in \delta(q_0, x) \quad \text{and} \quad p \in F.$$

The set of all strings accepted by A is defined as

$$T(A) = \{x \mid p \in \delta(q_0, x) \quad \text{and} \quad p \in F\}.$$

Example 4.12. Given a nondeterministic finite-state automaton

$$A = (\Sigma, Q, \delta, q_0, F)$$

where

$$\Sigma = \{0, 1\}$$
$$Q = \{q_0, q_1, q_2, q_3, q_4\}$$
$$F = \{q_2, q_4\}.$$

The state transition diagram of A is shown in Fig. 4.18. A typical sentence accepted by A is 01011 since $\delta(q_0, 01011) = q_2 \in F$. In general, $T(A)$ is the set of all strings containing either two consecutive 0's or two consecutive 1's.

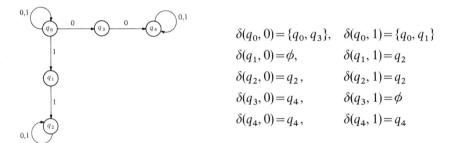

$$\delta(q_0, 0) = \{q_0, q_3\}, \quad \delta(q_0, 1) = \{q_0, q_1\}$$
$$\delta(q_1, 0) = \phi, \quad \delta(q_1, 1) = q_2$$
$$\delta(q_2, 0) = q_2, \quad \delta(q_2, 1) = q_2$$
$$\delta(q_3, 0) = q_4, \quad \delta(q_3, 1) = \phi$$
$$\delta(q_4, 0) = q_4, \quad \delta(q_4, 1) = q_4$$

Fig. 4.18. State transition diagram of A

The relationship between deterministic finite-state automata and non-deterministic finite-state automata and the relationship between the finite-state languages and the sets of strings accepted by finite-state automata can be expressed by the following theorems.

Theorem 4.1. Let L be a set of strings accepted by a non-deterministic finite-state automaton $A = (\Sigma, Q, \delta, q_0, F)$. Then there exists a deterministic finite-state automaton $A' = (\Sigma', Q', \delta', q_0', F')$ that accepts L. The states of A' are all the subsets of Q, i.e., $Q' = 2^Q$, and $\Sigma' = \Sigma$. F' is the set of all states in Q' containing a state of F. A state of A' will be denoted by $[q_1, q_2, \ldots, q_i] \in Q'$ where $q_1, q_2, \ldots, q_i \in Q$. $q_0' = [q_0]$. $\delta'([q_1, \ldots, q_i], a) = [p_1, p_2, \ldots, p_j]$ if and only if $\delta(\{q_1, \ldots, q_i\}, a) = \bigcup_{k=1}^{i} \delta(q_k, a) = \{p_1, p_2, \ldots, p_j\}$.

Since the deterministic and non-deterministic finite-state automata accept the same sets of strings, we shall not distinguish between them unless it becomes necessary, but shall simply refer to both as finite-state automata.

Theorem 4.2. Let $G=(V_N, V_T, P, S)$ be a finite-state grammar. Then there exists a finite-state automaton $A=(\Sigma, Q, \delta, q_0, F)$ with $T(A)=L(G)$, where

(i) $\Sigma = V_T$

(ii) $Q = V_N \cup \{T\}$

(iii) $q_0 = S$

(iv) if P contains the production $S \to \lambda$, then $F=\{S, T\}$, otherwise, $F=\{T\}$

(v) the state T is in $\delta(B, a)$ if $B \to a$, $B \in V_N$, $a \in V_T$ in in P; and

(vi) $\delta(B, a)$ contains all $C \in V_N$ such that $B \to aC$ is in P and $\delta(T, a) = \emptyset$ for each $a \in V_T$.

Theorem 4.3. Given a finite-state automaton $A=(\Sigma, Q, \delta, q_0, F)$. Then there exists a finite-state grammar $G=(V_N, V_T, P, S)$ with $L(G)=T(A)$, where

(i) $V_N = Q$

(ii) $V_T = \Sigma$

(iii) $S = q_0$

(iv) $B \to aC$ is in P if $\delta(B, a)=C$, $B, C \in q$, $a \in \Sigma$; and

(v) $B \to a$ is in P if $\delta(B, a)=C$ and $C \in F$.

Example 4.13. Given the finite-state grammar G_1 in Example 4.4, construct a finite-state automaton which will accept $L(G_1)$.

Let the (non-deterministic) automaton be

$$A = (\Sigma, Q, \delta, q_0, F)$$

where

$$\Sigma = V_T = \{a, b, c\}$$
$$Q = V_N \cup \{T\} = \{S, A_1, A_2, B_{10}, B_{20}, B_{30},$$
$$B_{21}, B_{31}, B_{32}, C_1, C_2, C_3, T\}$$
$$q_0 = S$$
$$F = \{T\}$$

and

$$\delta(S, a) = \{A_1, B_{10}\}$$
$$\delta(A_1, a) = \{A_2, B_{20}\}$$
$$\delta(A_2, a) = \{B_{30}\}$$
$$\delta(B_{10}, b) = \{C_1\}$$
$$\delta(B_{20}, b) = \{B_{21}\}$$
$$\delta(B_{21}, b) = \{C_2\}$$
$$\delta(B_{30}, b) = \{B_{31}\}$$
$$\delta(B_{31}, b) = \{B_{32}\}$$
$$\delta(B_{32}, b) = \{C_3\}$$
$$\delta(C_1, c) = \{T\}$$
$$\delta(C_2, c) = \{C_1\}$$
$$\delta(C_3, c) = \{C_2\}$$
$$\delta(T, a) = \delta(T, b) = \delta(T, c) = \emptyset .$$

Then, by Theorem 4.2, $T(A) = L(G_1)$.

By Theorem 4.1, a deterministic automaton A' can be constructed such that $T(A') = L(G_1)$.

4.6.2 Syntax Analysis of Context-Free Languages

When a context-free language is used to describe a class of patterns, the corresponding recognition device (or acceptor) is, in general, a non-deterministic pushdown automaton. Not every non-deterministic pushdown automaton can have an equivalent deterministic pushdown automaton. Therefore, the process or the algorithm of performing the recognition, called "syntax analysis" "parsing" is in general a non-deterministic procedure. The output of the syntax analyzer usually includes not only the decision of accepting the string generated by the given grammar, but also the derivation tree of the string which, in turn, gives the complete structural description of the pattern. Alternatively speaking, given a sentence x and a context-free (or context-free programmed) grammar G, construct a self-consistent derivation tree to fill the interior of the following triangle [4.99]. If the attempt is successful, $x \in L(G)$. Otherwise, $x \notin L(G)$.

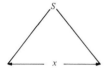

Consider the grammar G_2 in Example 4.4. The derivation tree of the sentence $x = a^2 b^2 c^2$ is

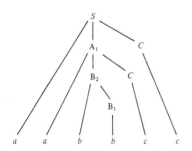

$$S \Rightarrow aA_1C \Rightarrow aaB_2CC \Rightarrow aabB_1CC$$
$$\Rightarrow aabbCC \Rightarrow aabbcC \Rightarrow aabbcc = a^2b^2c^2$$

or

$$S \overset{*}{\Rightarrow} a^2b^2c^2 \ .$$

It is in principle unimportant how we attempt to fill the interior of the triangle. We may do it from the top (the root of the tree) towards the bottom, called "top-down" parsing,

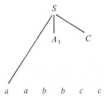

or from the bottom towards the top, called "bottom-up" parsing.

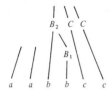

A number of top-down and bottom-up parsing algorithms have been developed [4.99, 100]. Unless for special classes of grammars, backtrackings are often required because of the nondeterministic nature of the parsing processes. In the following, a parsing algorithm for general context-free languages proposed by Earley is briefly presented [4.100].

Let $G=(V_N, V_T, P, S)$ be a context-free grammar and let $x=a_1 a_2 \dots a_n$ be a string in V_T^*. An object of the form $[A \rightarrow X_1 X_2 \dots X_k \cdot X_{k+1} \dots X_m, i]$ is called an item for x if $A \rightarrow X_1 X_2 \dots X_m$ is a production in P. For each integer j, $0 \leq j \leq n$, we can construct a list of items I_j such that $[A \rightarrow \alpha \cdot \beta, i]$ is in I_j for $0 \leq i \leq j$ if and only if for some γ and δ we have

$$S \overset{*}{\Rightarrow} \gamma A \delta$$

where

$$\gamma \overset{*}{\Rightarrow} a_1 \dots a_i, \text{ and } \alpha \overset{*}{\Rightarrow} a_{i+1} \dots a_j.$$

The sequence of lists $I_0, I_1, \dots, I_n$ is called the parse lists for the string x. It is noted that x $L(G)$ if and only if there is some item of the form $[S \rightarrow \alpha \cdot, 0]$ in I_n.

The procedure of constructing the parse lists $I_0, \dots I_n$ for x consists of the following:

 I) Construction of I_0
  1) If $S \rightarrow \alpha$ is a production in P, add $[S \rightarrow \cdot \alpha, 0]$ to I_0.
  2) Perform the following steps with $j=0$ until no new items can be added to I_0:
   a) If $[A \rightarrow \alpha \cdot B\beta, i]$ is in I_j and $B \rightarrow \gamma$ is a production in P, add $[B \rightarrow \cdot \gamma, j]$ to I_j.

b) If $[A \rightarrow \alpha \cdot, i]$ is in I_j, then for all items in I_i of the form $[B \rightarrow \beta \cdot A\gamma, k]$ add $[B \rightarrow \beta A \cdot \gamma, k]$ to I_j.

II) Construction of I_j from I_{j-1}

  3) For all $[A \rightarrow \alpha \cdot a_j \beta, i]$ in I_{j-1}, add $[A \rightarrow \alpha a_j \cdot \beta, i]$ to I_j.

  4) Perform (2) to I_j.

Example 4.14. For the grammar G_2 in Example 4.4 and the string $x = abc$, we can construct the following parse lists according to Earley's algorithm.

I_0	I_1
$S \rightarrow \cdot A_1 C, 0$	$S \rightarrow a \cdot A_1 C, 0$
	$A_1 \rightarrow \cdot b, 1$
	$A_1 \rightarrow \cdot aB_2 C, 1$
	$A_1 \rightarrow \cdot aA_2 C, 1$

I_2	I_3
$A \rightarrow b \cdot, 1$	$C \rightarrow c \cdot, 2$
$S \rightarrow aA_1 \cdot C, 0$	$S \rightarrow aA_1 C \cdot, 0$
$C \rightarrow \cdot c, 2$	

Since $[S \rightarrow aA_1 C \cdot, 0]$ is in I_3, x is in $L(G_2)$. The derivation tree can also be easily constructed using the information from the parse lists.

For an arbitrary context-free grammar, Earley's parsing algorithm requires time $0(n^3)$ to parse a string with lenth n. If the grammar is unambiguous, the time variation is quadratic. If we can limit the pattern grammar in a special class of context-free grammars, such as $LR(k)$ grammars or precedence grammars, then a more efficient (linear time variation) parsing algorithm can be applied [4.100].

4.7 Concluding Remarks

In this chapter, we have demonstrated that languages can be used to describe complex patterns. Consequently, syntax analysis procedures can be used to implement the pattern recognition process. It should be noted that, for many practical applications, often both syntactic and decision-theoretic approaches are used [4.12, 101]. For example, decision-theoretic approaches are usually effective in the recognition of pattern primitives. This is primarily due to the fact that the structural information of primitives is considered not important and the (local) measurements taken from the primitives are sensitive to noise and distortion. On the other hand, in the recognition of subpatterns and the pattern itself which are rich in structural information, syntactic approaches are therefore required. Also, in some practical applications, a certain amount of uncertainty exists in the process under study. For example, due to the presence of noise and variations in the pattern measurements, ambiguities often occur in the languages describing real-data patterns. In order to describe and recognize noisy patterns under possible ambiguous situations, the use of stochastic languages has recently been suggested [4.102–108].

A stochastic grammar is a 4-tuple $G_s = (V_N, V_T, P_s, S)$ where P_s is a finite set of stochastic productions and all the other symbols are the same, as defined in Section 4.4. For a stochastic context-free grammar, a production in P is of the form

$$A_i \xrightarrow{\ p_{ij}\ } \alpha_j, \quad A_i \in V_N, \quad \alpha_j \in (V_N \cup V_T)^*$$

where p_{ij} is called the production probability. The probability of generating a string x, called the string probability $p(x)$, is the product of all production probabilities associated with the productions used in the generation of x. The language generated by a stochastic grammar consists of the strings generated by the grammar and their associated string probabilities.

By associating probabilities with the strings, we can impose a probabilistic structure on the language to describe noisy patterns. The probability distribution characterizing the patterns in a class can be interpreted as the probability distribution associated with the strings in a language. Thus, statistical decision rules can be applied to the classification of a pattern under ambiguous situations (for example, use the maximum-likelihood or Bayes decision rule). Furthermore, because of the availability of the information about production probabilities, the speed of syntactic analysis can be improved through the use of this information [4.108, 109]. Of course, in practice, the production probabilities will have to be inferred from the observation of relatively large numbers of pattern samples [4.105].

Other approaches for the recognition of distorted or noisy patterns using syntactic methods include the use of transformational grammar [4.74] and the application of error-correcting parsing techniques [4.110]. In the use of error-correcting parsing as a recognition procedure, different types of primitive extraction error (substitution, deletion and insertion) are introduced. The original pattern grammar is modified by taking these errors into consideration. The recognition process is then based on the parser designed according to the modified grammar. The error-correcting capability of this class of parsers can be achieved by using either a minimum-distance or a maximum-likelihood decision criterion [4.110, 111].

References

4.1 K. S. Fu: *Sequential Methods in Pattern Recognition and Machine Learning* (Academic Press, New York 1968)

4.2 G. S. Sebestyen: *Decision Processes in Pattern Recognition* (Macmillan, New York 1962)

4.3 N. J. Nilsson: *Learning Machines-Foundations of Trainable Pattern-Classifying System* (McGraw-Hill, New York 1965)

4.4 J. M. Mendel, K. S. Fu: *Adaptive, Learning and Pattern Recognition Systems: Theory and Applications* (Academic Press, New York 1970)

4.5 W. Meisel: *Computer-Oriented Approaches to Pattern Recognition* (Academic Press, New York 1972)

4.6 K. Fukunaga: *Introduction to Statistical Pattern Recognition* (Academic Press, New York 1972)

4.7 E. A. Patrick: *Fundamentals of Pattern Recognition* (Prentice-Hall, Englewood Cliffs, N.J. 1972)

4.8 H. C. Andrews: *Introduction to Mathematical Techniques in Pattern Recognition* (Wiley, New York 1972)

4.9 R. O. Duda, P. E. Hart: *Pattern Classification and Scene Analysis* (Wiley, New York 1973)

4.10 C. H. Chen: *Statistical Pattern Recognition* (Hayden Book Company, Washington, D.C. 1973)

4.11 T. Y. Young, T. W. Calvert: *Classification, Estimation, and Pattern Recognition* (American Elsevier, New York 1973)

4.12 K. S. Fu: *Syntactic Methods in Pattern Recognition* (Academic Press, New York 1974)

4.13 W. F. Miller, A. C. Shaw: Proc. AFIPS Fall Joint Computer Conf. (1968)

4.14 R. Narasimhan: Report 121 (Digital Computer Laboratory, University of Illinois, Urbana, Illinois 1962)

4.15 Special Issues of *Pattern Recognition* on Syntactic Pattern Recognition, Vol. 3, No. 4, 1971 and Vol. 4, No. 1, 1972

4.16 N. V. Zavalishin, I. B. Muchnik: Automatika i Telemekhanika **1969**, 86

4.17 Ya. Z. Tsypkin: *Foundations of the Theory of Learning System* (Nauka, Moscow 1970)

4.18 M. A. Aiserman, E. M. Braverman, L. I. Rozonoer: *Potential Function Method in Theory of Learning Machines* (Nauka, Moscow 1970)

4.19 K. S. Fu: *Pattern Recognition and Machine Learning* (Plenum Press, New York 1971)

4.20 A. G. Arkadev, E. M. Braverman: *Learning in Pattern Classification Machines* (Nauka, Moscow 1971)

4.21 R. Narasimhan: On the description, generation, and recognition of classes of pictures. In *Automatic Interpretation and Classification of Images;* ed. by A. Grasselli (Academic Press, New York 1969)

4.22 W. Stallings: Computer Graphics and Image Processing **1**, 47 (1972)

4.23 T. Sakai, M. Nagao, H. Terai: Inform. Processing **10**, 10 (1970)

4.24 S. K. Chang: IEEE Trans. Systems, Man and Cybernetics SMC-**3**, 257 (1973)

4.25 R. H. Anderson: Syntax-Directed Recognition of Hand-Printed Two-Dimensional Mathmathics, Ph.D. Thesis. Harvard University, Cambridge, Mass. (Jan. 1968)

4.26 S. K. Chang: Inform. Sciences **2**, 253 (1970)

4.27 A. C. Shaw: Rept. SLAC-84, Stanford Linear Accelerator Center, Stanford, California (March 1968)

4.28 B. K. Bhargava, K. S. Fu: "Application of Tree System Approach to Classification of Bubble Chamber Photographs"; Techn. Rept. TR-EE 72–30, School of Electr. Eng., Purdue University, W. Lafayette, Indiana (Nov. 1972)

4.29 R. S. Ledley, L. S. Rotolo, T. J. Golab, J. D. Jacobson, M. D. Ginsburg, J. B. Wilson: In *Optical and Electro-Optical Information Processing*, ed. by J. T. Tippett, D. Beckowitz, L. Clapp, C. Koester and A. Vanderburgh, Jr. (MIT Press, Cambridge, Mass. 1965) p. 591

4.30 B. Moayer, K. S. Fu: "A Syntactic Approach to Fingerprint Pattern Recognition"; Proc. First International Joint Conference on Pattern Recognition, Oct. 30-Nov. 1, 1973, Washington, D.C. A more complete version of the paper was published in: Pattern Recognition 7, No. 1 (1975)

4.31 B. Moayer, K. S. Fu: "Syntactic Pattern Recognition of Fingerprints"; Tech. Report TR-EE 74-36, School of Elec. Engr., Purdue University, W. Lafayette, Indiana (Dec. 1974)

4.32 W. J. Hankley, J. T. Tou: Automatic Fingerprint Interpretation and Classification via Con-
      textural Analysis and Topological Coding

4.33 R. De Mori: IEEE Trans. Audio and Electroacoustics AU-21, 89 (1973)

4.34 A. Kurematsu, M. Takeda, S. Inoue: A Method of Pattern Recognition Using Rewriting
      Rules, 2nd Intern. Joint Conf. Artificial Intelligence, London (September 1971) pp. 248–257

4.35 R. H. Anderson: "Syntax-Directed Recognition of Hand-Printed Two-Dimensional Mathe-
      matics", in *Interactive Systems for Experimental Applied Mathematics*, ed. by M. Klerer and
      J. Reinfelds (Academic Press, New York 1968)

4.36 T. Vamos, Z. Vassy: "Industrial Pattern Recognition Experiment—A Syntax Aided Ap-
      proach"; Proc. First Intern. Joint Conf. on Pattern Recognition, Washington, D.C. (October
      30-November 1, 1973)

4.37 A. W. Laffan, R. C. Scott: "A New Tool for Automatic Pattern Recognition: A Context-
      Free Grammar for Plane Projective Geometry"; Proc. 2nd Intern. Joint Conf. Pattern Recog-
      nition, Lyngby-Copenhagen, Denmark (August 13–15, 1974)

4.38 R. L. Grimsdale, F. H. Summer, C. J. Tunis, T. Kilburn: Proc. IEE 106 B, 210 (1959); re-
      printed in *Pattern Recognition* (Wiley, New York 1966) pp. 317–338

4.39 M. Eden, M. Halle: *Proc* 4th *London Symp. Information Theory* (Butterworth, London 1961)
      pp. 287–299

4.40 L. D. Earnest: In *Information Processing*, ed. by C. M. Poplewell (North Holland Publishing
      Co., Amsterdam 1963) pp. 462–466

4.41 P. Mermelstein, M. Eden: Inform. and Control 7, 255 (1964)

4.42 M. Eden, P. Mermelstein: *Proc.* 16th *Annual Conf. Engineering in Medicine and Biology* (1963)
      pp. 12–13

4.43 H. Freeman: IEEE Trans. Elec. Comp. EC-10, 260 (1961)

4.44 H. Freeman: Proc. National Electr. Conf. 18, 312 (1962)

4.45 P. J. Knoke, R. G. Wiley: Proc. IEEE Comp. Conf. 1967, p. 142

4.46 J. Feder: Inform. and Control 13, 230 (1968)

4.47 H. Freeman, S. P. Morse: J. Franklin Inst. 284, 1 (1967)

4.48 J. Feder, H. Freeman: IEEE Intern. Conv. Record, Part 3, 1966, pp. 69–85

4.49 C. T. Zahn: SLAC Rpt. 72 (Stanford Linear Accelerator Center, Stanford, Calif. 1966)

4.50 H. Freeman, J. Garder: IEEE Trans. Elec. Comp. EC-13, 118 (1964)

4.51 R. Narasimhan: Comm. ACM 9, 166 (1966)

4.52 R. J. Spinrad: Inform. and Control 8, 124 (1965)

4.53 J. F. O'Callaghan: "Problems in On-Line Character Recognition" in *Picture Language
      Machines*, ed. by S. Kaneff (Academic Press, New York 1970)

4.54 M. Nir: "Recognition of General Line Patterns with Application to Bubble-Chamber Photo-
      graphs and Handprinted Characters", Ph. D. Thesis, Moore School of Electrical Engineering,
      University of Penn (Dec. 1967)

4.55 R. Narsimhan: Inform. and Control 7, 151 (1964)

4.56 J. W. Butler, M. K. Butler, A. Stroud: "Automatic Classification of Chromosomes"; Proc.
      Conf. Data Acquisition and Processing in Biology and Medicine, New York 1963)

4.57 H. C. Lee, K. S. Fu: "A Syntactic Pattern Recognition System with Learning Capability",
      Proc. COINS-72 (Dec. 1972)

4.58 A. Grasselli: "On the Automatic Classification of Fingerprints"; in *Methodologies of Pat-
      tern Recognition*, ed. by S. Watanabe (Academic Press, New York 1969)

4.59 G. Levi, F. Sirovich: Inform. Sci. 4, 327 (1972)

4.60 M. Nagao: "Picture Recognition and Data Structure"; in *Graphic Languages*, ed. by F. Nake
      and A. Rosenfeld (North-Holland Publishing Co., Amsterdam, London 1972)

4.61 M. D. Kelley: "Visual Identification of People by Computer"; Ph. D. Thesis Dept. of Com-
      puter Science, Stanford University, Stanford, Calif. (June 1970)

4.62 L. G. Roberts: In *Optical and Electro-Optical Information Processing*, ed. by J. T. Tippett,
      D. Beckowitz, L. Clapp, C. Koester and A. Vanderburgh, Jr. (MIT Press, Cambridge, Mass.
      1965) p. 159

4.63 R. O. Duda, P. E. Hart: "Experiments in Scene Analysis"; Proc. First National Symposium
      on Industrial Robots, Chicago (April 1970)

4.64 J. A. Feldman et al.: "The Stanford Hand-Eye Project"; Proc. First Intern. Joint Conf.
      Artificial Intelligence, Washington, D.C. (May 1969)

4.65   T.Pavlidis: Pattern Recognition **1**, 165 (1968)

4.66   A.Rosenfeld, J.P.Strong: "A Grammar for Maps", in *Software Engineering*, Vol. 2, ed. by J.T.Tou (Academic Press, New York 1971)

4.67   T.Pavlidis: Pattern Recognition **4**, 5 (1972)

4.68   T.Pavlidis: Structural pattern recognition: Primitives and juxtaposition, in *Frontiers of Pattern Recognition*, ed. by S.Watanabe (Academic Press, New York 1972)

4.69   M.L.Minsky, S.Papert: Project MAC Progress, Rpt. IV (MIT Press, Cambridge, Mass. 1967)

4.70   A.Guzman: Proc. AFIPS FJCC **33**, Pt. 1, 291 (1968)

4.71   C.R.Brice, C.L.Fennema: Artificial Intelligence **1**, 205 (1970)

4.72   K.S.Fu, T.L.Booth: IEEE Trans. SMC-**5**, (Jan. and July 1975)

4.73   J.Feder: Inform. Sci. **3** (1971)

4.74   M.C.Clowes: Transformational grammars and the organization of pictures, in *Automatic Interpretation and Classification of Images,* ed. by A.Grasselli (Academic Press, New York 1969)

4.75   Laveen Kanal, B.Chandrasekaran: On linguistic, statistical and mixed models for pattern recognition, in *Frontiers of Pattern Recognition,* ed. by S.Watanabe (Academic Press, New York 1972)

4.76   R.Narsimhan: Picture languages, in *Picture Language Machines,* ed. by S.Kaneff (Academic Press, New York 1970)

4.77   W.E.Underwood, L.N.Kanal: "Structural Description, Transformational Rules and Pattern Analysis"; Proc. First Intern. Joint Conf. Pattern Recognition, Washington, D.C. (October 30–November 1, 1973)

4.78   T.G.Evans: "A Formalism for the Description of Complex Objects and Its Implementation", Proc. Fifth Intern. Congress on Cybernetics, Namur, Belgium (Sept. 1967)

4.79   M.L.Minsky: Proc. IRE **49**, 8 (1961)

4.80   M.B.Clowes: Pictorial relationships — A syntactic approach, in *Machine Intelligence IV,* ed. by B.Meltzer and D.Michie (American Elsevier, New York 1969)

4.81   T.G.Evans: Descriptive pattern analysis techniques, in *Automatic Interpretation and Classification of Images*, ed. by A. Grasselli (Academic Press, New York 1969)

4.82   H.G.Barrow, J.R.Popplestone: In *Machine Intelligence 6*, ed. by B.Meltzer and D.Michie (Edinburgh University Press, Edinburgh 1971) pp. 377–396

4.83   R.A.Kirsch: IEEE Trans. Elec. Comp. EC-**13**, 363 (1964)

4.84   M.F.Dacey: Pattern Recognition **2**, 11 (1970)

4.85   D.M.Milgram, A.Rosenfeld: *IFIP Congress 71* (North-Holland, Amsterdam, August 1971, Booklet TA-2) pp. 166–173

4.86   A.C.Shaw: Inform. and Control **14**, 9 (1969)

4.87   A.C.Shaw: J. ACM **17**, 453 (1970)

4.88   J.L.Pfaltz, A.Rosenfeld: Proc. First Intern. Joint Conf. Artificial Intelligence, Washington, D.C. (May 1969) pp. 609–619

4.89   A.C.Shaw: Picture graphs, grammars, and parsing; in *Frontiers of Pattern Recognition,* ed. by S.Watanabe (Academic Press, New York 1972)

4.90   J.L.Pfaltz: "Web Grammars and Picture Description"; Technical Report 70–138, Computer Science Center, University of Maryland, College Park, Maryland (1970)

4.91   J.M.Brayer, K.S.Fu: "Web Grammars and Their Application to Pattern Recognition"; Technical Report 75-1, School of Electrical Engineering, Purdue University, W. Lafayette, Ind. 47907 (1975)

4.92   T.Pavlidis: J. ACM **19**, 11 (1972)

4.93   A.Rosenfeld: "Picture Automata and Grammars: An Annotated Bibliography", Proc. Symp. Computer Image Processing and Recognition, Vol. 2, Columbia, Mo. (Aug. 24–26, 1972)

4.94   T.Pavlidis: Graph theoretic analysis of pictures, in *Graphic Languages,* ed. by F.Nake and A.Rosenfeld (North-Holland, Amsterdam) 1972

4.95   W.S.Brainerd: Information and Control **14**, 217 (1969)

4.96   J.E.Donar: J. Computer System Sci. **4** (1970)

4.97   K.S.Fu, B.K.Bhargava: IEEE Trans. C-**22**, 1087 (1973)

4.98   B.K.Bhargava, K.S.Fu: "Transformation and Inference of Tree Grammars for Syntactic Pattern Recognition", Proc. IEEE Intern. Conf. Systems, Man and Cybernetics, Dallas, Texas (Oct. 2–4, 1974)

4.99   J. M. FOSTER: *Automatic Syntactic Analysis* (American Elsevier, New York 1970)

4.100   A. V. AHO, J. D. ULLMAN: *The Theory of Parsing, Translation, and Compiling*, Vol. 1, Parsing (Prentice-Hall, Englewood Cliffs, N. J. 1972)

4.101   F. W. BLACKWELL: "Combining Mathematical and Structural Pattern Recognition"; Proc. Second Intern. Joint Conf. Pattern Recognition, Copenhagen, Denmark (Aug. 13–15, 1974)

4.102   V. GRENANDER: "Syntax-Controlled Probabilities"; Tech. Rept., Division of Applied Math., Brown University, Providence, Rhode Island (1967)

4.103   K. S. FU: Syntactic pattern recognition and stochastic languages, in *Frontiers of Pattern Recognition*, ed. by S. WATANABE (Academic Press, New York 1972)

4.104   V. A. KOVALEVSKY: "Sequential Optimization in Pattern Recognition and Pattern Description"; *Proc. IFIP Congress,* Amsterdam, Holland (1968)

4.105   K. S. FU: "Stochastic Languages for Picture Analysis"; U.S.-Japan Seminar on Picture and Scene Analysis, Kyoto, Japan (July 23–27, 1973)

4.106   L. W. FUNG, K. S. FU: "Stochastic Syntactic Classification of Noisy Patterns"; Proc. Second Intern. Joint Conf. Pattern Recognition, Copenhagen, Denmark (Aug. 13–15, 1974)

4.107   V. DIMITROV: "Multilayered Stochastic Languages for Pattern Recognition"; Proc. First Intern. Joint Conf. Pattern Recognition, Washington, D.C. (October 30–November 1, 1973)

4.108   H. C. LEE, K. S. FU: IEEE Trans. C-**21**, 660 (1972)

4.109   T. HUANG, K. S. FU: Computer Graphics and Image Processing **1**, 257 (1972)

4.110   A. V. AHO, T. G. PETERSON: SIAM J. Comp. **1**, 305 (1972)

4.111   L. W. FUNG, K. S. FU: IEEE Trans. C-**24**, 662 (1975)

4.112   M. G. THOMASON, R. C. GONZALEZ: "Classification of Imperfect Syntactic Pattern Structures"; Proc. Second Intern. Joint Conf. Pattern Recognition, Copenhagen, Denmark (Aug. 13–15, 1974)

4.113   R. BAJCSY, L. I. LIEBERMAN: "Computer Description of Real Outdoor Scenes"; Proc. Second Intern. Joint Conf. Pattern Recognition, Copenhagen, Denmark (Aug. 13–15, 1974)

4.114   K. HANAKATA: "Feature Selection for Compact Pattern Description"; Proc. First Intern. Joint Conf. Pattern Recognition, Washington, D.C. (October 30–November 1, 1973)

4.115   S. L. HOROWITZ, T. PAVLIDIS: "Picture Segmentation by a Directed Split-and-Merge Procedure"; Proc. Second Intern. Joint Conf. Pattern Recognition, Copenhagen, Denmark (Aug. 13–15, 1974)

4.116   T. PAVLIDIS: Structural pattern recognition: Primitives and juxtaposition relations, in *Frontiers of Pattern Recognition*, ed. by S. WATANABE (Academic Press, New York 1972)

4.117   S. KANEFF (ed.): *Picture Language Machines* (Academic Press, New York 1970)

4.118   A. ROSENFELD: Isotonic grammars, parallel grammars, and picture grammars, in *Machine Intelligence VI,* (Edinburgh University Press, Edinburgh 1971)

4.119   K. TANAKA, J. TOYODA, N. ABE: "Some Studies on Web Grammars"; Proc. First Intern. Joint Conf. Pattern Recognition, Washington, D.C. (October 30–November 1, 1973)

4.120   F. NAKE, A. ROSENFELD (eds.): *Graphic Languages* (North-Holland, Amsterdam 1973)

4.121   Y. E. CHO: "The Generating Properties of Context-Free Picture Grammars"; Proc. Second Intern. Joint Conf. Pattern Recognition, Copenhagen, Denmark (Aug. 13–15, 1974)

4.122   R. S. LEDLEY: *Programming and Utilizing Digital Computers* (McGraw-Hill, New York 1972)

4.123   J. ALBUS: "Electrocardiogram Interpretation Using a Stochastic Finite-State Model"; Proc. Conf. Computer Graphics, Pattern Recognition and Data Structure, Los Angeles, California (May 14–16, 1975)

5. Picture Recognition*

A. ROSENFELD and J. S. WESZKA

With 17 Figures

This chapter reviews methods of measuring properties of pictures, and extracting objects from pictures, for purposes of picture recognition and description. Subjects covered include

1) Properties of regions in pictures—in particular, textural properties.
2) Detection of objects in pictures—template matching, edge detection.
3) Properties of detected objects—projections, cross-sections, moments.
4) Object extraction—thresholding, region growing, tracking.
5) Properties of extracted objects—connectedness and counting, area and perimeter, compactness, convexity, elongatedness.
6) Object and picture representation—boundaries, skeletons, relational structures.

5.1 Introduction

This chapter describes methods of measuring properties of pictures, and extracting objects from pictures, for purposes of pattern recognition. Properties of pictures, or of objects that have been extracted from pictures, can serve as features for statistical picture classification; while the extracted objects can serve as primitives for syntactic pattern recognition of the pictures.

Section 5.2 discusses properties that are appropriate to measure for uniform regions in a picture. These are primarily properties that characterize the texture of the region. The dependence of these properties on the picture's grayscale, and methods of normalizing the grayscale, are also treated.

In Section 5.3, we consider how to detect objects in a picture, by matching parts of the picture against templates. Objects of known shape can be detected using templates that have the given shape; objects of unknown shape, that contrast with their backgrounds, can be detected using edge- or curve-like templates. The techniques in this section detect positions where objects are likely to be present, but do not explicitly "extract" the objects from the picture; the latter problem will be treated in Section 5.5.

Section 5.4 discusses properties that are appropriately measured for regions in a picture that contain an object on a background. These properties include moments, coefficients in orthonormal expansions, as well as properties derived from projections or cross-sections of the regions. The dependence of these prop-

* The support of the Information Systems Branch, Office of Naval Research, under Contract N00014-67A-0239-0012, is gratefully acknowledged, as is the help of SHELLY ROWE in preparing this paper.

erties on the positions, orientations, and size of the objects, and methods of normalizing with respect to these geometrical parameters, are also considered.

Object extraction from a picture is treated in Section 5.5. This process produces explicit "overlays", usually in the form of two-valued pictures having
value 1 at object points and 0 at background points. The methods used include
thresholding (preceded by suitable processing of the picture, if necessary), tracking,
and region growing.

In Section 5.6, we discuss geometrical properties of objects, including connectedness (and methods of counting connected components), area and perimeter, extent, compactness, convexity, and elongatedness.

Section 5.7 is devoted to methods of representing objects, in particular using
their borders or their "skeletons". The representation of a picture by a relational
structure, involving objects, their properties, and relationships among them, is
also briefly discussed.

Techniques for the analysis of three-dimensional scenes are not covered in
this paper; see [5.1] for an introduction to this topic. We also do not cover picture
processing for purposes other than recognition—image coding, enhancement,
restoration, etc.

The subject of picture recognition has a large literature; only selected topics
are treated, on an expository level, in this chapter. Additional details can be
found in textbooks [5.1–3], while a large collection of references to the English-
language literature can be found in a continuing series of survey papers
[5.4–7] by the first author of this chapter. References on standard methods
of picture analysis will not be given here; see [5.1–7]. We will, however,
give a few references to recent developments of special interest, to which the
reader can refer for detailed discussions of methods that could not be covered in
the present brief paper.

5.2 Properties of Regions

In many cases, pictures can be regarded as made up of more or less uniformly
textured regions, or as containing objects on a background, where the objects
differ in texture from the background. Thus textural properties of regions in a
picture are often of importance for picture description. This section discusses
some of the commonly used textural properties.

Visual texture is a difficult concept to define, but it is commonly said to involve
the repetitive occurrence of local patterns in the given region. Thus one can describe
a texture by describing these local patterns and the rules for their arrangement. A
good collection of papers on the analysis, synthesis, and perception of texture can be
found in [5.8]. Selected approaches will be briefly reviewed in the next three
subsections.

5.2.1 Analysis of the Power Spectrum

One way of analyzing local pattern arrangement in a region is to examine the
power spectrum of the region, i.e., the squared magnitude of the region's two-

dimensional Fourier transform. If the gray level at position (x, y) in the region is $f(x, y)$, then this Fourier transform is defined by

$$F(u, v) = \mathscr{F}(f(x, y)) = \int\int_{-\infty}^{\infty} e^{-2\pi i(ux + vy)} f(x, y) dx dy$$

so that the power spectrum is $|F(u, v)|^2 = F(u, v)F^*(u, v)$, where $F^*(u, v)$ is the complex conjugate of $F(u, v)$. If the arrangement of local patterns over the region is periodic, say with period (u_0, v_0), then the power spectrum will have a high value at $(s/u_0, s/v_0)$, where s is the diameter of the region. Thus if the region is "busy", i.e., the patterns are fine-grained and closely spaced, the high values in the power spectrum will be spread out far from the origin, while for a coarsely textured region, the high values in the spectrum will be concentrated close to the origin. If the patterns, or their arrangement, are directionally biased, the spread of high values in the spectrum will be biased in the perpendicular direction; for example, horizontal streaks in the region will give rise to a vertical streak in the spectrum. These phenomena are illustrated in Fig. 5.1a–b.

A useful set of textural properties can be defined that take advantage of these properties of the power spectrum. Specifically, let (r, θ) be polar coordinates in the (u, v) plane, and suppose that we integrate $|F(u, v)|^2$ with respect to r and with respect to θ, i.e., we compute

$$F_1(r) = \int_0^{2\pi} |F(u, v)|^2 d\theta \quad \text{and} \quad F_2(\theta) = \int_0^{\infty} |F(u, v)|^2 dr .$$

If we wish, we can approximate these integrals by averaging the $|F(u, v)|^2$ values over a set of thin rings centered at the origin, and over a set of narrow angular sectors emanating from the origin, respectively. The results, for the pictures of Fig. 5.1a, are shown in graph form in Fig. 5.1c–d. (These results were obtained using the discrete Fourier transform of f, rather than the ordinary Fourier transform.) The degree of spread of the high values in $|F(u, v)|^2$ appears in the $F_1(r)$ graph as the rate of falloff from the peak at the origin; while directional biases in the high values appear as peaks in the $F_2(\theta)$ graph.

The values of $F_1(r)$ and $F_2(\theta)$, for specific choices of r and θ, can be used as textural properties. Alternately, we can compute measures of the spread or peakedness of these functions, e.g., the moment of inertia of $F_1(r)$ about the origin [i.e., $\int_0^{\infty} r^2 F_1(r) dr$], or the variance of $F_2(\theta)$.

5.2.2 Analysis of Local Property Statistics

An alternative approach to analyzing texture is to examine the frequency distribution of values of various local properties over the given region. A useful type of local property, in this connection, is a directional difference of averages taken over adjacent, non-overlapping neighborhoods in the picture. Let $A^{(r)}(x, y)$ denote the average of the gray levels ($f(x, y)$'s) in a neighborhood of radius r centered at (x, y); then a difference of non-overlapping A's in direction θ is defined by

$$D^{(r, \theta)}(x, y) = A^{(r)}(x + r \cos\theta, y + r \sin\theta) - A^{(r)}(x - r \cos\theta, y - r \sin\theta)$$

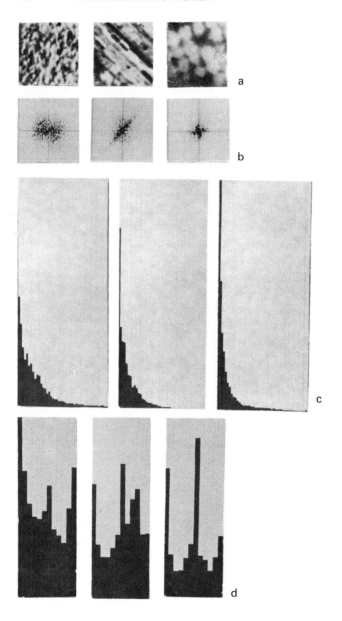

Fig. 5.1a–d. Texture analysis based on the power spectrum.

a) Input pictures, $f(x, y)$.

b) Power spectra, $\left| \int\!\!\int\limits_{-\infty}^{\infty} e^{-2\pi i(ux + vy)} f(x, y) dx dy \right|^2 \equiv |F(u, v)|^2$, for the pictures in a).

c) Ring averages, $\int_0^{2\pi} |F(u, v)|^2 d\theta$, for a discrete set of rings (one unit wide).

d) Sector averages, $\int_0^{\infty} |F(u, v)|^2 dr$, for a discrete set of sectors ($15°$ wide, starting at $-7\frac{1}{2}°$)

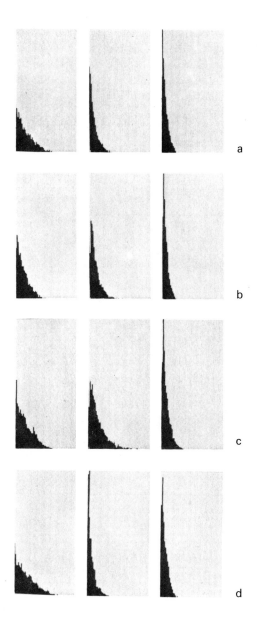

5.2a–d. Texture analysis based on local property statistics. Histograms of $D^{(r,\theta)}$, for the pictures in Fig. 5.1a, using four values of (r, θ):

Part	(r, θ)	Mean values, for the three pictures		
a)	$(1, 0)$	9.5	5.2	3.4
b)	$(1, \pi/2)$	7.2	6.1	3.2
c)	$(\sqrt{2}, \pi/4)$	12.3	4.8	4.2
d)	$(\sqrt{2}, 3\pi/4)$	10.4	9.4	4.7

If the texture in the region is "busy", $D^{(r,\theta)}$ should tend to have high values for small values of r; while if the texture is coarse, small r's should yield low values of D. If the texture has directional biases, the values of D will be higher for some θ's than for others; for example, if the texture is horizontally streaked, and we take r to be half the width of the streaks, then $D^{(r,\pi/2)}$ should be greater, on the average, than $D^{(r,0)}$.

Histograms of $D^{(r,\theta)}$, for $(r, \theta) = (1, 0)$, $(1, \pi/2)$, $(\sqrt{2}, \pi/4)$, and $(\sqrt{2}, 3\pi/4)$, are shown in Fig. 5.2a–d for the pictures in Fig. 5.1a. Statistics of these histograms,

Fig. 5.3a

	0–7	8–15	16–23	24–31	32–39	40–47	48–55	56–63
0– 7	290	214	122	49	11	5	1	0
8–15	214	145	223	173	66	33	12	1
16–23	122	223	106	180	130	97	39	5
24–31	49	173	180	94	180	131	90	23
32–39	11	66	130	180	118	191	132	64
40–47	5	33	97	131	191	129	221	88
48–55	1	12	39	90	132	221	150	215
56–63	0	1	5	23	64	88	215	304

	0–7	8–15	16–23	24–31	32–39	40–47	48–55	56–63
0– 7	398	165	28	5	7	0	0	0
8–15	165	257	206	91	18	14	1	0
16–23	28	206	215	235	83	16	10	0
24–31	5	91	235	181	240	64	16	1
32–39	7	18	83	240	194	219	55	4
40–47	0	14	16	64	219	220	246	21
48–55	0	1	10	16	55	246	245	183
56–63	0	0	0	1	4	21	183	394

	0–7	8–15	16–23	24–31	32–39	40–47	48–55	56–63
0– 7	367	224	15	6	0	0	0	0
8–15	224	257	221	36	4	0	0	0
16–23	15	221	268	230	22	0	0	0
24–31	6	36	230	241	229	18	1	0
32–39	0	4	22	229	273	212	2	0
40–47	0	0	0	18	212	285	204	8
48–55	0	0	0	1	2	204	336	136
56–63	0	0	0	0	0	8	136	437

5.3a–d. Texture analysis based on joint gray level statistics. Matrices $M^{(\Delta x, \Delta y)}$, for the pictures in Fig. 5.1a, using four values of $(\Delta x, \Delta y)$:

Part	$(\Delta x, \Delta y)$	Moment of inertia about main diagonal, for the three pictures (scaled)		
a)	(1, 0)	9.7	3.5	1.4
b)	(0, 1)	5.7	4.9	1.2
c)	(1, 1)	11.7	10.7	2.6
d)	(1, −1)	15.6	3.5	2.0

such as their means or standard deviations, can be used as textural properties; the means are tabulated in Fig. 5.2. Other local properties can also be used in place of $D^{(r,\theta)}$; examples may be found in [5.8].

5.2.3 Analysis of Joint Gray Level Statistics

Still another method of texture analysis which has received considerable attention [5.9] is based on examining the *joint* frequency distribution of pairs of gray levels, at various separations $(\Delta x, \Delta y)$ over the region. If we divide the grayscale into n intervals, we can represent such a distribution by an n-by-n matrix $M^{(\Delta x, \Delta y)}$ whose (h, k) element m_{hk} is the number of times that a point having gray level in the kth interval occurs in position $(\pm \Delta x, \Delta y)$ relative to a point having gray level in the hth interval. For example, in the case of the picture

$$112$$
$$344$$
$$411$$

Fig. 5.3b

	0–7	8–15	16–23	24–31	32–39	40–47	48–55	56–63
0– 7	342	217	43	14	2	1	0	0
8–15	217	193	240	117	41	9	2	0
16–23	43	240	154	238	114	51	13	0
24–31	14	117	238	122	220	122	47	6
32–39	2	41	114	220	126	230	125	32
40–47	1	9	51	122	230	148	249	66
48–55	0	2	13	47	125	249	185	210
56–63	0	0	0	6	32	66	210	353

	0–7	8–15	16–23	24–31	32–39	40–47	48–55	56–63
0– 7	347	188	45	17	14	7	1	1
8–15	188	231	225	82	38	15	3	0
16–23	45	225	185	247	92	20	11	2
24–31	17	82	247	170	214	76	36	3
32–39	14	38	92	214	175	224	67	14
40–47	7	15	20	76	224	191	262	34
48–55	1	3	11	36	67	262	213	200
56–63	1	0	2	3	14	34	200	382

	0–7	8–15	16–23	24–31	32–39	40–47	48–55	56–63
0– 7	398	190	9	0	0	0	0	0
8–15	190	295	212	29	1	0	0	0
16–23	9	212	287	211	18	0	0	0
24–31	0	29	211	267	223	21	0	0
32–39	0	1	18	223	278	218	7	0
40–47	0	0	0	21	218	288	194	4
48–55	0	0	0	0	7	194	316	141
56–63	0	0	0	0	0	4	141	425

Fig. 5.3c

	0–7	8–15	16–23	24–31	32–39	40–47	48–55	56–63
0– 7	249	221	104	71	13	9	4	0
8–15	221	139	205	146	85	46	16	3
16–23	104	205	103	167	143	106	50	10
24–31	71	146	167	89	171	138	95	32
32–39	13	85	143	171	92	187	149	71
40–47	9	46	106	138	187	111	213	103
48–55	4	16	50	95	149	213	137	201
56–63	0	3	10	32	71	103	201	290

	0–7	8–15	16–23	24–31	32–39	40–47	48–55	56–63
0– 7	272	198	77	46	38	23	14	4
8–15	198	170	189	136	73	34	17	12
16–23	77	189	143	223	113	59	34	15
24–31	46	136	223	117	183	104	60	19
32–39	38	73	113	183	129	197	102	39
40–47	23	34	59	104	197	136	230	97
48–55	14	17	34	60	102	230	156	215
56–63	4	12	15	19	39	97	215	295

	0–7	8–15	16–23	24–31	32–39	40–47	48–55	56–63
0– 7	332	234	40	12	1	0	0	0
8–15	234	218	231	81	14	1	0	0
16–23	40	231	222	235	69	5	0	0
24–31	12	81	235	182	239	63	2	0
32–39	1	14	69	239	216	223	35	1
40–47	0	1	5	63	223	236	205	32
48–55	0	0	0	2	35	205	278	167
56–63	0	0	0	0	1	32	167	395

if we divide the gray levels into two intervals, (1,2) and (3,4), we have

$$M^{(1,0)} = \begin{pmatrix} 6 & 1 \\ 1 & 4 \end{pmatrix}; \quad M^{(0,1)} = \begin{pmatrix} 0 & 5 \\ 5 & 2 \end{pmatrix};$$

and so on for other values of $(\Delta x, \Delta y)$. The matrices for $(\Delta x, \Delta y) = (1, 0), (0, 1), (1, 1),$ and $(1, -1)$, using eight gray level intervals, are shown in Fig. 5.3a–d for the pictures in Fig. 5.1a.

If the given region is coarsely textured, then for small values of $\sqrt{(\Delta x)^2 + (\Delta y)^2}$ we can expect to see the entries in the $M^{(\Delta x, \Delta y)}$ matrix concentrated near the main diagonal, since pairs of points separated by $(\Delta x, \Delta y)$ will tend to have similar gray levels. For a busy texture, on the other hand, these entries will be more spread out. For a texture with directional biases, the amount of spread will depend on the direction $\tan^{-1}(\Delta y/\Delta x)$. These remarks suggest that the moment of inertia

Fig. 5.3d

	0–7	8–15	16–23	24–31	32–39	40–47	48–55	56–63
0– 7	224	189	134	88	32	19	9	1
8–15	189	108	202	171	103	69	37	13
16–23	134	202	88	135	135	114	70	25
24–31	88	171	135	81	143	142	107	51
32–39	32	103	135	143	87	158	158	99
40–47	19	69	114	142	158	96	205	125
48–55	9	37	70	107	158	205	114	188
56–63	1	13	25	51	99	125	188	249

	0–7	8–15	16–23	24–31	32–39	40–47	48–55	56–63
0– 7	376	133	26	15	12	5	1	1
8–15	133	286	201	59	24	5	4	0
16–23	26	201	234	218	57	21	5	1
24–31	15	59	218	200	236	56	17	4
32–39	12	24	57	236	212	190	54	6
40–47	5	5	21	56	190	255	211	18
48–55	1	4	5	17	54	211	289	113
56–63	1	0	1	4	6	18	113	424

	0–7	8–15	16–23	24–31	32–39	40–47	48–55	56–63
0– 7	345	222	33	4	1	0	0	0
8–15	222	230	261	52	2	0	0	0
16–23	33	261	220	240	43	7	0	0
24–31	4	52	240	208	240	44	1	0
32–39	1	2	43	240	233	238	24	0
40–47	0	0	7	44	238	242	211	17
48–55	0	0	0	1	24	211	289	152
56–63	0	0	0	0	0	17	152	410

of $M^{(\Delta x, \Delta y)}$ about its main diagonal, i.e., $\sum_{h,k}(h-k)^2 m_{hk}$, may be a useful textural property. It is shown, for the matrices mentioned above, in Fig. 5.3. A variety of other textural properties derived from $M^{(\Delta x, \Delta y)}$ matrices are discussed in [5.9].

5.2.4 Grayscale Normalization

The values of the textural properties defined above are sensitive to overall changes in the given picture's grayscale. For example, if the gray levels of the picture are multiplied by a constant c, then the power spectrum values, and the features derived from them, are multiplied by c^2. Similarly, the $D^{(r,\theta)}$ values are multiplied by c, while the $M^{(\Delta x, \Delta y)}$ matrices should also tend to be spread away from (or compressed toward) the main diagonal to a degree that depends on c. Other types of changes in the picture's grayscale will have more complicated effects on textural property values.

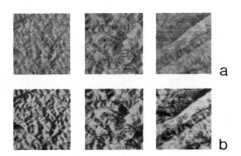

a

b

Fig. 5.4a and b. Grayscale normalization: Forcing each gray level to occur equally often. a) Input pictures. b) Results of normalization

If we want our textural properties to be invariant under grayscale changes, we can "normalize" the picture's grayscale before measuring the properties. One common way of doing this is to force the picture to have some standard frequency distribution of gray levels, e.g., a uniform distribution, in which all gray levels occur equally often. If there are n gray levels, we can do this by taking the n^{-1}th of the picture points having lowest gray level, and giving them all level 1; then taking the next lowest n^{-1}th and giving them level 2; and so on, with exact ties being resolved arbitrarily. (A more detailed description of this method can be found, e.g., in [5.9].) The results of forcing a set of pictures to have uniform gray level distributions are shown in Fig. 5.4. It is seen that the textures of these transformed pictures are essentially unchanged, though their grayscales are now "harsher".

5.3 Detection of Objects

Textural properties are appropriate descriptors for a uniform region in a picture, but not for a region that consists of an object on a background, or that overlaps two or more differently textured parts of the picture. In this section we discuss methods of detecting the presence of objects, or of edges between differently textured regions.

5.3.1 Template Matching

An object of known shape (and size) can be detected by matching the picture against a template having the given shape. This must be done for every possible position and orientation of the object. (Methods of speeding up the matching process will be discussed below.) The following are some standard measures of the degree of match between a picture $f(x, y)$ and a template T whose gray level at (x, y) is $t(x, y)$:

$$\max_{x, y \text{ in } T} |f(x, y) - t(x, y)|, \tag{5.1}$$

$$\int\int_T |f(x, y) - t(x, y)| dx dy, \tag{5.2}$$

$$\int\int_T [f(x, y) - t(x, y)]^2 dx dy. \tag{5.3}$$

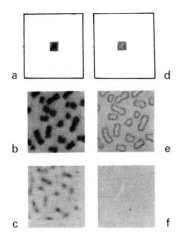

a

b

c

d

e

f

Fig. 5.5a–f. Template matching using the correlation coefficient. a) Template. b) Picture. c) Values of the correlation coefficient (nonlinearly scaled) for all possible shifts of a) relative to b). d) Outline template. e) Differentiated picture (see Subsect. 5.3.2). f) Same as c), using d) and e) in place of a) and b)

These measures are all zero for a perfect match, and have high values for poor matches. They differ, however, in the types of errors to which they are sensitive. For example, if $f(x, y) = t(x, y)$ except at a few points, where $|f(x, y) - t(x, y)|$ is large, measure (5.1) will show a large amount of mismatch, whereas measures (5.2) and (5.3) will show negligible mismatch. On the other hand, if $|f(x, y) - t(x, y)|$ is everywhere non-zero but small, e.g., $f(x, y) = t(x, y) + \varepsilon$, then measure (5.1) yields a small mismatch, ε, while measures (5.2) and (5.3) yield large mismatches, $\varepsilon|T|$ and $\varepsilon^2|T|$, respectively, where $|T|$ is the area of the template T.

A useful match measure that can be derived from (5.3) is the correlation coefficient

$$\frac{\int\int_T f(x, y)t(x, y)dxdy}{\sqrt{\int\int_T f^2(x, y)dxdy \int\int_T t^2(x, y)dxdy}}. \tag{5.4}$$

It can be shown that this always has value between 0 and 1, with value 1 being achieved if and only if $f(x, y) \equiv ct(x, y)$ for some positive constant c. In fact, measure (5.4) is evidently unaffected if the picture's grayscale is multiplied by a constant, unlike measures (5.1)–(5.3), which should be used only in conjunction with some form of grayscale normalization (see Section 5.2.4).

A template, a picture, and the values of the correlation coefficient (5.4) for all positions of the template relative to the picture, are shown in Fig. 5.5a–c. It will be noted that there are many near-misses—i.e., relatively high values appear even at positions where the match of template to picture is not very close. The matches are also not very sharply localized; match values drop off relatively slowly around a position of perfect match. These problems can be solved by using a template that resembles the outline of the desired object, rather than the solid object. Such a template is shown in Fig. 5.5d, and its match values with a derivative of the picture (Fig. 5.5e) are shown in Fig. 5.5f.

The process of matching a template against a picture in all possible positions is computationally costly. To reduce its cost, one can attempt to eliminate positions in which a match is unlikely, e.g., by measuring some simple property of the picture f (a textural property, say) in every position, and ignoring positions where this value differs too greatly from the value of the given property for the template t. Further reduction can be achieved by using a mismatch measure that can be expected to grow rapidly, as f and t are compared point by point, unless f actually matches t; thus a position where there is no match can be rejected, by the mismatch measure exceeding a threshold, after only a partial comparison has been made. More details on these methods of reducing the cost of template matching can be found in [5.10–11].

It is often unrealistic to assume that the shapes of the objects being looked for are known exactly; it would be more appropriate to use "templates" that could tolerate limited amounts of geometrical distortion. Two approaches to this problem have recently been investigated. In one of these [5.12], parameters that control the shape of the template are varied in an attempt to improve the degree of match. In the other [5.13], the template is regarded as made up of subtemplates joined by "springs", and one attempts to find positions of these subtemplates which maximize their degrees of match with the picture, while at the same time minimizing the tensions in the springs.

5.3.2 Edge Detection

Even if we do not know the shapes of the objects, we often do know something about how they differ from their background, e.g., that there should be a more or less abrupt change in gray level, in color, or in texture, at the boundary between objects and background. Under these circumstances, we should be able to detect the presence and location of an object by detecting such abrupt changes, or "edges". In the following paragraphs we discuss some basic methods of edge detection.

Abrupt changes in gray level can be detected by applying some type of derivative operation to the given picture; the result should have high values where edges are present, and low values elsewhere. If we do not know the directions of the desired edges, this operation should be isotropic (i.e., direction-independent). A simple isotropic derivative operation is the *gradient*; for the picture $f(x, y)$, this is the vector-valued function whose magnitude and direction are

$$\sqrt{(\partial f/\partial x)^2 + (\partial f/\partial y)^2} \quad \text{and} \quad \tan^{-1}[(\partial f/\partial y)/(\partial f/\partial x)] \,.$$

(For digital pictures, these derivatives must be replaced by differences, and we can approximate the magnitude by using the sum or maximum of the absolute values, rather than the square root of the sum of the squares, if desired.) Another useful isotropic operation is the *Laplacian*

$$\frac{\partial^2 f}{\partial x^2} + \frac{\partial^2 f}{\partial y^2} \,,$$

but this usually does not respond as strongly to edges as does the gradient. The magnitudes of the gradient and Laplacian, for the same set of pictures as in Fig. 5.1a, are shown in Fig. 5.6.

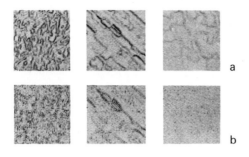

a

b

Fig. 5.6a and b. Magnitudes of derivative operations (using digital approximations) for the pictures in Fig. 5.1a. a) Gradient (multiplied by 2). b) Laplacian (multiplied by 4)

a

b

Fig. 5.7a and b. Vertical line detection. a) Input picture: Vertical dark line in noise. b) Output of vertical line detection operator for a)

When the picture is noisy, simple derivative operations may not be very useful in detecting edges. Under such circumstances, it may be more advisable to treat edge detection as a classification problem: given the observed gray levels in some neighborhood on the picture, is it more likely that they arise from an edge or from a uniform region? A detailed treatment of this approach may be found in [5.14]. Another possibility is to determine a step edge that best fits the observed gray levels, and to decide in favor of an edge being present if the height of this step exceeds some threshold; on this approach see [5.15–16].

Edges of known orientations and shapes can best be detected using "edge templates". For example, if we are looking for straight, vertical edges, we can sum the gray levels in two parallel, adjacent vertical strips, and subtract the results; the magnitude of this difference will be high if a straight vertical edge is present in that position. The same approach is commonly used to detect lines in a picture; we can sum the gray levels in three adjacent strips along the direction of the desired line, and subtract the sum along the center strip from the average of the sums along the flanking strips, obtaining a high magnitude of difference when a line that contrasts with its background runs down the center strip. Smooth curves can also be detected in this way (if we use strips in many orientations at each point), since locally they resemble lines, provided that they are not too sharply curved. An example of vertical line detection by this method is shown in Fig. 5.7. A disadvantage of this template approach is that it will give higher values for a high-contrast edge, or isolated point, than it will for a low-contrast line. On nonlinear line-detection "templates" that are not subject to this disadvantage see [5.17].

Objects that differ texturally from their backgrounds have edges that are characterized by changes in local property statistics, rather than by simple steps

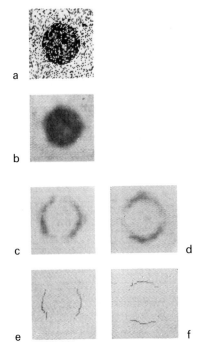

a

b

c

d

e

f

Fig. 5.8 a–f. Detection of texture edges. a) Input picture: Noisy dark region on a noisy light background. b) Result of averaging a), using a 8-by-8 square averaging neighborhood at each point. c–d) Horizontal and vertical differences of adjacent, non-overlapping averages that touch at each point of a). e–f) Horizontal and vertical maxima (respectively) of c–d)

in gray level. A straightforward approach to detecting such edges is to compute the appropriate local property at each point of the picture, and then look for pairs of adjacent neighborhoods in which the local property values differ significantly. For example, Fig. 5.8a shows a picture containing an object that has different gray level statistics from its background; this object can be detected by averaging the gray level over a neighborhood of every point (i.e., blurring the picture; Fig. 5.8b), and then taking differences of these averages in various directions (Fig. 5.8c–d), analogous to directional derivatives. As these figures show, edge detection based on differences of averages yields thick edges, since the edge is detected at many nearby positions; if desired, thin edges can be obtained by a nonmaximum suppression process (Fig. 5.8e–f). Further details on this approach may be found in [5.17–18].

5.4 Properties of Detected Objects

Suppose that a region in a picture contains an object on a background; to find such regions, we can look for places where there are good matches of templates with the picture. In this situation, we can obtain useful information about the object even without explicitly extracting it from the background, provided that we have at least a general idea about how the object and background differ. This section discusses properties that it may be useful to measure under such circumstances.

Input pictures	Moments for the pictures				
	m_{20}	m_{11}	m_{02}	m_{30}	m_{03}
0	6.96	0	16.25	0	0
1	1.41	−0.96	19.61	−0.10	10.18
2	8.69	1.88	21.50	2.34	9.00
3	8.03	0	20.82	−7.31	0
4	6.07	0.06	10.80	−9.27	7.38
5	9.19	−1.88	20.51	0	−27.56
6	8.69	1.16	17.36	2.34	14.80
7	6.80	4.00	18.76	4.36	−53.01
8	9.19	0	17.66	0	0
9	7.97	−0.69	15.61	−3.96	−18.18

Fig. 5.9. Moments for a set of numerals

5.4.1 Moments

Suppose, for concreteness, that the object has generally higher gray level than the background. Then we can get a good idea of the position of the object in the region, and of its extent in various directions, by computing *moments* of the picture's gray levels $f(x, y)$ over the region. The (i, j) *moment* of $f(x, y)$ over the region R is defined as

$$m_{ij} = \int \int_R x^i y^j f(x, y) dx dy .$$

The coordinates $(\bar{x}, \bar{y})$ of the *centroid* of R (its "center of gravity", if we think of gray level as corresponding to mass) are $\bar{x} = m_{10}/m_{00}$, $\bar{y} = m_{01}/m_{00}$. If we choose a coordinate system with $(\bar{x}, \bar{y})$ as the origin, the moments $\bar{m}_{ij}$ in this coordinate system (which are called "central moments") indicate how the gray levels in R are distributed relative to the centroid. For example, $\bar{m}_{20}$ and $\bar{m}_{02}$ are the moments of inertia of R around vertical and horizontal lines through the centroid, respectively; if $\bar{m}_{20}$ is greater than $\bar{m}_{02}$, the object is likely to be horizontally elongated, since the high gray levels are more spread out horizontally than they are vertically. The asymmetry of the object about these vertical and horizontal lines can be measured by the magnitudes of the moments $\bar{m}_{30}$ and $\bar{m}_{03}$, which are zero if there is perfect symmetry. The first few moments for a set of pictures of numerals are shown in Fig. 5.9. All m's should have overbars.

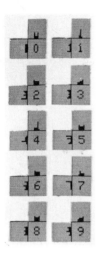

Fig. 5.10. Horizontal and vertical projections
of the pictures in Fig. 5.9a

Other types of information about the arrangement of gray levels in a region can be obtained by computing the Fourier coefficients of $f(x, y)$, i.e.,

$$\int\int_R f(x, y) \sin(ux + vy)dxdy \quad \text{or} \quad \int\int_R f(x, y) \cos(ux + vy)dxdy .$$

If a particular coefficient is high, the gray level should tend to be periodically distributed (with a given period, phase, and orientation). Coefficients in other orthogonal expansions of f—e.g., Walsh coefficients—can also be useful. The orthogonality of the basis functions insures that properties measured in this way will be uncorrelated.

5.4.2 Projections and Cross-Sections

We can also get an idea of how the gray levels in R are distributed by examining the *projections* of $f(x, y)$ in various directions. For example, the projections of f in the x and y directions are

$$\int_R f(x, y)dx \quad \text{and} \quad \int_R f(x, y)dy .$$

These projections, for the same set of numerals used in Fig. 5.9, are shown in graph form in Fig. 5.10. (Projections in a sufficient number of directions contain enough information, in principle, to reconstruct the picture; but we shall not pursue this subject here.) It is seen that, for objects having higher gray levels than their backgrounds, peaks in the projections can indicate the locations of major parts of the objects. Numerical properties of projections, such as their (one-dimensional) moments, Fourier coefficients, etc., can be useful as object descriptors.

More detailed information about the arrangement of gray levels in the region R can be obtained by examining *cross-sections* of $f(x, y)$ in various directions; e.g., the cross-sections in the x direction are just the functions $f(x, y_0)$ for par-

Character	Section	Number of runs of black points	Average run length
0	T	1	2
	M	2	1
	B	1	2
1	T	1	1
	M	1	1
	B	1	3
2	T	1	3
	M	1	3
	B	1	5
3	T	1	3
	M	1	2
	B	1	3
4	T	1	1
	M	2	1
	B	1	1
5	T	1	5
	M	1	4
	B	1	3
6	T	1	3
	M	1	4
	B	1	3
7	T	1	5
	M	1	1
	B	1	1
8	T	1	3
	M	1	3
	B	1	3
9	T	1	3
	M	1	4
	B	1	2

Fig. 5.11. Characteristics of three horizontal cross-sections (T = top, M = middle, B = bottom) of the pictures in Fig. 5.9a: number of runs of black points, and average run length

ticular values of y_0. Here again, for an object having high gray level, peaks in the cross-sections correspond to object parts. Some features of three horizontal cross-sections of each character in Fig. 5.9a are shown, in table form, in Fig. 5.11. Comparison of successive cross-sections can give useful information about object shape, in terms of how the peaks shift, expand, shrink, merge, and split as we track them from one cross-section to the next.

5.4.3 Geometrical Normalization

The values of moments, projections, etc. all depend on the position and orientation of the object in the given region. We can obtain properties that are invariant under translation or rotation of the object by using suitable combinations of

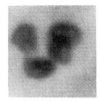

a

b

c

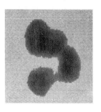

d

Fig. 5.12a–d. Geometrical normalization. a) Input picture (gray level range 0 to 63). b) Result of setting the gray levels (<32) of background points in a) to zero. c) Result of normalizing b) by rotating the object to make its principal axis vertical. d) Result of normalizing b) by rotating the object to make its least-area circumscribed rectangle upright

moments. For example, the central moments $\bar{m}_{ij}$ are invariant under translation; and the moment of inertia of the region R around its centroid, $\bar{m}_{20}+\bar{m}_{02}$, is invariant under rotation.

We can also use moments to "normalize" the position and orientation of the object, so that its projections, cross-sections, etc. can also be used to derive invariant properties of it. In fact, by using a coordinate system with origin at the centroid, we immediately obtain translation invariance. To get rotation invariance, we can find the line $y = x \tan \theta$, through this origin, about which the moment of inertia of R is least; i.e., we find the θ (which will usually be unique) such that

$$\int\int (x \sin \theta - y \cos \theta)^2 f(x, y) dx dy = \bar{m}_{20} \sin^2 \theta - 2\bar{m}_{11} \sin \theta \cos \theta + \bar{m}_{02} \cos^2 \theta$$

is as small as possible. (This line is called the *principal axis* of R.) We can then choose a rotated coordinate system in which this line is, say, vertical; this will tend to align the object so that it is elongated in the y direction. An example of a picture that has been normalized in this way is shown in Fig. 5.12a–c.

If the object has been explicitly extracted from the picture, another method of geometrical normalization can be used. We can circumscribe rectangles (say) around the object, and find an orientation for which the area of the circumscribed rectangle is least (again, this will usually be unique). We can then choose a rotated coordinate system in which the long sides of this minimum-area rectangle are, say, vertical. This too will tend to align the object so that it is vertically elongated; but for bent objects, it does not always yield the same orientation as the principal axis method, as we see in Fig. 5.12d.

Still another approach to geometrical normalization is to use a transform of the picture that is invariant under geometrical operations on the picture. For example, the autocorrelation and the power spectrum of f,

$$f \otimes f = \iint_{-\infty}^{\infty} f(x, y) f(x+h, y+k) dx dy \text{ and } | \iint_{-\infty}^{\infty} f(x, y) e^{-2\pi i (ux + vy)} dx dy |^2$$

both remain invariant if the original picture f is translated. Rotation and scale invariance can be obtained in analogous ways, using polar-coordinate transforms.

5.5 Object Extraction

In this section we consider methods of explicitly extracting objects from a picture. The output of the extraction process must be a specific decision as to which points of the picture belong to the objects, and which to the background. (More generally, one can *segment* a picture into meaningful parts (not necessarily objects and background); here the result must explicitly indicate which points belong to each part.) The results of this decision can be expressed in the form of an "overlay", in register with the original picture; this overlay can be thought of as a two-valued picture that has value 1 at points belonging to the objects, and value 0 at points of the background.

5.5.1 Thresholding

If the objects occupy a distinctive gray level range—e.g., they have higher gray levels than the background—then they can be extracted by *thresholding*; in other words, for some threshold value θ, we can create an overlay $o(x, y)$ defined by

$$o(x, y) = 1 \quad \text{if} \quad f(x, y) \geq \theta; \quad = 0 \text{ otherwise}$$

where $f(x, y)$ is the gray level of the given picture at (x, y). If we want to preserve information about the gray levels of the objects, while still distinguishing them from the background, we can perform "semi-thresholding" rather than thresholding—i.e., we can create a new picture $s(x, y)$ such that

$$s(x, y) = f(x, y) \quad \text{if} \quad f(x, y) \geq \theta; \quad = 0 \text{ otherwise} .$$

The results of thresholding and semithresholding the picture in Fig. 5.12a, using various threshold levels, are shown in Fig. 5.13.

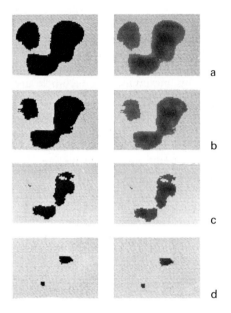

a

b

c

Fig. 5.13 a–d. Thresholding, Results of thresholding and semithresholding the picture in Fig. 5.12a at a) 35, b) 40, c) 45, d) 50. (Fig. 5.12b showed the same picture semithresholded at 32)

d

Fig. 5.14. Histogram of the gray levels in the picture in Fig. 5.11a

As Fig. 5.13 shows, proper choice of threshold is very important if one wants to extract objects correctly. A commonly used method of threshold selection is based on examining the histogram of the picture's gray levels. If the object and background gray level ranges are different, there should be peaks on this histogram corresponding to these ranges, separated by a valley corresponding to the intermediate gray levels that occur only rarely in the picture. The histogram for the picture in Fig. 5.12a is shown in Fig. 5.14. Note that the thresholds 32 and 35 used in Figs. 5.12b and 5.13a are at or near the valley bottom on this histogram.

The proper choice of threshold may vary from place to place in a picture; it may be preferable to threshold a picture piecewise. In fact, if we examine a small window of a picture, and discover that it has a strongly bimodal histogram, we can conclude that the window contains an object, or that an edge cuts across it [5.19]. When suitable thresholds have been chosen, say at the valley bottoms, for the windows that have bimodal histograms, we can assign thresholds to the non-bimodal windows by interpolation. It should be pointed out that if a picture has

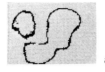
a

b

c

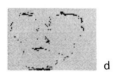
d

Fig. 5.15a–d. Outline extraction by thresholding. a) Result of displaying gray levels 35 to 38 in the picture in Fig. 5.12a as black, and all other levels as white. b) Same, using only levels 35 to 37. c) Result of displaying points of this picture at which the gradient has values ≥ 3 as black, and all other points as white. d) Same, using only values ≥ 4

a multimodal histogram, it is not in general safe to segment it by using thresholds at the bottoms of all of the valleys between the peaks, since there will be no way of distinguishing points that belong to a region of intermediate gray level from points that belong to transition zones between high and low gray level regions.

Outlines of objects, rather than the objects themselves, can be extracted in two ways. One approach is to "threshold" so as to extract points having a narrow range of gray levels, such as might be expected to occur just on the border between objects and background. Examples of this method are shown in Fig. 5.15a–b. The other approach is to apply an edge-sensitive operation to the picture, e.g., a gradient operation, and threshold the results; this should yield points on or near edges of objects, where the gradient has high values. Results obtained using this method are shown in Fig. 5.15c–d.

If an object differs texturally from its background, rather than occupying a distinctive range of gray levels, it cannot be extracted by simple gray level thresholding. For example, in the picture shown in Fig. 5.8a, both the object and the background have the same set of gray levels; they differ only in the probabilities of these gray levels. In cases like this, however, one can often convert the picture into a new form in which the objects and background do have different gray level ranges. Thus, in the case of Fig. 5.8a, if we simply blur the picture (as shown in Fig. 5.8b), we obtain a new picture in which the object is now generally darker than the background. The histogram of gray levels of this picture is shown in Fig. 5.16a; it now has peaks corresponding to the object and background gray level ranges. If we threshold at the bottom of the valley between these peaks, we obtain the reasonable result shown in Fig. 5.16b.

a

Fig. 5.16a and b. Extraction of a textured object by averaging and thresholding. a) Histogram of the gray levels in the picture in Fig. 5.8b. b) Result of thresholding this picture at 32 (near the bottom of the valley on the histogram)

b

5.5.2 Region Growing

A more flexible approach to object extraction or segmentation is to "grow" the objects, or the regions, by successively adding points, or merging subregions, if appropriate acceptance conditions are satisfied. This approach makes it possible to adjust the acceptance criteria in the course of the region growing process, so that they can depend on the textures and shapes of the growing regions, if desired. Object extraction by thresholding, on the other hand, applies a single fixed acceptance criterion to all points of the picture simultaneously.

A very simple example of object growing uses a high threshold to find "cores" of objects, and they are then allowed to grow by repeatedly adding adjacent points to them provided that these points exceed a certain lower threshold. This technique can be illustrated by referring to Figs. 5.12 and 5.13. By taking the high threshold as 45 or 50, we extract points belonging to two of the three objects. The growing process, using a lower threshold of 35 or 40, could then be used to extract the two objects, but not the third, even though it contains many points whose gray levels exceed the lower threshold.

As already mentioned, the criteria used to accept new points into an object can vary as the object grows (and not stay the same throughout the growth process, as in the example just given). The criteria can thus be made to depend on the object's shape and texture. As an example, suppose that we want to extract objects that have fairly constant gray level and fairly simple shape. We can start with "object cores" that are connected components of constant gray level; and we can merge two adjacent components if this will result in a more compact shape (see Subsection 5.6.2 on measures of shape compactness), provided that the gray levels of the components do not differ too greatly. This process can be repeated, merging unions of components provided the shape remains compact and the average gray levels do not greatly differ. A region growing procedure of this kind is described in [5.20].

Another way of segmenting a picture is to start with a standard partition of it, say into grid squares. We split a square (say into quadrants) if its gray level is too highly variable; and we merge neighboring squares if their gray levels are similar. This process can be used to obtain a partition into pieces that are unions of squares, where the gray level (or some other property, if desired) is uniform, within some tolerance, on each piece. On procedures of this kind see [5.21].

5.5.3 Tracking

A special type of "region growing" is *tracking*, where one begins at a point lying on an edge or curve, and successively accepts neighboring edge or curve points until the entire object border, or the entire curve, has been traversed. Here again, the acceptance criteria can depend both on the contrast of the edge or curve and on its shape. For example, one can look for high-contrast neighboring points, subject to the constraint that the curvature of the resulting edge or curve be small. If following the path of highest contrast leads to high curvature, one can back-track. Some recent examples of edge and curve tracking methods can be found in [5.22, 23].

Edge and curve detection operations (Subsection 5.3.2) often yield incomplete or broken results, since there may not be high contrast with the background at all points of the edge or curve. Edge and curve tracking, on the other hand, can be designed to bridge gaps, by looking for high-contrast points in a zone that extends the portion of the edge or curve already found.

A special case of tracking is *raster tracking*, where the edges or curves are tracked from row to row of the picture (so that the tracking is based on a row-by-row scan resembling a TV raster). Here the positions where the current row hits an edge or curve are noted, and hits are looked for in nearby positions on the next row (or within the next few rows, if we want to be able to bridge gaps). It is relatively straightforward to track any number of edges or curves simultaneously in this way, provided that they do not become very oblique (at the worst: tangential) to the raster lines.

5.6 Properties of Extracted Objects

Once we have explicitly extracted objects from a picture, we can analyze their geometrical properties. These include connectedness, size (area, perimeter, extent), and shape (compactness, convexity, elongatedness, etc.). These and other geometrical properties are the subject of this section. In what follows, S denotes an object, or more generally, an arbitrary finite set of digital picture points.

5.6.1 Connectedness

We say that two points (x_0, y_0) and (x_n, y_n) of S are *connected* in S if there exists a sequence of points of S, $(x_0, y_0), (x_1, y_1), \ldots, (x_n, y_n)$, such that (x_k, y_k) is a neighbor of (x_{k-1}, y_{k-1}), $1 \leq k \leq n$. Such a sequence of points is called a *path* in S. A maximal set of mutually connected points of S is called a *connected component* of S. If S has only one connected component, it is called *connected*.

There are two versions of the above definitions (and of many of the other definitions in this section), depending on whether or not diagonally adjacent points are considered to be neighbors. (Horizontally or vertically adjacent points, i.e., with $|x_k-x_{k-1}|+|y_k-y_{k-1}|=1$, are always regarded as neighbors, so that a point always has four neighbors; but we may or may not allow the additional four points, with $(x_k-x_{k-1}, y_k-y_{k-1})=(\pm1, \pm1)$, to be called neighbors also.)

For example, if S consists of two diagonally adjacent points, $\begin{smallmatrix}p\\&p\end{smallmatrix}$, it is connected in the 8-neighbor sense, but not in the 4-neighbor sense. If we used a hexagonal rather than a square grid for our digital pictures, this ambiguity would not arise, and a point would always have six neighbors.

Let $\bar{S}$ be the complement of S; this includes all the points that lie outside the picture. If S has more than one connected component, then all but one of its components are *holes* in S; the remaining component, which contains the points outside the picture, is called the *background* of S. It turns out that if we want certain basic properties of connectedness to be valid, and if we want certain algorithms to work, we must use opposite types of connectedness for S and for $\bar{S}$—i.e., if we use 4-neighbor connectedness for S, then we must use 8-neighbor connectedness for $\bar{S}$, and vice versa. Thus if S consists of the four points $\begin{smallmatrix}&p&\\p&&p\\&p&\end{smallmatrix}$ it is connected in the 8-neighbor sense, and has a hole (since we use 4-neighbor connectedness for $\bar{S}$); but it is not connected in the 4-neighbor sense, and has no holes, if we use 8-neighbor connectedness for $\bar{S}$. On the other hand, $\begin{smallmatrix}ppp\\p&&p\\ppp\end{smallmatrix}$ is connected, and has a hole, in both senses. (In the case of a hexagonal grid, we can use 6-neighbor connectedness for both S and $\bar{S}$.) On the theory of digital connectedness see [5.24–26].

The *border* of S consists of those points of S that are neighbors of points of $\bar{S}$; the remainder of S is called its *interior*. For example, in the nine point object $\begin{smallmatrix}bbb\\bib\\bbb\end{smallmatrix}$ we have labelled the border points b and the interior point i. A border point of S is called a *simple* point if deleting it from S would not disconnect the part of S inside its neighborhood; in other words, the point (x, y) of S is simple provided that, for any two neighbors of (x, y) that lie in S, there is a path in S, consisting of neighbors of (x, y), that joints the two given neighbors. For example, if the neighborhood of p is $\begin{smallmatrix}n\\p\\n\end{smallmatrix}$, then p is simple in the 4-neighbor sense (since the diagonal neighbor can be ignored), but not in the 8-neighbor sense; while if the neighborhood is $\begin{smallmatrix}n\\np\end{smallmatrix}$, then p is simple in the 8-neighbor sense but not in the 4-neighbor sense. We will need to use simple points in defining "thinning" operations in Subsection 5.6.3.

One often wants to *count* the connected components of a given S, since this is a useful property of S. If none of the components has holes, this can be done in a single row-by-row scan of the picture, as follows: On the top row, count 1 for every run of points of S. On succeeding rows, for each run of points of S that is adjacent to k such runs on the preceding row (where $k \geq 0$), add $1 - k$ to the count. When the scan is complete, it can be shown that the count will equal the total number of components of S. (If the components do have holes, the count will instead equal the number of components minus the number of holes.)

To count the components when they may have holes, one must in effect assign a unique "label" to the points of each component. On the first row, each run of points of S gets its own label; on subsequent rows,
a) if a run is adjacent to no runs on the previous row, it gets a new label;
b) if it is adjacent to just one run on the previous row, it gets that run's label;
c) if it is adjacent to several runs on the previous row, it gets one of their labels, and the other labels, if any, are noted to be equivalent to that label.
When the scan is complete, the number of inequivalent labels used is equal to the number of components. The areas of the components can be determined at the same time, by keeping count of how many times each label was used, and when labels are found to be equivalent, combining their counts.

5.6.2 Size, Compactness, and Convexity

As just indicated, the area of a set S of digital picture points is just the number of points in S. The *perimeter* of S can be defined as the number of border points of S (i.e., as the area of S's border). Alternatively, it can be defined as the number of adjacencies between points of S and points of $\bar{S}$, i.e., the number of pairs of neighboring points such that the first point is in S and the second in $\bar{S}$. This latter definition is essentially the number of moves that one must make in order to follow the border of S completely around; it is always greater than the area of the

border. For example, if S is $\begin{smallmatrix}ppp\\ppp\end{smallmatrix}$, its perimeter in the first sense is 8, in the second

sense 12; if S is $\begin{smallmatrix}ppp\\ppp\end{smallmatrix}$, its perimeters are 3 and 8, respectively; while $\begin{smallmatrix}p\\p\\p\end{smallmatrix}$ has perimeters 3 and 12, respectively.

The *compactness* of S is often measured by A/P^2, where A is its area and P its perimeter. In the real plane, this is greatest $(=4\pi)$ for circles, and is smaller for all other figures. In the digital case, however, it is greatest for certain squares or octagons, depending on how we measure perimeter [5.27].

The *extent* of S in a given direction is the length of its projection perpendicular to that direction. For example, the *height*, or vertical extent, of S, is the number of rows of the picture that S occupies; while its *width*, or horizontal extent, is the number of columns that it occupies. The *diameter* of S is its greatest extent in any direction—or, equivalently, the greatest distance between any two points of S.

S is called *convex* if its cross-section along any line consists of at most a single line segment—or, equivalently, if any line segment whose endpoints are in S must lie entirely in S. This definition must be relaxed somewhat in the digital case to allow small concavities that arise from the digitization process. For example, $\begin{smallmatrix}p\\pp\end{smallmatrix}$ is (digitally) convex, but

$\begin{smallmatrix}\ p\\\ p\\ppp\end{smallmatrix}$

is not. It is easily seen that if S is convex, it must be connected, and can have no holes. The smallest convex set containing S is called the *convex hull* of S.

The theory of digital convexity was first discussed in [5.28]. Algorithms have been developed for constructing the convex hull of S, for breaking an arbitrary S up into convex parts, and for finding concavities in S or "shadows" of S (e.g., points of $\bar{S}$ that are behind points of S when we take cross-sections in various directions); the details will be omitted here.

5.6.3 Arcs, Curves, and Elongatedness

In the digital case, S is called a *closed curve* if it is connected, and every point of S has exactly two neighbors in S. For example, $\begin{smallmatrix} & p & \\ p & & p \\ & ppp & \end{smallmatrix}$ is a closed curve in the 8-neighbor sense, while $\begin{smallmatrix} & p & \\ p & & p \\ & ppp & \end{smallmatrix}$ is a closed curve in the 4-neighbor sense (but not vice versa). S is called an *arc* if it is connected, and all but two of its points have exactly two neighbors in it, while the two exceptional points (the *endpoints*) each have exactly one neighbor. The *slope* of an arc or curve at a point, if defined by the directions to the neighbors, is always a multiple of 45° (or 90°, if points are only allowed to have four neighbors). For many purposes, it is more useful to define slope in terms of the directions to points several steps away along the arc or curve; the farther away we go, the more values become possible, and our choice of how far away to go depends on how fine a level of detail we want in our description of the curve. Similarly, the *curvature* at a point can be defined as the difference between the slopes on the two sides of the point.

Angles on a curve can be defined as local maxima of the curvature [5.29]. Points of *inflection* can be defined as zero-crossings of the curvature; these points separate the curve into successive convex and concave pieces. For an arc to be a *straight line* segment, its slope must be approximately constant; it turns out that this implies that the directions between successive pairs of neighbors along the arc take on at most two values, differing by 45°, where at least one of these values occurs only in runs of length 1, while the other value occurs in runs whose lengths are as equal as possible [5.30]. Thus $\begin{smallmatrix} & pp & \\ ppp & \\ ppp & \end{smallmatrix}$ is a straight line segment (in the 8-neighbor sense), but $\begin{smallmatrix} p & \\ ppp & \end{smallmatrix}$ and $\begin{smallmatrix} pp & \\ p & p \end{smallmatrix}$ are not.

S is *elongated* if its greatest extent is much larger than its least extent. However, this definition does not cover all the situations in which we would want to call S elongated, since a coiled snake is elongated even though its overall shape is circular. We can develop a better definition by introducing the concepts of *shrinking* and *expanding* the set S. Let $S^{(1)}$ be the result of adding to S all points of $\bar{S}$ that are neighbors of points of S, and let $S^{(k)}$ be the result of repeating this process k times $(k = 1, 2, \ldots)$. Thus if S consists of a single point p, $S^{(1)}$ is $\begin{smallmatrix} & p & \\ ppp & \\ & p & \end{smallmatrix}$,

$$p$$
$$ppp$$
and $S^{(2)}$ is $ppppp$, in the 4-neighbor sense, while in the 8-neighbor sense they are
$$ppp$$
$$p$$
$$ppppp$$
$$ppp \qquad ppppp$$
ppp and $ppppp$, respectively. Similarly, let $S^{(-1)}$ be the result of deleting from
$$ppp \qquad ppppp$$
$$ppppp$$
S all points that are neighbors of points of $\bar{S}$, and let $S^{(-k)}$ be the result of repeating
$$p$$
$$ppp$$
this process k times ($k=1, 2, \ldots$). Thus if S is $ppppp$, $S^{(-1)}$ in the 4-neighbor sense
$$ppp$$
$$p \qquad\qquad p$$
is ppp, while in the 8-neighbor sense it is just p.
$$p$$

p

If we shrink and then re-expand, e.g., $(S^{(-k)})^{(k)}$, it is not hard to see that we may not get our original S back; but it can be shown that we must get a subset of it, i.e., we can never get points that were not in S. Let S_k^* be the set of points that we do not get back, and let C be a connected component of S_k^*. Since every point of C must have disappeared under k-step shrinking, the "width" of C is at most $2k$ (i.e., every point of C is at distance at most $2k$ from the complement $\bar{C}$). Suppose that C has area, say, $12k^2$; then its "length", defined as area/width, is at least $6k$. Since this length is three times the width, we can legitimately call C "elongated". Thus if we shrink and re-expand S, the large connected components of points that we lose (large in comparison with the amount of shrinking that we used) are *elongated parts* of S. For example, if S is

$$ppppp$$
$$ppppppppp$$
$$ppppppppp$$
$$pppp$$
$$p$$

then $S^{(-1)}$ is $\qquad pp$ $\qquad\qquad$ (in the 8-neighbor sense)
$$pp$$

$$pppp$$
and $(S^{(-1)})^{(1)}$ is $\quad pppp$.
$$pppp$$
$$pppp$$

We have thus lost three components, two of them consisting of only one point each, while the third consists of 12 points, and is elongated. Further discussion of how this method can be made to work in the presence of noise, and of how a similar scheme involving expansion and re-shrinking can be used to detect clusters of points in a set S, may be found in [5.31–32].

If S is everywhere elongated, it can be *thinned* by removing border points from it, provided that the points removed are simple (see Subsection 5.6.1) and have more than one neighbor in S; these conditions guarantee that the thinning process will not disconnect S, and will not shrink arcs that are already thin. Even if all such border points on one side of S (e.g., the points whose right-hand neighbors are in $\bar{S}$) are removed at once, it can be shown that S will not disconnect; but if points are removed on all sides at once, S may even vanish completely,

e.g., if S is $\begin{matrix} ppppp \\ ppppp \end{matrix}$. More complex thinning algorithms can be used to remove border points on two sides at a time; see, e.g., [5.33]. It should be noted that thinning will not necessarily produce a "thin" object; for example, if S is

$$\begin{matrix} p\ p\ p \\ ppp \\ ppppp \\ ppp \\ p\ p\ p \end{matrix}$$

then thinning has no effect on it.

5.7 Representation of Objects and Pictures

In this section we discuss methods of representing objects that have been extracted from a picture; in particular, using borders or "skeletons" as representations. We also discuss the representation of pictures by relational structures involving objects or regions, their properties, and relationships among them.

5.7.1 Borders

An object is completely determined if we know its *borders*, provided that we also know which side of each border is inside the object and which is outside. Note that an object may have more than one border, if it has holes. Note also that two borders may have points in common, if a hole is near the outside edge of the object; and that a border may pass through the same point twice, if the object is "thin" at that point. Nevertheless, for any given border, simple algorithms exist that will "follow" or track it completely around, starting from any point of it (and given a neighbor of that point which lies outside the object); see, e.g., [5.24].

The sequence of moves that we make while following a border take us repeatedly from a point to one of its neighbors; if 8-neighbor adjacency is used in defining "border", this neighbor must be one of the four horizontal and vertical neighbors, while if 4-neighbor adjacency is used, successive points on the border can also be diagonal neighbors. For concreteness, let us make the latter assumption. Thus the moves can be specified by 3-bit numbers indicating which one of the eight neighbors of the current border point is the next border point; e.g., we can use the convention

$$\begin{matrix} 321 \\ 4p0 \\ 567 \end{matrix}$$

to designate p's eight neighbors by the numbers $0, \ldots 7$. The sequence of moves around the border is thus completely determined by specifying a string of 3-bit numbers. Conversely, any such string defines an (8-neighbor) path of points in the picture, if we are given the starting point. This method of representing object borders—or more generally, arbitrary paths—by strings of 3-bit numbers is called

$$ppp$$
$$p \quad p$$

chain coding. For example, the path $pppp$, starting from its left end, has the

$$p$$
$$p$$

chain code 00012446666. A detailed review of chain coding can be found in [5.34].

If we are given the chain codes of all the borders of an object, as well as a starting point for each chain, and a neighbor of that point which lies outside the object, we can reconstruct the object completely. To do this, we move as directed by each chain code and put down 1's in the (initially blank) picture, while putting down 0's at neighboring points that lie outside the object (these are always determinable, since the initial such point is given). When all the object's borders have been "painted" in this way, we can fill in the interior of the object by letting 1's expand into blanks (but not into 0's).

The border chain codes give a translation-invariant description of an object, since the position of the set of starting points can be chosen arbitrarily. However, this description is not rotation-invariant; in fact, if we rotate a curve, its chain code changes in nontrivial ways (unless the rotation is by a multiple of 90°, in which case we need only add a multiple of 2, modulo 8, to each code). For

$$p$$
$$p$$

example, the line segment $\quad p \quad$ has chain code 11111, but if we rotate it by

$$p$$
$$p$$
$$p$$

$-45°$, it becomes (approximately) $pppppppp$, which has chain code 0000000; this increase in length is needed to compensate for the fact that horizontal and vertical steps are only $1/\sqrt{2} = 0.7$ as long as diagonal steps.

We can obtain a rotation-invariant description of a closed curve by using Fourier methods. (Of course, this description is no longer digital.) For example, let $\theta(s)$ be the slope of the curve at position s (measured along the curve, from an arbitrary starting point). Thus $\theta(s)$ is a periodic function, whose period is the perimeter of the curve. If we expand $\theta(s)$ in a Fourier series, the (squared) magnitudes of the series coefficients are rotation-invariant properties of the curve. For a more detailed discussion of this approach, see [5.35]; other types of Fourier descriptors can also be defined. Approximations to the shape of the curve can be obtained by truncating the series.

5.7.2 Skeletons or "Medial Axes"

A very different way of describing an object is in terms of its "skeleton", which can be defined as follows: At each point p of the object S, there is a largest circle C_p centered at p that is entirely contained in the object. (If p is on the border of S, C_p has radius 0.) The circle C_p may be contained in another circle C_q; we can

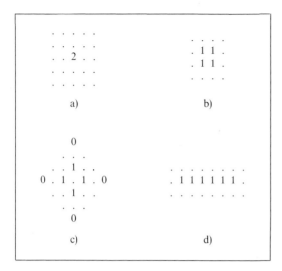

Fig. 5.17. Skeletons of some simple objects. Each skeleton point p is labeled with its associated radius r_p; the remaining points of the original objects are marked by dots

discard C_p in that case. It is easily seen that S is the union of the remaining circles. The set of centers p and radii r_p of these maximal circles C_p is called the *skeleton* of S; it is clear that when the skeleton is specified, S is completely determined.

In the digital case, it is convenient to use squares (S_p) instead of circles; the reasoning in the preceding paragraph remains valid when we do this. It is easily seen that if S_p is contained in S_q, there is some neighbor p' of p such that S_p is contained in $S_{p'}$; thus the points of the skeleton are just those points for which r_p is a local maximum. Unfortunately, this implies that the skeleton is quite disconnected; two neighboring points p and p' cannot both be skeleton points unless $r_p = r_{p'}$. The skeleton is a somewhat less economical way of representing an object than is the border chain code. The skeleton points of some simple objects are shown in Fig. 5.17.

The most natural way of finding the skeleton of a given object is by shrinking and re-expanding it. In the notation used in Subsection 5.6.3, the skeleton points of radius k are just the points that are in $S^{(-k)}$ but not in $(S^{(-k-1)})^{(1)}$ [5.36]. On a method of finding the skeleton using two raster scans of the picture, in opposite directions, see [5.37]. Given the skeleton, the object can be reconstructed by simply expanding each skeleton point a number of times equal to its associated radius. The 8-neighbor expansion (and shrinking) should be used here, if the squares S_p are supposed to have horizontal and vertical sides; if we prefer to use diagonally oriented squares S_p (i.e., diamonds), 4-neighbor expansion and shrinking should be used. Alternating 4 and 8 yields octagons instead of squares [5.31].

5.7.3 Relational Structures

When objects have been extracted from a picture, or the picture has been segmented into regions, it becomes possible to contruct *descriptions* of the picture. Such descriptions can include

a) Representations of the objects (or regions);
b) Properties of the objects—color, texture, shape, etc.;
c) Relations among objects.

Under this last heading, geometrical relations are of particular interest. Some of these are easy to define, e.g., "is adjacent to" or "is inside of" (S is inside T if any path from S to the edge of the picture must pass through T). Others are much fuzzier, e.g., "is near" or "is to the left of". (This last example does not seem to have any simple definition, though it can be roughly defined by a combination of conditions such as the following: S is to the left of T if the centroid of S is farther left than the left-most point of T, and no point of S is as far to the right as the right-most point of T [5.38].)

A relational structure can be represented by a labeled directed graph in which each node represents an object (or region), and is labeled with a list of property values for that object; and arcs join pairs of related regions, and are labeled with lists of relation values. Note that properties and relations can have numerical values (e.g., area or distance); literal or nominal values (e.g., color = red, blue, etc.); or truth values (e.g., convexity, adjacency). Alternatively, the nodes of the graph can represent either objects, properties, or instances of relations; the arc between an object node and a property node is labeled with the value of that property for that object, while the arcs between a pair of object nodes and a relation instance node are labeled with the value of that relation for that pair of objects. (A node is needed for each instance of a relation, if we want to be able to determine which pairs of objects are related.) Relational structures can also be represented in other ways; for some examples, as well as a discussion on how to detect matches between such structures, see [5.39]. More specialized classes of relational structures can be defined for representing line drawings; such structures are widely used in computer graphics [5.40].

"Generalized" relational structures, in which the information is only partially specified, can be used as *models* for classes of pictures [5.38]. Such models play a very important role in analyzing pictures of the given class, since they determine what type of segmentation is wanted, what types of properties should be measured, and so on. Moreover, when the picture analysis process is guided by a model, it becomes possible to adjust the operations used, depending on which part of the picture is being analyzed; for example, when we have identified something in one part of the picture, the model can tell us where to look for other things. For practical scene analysis purposes, it is generally more effective to embody such knowledge about the given class of pictures in the picture analysis programs themselves, rather than in a formal model represented by a data structure.

References

5.1   R.O. DUDA, P.E. HART: *Pattern Classification and Scene Analysis* (Wiley, New York 1973)
5.2   A. ROSENFELD: *Picture Processing by Computer* (Academic Press, New York 1969)
5.3   A. ROSENFELD, A.C. KAK: *Digital Picture Processing* (Academic Press, New York 1976)
5.4   A. ROSENFELD: Computing Surveys 1, 147 (1969)
5.5   A. ROSENFELD: Computing Surveys 5, 81 (1973)
5.6   A. ROSENFELD: Computer Graphics and Image Processing 1, 394 (1972)
5.7   A. ROSENFELD: Computer Graphics and Image Processing 3, 178 (1974)

5.8   B. S. LIPKIN, A. ROSENFELD: *Picture Processing and Psychopictorics* (Academic Press, New York 1970) pp. 289–370

5.9   R. M. HARALICK, K. SHANMUGAM, I. DINSTEIN: IEEE Trans. Systems, Man, and Cybernetics SMC-**3**, 610 (1973)

5.10 D. I. BARNEA, H. F. SILVERMAN: IEEE Trans. Computers C-**21**, 179 (1972)

5.11 R. N. NAGEL, A. ROSENFELD: Proc. IEEE **60**, 242 (1972)

5.12 B. WIDROW: Pattern Recognition **5**, 175 (1973)

5.13 M. A. FISCHLER, R. A. ELSCHLAGER: IEEE Trans. Computers C-**22**, 67 (1973)

5.14 A. K. GRIFFITH: J. Assoc. Computing Machinery **20**, 62 (1973)

5.15 M. HUECKEL: J. Assoc. Computing Machinery **18**, 113 (1971)

5.16 M. HUECKEL: J. Assoc. Computing Machinery **20**, 634 (1973)

5.17 A. ROSENFELD, M. THURSTON: IEEE Trans. Computers C-**20**, 562 (1971)

5.18 A. ROSENFELD, M. THURSTON, Y-H. LEE: IEEE Trans. Computers C-**21**, 677 (1972)

5.19 C. K. CHOW, T. KANEKO: In *Frontiers of Pattern Recognition*, ed. by S. WATANABE (Academic Press, New York 1972) pp. 61–82

5.20 C. R. BRICE, C. L. FENNEMA: Artificial Intelligence **1**, 205 (1970)

5.21 S. L. HOROWITZ, T. PAVLIDIS: Proc. 2nd Intern. Joint Conf. Pattern Recognition **1974**, 424

5.22 U. MONTANARI: Comm. Assoc. Computing Machinery **14**, 335 (1971)

5.23 A. MARTELLI: Computer Graphics and Image Processing **1**, 169 (1972)

5.24 A. ROSENFELD: J. Assoc. Computing Machinery **17**, 146 (1970)

5.25 A. ROSENFELD: J. Assoc. Computing Machinery **20**, 81 (1973)

5.26 A. ROSENFELD: Information and Control **26**, 24 (1974)

5.27 A. ROSENFELD: IEEE Trans. Systems, Man, and Cybernetics SMC-**4**, 221 (1974)

5.28 J. SKLANSKY: Pattern Recognition **2**, 3 (1970)

5.29 A. ROSENFELD, E. JOHNSTON: IEEE Trans. Computers C-**22**, 875 (1973)

5.30 A. ROSENFELD: IEEE Trans. Computers C-**23**, 1264 (1974)

5.31 A. ROSENFELD, J. L. PFALTZ: Pattern Recognition **1**, 33 (1968)

5.32 A. ROSENFELD, C. M. PARK, J. P. STRONG: EASCON '69 Record **1969**, 264

5.33 R. STEFANELLI, A. ROSENFELD: J. Assoc. Computing Machinery **18**, 255 (1971)

5.34 H. FREEMAN: Computing Surveys **6**, 57 (1974)

5.35 C. T. ZAHN, R. Z. ROSKIES: IEEE Trans. Computers C-**21**, 269 (1972)

5.36 J. C. MOTT-SMITH: In *Picture Processing and Psychopictorics*, ed. by B. S. LIPKIN and A. ROSENFELD (Academic Press, New York 1970) pp. 267–278

5.37 A. ROSENFELD, J. L. PFALTZ: J. Assoc. Computing Machinery **13**, 471 (1966)

5.38 P. H. WINSTON: "Learning structural descriptions from examples", AI TR-231 (MIT, Cambridge, Mass. 1970)

5.39 H. G. BARROW, R. J. POPPLESTONE: In *Machine Intelligence* 6, ed. by B. MELTZER and D. MICHIE (University Press, Edinburgh 1971) pp. 377–396

5.40 R. WILLIAMS: Computing Surveys **3**, 1 (1971)

6. Speech Recognition and Understanding

JARED J. WOLF

With 6 Figures

Speech is man's most natural channel of communication, so it is only natural that it should be the subject of much work in pattern recognition. Recognizing speech is difficult, for the nature of the speech communication process is such that the resulting acoustic signal is highly encoded and full of contextual dependencies. Speech perception on the part of a human listener requires him to utilize his linguistic knowledge to undo the encoding. Machines that aspire to recognize the same signal must be able to apply similar constraints. Current work in automatic speech recognition ranges from systems that recognize isolated words from limited vocabularies to systems that "understand" the meaning of naturally spoken sentences, using higher level linguistic constraints in addition to the information derived from the speech signal itself. This chapter describes the techniques developed and the progress made in speech recognition and understanding in the early 1970's.

6.1 Principles of Speech, Recognition, and Understanding

6.1.1 Introduction

The study of speech recognition has been a part of pattern recognition research for as long as it has been meaningful to talk of pattern recognition itself, if only because of the extremely "everyday" nature of speech. We are so accustomed to communicating with others (with little apparent effort) by means of speech that is seems only natural that we should strive towards communicating with machines in the same way.

The speech signal carries many messages. In addition to the linguistic message, the identification of which we call "speech recognition", the speech signal carries information about the speaker's identity, his language, his physical and emotional state, and his geographical and societal background. Transmitting a linguistic message is most often the primary purpose of speech communication, and it is the recognition of this message by machines that would be most useful.

Aside from sheer laziness, why should one wish to communicate with machines by speaking to them? As implied by the "laziness" argument, speech is the primary and most natural output channel of human communication. It allows a higher data rate than other output channels, it allows communication without specialized training, it leaves the body free for other activities, and it can be transmitted by means of inexpensive and readily available terminal equipment. [For a more complete discussion of these attractive features (and some less attractive ones as well), see [6.1–4]]. To such practical justifications for work on speech recognition should be added its contribution towards improved understanding of human communication processes, both natural language in general and speech production and perception in particular.

There is presently a great deal of work going on in the general area of automatic speech recognition, both in building speech recognition systems and in research relevant to the support of speech recognition efforts. To appreciate the magnitude and diversity of this work, one need only refer to the proceedings of the IEEE Symposium on Speech Recognition [6.5,6], the Stockholm Speech Communication Seminar [6.7], the Leningrad Symposium on Auditory Analysis and Perception of Speech [6.8], the IEEE 1972 Conference on Speech Communication and Processing [6.9], the biannual meetings of the Acoustical Society of America, or any of a dozen conferences on acoustics, phonetics, pattern recognition, information theory, communications, and computer applications. A rich literature is growing in the IEEE Transactions on Acoustics, Speech, and Signal Processing (formerly Transactions on Audio and Electroacoustics), the International Journal of Man-Machine Studies, the Journal of the Acoustical Society of America, and others.

It may be a mark of maturity that it is now reasonable to identify subfields within the general field of speech recognition. The precise position of a dividing line is not quite clear at this point, but between recognition of isolated words at one extreme and understanding of continuous speech at the other there lie vast differences in approach and philosophy. I shall elaborate on this in Subsection 6.1.3. In the remainder of this section, I shall discuss the nature of the speech communication process and how it influences approaches to automatic recognition. Section 6.2 presents some recent developments in automatic speech recognition, and Section 6.3 is devoted to the newest development in the field, *speech understanding*. Section 6.4 presents some modest assessments of the future of the field.

This chapter will not cover to any great extent the past history of the field of speech recognition. Rather it is intended to bring up to date the existing collection of surveys of the field: the early surveys by FATEHCHAND [6.10], and DAVID and SELFRIDGE [6.11], the excellent articles by LINDGREN [6.12,13], which also present much basic acoustic-phonetics, the report by HYDE [6.14], which contains an excellent discussion following the survey, and the chapters by HILL [6.2] and LEA [6.15], which extend the coverage to about 1970. DENES [6.16] gave a historical perspective on the techniques employed from the earliest days of speech recognition to the present day. For more recent reports, see [6.17] and the references cited at the beginning of this section. For papers of a more philosophical bent, see [6.18–25]. For coverage of work in the Soviet Union, not very well referenced in the West, see [6.26–31].

6.1.2 The Nature of Speech Communication

Speech is a complex sound produced by the human vocal apparatus, which consists of organs primarily used for breathing and eating: the lungs, trachea, larynx, throat, mouth, and nose. The source of energy for the production of these sounds is the reservoir of air in the lungs. Sound is generated in two ways. If air is forced through the larynx with the vocal folds appropriately positioned and tensioned, it sets them into oscillation, so that they release puffs of air in a quasi-periodic fashion at rates of about 80 to 200 Hz for male speakers, faster for women and children. This glottal source is rich in harmonics, and it excites the acoustic resonances of the vocal tract above the larynx, which filter the sound. These sharp resonances, called *formants*, are determined by the shape of the throat, mouth, and, if the velum (soft palate) is open, the nasal cavity. It is through manipulation of the vocal tract shape by the articulators (tongue, jaw, lips and velum) that we control the formant frequencies that differentiate the various *voiced* speech sounds. These are the vowels, nasal consonants, liquids (/r/ and /l/), and glides (/w/ and /y/). Only the lowest three or four formants, up to about 4 kHz, are perceptually significant.

The other sound source used in speech is turbulent noise, produced by forcing air through some constriction (such as between the tongue and teeth in th-sounds) or by an abrupt release of pressure built up at some point of closure in the vocal tract (such as behind the lips in a /p/). The spectral peaks associated with these *fricated* sounds generally lie between 2 and 8 kHz and are primarily determined by the position and the shape of the constriction. Some sounds, the *voiced frica-tives*, such as /z/ and /v/, have both voiced and turbulent excitation.

Distinguishable differences in the voice signal can be produced by quite small changes in the way the vocal tract is manipulated, so a very large number of sounds can be produced. For the communication of language, however, only a restricted number of sounds, or more accurately, sound classes, are used. Words in English are made up of only 40 or so of these *phonemes*, which correspond roughly to the pronunciation symbols in a dictionary. (Phonemic symbols are conventionally enclosed by virgules, e.g., /t/.) Since there are relatively few of these elemental sound units, most speech recognition systems choose phonemes or phoneme-like units as the units of recognition.

This concept of elemental units does not reduce speech recognition to the sequential recognition of 40 or so fixed patterns. The acoustic realizations of phonemes in real speech are drastically different from their characteristics in isolated environments. When phonemes are strung together into words, the acoustic characteristics of successive phonemes become overlapped, due to the dynamics of the articulators and the tendency for an articulator to anticipate the position it will next assume. (For example, when you say the /t/ of the word "tin", the lips are spread apart, but in "twin", they are pursed together. Since the lips are not used for the articulation of the /t/, they are free to assume the position for the following phoneme). These context effects, along with effects due to linguistic stress, speed of talking, the size of a particular speaker's vocal tract, and variation in the way a speaker says a given word from repetition to repetition make the decoding of the speech signal a non-trivial problem. To be sure, the speech wave does contain much information directly related to the phonemes intended by the speaker, but the details of the coding are complex [6.32–35].

The phonemes themselves can be grouped into classes according to the ways they can modify and affect one another when they are in proximity in normal speech. It is convenient to describe these classes in terms of about fifteen binary *distinctive features* [6.13, 36–38], most of which have straightforward articulatory and acoustic attributes, such as voiced/unvoiced, nasal/non-nasal, fricated/unfricated, tongue position: back/front, high/low, etc. Distinctive features have proved to be quite powerful in describing the phonological changes that underlie the contextual effects referred to above. For that reason, some speech recognition systems use them as recognition units or as ways of organizing their recognition of phoneme-sized units.

Knowledge of the mechanism of production of speech sounds is certainly essential for a speech recognizer, but it is not sufficient for unraveling the speech code. It is equally as important to consider the speech communication process from a broader viewpoint.

"Speech is a form of communication between human beings which involves the generation and reception of a complex acoustic signal. The process by which thoughts in the mind of the talker are communicated, and so form reciprocal thoughts in the mind of the listener, may be thought of as a coding operation which takes place over a hierarchy of processing levels. At the highest level we have the thoughts, or possibly the fundamental concepts which give rise to these thoughts. The thoughts are encoded on a lower level, which we shall refer to as the linguistic level, in the form of words. The words are encoded on successively lower levels, involving neural processing and articulatory movements, until the lowest level is reached with the acoustic signal." Hyde [Ref. 6.14, p. 2]

Each level of encoding adds redundancy to the eventual acoustic signal. Choosing the words to express the thoughts employs the redundancy of the grammatical structure of the language and the semantics of the particular topic of discourse. Intonation and timing provide cues to the grammatical structure. The acoustic realization of the phonemes involves many redundant cues, so many in fact that a speaker is permitted considerable variation in just how he pronounces them. He may even leave some phonemes out entirely. This sloppiness is permissible because the speaker knows that the listener can use the redundancies to understand the message [6.39].

"... and how little we actually hear, we realize when we go to a foreign theatre; for there what troubles us is not so much that we cannot understand what the actors say as that we cannot hear their words. The fact is that we hear quite as little under similar conditions at home, only our mind, being fuller of English verbal associations, supplies the requisite material for comprehension upon a much slighter auditory hint." James [Ref. 6.40, p. 159].

This quotation makes two points of relevance to speech recognition. Perhaps James's principal point is that speech communication is not accomplished via the acoustic signal alone, but also by reference to the structure of the language and the semantic context of the verbal communication. The second point is that the discreteness of the words of spoken language as we perceive it is absent in the speech signal; it is obscured by the levels of encoding between the words and the spoken utterance; it is reconstructed by the listener through his linguistic competence. An automatic speech recognition system faced with the same input signal must be capable of doing a similar reconstruction.

6.1.3 Approaches to Automatic Recognition

Early work in automatic speech recognition assumed that the information necessary for recognition was contained in the speech signal alone. Once the basic principles of the acoustic coding of the phonemes were uncovered, simple extensions of the vocabularies would lead to recognition of virtually unlimited speech. The error of such a simplistic viewpoint soon became apparent, and it was recognized that "automatic speech recognition—as the human accomplishes it—will probably be possible only through the proper analysis and application of grammatical, contextual, and semantic constraints" [Ref. 6.33, p. 199]. Information would still need to be extracted from the speech signal, so work in this aspect of speech recognition has continued to evolve. Speech recognition work utilizing phoneme-sequential probabilities was reported in 1958 [6.41], but the very real difficulties involved in understanding how to apply higher level constraints prevented any real progress on this front until the late 1960's. Even now, it should be said that this work is only beginning.

A rough idea of the potential contribution of the higher level linguistic sources of knowledge may be inferred from the results of the spectrogram reading experiments of KLATT and STEVENS [6.42]. Human experts attempting to read spectrograms (plots of energy vs. time and frequency, used by speech researchers) of spoken sentences produced error rates on the order of 25% in making only a "partial" phonetic transcription based on spectrographic evidence alone, yet they were able to achieve an error rate of only 4% in identifying the words of the sentences when permitted to make use of knowledge of the (200 word) vocabulary and of syntactic and semantic constraints.

In the mid-1960's it became apparent that one could build isolated-word recognizers of practical accuracy, given sufficient constraints from restricting the size of the vocabulary and training to the voice characteristics of individual speakers. This has effectively created a subfield within speech recognition, where techniques not applicable to more general applications may be used. For example, there is no word boundary problem, for the boundaries of the word coincide with the beginning and end of the utterance. Given a small enough vocabulary and the limited duration of the words, it is possible to recognize the words without necessarily segmenting the signal into linguistic elements such as phonemes; they can be treated as more abstract patterns of phonetically motivated measurements.

The distinction between such isolated word recognition and the more general problem of continuous speech recognition is one aspect of the division of the field mentioned in the Introduction 6.1.1. Continuous speech recognition, then, addresses the problem of recognizing utterances in which the words are strung together, as in normal conversational speech. This introduces the problem of coping with longer utterances, finding the boundaries between words, and coping with the way word pronunciations themselves may change due to the context. On the other hand, continuous speech is subject to prosodic, syntactic, and semantic constraints (which by and large do not apply to the isolated word situation), which provide additional levels of redundancy, if only they can be effectively applied.

In 1970, a study group convened by the Advanced Research Projects Agency (ARPA) of the United States Department of Defense was asked to consider the feasibility of building speech recognition systems of substantially greater power, which would build on recent advances in computational linguistics, artificial intelligence, and computer science to implement such higher-level sources of knowledge. The report of this group, in recommending the initiation of such a program of research and development, coined a new descriptor, *speech understanding*:

"We call the type of system to be investigated a *speech understanding* system. The inclusion of *understanding* is to distinguish the systems somewhat from *speech recognition* systems. It does not so much emphasize enhanced intellectual status, but emphasizes that the system is to perform some task making use of speech. *Thus, the errors that count are not errors in speech recognition, but errors in task accomplishment.* If the system can guess (infer, deduce, ...) correctly what the user wants, then its inability to determine exactly what the user said should not be held against it—even as for you and I." NEWELL et al. [Ref. 6.3, p. 6].

(This contrast introduces a terminological dilemma: does *speech recognition* refer to the general problem of making machines able to apprehend speech, or only to the subfield of that problem that is to be contrasted to *speech understanding?* I see little alternative but to use *speech recognition* for both senses, relying on context to distinguish between them. Hence until this point, I have been using the term in referring to the general field; in the following I shall use it to refer to an approach that is to be contrasted to the speech understanding approach).

In the past, the emphasis had generally been that the higher-level linguistic constraints would be used in order to recognize what the speaker had *said* (that is, his words); the ARPA study group proposed to shift the emphasis to the recognition of what the speaker *meant*. In other words, instead of applying the higher-level constraints to already recognized words, one should use those constraints as an integral part of the recognition process. They should guide the course of the recognition process rather than merely operate on the results of it. In spite of the ARPA group's disclaimer of "enhanced intellectual status" for the proposed systems, the work that this report engendered has led to research-oriented speech understanding systems in which these higher-level linguistic sources of knowledge are being applied in an effective way for the first time. This new development is the subject of Section 6.3.

A growing field within pattern recognition is the syntactic approach to pattern recognition, in which the techniques of formal linguistics are used to describe and analyze patterns with internal structure, most often pictures [6.43–48]. Syntactic pattern recognition attempts to model the structure of subpatterns within a larger pattern by means of a grammar of a formal (artificial) language. Speech is a pattern with considerable internal structure (e.g., phonemes and syllables within words, words within sentences, and sentences within dialogues). In fact, it is slightly ironical that many of the basic terms used in syntactic pattern recognition have been borrowed (and in the process, formalized) from natural linguistics (e.g. syntax, grammar, parsing, semantics). Speech recognition and understanding researchers generally use such terms in their natural linguistic sense. (N.B. In this chapter, all linguistic terminology is used in its natural linguistic sense, except for occasional explicit references to syntactic pattern recognition.) Outside of the obvious uses of the syntax of the words in an utterance, the techniques of syntactic pattern recognition have as yet made only a little impact on speech recognition and understanding research.

6.2 Recent Developments in Automatic Speech Recognition

6.2.1 Introduction

After the work on speech understanding had been initiated, it might have been reasonable to expect that speech recognition, as I have distinguished it above, would become overshadowed and less important. On the contrary, it now appears as vigorous as ever. There are two reasons for this: the support that such work can provide for more ambitious speech understanding systems and the growing practicality of limited capacity speech recognition systems.

To a first approximation, it may be said that any speech understanding system must have some sort of a speech recognizer as its interface to the speech signal itself. No amount of higher-level magic will permit the message to be understood without its having been listened to! The requirements on, and the form of, the "front end" of a speech understanding system are somewhat more general than in a limited speech recognition system, but both types of system can draw upon many of the same techniques of signal processing and acoustic-phonetic decision making logic. Furthermore, given the very large size of present speech understanding systems, it may be more practical in many cases to set certain kinds of general speech recognition research in the context of more limited systems.

A number of factors have combined to make limited capacity speech recognition systems, primarily word recognizers, much more practical than they have been in the past. The primary factor, of course, is the improvement in performance of such systems: sufficient accuracy, adaptability to the talker, and ability to function in spite of environmental noise. Secondly, the costs of implementing these systems as combinations of special purpose circuitry and small digital computers have been steadily decreasing. Finally, applications for limited speech recognizers have been identified and developed to the point where such systems are practical enough to become commercially viable.

6.2.2 Isolated Word Recognition

In the context of "isolated word recognition", "word" means a word or a short phrase that can be treated for recognition purposes as a single unit. Most recent isolated word recognizers do not attempt to segment the signal into phoneme-sized units and recognize each one individually. Instead the entire word is treated as an acoustic pattern according to the customary model of statistical pattern recognition: a set of measurements is made on the acoustic pattern, which is then classified by comparison with stored reference patterns. Structural relationships in the acoustic pattern are largely ignored. These systems make full use of the fact that their input is an isolated short utterance from a limited repertoire. The techniques employed are usually not generalizable to continuous speech. See, for example, [6.49–51].

One example of this type of system is the VOICE COMMAND SYSTEM introduced by Scope Electronics Inc. in 1971 and modified slightly since then [6.52]. In this system, the speech signal is transformed into short-time power spectra by a set of 16 bandpass filters covering the spectrum to 5 kHz. These spectra are read at a rate of 60 per second. These data are then read into a minicomputer and transformed by a "coding compressor" into a pattern 120 bits in length. The coding compression algorithm has not been published, but one of its actions in transforming a variable duration set of spectra into a fixed length pattern is to warp the time axis nonlinearly so as to distribute the changes of spectral energy equally across 8 time intervals. It is claimed that this eliminates problems caused by varying rates of articulation. A user must "train" the system by uttering five examples of each vocabulary item. Reference patterns and decision thresholds are formed from these training utterances. Recognition of a new utterance is accomplished by correlating the resulting 120 bit pattern against all the references and selecting the one whose correlation is highest, provided that a rejection threshold is also exceeded. In order for a new user to use the system, he must retrain it with examples of his own voice. For a 40 word vocabulary, about 97% accuracy is reported, where the 3% error includes both rejections and misclassifications.

Different feature extraction and classification techniques are used in the VIP-100 (Voice Information Processor) being offered by Threshold Technology Inc. (TTI) [6.53, 54]. In this system also, a short-time spectral analysis is performed by a set of bandpass filters. The filter outputs are processed by special spectral shape and spectral change detectors (realized in hardware) into a sequence of values of 32 binary acoustic features similar to those described by Martin [6.55]. Five of these features are broad-class features such as vowel/vowel-like, long pause, short pause, unvoiced noise-like consonant, and burst. The remaining 27 features represent measurements corresponding to phoneme-like events. These binary features form the input to a minicomputer, which performs the other functions of the system. Time normalization is performed by dividing the duration of the word into 16 equal time segments and forming an equivalent 32 bit pattern for each. The resulting 512 bit pattern thus represents the word. Recognition is accomplished by a weighted correlation between the test pattern and all reference patterns. Correlations are also performed after shifting the two patterns one time segment in each direction, and the reference word producing the highest overall correlation is selected, providing that the second best correlation is not too close to the best. As in the previous system, the reference patterns for the vocabulary set are formed from training utterances by the particular speaker. Accuracies greater than 99% for 32 word vocabularies have been reported [6.56].

Isolated word recognition systems are also being applied to tasks where multiple-word utterances are needed. This, of course, requires that the user pause for at least a fraction of a second between words. The system may provide a visual display of the words recognized and require the user to confirm the correctness of all the words in the utterance before taking action on it. In a television tube quality control application, TTI's system displays to the inspector (who must use both hands to handle and measure the tube) the type of measurement it expects next. If the spoken measurement is outside the expected range of variation, the system takes a special action, such as flashing a light [6.57].

In another TTI application, programming of numerically controlled machine tools, the user examines a blueprint and speaks a specification of each action the tool is to take [6.58]. The numerical control "language" has a simple but rigid syntax: each specification begins with a command, followed by directions, coordinates, and measurements in a particular order. Once the initial word is recognized, the visual display prompts the user for the information required to follow and also displays his responses as recognized. The syntax of the application language allows the system to recognize each word from a *subvocabulary* of only those words that are appropriate at each point in the sequence. Such an application may have 100 or more words in its total vocabulary, but at each point, only 20 to 30 may be meaningful, and it is from those reduced sets that the system need make its choice. This is an example of how syntactic and semantic constraints can be used to increase the capabilities of even a limited capacity isolated word recognition system. A very similar system has recently been described by HATON [6.59].

Another type of pattern-matching isolated word recognizer was recently described by ITAKURA [6.60]. In this system, the speech signal is represented by linear prediction coefficients (LPC) computed from the windowed speech waveform at 15 ms intervals. Linear prediction is a type of analysis in which the signal is modeled as the output of an all-pole filter, which is particularly appropriate for speech [6.61–66]. ITAKURA has shown that the residual prediction error is an appropriate distance metric in the LPC space. A word is recognized by comparing its LPC description with those of a set of reference patterns representing the vocabulary items. A dynamic programming algorithm effectively warps the time axis of the unknown word to achieve the best fit to each reference pattern. In the experiment described, the reference patterns were single examples of 200 Japanese place names spoken by a single speaker. For 2000 test utterances by the same speaker, spoken over a 3 week period, a recognition rate of 97.3%, rejection rate of 1.65%, and error rate of 1.05% were reported. The system operated with speech transmitted through the telephone system and included automatic spectral normalization to compensate for variations in transducer and transmission response.

A somewhat different use of syntactic constraints is found in an "isolated utterance sentence recognition system" described by NEELY and WHITE [6.67]. The input to the system is a sentence spoken with pauses between the words. The system consists of an isolated word recognizer followed by a syntax analyzer. The word recognizer uses a "character string" mapping and comparison technique [6.68] to produce a list of candidate words ordered by confidence. The syntax analyzer chooses the best word sequence from the sequence of candidate lists according to a very simple syntactic criterion. The grammar is preprocessed to prepare a "binary context" table of all pairs of words that can legally occur adjacent in a sentence. The word from the candidate lists that is identified with the highest degree of confidence is selected as the anchor point for the syntax checking; this word is assumed to be correct. The words to the immediate right and left of the anchor word are then examined. If the top candidate is consistent with the anchor word according to the binary context table, it is accepted; otherwise succeeding word candidates are examined until one is accepted. Then the words adjacent to the newly accepted words are examined in a similar way. If a candidate list becomes exhausted, the system backtracks, rejects a previously accepted word, and continues from there. The process continues until all the words in the sentence pass the pairwise syntactic consistency check or all possible combinations have been exhausted, in which case the sentence is rejected. Results were given for a 36 word vocabulary and a context-free grammar of 13 production rules. For 200 spoken sentences averaging 4 words each, without the syntax checking, 93% of the words and 70% of the sentences were correctly recognized. With the syntax checking, the accuracies increased to 95% and 80%, respectively. All of the anchor words were correctly recognized.

Some word recognizers exploit rather than ignore the syllabic and phonemic structure of the utterance. Many of the techniques employed in these systems are generalizable to continuous speech recognition and understanding. See, for example, [6.29, 30, 69–71].

An interesting example of such a system was described by MEDRESS [6.72]. As in many systems, a short-time spectral analysis is performed by a 36-channel filter bank. This spectral representation is then examined in detail by segmentation and distinctive feature estimation algorithms. The initial phase involves estimation of those features whose acoustic manifestations are least dependent on their phonemic environment and which appear most clearly in the acoustic signal; in the second phase, other more dependent and less reliable features are determined by utilizing phonological constraints on the word structure and additional measurements that depend on the initial measurements. For example, if it is clear that the word begins with a $/t/$, then the only phonemes that can follow it are a vowel, $/r/$, or $/w/$, so the recognizer need not consider any other possibilities. The description of the word that results from the two phases of recognition may or may not be sufficiently complete to assign a single phonemic label to each segment, depending on the phonological constraints and whether the acoustic evidence was clear enough to permit a decision to be made about every feature (that is, a specific phoneme is specified as the intersection of several features, so an incomplete feature analysis may specify a small class of phonemes). The resulting description is then compared with the dictionary pronunciations for all vocabulary entries. If no match or more than one match is found, then various error handling techniques are possible, but these had not been implemented in the system described. A 105 word vocabulary of single-syllable, single-morpheme words was used; the recognition algorithms were organized so as to exploit the phonological constraints for such words. With the exception of initial $/y/$ and nasals, a phonemic recognition rate of over 90% was achieved for a set of utterances used to formulate the recognition algorithms, for new repetitions by the same (three) speakers, and for new utterances by four other speakers (all adult male). Little difference in performance was noted for the new speakers. It was felt that the hierarchical structure of robust decisions contributed to the ability to recognize the words spoken by new speakers. (For $/y/$ and nasals, the generalizability to new speakers was not good).

In another implementation of a similar system [6.73], the vocabularies were composed of multisyllable words or short sentences. Instead of every segment, only the initial consonant cluster and vowel and the final consonant cluster were examined, and strident fricatives were located. The lexical search procedure contained no error recovery for the cases where no match or more than one match was found. Average word recognition accuracies of 94% for a 100 word list and 95% and 92% for two 60 sentence lists were reported for five speakers, only one of whom had been used to tune up the system.

6.2.3 Continuous Speech Recognition

Continuous speech recognition (CSR) implies working with a speech signal in which the words are not isolated, but continuously strung together, as in normal speech. Although an ultimate aim of CSR is the specification of the words spoken, many systems have less ambitious goals, such as the recognition of particular words in the speech signal (word spotting) or recognition only into a sequence of phonemes. Other system, however, do use vocabulary and linguistic contraints in order to attempt to deduce the words themselves.

Work on various aspects of CSR dates from the first use of computers and speech [6.74, 75], but the system by REDDY [6.76–78] was the first to segment and recognize a fairly complete set of phoneme-sized units for unrestricted speech. REDDY'S system used no preprocessing hardware; the signal itself was sampled by an analog-to-digital converter. Segmentation into phoneme-sized units was based on amplitude and zero-crossing information, and classification was based on parameters derived from one (or possibly more) Fourier series expansion of a short interval during each segment. A phoneme recognition accuracy of about 81% was achieved for utterances from a single speaker.

REDDY'S work led directly to that of VICENS [6.79], who used slightly more hardware processing of the signal (amplitude and zero-crossings in three hardware-filtered frequency bands), also segmented the signal into phoneme-sized units, and then labeled them from an alphabet of fifteen classes (9 vowel classes, 2 fricative classes, and individual classes for nasals, consonants, stops, and transitions). Recognition at the word level was then accomplished by comparison with a lexicon. Time constraints prevented searching the entire lexicon, so heuristics based on the most robust acoustic characteristics were used to direct and limit the search. The word comparison algorithms posited one-to-one correspondences for the more robust segments first, then fit the less robust ones. They allowed for the possibility of missing or extra segments and for certain errors in labeling. VICENS constructed both isolated word recognizers (one of which was syntax-directed, similar to those described in the previous subsection) and a continuous speech recognizer. This last system is the most important, even though it boasted only a 16 word vocabulary and an extremely rigid syntax in which only 192 sentences were possible, because it used the syntactic constraints to deduce the possible locations of words in the continuous acoustic stream. This system could recognize about 85% of the sentences spoken by the two speakers used to train the lexicon, corresponding to a word recognition accuracy of 96%.

A CSR project of somewhat larger scope was conducted for several years by IBM [6.80–82]. The system consisted of two stages, an acoustic processor followed by a linguistic processor. In the acoustic processor, the signal was spectrally analyzed by a hardware filter bank. The spectra were grouped into phoneme-sized segments by segmentation algorithms. These segments were then analyzed by a "steady-state classifier", which produced a phonemic label for each segment, and by a "dynamic classifier", which considered the region from the center of one segment to the center of the next as the transition of a phoneme pair. A "dual classifier" then reconciled these two descriptions into a single phoneme string, which was fed to the linguistic processor. The linguistic processor used the syntax of the language, the pronunciations of the vocabulary items, including how those pronunciations can vary, and statistics describing the language and the behavior of the acoustic processor to convert the errorful phoneme string into a word sequence. In 1973, with a 250 word vocabulary and a context-free grammar permitting 14 million possible sentences, the following results based on 153 sentence-length utterances by five speakers were reported: 38% of the utterances were correctly decoded, 43% were incorrectly decoded, and 19% failed to be completely analyzed. On a word basis, 78% of the words in these utterances were correctly identified [6.82]. This project has since been carried on by Rockwell International. In 1974, for a roughly comparable vocabulary and grammar, sentence accuracies for six speakers ranging from 33% to 89% were reported [6.83].

IBM has since embarked on a larger, more ambitious, and longer-term CSR project, having as its eventual goal a vocabulary of 10000 words and little restriction on the grammar. The overall system design is apparently similar to the previous system, i.e., acoustic processing producing a noisy phonemic string, followed by statistical linguistic decoding [6.84–86].

The DRAGON speech recognition system by BAKER [6.87–90] takes a somewhat different approach to the representation of the sources of knowledge needed to perform continuous speech recognition. A single abstract model, that of a probabilistic function of a Markov process, is used at every level of representation: acoustic, lexical, syntactic, etc. The relations between a sequence of observations (e.g., a sequence of acoustic parameter values) and a "hidden" Markov process (e.g., the underlying sequence of phonemes) are represented by matrices of Markov transition probabilities and probabilities relating the observations to the "hidden" Markov states. Given that the required knowledge can be satisfactorily represented in this manner, the matching procedure in such a system consists of evaluating the *a posteriori* probability of the sequence of interest, and the search of the problem space may be done in an optimal fashion by a relatively efficient algorithm. These principles have been implemented in a CSR system embodying fairly basic knowledge at the acoustic-phonetic, lexical, and syntactic levels. For a total of 61 sentences from three tasks, with vocabularies ranging from 24 to 195 words, word recognition accuracies on the order of 90% were reported; sentence accuracies were not given [6.89].

Before going on to discuss total speech understanding systems, let me simply mention six other recent CSR projects. MARTIN [6.56] built a system that recognized connected sequences of the ten digits, using filter bank spectral analysis, feature abstraction by analog-threshold logic, and word recognition by sequential logic that took into account alternate pronunciations of the words. No adaptation to the speaker was required. For 34000 spoken digits by 155 talkers from all the major dialect areas of the United States, digit-recognition accuracies of 88–94% were reported. DE MORI and his colleagues have made extensive use of syntactic pattern recognition techniques at the acoustic parametric level in building an acoustic processor that is intended to become the "front end" for a speech understanding system [6.91–93]. DERKACH and his colleagues have built an experimental CSR system with a 300 word vocabulary and a hierarchical structure that includes syntactic and semantic analyses [6.31]. LEA [6.94] has demonstrated that the voice fundamental frequency contour can be used to detect the majority of syntactic constituent boundaries in English sentences. Such a technique suggests that prosodic cues can be used to form syntactic hypotheses that can be used to guide phonetic recognition within constituents [6.94,95]. Lɪ and his colleagues investigated the nature of the interaction between segmental and prosodic features (particularly syllable stress) in the context of a "word spotting" application [6.96]. WILLEMS built a prosodic recognizer that recognizes the structure of spoken English numbers (zero to nine hundred ninety-nine) from the speech envelope and fundamental frequency contour only [6.97].

6.3 Speech Understanding

6.3.1 Introduction

The term "speech understanding" was introduced into the literature in the report by NEWELL et al. [6.3] to denote the type of speech recognition system that would make heavy use of higher level linguistic constraints in order to perform a task using speech input. The use of the word "understanding" in this context does not mean a broad comprehension of the world in general, but rather an ability to deal with the meaning of an utterance within a narrowly defined domain of discourse. We must say "narrowly defined" because that is a fair description of our current ability to deal with the representation of meaning.

The NEWELL report does not fully define the distinction between speech recognition and speech understanding systems, although it does address the issue. WALKER makes the distinction somewhat clearer:

"In contrast to the goals of speech *recognition*, the goals of speech *understanding* are both broader and narrower. Speech recognition efforts have been directed toward providing an orthographic transcription of the sounds and words corresponding to the acoustic signals of arbitrary utterances. Although the vocabulary might be limited, the intent is to process arbitrary utterances, essentially independent of context. Speech understanding is broader because it seeks to interpret the meaning of an utterance rather than just identify its form. It is narrower, because it can expect to process only those utterances that are relevant to a particular task domain." [Ref. 6.98, pp. 4–5]

The distinction has to do with the orientation toward a particular task; that orientation provides a means through which semantic constraints can be applied to the recognition of the meaning of the utterance. One can take as the defining property of a speech understanding system that it builds up a representation of the meaning of the utterance, either explicitly or implicitly, and that the process of building this meaning representation contributes to the recognition process itself.

In the VICENS system [6.79], no separate semantic representation was built up, but the semantics was implicit in the syntactic representation. In fact, this system was used to control the Stanford HAND-EYE system, so it qualifies as the first speech understanding system, however rudimentary its capabilities. Also qualifying under this definition are the syntax-directed isolated word recognition systems mentioned earlier [6.58, 59, 79], although it must be said that as one approaches the extremes of simplicity, the distinction between recognition and understanding becomes less clear and less relevant.

The NEWELL report resulted in the establishment of a five-year project in speech understanding research by ARPA in 1971. The goals of that project are set down in the report:

"The system should accept continuous speech from many cooperative speakers of the general American dialect, in a quiet room over a good quality microphone, allowing slight tuning of the system per speaker, but requiring only natural adaptation by the user, permitting a slightly selected vocabulary of 1000 words, with a highly artificial syntax and a [manageable] task ..., with a simple psychological model of the user, providing graceful interaction, tolerating less than 10% semantic error, in a few times real time, and be demonstrable in 1976 with a moderate chance of success." [Ref. 6.3, p. 2]

(The "few times real time" goal should be interpreted in light of the fact that the report also made assumptions about the availability of computer systems substantially faster than existing machines [Ref. 6.3, p. 32].)

The project established efforts toward building such systems at Bolt Beranek and Newman Inc. (BBN), Carnegie-Mellon University (CMU), MIT Lincoln Laboratory, Stanford Research Institute (SRI), and System Development Corporation (SDC). More specialized research efforts were established at UNIVAC, University of Michigan (later University of California at Berkeley), Speech Communications Research Laboratory, and Haskins Laboratories. According to the guidelines for the project, during the first two years, each of the systems contractors constructed a complete, but preliminary speech understanding system. In 1973 the five systems were reviewed; BBN, CMU, and a combined SRI-SDC project were selected to continue the development of speech understanding systems.

In Subsection 6.3.2, I shall briefly discuss the different sources of knowledge that a speech understanding system can bring to bear on the task of understanding an utterance. Subsection 6.3.3 will illustrate how these sources of knowledge are being applied in present speech understanding systems.

6.3.2 Relevant Sources of Knowledge

Because of the magnitude of the problem that the present speech understanding systems are attacking, it has become a premise that information from as many relevant sources of knowledge as possible should be brought to bear in aid of the recognition process. In the broadest sense, the relevant sources of knowledge for speech understanding are the same as for speech recognition. However, as the previous section has shown, past speech recognition work has concentrated on those areas concerned with the phonetic description of the speech signal. The higher-level linguistic areas were largely unexplored territory, as was the matter of how to apply those sources of knowledge to the problem. Furthermore, the higher aspirations of the current work and the ways in which the higher levels can contribute to the recognition process imply the possibility of different techniques even at the phoneme and word recognition levels.

A speech understanding system must treat the utterance at many levels, from the speech signal itself to the representation of meaning from which action is derived. There is some latitude in determining which intermediate levels are used, but they probably must include the following:

1) Processed representation(s) of the speech signal (spectra, fundamental frequency, other parametric representations)
2) At least one subword level (phonetic, phonemic, syllabic, etc.)
3) Morpheme or word
4) Syntactic structure(s)
5) Semantic structure(s).

Sources of knowledge relate the representation at one level to those at others. Speech recognition/understanding is an *analytic* process, in that it seeks to transform an utterance into a meaning. Many of the knowledge sources are known or best expressed in the opposite, or *generative* direction (for example, syntax). Expressing such knowledge in the reverse direction or organizing the system in such a way that generative knowledge is used in its preferred direction is a major problem faced by speech understanding researchers.

The NEWELL report [6.3] summarizes the states of the available sources of knowledge as of 1970. More recent viewpoints are referenced in the text below.

a) Signal Processing and Signal Representation

A wide variety of methods for processing the speech signal and representing its relevant properties is available in the literature on speech processing and speech recognition [6.33, 99, 100]. If cost and computation time are not limiting factors, processing the sampled and quantized speech signal by computer program (e.g., digital filtering, Fast Fourier Transform, linear prediction, and measures derived from them) offers the most precision and flexibility. Signal processing computers today can compute such algorithms in about real time, but at considerable cost. Conventional analog filtering (e.g., filter bank spectral analysis) is fast and cheap, but more limited in precision and versatility. Linear prediction [6.61–66], the newest analysis method, appears to offer advantages in the form of the spectral modeling involved, and it appears to be especially appropriate for estimating the formants of vowel-like sounds. Fundamental frequency, a primary carrier of the prosodic form of an utterance, can be estimated by special purpose hardware or by various algorithms operating on the digitized signal [6.101–104].

b) Phonemic Segmentation and Labeling

Here again, the entire body of knowledge of acoustic-phonetics, which attempts to systematize the relation between the acoustic properties of the speech signal and the phonemic entities which underlie them, coincides precisely with the theoretical and experimental principles with which speech recognition has been working for many years. The effective use of higher-level linguistic constraints removes some of the burden of recognition from the phonemic segmentation and recognition component of a system, but it cannot do this completely. Proper use of the segmental information in the signal will always be important. If it is not done well enough, the higher levels will be faced with so much uncertainty (or error) that they will become ineffective. The higher the performance at this level, the wider can be the syntactic and semantic aspirations of the system.

The presence of significant higher level sources of knowledge has another implication at this level. It makes possible the direct use of the body of acoustic-phonetic knowledge in generative form, which is becoming quantitatively systematized by work in speech synthesis, but which has always been the preferred form of description for many phonetic phenomena [6.21, 22]. For example, in the KLATT and STEVENS experiment on the reading of spectrograms [6.42], in which the experimenters were assisted by a computer program to match a phonetic transcription against a dictionary of 200 words, the experimenters reported that their ability to transcribe the details of the spectrogram was far overshadowed by their ability to verify a particular word hypothesis. The reason for this is simple. The acoustic properties of the phonemes are highly dependent on their context. In the analytic direction, this context must be inferred; in the generative direction, the context is known and may be taken into account. Indeed, the implementation of this kind of verification of word hypotheses ("analysis by synthesis") is being attempted in present speech understanding systems [6.105–107].

c) Phonology and Lexical Representation

Words are pronounced differently in continuous speech than they are in isolation, principally due to effects of speaking rate and to contextual effects at word boundaries. For example, the words "did you" are often pronounced "dija" when embedded in a naturally spoken sentence. These effects are not simply sloppy articulation; they are real phenomena found in normal continuous speech. Much of this phonological variation can be described by general phonological rules. It is clear that a speech understanding system, which must cope with the pronunciations encountered in continuous speech, must take these phenomena into account. Multiple pronunciations in the system's dictionary can account for within-word variations, but variations across word boundaries, as in the example above, must also be handled. The current work in speech understanding has stimulated work along these lines [6.108–110], and phonological rules are being experimentally implemented in speech understanding systems [6.86, 107, 111, 112].

d) Syntax

In this case also, modern theories of grammar are usually generative in form, and building text parsers that reverse them has proved cumbersome. Text parsers for artificial languages and subsets of natural language using other formalisms do exist [6.113], but they are not directly applicable to speech understanding for several reasons.

1) Text parsers assume as input the exact words of the sentence. In a speech understanding system, the boundaries between the words are not distinct, and many of the words recognized from the utterance will in fact be wrong. More generally, words recognized from the utterance must be regarded as hypotheses, so at any one point in the utterance, the parser must be able to cope with a list of such hypotheses, not just one.

2) Text parsers usually make particular use of the function words in a sentence. In speech, these small words are often the least distinct, and hence the least reliably recognized of all.

3) Text parsers are usually organized to proceed from left to right across a sentence. In a speech understanding system there may be no words available at some point, so it must be able to deal with gaps in the input.
4) The building of syntactic structures, while useful for semantic interpretation, does not in itself contribute to the process of understanding an unknown utterance. A syntactic component of a speech understanding system should ideally be able to make judgments of syntactic goodness of hypothesized word sequences and use partially constructed structures to make predictions to fill the gaps.

In short, significant adaptations of existing text parsing techniques are necessary to make them useful for speech understanding. For a summary of such techniques, see [6.113], and for descriptions of the syntactic components of current speech understanding systems, see [6.114–118].

e) Prosodics

Speech lacks the punctuation marks which help to denote syntactic structure in written text, but much of the same information is encoded in the prosodic contour of an utterance, comprising intonation, stress, pauses, and other durational information. Stress also affects the acoustic realization of the phonemes and the applicability of certain phonological rules, so prosodic information is potentially useful at many levels. Unfortunately our understanding of the ways in which these cues are encoded in prosodic parameters is much less clear than in the case of written punctuation. The use of prosodic information in speech understanding is being studied [6.94–96, 119, 120], but it has not yet been incorporated into speech understanding systems.

f) Semantics and Pragmatics

I have grouped these two areas together because the boundary between them is indistinct. Semantics certainly deals with the relations among the words and concepts appropriate to the task domain. As with syntax, a semantics component should ideally be able not only to build semantic structures, but also to offer judgments of semantic goodness and to make proposals in order to limit the searches performed by other components of the system.

In systems where the user enters into an interactive dialogue with the systems, it is useful to model the user's state, the discourse, and the state of the task, in order to be able to judge the appropriateness of a hypothesized utterance, to formulate a response, and to predict what sorts of things the user might say in the following utterances. These considerations fall into the area of pragmatics, but it is difficult to say where semantics leaves off and pragmatics begins.

At this time there appear to be few pragmatic principles of much generality; the techniques currently being implemented have much to do with the characteristics and limitations of the individual task domains. The work in Artificial Intelligence on the representation of knowledge and modeling user performance is the principal basis of these sources of knowledge [6.113, 121–125].

g) Organization of Complex Knowledge-Based Systems

This is not a knowledge source in the sense used above, but it is an area of computer science which has much to contribute to solving the problem. This area deals with the overall problem of organizing and controlling a large system made up of as many diverse components as a speech understanding system requires. Once again, the background and experience of Artificial Intelligence provide many of the concepts and techniques required in the application to the speech understanding problem. Among them are:

1) Representation of partial and uncertain knowledge for future use and refinement.
2) Search strategies in combinatorial solution spaces.
3) The concept of non-determinism (if at a choice point, a decision is not possible based on the available information, following out the consequences of taking every path leading from that point).
4) Handling multiple hypotheses.
5) Scoring mechanisms for combining evaluations from multiple idiosyncratic knowledge sources.
6) Advanced programming languages for treating such concepts.

See [6.122, 126–130].

6.3.3 Present Speech Understanding Systems

Today it is a historical fact that a discussion of speech understanding work must be largely concerned with the ARPA speech understanding research project, but it should not be inferred that they are, or claim to be, one and the same. In order to illustrate the current state of the art, I shall describe some of the salient points of the ARPA project systems. Let me emphasize that this represents a snapshot (taken in 1974) of ongoing research and development projects. Even at the time of writing, these descriptions no longer reflect the current status of these projects in many ways; substantial changes have been and are being made.

Each system is oriented to one or more task domains. The task domain serves to define the vocabulary and to provide a context within which specific syntactic, semantic, pragmatic, and control aspects can be explored. It is to be hoped that many of the techniques developed in such specific contexts can be generalized.

a) BBN SPEECHLIS

In order to illustrate some of the concepts and methods involved in speech understanding systems research, I shall go into somewhat more detail discussing the system I am most familiar with, SPEECHLIS, the speech understanding system under development at Bolt Beranek and Newman Inc. [6.125, 131].

The initial task domain selected for SPEECHLIS was the (already existing) domain of the LUNAR system [6.132, 133], a natural English text question-answering system dealing with chemical analyses of the Apollo 11 moon rocks.

The LUNAR system understands and answers such questions as:

"Give me all lunar symples with magnetite."
"What is the average concentration of rubidium in high-alkali rocks?"
"List potassium/rubidium ratios for samples not containing silicon."

The subdomain selected for SPEECHLIS contains a vocabulary of about 250 words and a habitable subset of natural English grammar (declarative, imperative, and interrogative sentences with sentential complements, and relative and reduced relative clauses). A second task domain dealing with travel budget management was adopted later, but the system has not yet been run in that task. These domains will eventually be expanded to fill a 1000 word vocabulary.

The design of SPEECHLIS evolved from the KLATT and STEVENS spectrogram reading experiments mentioned earlier [6.42]. The computer protocols of their experimental trials provided valuable insights into their strategies for interpreting the spectrographic representation of a spoken sentence. In effect, the experimenters were simulating a speech understanding system. In order to go farther along these lines, a technique of "incremental stimulation" was developed, in which the various individual components of a speech understanding system were "implemented" with human simulations [6.134]. As each human simulator gained insight into the role of his component in understanding an utterance, he attempted to replace parts of his mental processing with computer programs to carry out these functions. If successful, he gradually built himself out of the component, remaining only in the role of monitoring performance and considering improvements in the algorithms.

From the spectrogram reading and incremental simulation experiments it became apparent that at least seven conceptual components were identifiable, as illustrated in Fig. 6.1. With the exception of a pragmatics component, initial versions of these have been implemented as parts of SPEECHLIS. (Initial capital letters on the words "syntax" and "semantics" in the following will indicate reference to parts of the SPEECHLIS system).

An acoustic feature extraction and segmental recognition component analyzes the acoustic signal [6.135]. A number of parameters are computed from the signal, such as the poles of a 14-pole linear prediction (LP) analysis of the 0–5 kHz region of the spectrum, fundamental frequency, total energy, energy at low and high frequencies, spectral derivatives, and poles of a two-pole LP analysis [6.136].

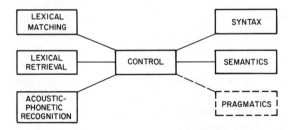

Fig. 6.1. Organization of the BBN SPEECHLIS speech understanding system. (The pragmatics module was not implemented in the system as described)

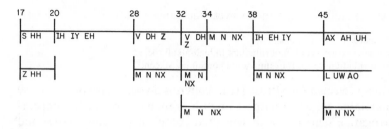

Fig. 6.2. Initial part of a segment lattice from the analysis of an utterance beginning, "Give me all ...". The numbers represent time in centiseconds. The segment labels use a computer representation of phonemic symbols (IH = the vowel in "bit", IY = the vowel in "beet", DH = the first sound in "the", etc. In this notation, the utterance would be transcribed as G IH V M IY AO L...)

These parameters are used by non-deterministic segmentation, feature extraction, and segment labeling algorithms to produce a partial phonetic transcription in the form of a *segment lattice*, an example of which is shown in Fig. 6.2. The segment lattice compactly represents alternative segmentations of the signal and alternative labels for the individual segments. Not shown in Fig. 6.2 are confidence estimates for each boundary and each segment label.

The segment lattice is then processed by a phonological rule component, which augments the lattice with branches for possible underlying sequences of phonemes that could have resulted in the observed acoustic sequences [6.107]. Associated with each added branch is a predicate function, which is later used by the word matcher to check for the applicability of the given phonological rule based on the specific word spelling and the necessary context. In this manner, the phonological rules are both analytic and partially generative. Other generative rules are applied ahead of time to the dictionary phonetic spellings of words.

The lexical retrieval component retrieves words from the lexicon on the basis of the information in the segment lattice and knowledge of the vocabulary. These words are then matched against the input signal by a word matching or word verification component.

The word verification component, given a particular word and a particular location in the input signal, determines the degree to which the word matches the signal [6.107]. In the present system, the word matching is done against the segment lattice only, by comparing the phonetic spellings of the word against all paths through a given region of the lattice. Since the segment lattice contains errors, the word matching is mediated by a phonetic similarity matrix for evaluating non-exact segment matches, phonologically motivated deletion likelihoods for each segment in a word, and rudimentary duration cues based on the vowel tenseness and stress markings in the phonetic spelling of the word. A score is assigned to each word match, based on how well the phonetic spelling matches the segment lattice. Word matches whose scores exceed a threshold are entered into a *word lattice*, which is a structure analogous to the segment lattice, but consisting of words instead of segment descriptions.

The syntactic component makes use of the Augmented Transition Network (ATN) formalism [6.113, 137, 138]. The grammar, whose scope was described above, and the parser have been specially adapted to the tasks of judging the grammaticality of a hypothesized partial interpretation of the utterance and proposing words or syntactic categories to extend a partial interpretation [6.115, 116].

The semantic component is capable of noticing coincidences between semantically related words that have been found at different places in the utterance, judging the meaningfulness of a hypothesized interpretation, and predicting particular words or specific classes of words for extending a partial interpretation [6.121, 139]. It makes use of a semantic association network [6.140, 141] to describe the relations among words and concepts, and case frames [6.142] to describe how these relationships hold and how they may be expressed in an utterance. The implementation of semantic procedures for answering questions using the data base has not yet been implemented in SPEECHLIS, as it had in LUNAR. Some pragmatic inferences have been identified and embedded in the control strategy, but no systematic pragmatics component has been implemented.

The control component incorporates the capabilities of all the sources of knowledge into an overall strategy for inferring an interpretation of the utterance. It must resolve such questions as where in the utterance to look for word matches, what thresholds to set on word match quality, when to temporarily abandon a given region of the utterance to concentrate on another region, how and where to use syntactic, semantic, and pragmatic information, and how to interpret and combine evaluation scores from the diverse knowledge sources in order to select which of many competing partial interpretations to work on next [6.130].

Interacting with the word lattice, the higher-level components of the system (Syntax and Semantics) form internal data objects called *theories* representing hypotheses about the original utterance. A theory contains a non-overlapping collection of word matches that are postulated to be in the utterance, together with syntactic, semantic and pragmatic information about the relationships among the words and scores representing the evaluations of the theory by the various knowledge sources. Theories grow and change as additional bits of evidence for or against them are found. A primary mechanism for accomplishing this is the creation of *monitors*. A monitor is a trap set by a hypothesis for new information that, if found, would result in a change or extension of the monitoring hypothesis. However, the reprocessing that is called for when a monitor is noticed is not done immediately. Rather an *event notice* is created, pointing to the monitor and the new evidence. This event notice is later evaluated by the control component to decide when and if to process it. This allows several new pieces of information to accumulate and be compared before choosing one to be processed, thus preventing wasteful depth-first searches. In addition to waiting for new information (by setting monitors), the higher-level components can also actively seek out information. One way this is done is by means of *proposals*. A proposal is a request to match a particular word or set of words at some point in the utterance. Any of the higher-level components can set monitors and make proposals.

The first activity of the control program is to call the acoustic-phonetic and phonological components to construct an initial segment lattice from the speech signal. A word lattice of robust word matches is then constructed by the lexical retrieval and matching components, which scan the segment lattice for "good", "big" word matches. In addition, a set of words that are pragmatically likely to begin an utterance is proposed at the beginning of the segment lattice. As each such word match is found, it is entered into the word lattice and given to the semantic component for analysis. If the word has semantic content, a theory is created for the word match, designating all semantic contexts in which it could appear. If a monitor is noticed indicating that a word fits into the semantic context of a theory that was created earlier, an event is created, associating the new word match with the old theory. Proposals for specific content words that are likely to appear adjacent to the new word match are created and added to the proposals queue. For each new word match, appropriate inflectional endings and auxiliary verbs are matched against the segment lattice and associated with the word match in the word lattice if they match well.

After the initial set of robust word matches has been examined, the proposals that are likely to be productive are processed, thus introducing new word matches and triggering a new round of semantic analysis. The events at the top of the event queue are then handed back to the semantic component for further processing. For each event, a new theory with an augmented semantic context is created and entered into the theory queue. This may result in additional events as Semantics makes new proposals or notices other word matches in the word lattice that fit into the modified context. In this way, Semantics assembles meaningful sets of content words.

As new theories are created, each is examined to determine whether it might be fruitful to call upon syntactic knowledge to develop further support for it. Since the number of possible parsings decreases with the number of adjacent or "close" word matches, this decision is made on the basis of the number of adjacent word matches in the theory, the size of the gaps between word match sequences, and the absence of unused content words in the word lattice that could be added to the theory by Semantics.

Syntactic knowledge is used to postulate grammatical structures that may obtain among the words in a theory. For example, in the case of

"... people done chemical analyses ... silicon",

Syntax could suggest that "people" is the subject of the verb "done", "chemical analyses" is the noun-phrase object, and that an auxiliary verb must appear somewhere in the utterance. Such grammatical information is checked for consistency with the postulated semantic structures, to determine, for example, whether it makes semantic sense for "people" to do something. Function words (e.g., determiners and prepositions) that are likely to appear adjacent to a sequence of word matches are proposed by Syntax in the context of these grammatical structures and added to the theory if they are found. Monitors are set for less likely contexts. Each small gap between sequences of word matches is analyzed, and a strong attempt is made to find a small word that fits, e.g., "for" or "of" before "silicon". Syntax can also call on Semantics directly to check the consistency of a hypothesized grammatical constituent. In the above example, after Syntax parses "chemical analyses" as a noun phrase, it calls Semantics to verify its semantic consistency.

This process of monitoring, proposing, event processing, and theory refinement continues until one or more theories are formed that are consistent with the segment lattice, the pronunciations in the lexicon, the grammar of the language, and the semantic and pragmatic aspects of the task domain. Strategies for recognizing and recovering from a state where no theories are emerging as good candidates for the whole utterance are under study. The system, as implemented on a PDP-10 computer, is slow, requiring many hundreds of times real time to arrive at an interpretation of an utterance; the use of LISP to implement the higher-level components is one reason for this.

As was the strategy of the spectrogram readers, the overall strategy of SPEECHLIS is partially bottom-up, partially top-down. It relies on enough correct content words emerging from the initial scan of the segment lattice to start off the hypothesis formation activity of the higher-level components. One frequent problem so far has been that the segment lattice has not been good enough—too many errors and too much ambiguity. For this reason, the sytem as a whole has not been run on many sentences, so no overall performance figures can be given; performance evaluations for some test cases were given in [6.125, 130, 131]. Revision of the segmentation and labeling and lexical matching components is in progress, as are the refinement of the other components and the implementation of the second task domain, which will include an explicit pragmatics component.

b) CMU Hearsay

The speech understanding systems at Carnegie-Mellon University (CMU) are lineal descendants of the earlier work by REDDY [6.76] and VICENS [6.79] described in Section 6.2. Based on this experience, the CMU group has formulated a general model and framework for building speech understanding systems in which multiple sources of knowledge can be systematically applied and evaluated. This model consists of a small set of independent processes (embodying the knowledge sources) capable of contributing to the understanding process, using the "hypothesize and test" paradigm. Hearsay I, which was first demonstrated in June 1972, and Hearsay II are specific implementations of this model. The structure of the Hearsay I system is illustrated in Fig. 6.3.

The initial Hearsay I implementation was a chess playing system that accepted spoken moves [6.143–146]. Chess moves are expressible with a 31 word

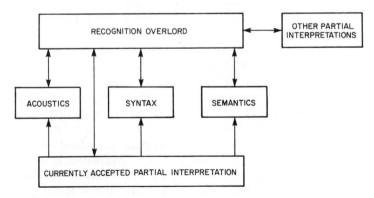

Fig. 6.3. Organization of the CMU Hearsay I speech understanding system

vocabulary and a finite context-free grammar of 18 production rules, which is capable of generating about five million sentences. Typical sentences are:

"Queen takes pawn."
"Knight to queen's bishop three."
"King bishop pawn moves to bishop four."

(A few other tasks with slightly more ambitious vocabularies have been implemented with Hearsay I by providing the appropriate vocabulary and grammar. However, no semantics components were implemented for these tasks).

A spoken sentence is analyzed by measuring the maximum amplitude and zero crossing count over 10 ms intervals for the original signal and for the outputs of five bandpass filters covering the range 200–6400 Hz. Each 10 ms datum is independently labeled as one of a set of phoneme-like classes by a modified nearest-neighbor classifier. Speaker-dependent training data can be incorporated in the reference information of this classifier. This string of labels, one for each 10 ms, is locally smoothed, and the labels are grouped into phoneme-like segments. The parameters and the labels are the representation of the acoustic data available to the acoustic recognizer.

The acoustic recognizer uses gross features of the acoustic data to propose words from the lexicon, and it verifies hypothesized words by doing more detailed comparisons of their phonetic spellings with the acoustic data. The syntactic recognizer predicts phrases from local context and verifies word sequences by means of syntactic consistency checks. A chess playing program keeps track of the board position and can generate a list of all legal moves, ordered by likelihood. The semantic recognizer uses this list to hypothesize moves likely to be expressed in the utterance and to evaluate the likelihood of hypothesized constructions.

The system operates in the following manner. Based on the "currently accepted partially recognized utterance" (initially null) one module hypothesizes a set of words for part of the unrecognized portion. These hypotheses are then evaluated by the other knowledge sources. If one is accepted at a high enough level of confidence, it is incorporated into the currently accepted partial interpretation, and other unrejected hypotheses are pushed on a stack for the purpose of backtracking if needed later. If the utterance still has unrecognized portions and the interpretation is still unclear, the cycle repeats. The recognition overlord, or control component, selects which module will hypothesize, evaluates the verification scores, decides which hypotheses to accept and reject, and decides when to abandon the current partial interpretation in favor of another.

In the SPEECHLIS system, the knowledge sources have specific cooperative roles in producing an interpretation of the utterance. In the Hearsay model, they are quite autonomous, interacting with each other only to the extent that they generate and verify hypotheses in the common data area. They are otherwise unaware of each other's presence or capabilities. This appears to make it easy to add a new knowledge source, by making it operate with the same paradigm as the others, at the same level of representation, in this case, the word. This is one of the objectives of their system design. It holds true, however, only for new knowledge sources that fit conveniently within the paradigm.

The performance of the Hearsay I system ranges from about 90% word accuracy on the 31-word chess task to about 50% on three other tasks with vocabularies up to 76 words and no semantic component in the system. Computation times on a PDP-10 computer system are on the order of 5 to 10 times real time.

Hearsay II is the successor to the Hearsay I system [6.117, 146–148]. It differs in that all information about the utterance is represented in a single, uniform, multi-level data base, and that a larger number of more detailed knowledge sources operate on this data base. The "hypothesize and test" paradigm of the knowledge sources can operate both within and between all levels of representation (parametric, segmental, ..., conceptual) in this structure. The activation of a knowledge source is data-driven, based on the occurrence of patterns in the data base that match templates specified by the knowledge source. Besides providing a way to specify knowledge sources independently, this also permits the exploitation of parallel execution; one of the implementations of Hearsay II is on a multiprocessor computer system designed to explore such operation. The task domain of the new system is the retrieval of wire-service news stories upon voice request.

c) SDC VDMS

The voice-controlled data management system (VDMS) under development at System Development Corporation (SDC) [6.149, 150] allows one to access a data base of information about the submarine fleets of the United States, Soviet Union, and United Kingdom. The vocabulary of the system is about 150 words. A context-free grammar of 35 recursive production rules gives an artificial, but English-like data management language with sentences such as:

"Print type where category equals nuclear."
"Total quantity where country equals USSR."
"Count where submerged speed greater than one and country equals USA."

The system organization is illustrated in Fig. 6.4. The operation of the system is strongly predictive, driven both from the parser and from a discourse level controller, which contains a user model and a "thematic memory". It is assumed that the user carries on a dialogue with the system. The user's state (e.g., system login, interactive query, report generation) is used to predict syntactic forms likely to be used in the next utterance. The thematic memory keeps track of the content words in the user's utterances and in the system responses, in order to predict words likely to occur in the next utterance. The parser uses a non-directional

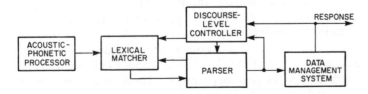

Fig. 6.4. Organization of the SDC VDMS speech understanding system

scanning approach, which means that it can begin processing at any point in the utterance at which there is a high probability of a correct match. Semantic constraints are inherent in the syntactic categories of the grammar.

The acoustic-phonetic processor [6.151–153] uses amplitude and zero-crossing information from three hardware bandpass filters covering 150–5000 Hz. Individual 10 ms segments are given labels from a set of five gross classes (silence, vowel-like, strong frication, unvoiced, other), grouped, and then further processed, using linear prediction analyses on the digitized signal. Vowels are tentatively identified by comparing the formant frequencies at selected times with speaker-dependent reference data; fricatives and plosive bursts are analyzed into five classes based on spectrum shape; nasals are identified as a single class. This combined symbolic and parametric data is used by the lexical matcher to verify specific words.

There is no bottom-up processing at the word level; words are matched only upon prediction by the parser or the discourse level controller. Given a word to be matched, the lexical matcher obtains an idealized phonemic spelling from the lexicon, expands it into a set of alternative pronunciations by a set of generative phonological rules [6.111], and attempts to match each one against the available acoustic-phonetic data. The matching procedures work on a syllable-by-syllable basis, with a separate analysis that attempts to compensate for coarticulation across syllable and word boundaries [6.106].

The acoustic-phonetic processor of the VDMS system is implemented on a Raytheon 704, and the lexical matching and linguistics component are implemented on an IBM 370/145. Only preliminary performance figures are available [6.150]; for ten dialogues of about ten sentences each by each of two speakers, 52% of the utterances were completely understood.

d) SRI Speech Understanding System

The task domain of Stanford Research Institute's (SRI) speech understanding system is a simulation of the actions required for the assembly, test, and repair of small mechanical devices, initially focusing on the repair of a leaky faucet [6.105, 154, 155]. The system appears to permit a fairly natural subset of English appropriate to this task, including such sentences as:

> "Can we fix a worn valve?"
> "The little brass washer is on the table."
> "Where are the washers for the faucet?"

The structure of the system is illustrated in Fig. 6.5. This system is also strongly predictive, with the parser playing the principal role. It coordinates information from the various knowledge sources to predict the sequence of words in the utterance, spoken in the context of a particular task. There is no grammar separate from the parsing program; it is contained in the structure of the parser itself. Semantic constraints (e.g., case frame information about individual verbs) also appear to be integrated into the parsing procedure. The acoustic component is used only to verify word predictions. A complete analysis of the utterance results in a program that operates on a model of the task domain ("world model").

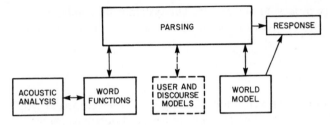

Fig. 6.5. Organization of the SRI speech understanding system. (The user and discourse models were not implemented in the system as described)

The execution of that program constitutes the understanding of the utterance, by retrieving information about the model in the case of a question or by changing the state of the model in the case of a command. The world model is also used during the parsing to determine whether or not definite noun phrases or prepositional phrases correspond to some portion of the model. Little user or discourse modeling is implemented, but research on this is in progress [6.124].

The parser uses a top-down, "best-first" strategy [6.114, 156]. As it proceeds from left to right across an utterance, each path emanating from each choice point is assigned a priority based on estimated likelihood of completion. The path with the highest priority is processed until it completes successfully or its priority falls below the next best one, due to events farther along the path. When a word is predicted at a specific point in the utterance, a "word function", which is a subprogram for verifying that particular word, is called. It returns a score that reflects the likelihood that the word is present. The priority of the parse path that led to the prediction is modified accordingly.

The speech signal is sampled and processed by four digital filters over 80–6800 Hz. These filter outputs are used to classify successive 10 ms intervals as vowel-like, voiced stop, voiced turbulence, unvoiced turbulence, silence, or transition. Three other digital filters over 1500–8000 Hz are used to subdivide turbulent intervals into six classes. A linear prediction analysis of voiced sounds provides frequency and bandwidth estimates of the first five formants.

A word function uses word-specific algorithms to reference these acoustic parameters in order to make a judgment as to the presence of the word at a specific point in the utterance [6.157]. Such a program is prepared after a detailed examination of acoustic data from that word in a variety of contexts. Word functions do not appear to take into account the neighboring contexts of the word if known. Speaker-dependent information must be incorporated into each word function separately. A total of 42 word functions is available to the system.

The parser contains syntactic and semantic specifications for almost 300 words, but the number of word functions is also a factor in determining the effective vocabulary. Results have been reported for the processing of 71 utterances using a 54 word vocabulary [6.105, 155]. The system completely parsed and responded to 51; 44 of those were understood correctly, including 6 in which the substitution of small function words did not affect the appropriateness of the response; the other 7 were processed incorrectly. The system is implemented on a PDP-10, and it requires on the order of 200 times real time to analyze an utterance.

e) Lincoln Speech Understanding System

The system organization of the speech understanding system developed at MIT Lincoln Laboratory [6.158–163] is illustrated in Fig. 6.6. A Phonetic Recognition module processes the speech signal and produces a sequence of acoustic-phonetic elements. Three different Linguistic Processors were developed [6.112, 159, 160, 164]; one called VASSAL has been used for the most experimentation and will be described here. The function of the Linguistic Processor is to hypothesize grammatical word sequences and match them against the string of acoustic-phonetic elements. A Functional Response module maintains a model of the task domain and uses it to help select or reject sentence candidates proposed by the Linguistic Processor. It also uses an accepted sentence to produce the requested action.

The system as implemented did not include a Functional Response module, due to the project's termination in 1974. The task domain of the Lincoln system is the vocal control of a data retrieval, analysis, and display facility that supports acoustic-phonetic research. The Lincoln system uses a finite context-free grammar of 111 production rules, which can generate almost five million sentences. As in the SDC system, the non-terminals of the grammar are semantic rather than syntactic categories. The grammar is constructed so that a successful parse yields a functional representation of the sentence that can be mapped into an executable process. A vocabulary of about 250 words is used, giving typical sentences like:

"Move to the next utterance."
"Put the right cursor on the third frame."
"Recompute the average energy in the second voiced region."

Some testing has also been done with a 500 word vocabulary and larger grammar.

The Phonetic Recognition module [6.165] bases its processing on linear predictive spectral analysis and voicing detection of a fundamental frequency extractor. Formants are tracked during voiced intervals [6.166], and an initial segmen-

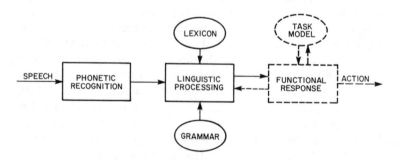

Fig. 6.6. Organization of the Lincoln speech understanding system. (The functional response module was not implemented)

tation into four broad acoustic classes is performed. More detailed segmentation and identification is then done within these initial segments. Vowels are identified by classification of formant frequency positions at their centers; glides, nasals, and diphthongs are detected, segmented, and identified by algorithms that make extensive use of formant trajectories. Most of the classification algorithms make use of speaker-dependent thresholds and formant targets. The result of these segmentation and identification algorithms is a string of phoneme-sized acoustic-phonetic elements called "APELs". Many APELs represent a single phoneme; some represent a phoneme class, such as nasals; a few others represent "deletable" segments, such as nasals that were detected with relatively low confidence. The segments of the output string may carry more than one APEL label; the top three choices are generally given for vowels, and one to three labels are given for consonants, depending on the results of the individual classification algorithms.

The Linguistic Processor uses the semantic grammar to hypothesize word sequences to be compared against the APEL string. The dictionary pronunciations are processed by phonological rules so that they include optional deletions and insertions. The word matching algorithm matches the word along the APEL string by aligning the vowels first, then mapping the consonants. Phoneme to APEL matches are computed using a similarity matrix derived from performance statistics of the Phonetic Recognition module. The process of word sequence proposal and matching proceeds top-down, left-to-right. A "best-first" heuristic, similar in philosophy to SRI's, selects the sentence fragment to be processed next. The priority in this case is a function of the word match scores and the length of the sentence fragment; the semantic grammar provides the allowable word sequences, but it does not modify the priorities of the different paths.

The system is implemented on the Lincoln TX-2 and FDP (fast digital processor) computers, the latter being used for the signal processing, formant tracking, and initial segmentation. The speech input is recorded in the TX-2 computer room using a close-talking noise canceling microphone. The recognition of an utterance requires on the order of 20 times real time. For a test of 275 sentences, chosen so as to span the entire grammar and spoken by 6 male speakers, sentence recognition accuracy of about 50% has been reported [6.163]. In another test of 116 less difficult sentences also by 6 male speakers, 74% sentence recognition was reported [6.160].

f) Conclusion

The diversity of approaches at the many levels of building a speech understanding system was an overtly planned feature of the ARPA speech understanding project. The space of possible approaches to a problem of this complexity is too vast to be explored by a single effort, and the nature of the interactions among multiple, diverse, imperfect knowledge sources can only be explored in the context of complete, functioning systems. The initial round of system building was designed to bring the project to that point, but it is still too early to evaluate the effectiveness of the different system philosophies.

Therefore a note of caution is in order regarding the performance figures cited above. They represent the performance of systems that by and large had been functioning as complete systems for only a short time. At such a point in an ongoing research project, a single number gives only the most global view of the performance of a system. It does not, for example, describe the severity of the errors, nor does it describe the performance of individual system components. (Some more detailed performance descriptions may be found in the references).

Furthermore, the initial systems differ greatly along the dimensions that reflect the goals of the project, in particular, the quality of the environment in which the speech is recorded, the size of the task domain, the size and complexity of the grammar, the use of semantics and pragmatics, and the processing time necessary to understand an utterance. The "few times real time" goal, while desirable, will probably not be met along with the others, for most of the systems are implemented on 1970 vintage computers, and, for the present, it is more important to make the systems research oriented for ease of examination and modification than to strip them for speed.

The systems as described above make no use of prosodic information contained in the utterance. This is an important topic, which has been under investigation by the more specialized research efforts of the ARPA project, and system builders are presently attempting to incorporate such information into their speech understanding systems. Also being incorporated to a much greater degree than described above are models of the task, the user, and the discourse. Needless to say, not just these topics, but all aspects of the current systems are being expanded and improved.

6.4 Assessment of the Future

LINDGREN, in his 1965 survey [6.12], quoted one researcher as saying that what the general speech recognition field needed then was "one good idea", but the progress made in the past ten years has not been due to a single good idea, or even to a small number of them. The sources of knowledge that must be tapped by advanced speech recognition and understanding systems are too numerous and diverse for any single idea to produce a dramatic breakthrough. Progress has been and will continue to be made only by the conception and synthesis of many "good ideas" stemming from all aspects of the speech communication process.

In the analysis of the speech signal, there are trade-offs in cost, speed, versatility, and precision among the many analog and digital signal processing techniques available. Therefore the selection of a method of signal analysis is and is likely to remain an open question. Over the past ten years, the improvements in our understanding and practice of digital signal processing together with its falling costs suggest that it will become even more widely used, not only for research, but also for practical applications. Volume production of entirely digital linear prediction vocoders is a likely possibility in the near future; the speech signal analysis component of such devices could very likely serve the signal processing needs of speech recognition and speech understanding systems.

The problem of handling the speaker-dependent differences in the speech signal is still far from solved. Training to examples of each speaker's words may be adequate for limited vocabulary pattern matching word recognizers which do not consider the structure of speech sounds. For other systems, the possibilities include speaker-independent recognition algorithms, recognition algorithms using thresholds and values that are derived from some kind of speaker calibration procedure, and algorithms that automatically adapt to the characteristics of the speaker. Some work has been done in the first [6.55, 72, 135, 167] and second [6.150, 165] of these areas; little has been done in the third. A closely related question is that of adapting to different conditions of background noise and transmission characteristics.

For continuous speech recognition and understanding systems, the development of techniques for using prosodic information will continue to be important, as will a better understanding of the phonological rules that govern changes in pronunciation. The relationships between specific task domains and syntactic, semantic, and pragmatic components must be more systematically understood so that building a recognition/understanding system for a new task can become a relatively straightforward job. As higher-level linguistic techniques become more widely applied, the distinction between continuous speech recognition and speech understanding for specific applications may be expected to fade.

With the exception of the pattern-matching word recognizers, the speech recognition and understanding systems described above fit into syntactic pattern recognition in its broadest sense. In all of these cases, some aspect of the structure of the pattern is exploited by the recognition process. Virtually the only use of syntactic pattern recognition techniques, however, is at the level of the syntax of the words within the sentence, and even there it is more related to natural and computational linguistics than to syntactic pattern recognition *per se*. There are at least two reasons for this apparent lack of intersection between these two fields. First, it is unclear how many of the sources of knowledge (e.g., semantics) can be expressed as a grammar. The recent reports by DE MORI [6.91–93] and by NEW-MAN et al. [6.168] suggest that syntactic techniques are suited to describing the contextual dependencies encountered at the level of acoustic parameters [6.35], and further developments may be expected here. Secondly, the syntactic approach is still sufficiently new and different that it simply has not had time to make an impact on a relatively established area of research. One can expect that more interaction between these two fields can only be mutually beneficial.

The progress in speech recognition and understanding techniques in the past five years, the pace of current research efforts, and the continuing developments in computer hardware and software should continue to bring speech recognition and understanding performance closer to the point of practicality. Isolated word recognition is just barely there now; it must continue to develop practical applications as well as to improve, for it faces stiff competition from other methods of data entry, such as optical sensing. Continuous speech recognition and understanding are farther away, but their prospects of reaching the point of practicality have never looked better.

Acknowledgement

I would like to thank the members of the BBN speech group for their help and comments on earlier versions of this chapter. I have borrowed liberally in places from their descriptions of the BBN SPEECHLIS system. The preparation of this chapter was supported in part by the Advanced Research Projects Agency of the Department of Defense and monitored by ONR under Contract No. N00014-75-C-0523.

References

6.1   R. Turn: "The Use of Speech for Man-Computer Communication"; Rand Corp., Santa Monica, Calif., Report R-1386-ARPA (1974)
6.2   D. R. Hill: In *Advances in Computers*, Vol. 11, ed. by F. L. Alt and M. Rubinoff (Academic Press, New York 1971) pp. 166–230
6.3   A. Newell, J. Barnett, J. W. Forgie, C. Green, D. Klatt, J. C. R. Licklider, J. Munson, D. R. Reddy, W. A. Woods: *Speech Understanding Systems: Final Report of a Study Group* (North-Holland Publishing Co., Amsterdam 1973)
6.4   W. A. Lea: IEEE Trans. Audio Electroacoust. AU-**16**, 184 (1968)
6.5   L. D. Erman (ed.): IEEE Symposium on Speech Recognition, Contributed Papers, April 15–19, 1974, Carnegie-Mellon Univ., Pittsburgh, Pa., IEEE Catalog No. 74 CHO 878-9 AE (1974)
6.6   D. R. Reddy (ed.): *Speech Recognition: Invited Papers presented at the IEEE Symposium* (Academic Press, New York 1975)
6.7   G. Fant (ed.): Proceedings of the Speech Communication Seminar, Aug. 1–3, 1974, Stockholm (Almqvist and Wiksell, Uppsala 1975) in press
6.8   The papers from sessions I and II are printed in Acustica **31**,(1974); the papers from sessions III, IV, and V are in G. Fant, M. A. A. Tatham (eds.): *Auditory Analysis and Perception of Speech* (Academic Press, London 1975)
6.9   C. P. Smith (ed.): Conference Record, 1972 Conference on Speech Communication and Processing, April 24–26, 1972, Newton, Mass., IEEE Catalog No. 72 CHO 596-7 AE (1972)
6.10   R. Fatehchand: In *Advances in Computers*, Vol. 1, ed. by F. Alt (Academic Press, New York 1960) pp. 193–229
6.11   E. E. David, O. G. Selfridge: Proc. IRE **50**, 1093 (1962)
6.12   N. Lindgren: IEEE Spectrum **2**, No. 3, 114 (1965)
6.13   N. Lindgren: IEEE Spectrum **2**, No. 4, 44 (1965)
6.14   S. R. Hyde: Automatic Speech Recognition: Literature Survey and Discussion, British Post Office Research Department Report No. 45 (1968); also in *Human Communication: A Unified View*, ed. by E. E. David, Jr. and P. B. Denes (McGraw-Hill Book Co., New York 1972) pp. 399–438
6.15   W. A. Lea: In *Current Trends in Linguistics*, Vol. 12, ed. by T. Sebeok (Mouton, The Hague 1972) pp. 1561–1620
6.16   P. B. Denes: In *Speech Recognition: Invited Papers presented at the IEEE Symposium*, ed. by D. R. Reddy (Academic Press, New York 1975) pp. 73–82
6.17   D. R. Hill: Int. J. Man-Machine Studies **4**, 383 (1972)
6.18   G. Fant: Speech Transmission Laboratory Quarterly Progress Report 1/70, Royal Institute of Technology, Stockholm (1970) p. 16, also in *Speech Sounds and Features*, ed. by G. Fant (MIT Press, Cambridge, Mass. 1973) pp. 202–215
6.19   J. R. Pierce: IEEE Spectrum **5**, No. 7, 44 (1968)
6.20   J. R. Pierce: J. Acoust. Soc. Am. **46**, 1049 (1969)
6.21   D. H. Klatt: In *Speech Recognition: Invited Papers presented at the IEEE Symposium*, ed. by D. R. Reddy (Academic Press, New York 1975) pp. 321–341
6.22   D. H. Klatt: Proc. Speech Communication Seminar, Aug. 1–3, 1974, Stockholm, Vol. 3 (Almqvist and Wiksell, Uppsala 1975) pp. 277–289
6.23   D. H. Klatt: Comments on Session 3: Automatic Recognition, Proc. Speech Communication Seminar, Aug. 1–3, 1974, Stockholm, Vol. 3 (Almqvist and Wiksell, Uppsala 1975) pp. IX–XXXII
6.24   D. J. Broad: Int. J. Man-Machine Studies **4**, 105 (1972)
6.25   K. W. Otten: In *Advances in Computers*, Vol. 11, ed. by F. L. Alt and M. Rubinoff (Academic Press, New York 1971) pp. 127–163
6.26   J. W. Falter, K. W. Otten: IEEE Trans. Audio Electroacoust. AU-**15**, 27 (1967)

6.27   N. G. ZAGORUIKO: Speech Transmission Laboratory Quarterly Progress Report 1/70, Royal Institute of Technology, Stockholm (1970) p. 32

6.28   V. M. VELICHKO, N. G. ZAGORUYKO: Int. J. Man-Machine Studies **2**, 223 (1970)

6.29   M. DERKACH: Speech Transmission Laboratory Quarterly Progress Report 1/70, Royal Institute of Technology, Stockholm (1970) p. 39

6.30   M. DERKACH, R. GUMETSKY, L. MISHIN: Proc. Conf. on Speech Communication and Processing, April 24–26, 1972, Newton, Mass. (1972) p. 338

6.31   M. DERKACH, R. GUMETSKY, B. GURIN, L. MISHIN: Proc. Speech Communication Seminar, Aug. 1–3, 1974, Stockholm, Vol. 3 (Almqvist and Wiksell, Uppsala 1975) pp. 393–400

6.32   P. B. DENES, E. N. PINSON: *The Speech Chain*, (Anchor Press, Garden City, N.Y. 1973)

6.33   J. L. FLANAGAN: *Speech Analysis, Synthesis, and Perception*, 2nd. ed. (Springer, Berlin, Heidelberg, New York 1972)

6.34   A. M. LIBERMAN, F. S. COOPER, D. P. SHANKWEILER, M. STUDDERT-KENNEDY: Psych. Rev. **74**, 431 (1967); also in *Human Communication: A Unified View*, ed. by E. E. DAVID, JR. and P. B. DENES (McGraw-Hill Book Co., New York 1972) pp. 13–50

6.35   A. M. LIBERMAN: Cognitive Psych. **1**, 301 (1970)

6.36   R. JAKOBSON, C. G. M. FANT, M. HALLE: *Preliminaries to Speech Analysis* (MIT Press, Cambridge, Mass. 1963)

6.37   G. FANT: *Speech Sounds and Features* (MIT Press, Cambridge, Mass. 1973)

6.38   N. CHOMSKY, M. HALLE: *The Sound Pattern of English* (Harper and Row, New York 1968)

6.39   R. JAKOBSON: Scientific American **227**, No. 3, 73 (1972)

6.40   W. JAMES: *Talks to Teachers on Psychology and to Students on Some of Life's Ideals* (Holt, New York 1899)

6.41   D. B. FRY, P. B. DENES: Language and Speech **1**, 35 (1958)

6.42   D. H. KLATT, K. N. STEVENS: IEEE Trans. Audio Electroacoust. AU-**21**, 210 (1973)

6.43   K.-S. FU, P. H. SWAIN: In *Software Engineering*, Vol. 2, ed. by J. J. TOU (Academic Press, New York 1971) pp. 155–182

6.44   Special issue on syntactic pattern recognition. Pattern Recognition **3**, (1971)

6.45   Special issue on syntactic pattern recognition. Pattern Recognition **4**, (1972)

6.46   L. KANAL: IEEE Trans. Inform. Theory IT-**20**, 697 (1974)

6.47   K.-S. FU: *Syntactic Methods in Pattern Recognition*, (Academic Press, New York 1974)

6.48   K.-S. FU: Chapter 4 in this volume

6.49   J. C. MILLER, P. W. ROSS, C. M. WINE: IEEE Trans. Audio Electroacoust. AU-**18**, 26 (1970)

6.50   M. T. CLARK: IEEE Trans. Audio Electroacoust. AU-**18**, 304 (1970)

6.51   J. N. SHEARME, P. F. LEACH: IEEE Trans. Audio Electroacoust. AU-**16**, 256 (1968)

6.52   J. W. GLENN, M. H. HITCHCOCK: Electron. **44**, 84 (1971)

6.53   M. B. HERSCHER, R. B. COX: Proc. Conf. on Speech Communication and Processing, April 24–26, 1972, Newton, Mass. (1972) p. 89

6.54   Technical Data VIP 100, Threshold Technology Inc., Cinnaminson, N.J.

6.55   T. B. MARTIN: "Acoustic Recognition of a Limited Vocabulary in Continuous Speech"; Ph. D. dissertation, Univ. of Pennsylvania, Philadelphia, Pa. (1970)

6.56   T. B. MARTIN: In *Speech Recognition: Invited Papers presented at the IEEE Symposium*, ed. by D. R. REDDY (Academic Press, New York 1975) pp. 55–71

6.57   Quality Progress **VI**, 12 (1973)

6.58   VNC-100 Programming System, Threshold Technology Inc., Cinnaminson, N. J.

6.59   J.-P. HATON: IEEE Trans. Acoust., Speech, Signal Processing ASSP-**22**, 416 (1974)

6.60   F. ITAKURA: IEEE Trans. Acoust., Speech, Signal Processing ASSP-**23**, 67 (1975)

6.61   F. ITAKURA, S. SAITO: Electron. Comm. in Japan **53 A**, 36 (1970)

6.62   B. S. ATAL, S. L. HANAUER: J. Acoust. Soc. Am. **50**, 637 (1971)

6.63   J. D. MARKEL: "Formant Trajectory Estimation from a Linear Least-Squares Inverse Filter Formulation"; Speech Comm. Res. Lab., Santa Barbara, Calif., Monograph 7 (1971)

6.64   J. MAKHOUL, J. WOLF: "Linear Prediction and the Spectral Analysis of Speech", Bolt Beranek and Newman Inc., Cambridge, Mass., Report 2304 (1972)

6.65   J. MAKHOUL: Proc. IEEE **63**, 561 (1975)

6.66   J. D. MARKEL, A. H. GRAY, JR.: *Linear Prediction of Speech* (Springer, Berlin, Heidelberg, New York 1976)

6.67   R. B. NEELY, G. M. WHITE: Proc. IFIP Congress 74 (North-Holland Publishing Co., Amsterdam 1974) p. 748

6.68   G. M. WHITE: Proc. Speech Communication Seminar, Aug. 1–3, 1974, Stockholm, Vol. 3 (Almqvist and Wiksell, Uppsala 1975) pp. 225–231

6.69   T. G. von KELLER: J. Acoust. Soc. Am. **49**, 1288 (1971)

6.70   L. BUISSON, G. MERCIER, J. Y. GRESSER, M. QUERRE, R. VIVES: Proc. Speech Communication Seminar, Aug. 1–3, 1974, Stockholm, Vol. 3 (Almqvist and Wiksell, Uppsala 1975) pp. 189–196

6.71   M. MLOUKA, J. S. LIENARD: Proc. Speech Communication Seminar, Aug. 1–3, 1974, Stockholm, Vol. 3 (Almqvist and Wiksell, Uppsala 1975) pp. 257–263

6.72   M. F. MEDRESS: "Computer Recognition of Single-Syllable English Words"; Ph. D. dissertation, MIT, Cambridge, Mass. (1969)

6.73   M. MEDRESS: Proc. Conf. on Speech Communication and Processing, April 24–26, 1972, Newton, Mass. (1972) p. 113

6.74   J. W. FORGIE, C. D. FORGIE: J. Acoust. Soc. Am. **31**, 1480 (1959)

6.75   G. W. HUGHES: "On the Recognition of Speech by Machine", Sc. D. dissertation, MIT, Cambridge, Mass. (1959); also MIT Res. Lab. of Electronics Tech. Report 395 (1961)

6.76   D. R. REDDY: "An Approach to Computer Speech Recognition by Direct Analysis of the Speech Wave"; Ph. D. dissertation, Standford Univ., Stanford, Calif. (1966); also Computer Science Dept., Stanford Univ., Tech. Report CS 49 (1966)

6.77   D. R. REDDY: J. Acoust. Soc. Am. **41**, 1295 (1967)

6.78   D. R. REDDY: J. Acoust. Soc. Am. **42**, 329 (1967)

6.79   P. VICENS: "Aspects of Speech Recognition by Computer", Ph. D. dissertation, Stanford Univ., Stanford, Calif. (1969); also Computer Science Dept., Stanford Univ., Tech. Report CS 127 (1969)

6.80   C. C. TAPPERT, N. R. DIXON, A. S. RABINOWITZ: IEEE Trans. Audio Electroacoust. AU-**21**, 225 (1973)

6.81   C. C. TAPPERT, N. R. DIXON: Proc. Third Joint Conf. on Artificial Intelligence, 20–23 August 1973, Stanford Univ., Stanford, Calif. (1973) p. 173

6.82   N. R. DIXON, C. C. TAPPERT: "Intermediate Performance Evaluation of a Multi-Stage System for Automatic Recognition of Continuous Speech", International Business Machines Corp., RADC-TR-73-16 (1973)

6.83   J. E. PAUL, JR., A. S. RABINOWITZ: Proc. IEEE Symp. Speech Recognition, April 15–19, 1974, Carnegie-Mellon Univ., Pittsburgh, Pa. (1974) p. 63

6.84   L. R. BAHL: Proc. IEEE Symp. Speech Recognition, April 15–19, 1974, Carnegie-Mellon Univ., Pittsburgh, Pa. (abstract) (1974) p. 55

6.85   F. JELINEK, L. R. BAHL, R. L. MERCER: IEEE Trans. Inform. Theory IT-**21**, 250 (1975)

6.86   P. COHEN, R. L. MERCER: Proc. IEEE Symp. Speech Recognition, April 15–19, 1974, Carnegie-Mellon Univ., Pittsburgh, Pa. (1974) p. 177

6.87   J. K. BAKER: IEEE Trans. Acoust., Speech, Signal Processing ASSP-**23**, 24 (1975)

6.88   J. K. BAKER: In *Speech Recognition: Invited Papers presented at the IEEE Symposium*, ed. by D. R. REDDY (Academic Press, New York 1975) pp. 521–542

6.89   J. K. BAKER: Speech Communication Seminar, Aug. 1–3, 1974, Stockholm, Vol. 3 (Almqvist and Wiksell, Uppsala 1975) pp. 401–408

6.90   J. K. BAKER: "Stochastic Modeling as a Means of Automatic Speech Recognition"; Ph. D. dissertation, Carnegie-Mellon Univ., Pittsburgh, Pa. (1974)

6.91   R. DE MORI: IEEE Trans. Audio Electroacoust. AU-**21**, 89 (1973)

6.92   R. DE MORI, P. LAFACE, E. PICCOLO: Proc. Speech Communication Seminar, Aug. 1–3, 1974, Stockholm, Vol. 3 (Almqvist and Wiksell, Uppsala 1975) pp. 233–238

6.93   R. DE MORI: Proc. IFIP Congress 74 (North-Holland Publishing Co., Amsterdam 1974) p. 753

6.94   W. A. LEA: IEEE Trans. Audio Electroacoust. AU-**21**, 249 (1973)

6.95   W. A. LEA, M. F. MEDRESS, T. E. SKINNER: IEEE Trans. Acoust., Speech, Signal Processing ASSP-**23**, 30 (1975)

6.96   K.-P. LI, G. W. HUGHES, T. B. SNOW: IEEE Trans. Audio Electroacoust. AU-**21**, 50 (1973)

6.97   Y. D. WILLEMS: "The Use of Prosodics in the Automatic Recognition of Spoken English Numbers"; Ph. D. dissertation, MIT, Cambridge, Mass. (1972)

6.98   D. E. WALKER: "Speech Understanding, Computational Linguistics, and Artificial Intelligence", Stanford Research Institute, Menlo Park, Calif., Artificial Intelligence Center Note 85 (1973)

6.99   R. SCHAFER, L. RABINER: In *Speech Recognition: Invited Papers presented at the IEEE Symposium*, ed. by D. R. REDDY (Academic Press, New York 1975) pp 99–150

6.100   R. SCHAFER, L. RABINER: PROC. IEEE **63**, 662 (1975)

6.101   A. M. NOLL: J. Acoust. Soc. Am. **41**, 293 (1967)

6.102   M. M. SONDHI: IEEE Trans. Audio Electroacoust. AU-**21**, 262 (1973)

6.103   B. GOLD, L. RABINER: J. Acoust. Soc. Am. **46**, 442 (1969)

6.104   J. D. MARKEL: IEEE Trans. Audio Electroacoust. AU-**20**, 367 (1972)

6.105   D. E. WALKER: Proc. IEEE Symp. Speech Recognition, April 15–19, 1974, Carnegie-Mellon Univ., Pittsburgh, Pa. (1974) p. 32

6.106   R. V. WEEKS: Proc. IEEE Symp. Speech Recognition, April 15–19, 1974, Carnegie-Mellon Univ., Pittsburgh, Pa. (1974) p. 154

6.107   P. ROVNER, J. MAKHOUL, J. WOLF, J. COLARUSSO: Proc. IEEE Symp. Speech Recognition, April 15–19, 1974, Carnegie-Mellon Univ., Pittsburgh, Pa. (1974) p. 160

6.108   B. T. OSHIKA, V. W. ZUE, R. V. WEEKS, H. NEU, J. AURBACH: IEEE Trans. Acoust., Speech, Signal Processing ASSP-**23**, 104 (1975)

6.109   M. H. O'MALLEY, A. COLE: Proc. IEEE Symp. Speech Recognition, April 15–19, 1974, Carnegie-Mellon Univ., Pittsburgh, Pa. (1974) p. 193

6.110   J. FRIEDMAN: IEEE Trans. Acoust., Speech, Signal Processing ASSP-**23**, 100 (1975)

6.111   J. A. BARNETT: Proc. IEEE Symp. Speech Recognition, April 15–19, 1974, Carnegie-Mellon Univ., Pittsburgh, Pa. (1974) p. 188

6.112   J. W. KLOVSTAD, L. F. MONDSHEIN: IEEE Trans. Acoust., Speech, Signal Processing ASSP-**23**, 118 (1975)

6.113   W. A. WOODS: In *Speech Recognition: Invited Papers presented at the IEEE Symposium*, ed. by D. R. REDDY (Academic Press, New York 1975) pp. 345–400

6.114   W. H. PAXTON: Proc. IEEE Symp. Speech Recognition, April 15–19, 1974, Carnegie-Mellon Univ., Pittsburgh, Pa. (1974) p. 218

6.115   M. BATES: IEEE Trans. Acoust., Speech, Signal Processing ASSP-**23**, 112 (1975)

6.116   M. A. BATES: "Syntactic Analysis in a Speech Understanding System"; Ph. D. dissertation, Harvard University, Cambridge, Mass. (1975); also Bolt Beranek and Newman Inc., Cambridge, Mass., Report 3116 (1975)

6.117   E. RICH: Proc. IEEE Symp. Speech Recognition, April 15–19, 1974, Carnegie-Mellon Univ., Pittsburgh, Pa. (1974) p. 242

6.118   R. B. NEELY: "On the Use of Syntax and Semantics in a Speech Understanding System"; Ph. D. dissertation, Stanford Univ., Stanford, Calif. (1973)

6.119   M. H. O'Malley, D. R. Kloker, D. Dara-Abrams: IEEE Trans. Audio Electroacoust. AU-**21**, 217 (1973)

6.120   W. A. LEA: "Prosodic Aids to Speech Recognition: V. A Summary of Results to Date", Sperry Univac DSD, St. Paul, Minn., Report No. PX 11087 (1974)

6.121   B. NASH-WEBBER: "Semantics and Speech Understanding", Bolt Beranek and Newman Inc., Cambridge, Mass., Report No. 2896 (1974)

6.122   T. WINOGRAD: "Five Lectures on Artificial Intelligence", Stanford Univ., Stanford, Calif., Artificial Intelligence Laboratory Memo AIM-246 (1974)

6.123   J. J. ROBINSON: In *Speech Recognition: Invited Papers presented at the IEEE Symposium*, ed. by D. R. REDDY (Academic Press, New York 1975) pp. 401–427

6.124   B. G. DEUTSCH: Proc. IEEE Symp. Speech Recognition, April 15–19, 1974, Carnegie-Mellon Univ., Pittsburgh, Pa. (1974) p. 250

6.125   W. A. WOODS, M. BATES, B. BRUCE, J. COLARUSSO, C. COOK, L. GOULD, D. GRABEL, J. MAKHOUL, B. NASH-WEBBER, R. SCHWARTZ, J. WOLF: "Natural Communication with Computers", Final Report—Volume 1: Speech Understanding Research at BBN, Bolt Beranek and Newman Inc., Cambridge, Mass., Report 2976 (1974)

6.126   A. NEWELL: In *Speech Recognition: Invited Papers presented at the IEEE Symposium*, ed. by D. R. REDDY (Academic Press, New York 1975) pp. 3–54

6.127   D. R. REDDY, L. D. ERMAN: In *Speech Recognition: Invited Papers presented at the IEEE Symposium*, ed. by D. R. REDDY (Academic Press, New York 1975) pp. 457–479

6.128   V. R. LESSER: In *Speech Recognition: Invited Papers presented at the IEEE Symposium*, ed. by D. R. REDDY (Academic Press, New York 1975) pp. 481–499

6.129   J. A. BARNETT: In *Speech Recognition: Invited Papers presented at the IEEE Symposium*, ed. by D. R. REDDY (Academic Press, New York 1975) pp. 500–520

6.130   P. ROVNER, B. NASH-WEBBER, W. A. WOODS: IEEE Trans. Acoust., Speech, Signal Processing ASSP-**23**, 136 (1975)

6.131   W. A. WOODS: IEEE Trans. Acoust., Speech, Signal Processing ASSP-**23**, 2 (1975)

6.132   W. A. WOODS: 1973 Nat. Computer Conference and Exposition, AFIPS Conf. Proceedings **42**, 441 (1973)

6.133   W. A. WOODS, R. M. KAPLAN, B. NASH-WEBBER: "The Lunar Sciences Natural Language Information System: Final Report"; Bolt Beranek and Newman Inc., Cambridge, Mass., Report 2378 (1972)

6.134   W. A. WOODS, J. MAKHOUL: Proc. Third Int. Joint Conf. Artificial Intelligence, 20–23 August 1973, Stanford Univ., Stanford, Calif., (1973) p. 200; also Artificial Intelligence **5**, 73 (1974)

6.135   R. SCHWARTZ, J. MAKHOUL: IEEE Trans. Acoust., Speech, Signal Processing ASSP-**23**, 50 (1975)

6.136   J. MAKHOUL, J. WOLF: "The Use of a Two-Pole Linear Prediction Model in Speech Recognition", Bolt Beranek and Newman Inc., Cambridge, Mass., Report 2357 (1973)

6.137   W. A. WOODS: Comm. ACM **13**, 591 (1970)

6.138   W. A. WOODS: In *Natural Language Processing*, ed. by R. RUSTIN (Algorithmics Press, New York 1973) pp. 111–154

6.139   B. NASH-WEBBER: IEEE Trans. Acoust., Speech, Signal Processing ASSP-**23**, 124 (1975)

6.140   M. R. QUILLIAN: In *Semantic Information Processing*, ed. by M. MINSKY (MIT Press, Cambridge, Mass. 1965) pp. 227–270

6.141   S. SHAPIRO: "A Data Structure for Semantic Information Processing", Ph. D. dissertation, Univ. of Wisconsin, Madison, Wisc. (1971)

6.142   C. FILLMORE: In *Universals in Linguistic Theory*, ed. by E. BACH and R. HARMS (Holt, Rinehart, and Winston, Chicago 1968) pp. 1–90

6.143   D. R. REDDY, L. D. ERMAN, R. B. NEELY: IEEE Trans. Audio Electroacoust. AU-**21**, 229 (1973)

6.144   D. R. REDDY, L. D. ERMAN, R. D. FENNELL, R. B. NEELY: Proc. Third Joint Conf. Artificial Intelligence, 20–23 August 1973, Stanford Univ., Stanford, Calif. (1973) p. 194

6.145   L. D. ERMAN: "An Environment and System for Machine Understanding of Connected Speech", Ph. D. dissertation, Stanford Univ., Stanford, Calif. (1974)

6.146   V. R. LESSER, R. D. FENNELL, L. D. ERMAN, D. R. REDDY: IEEE Trans. Acoust., Speech, Signal Processing ASSP-**23**, 11 (1975)

6.147   L. SHOCKEY, L. D. ERMAN: Proc. IEEE Symp. Speech Recognition, April 15–19, 1974, Carnegie-Mellon Univ., Pittsburgh, Pa. (1974) p. 208

6.148   L. D. ERMAN, V. R. LESSER: "A Multi-Level Organization for Problem Solving Using Many, Diverse, Cooperating Sources of Knowledge", Technical Report, Computer Science Department, Carnegie-Mellon University (1975)

6.149   J. BARNETT: IEEE Trans. Audio Electroacoust. AU-**21**, 185 (1973)

6.150   R. B. RITEA: Proc. IEEE Symp. Speech Recognition, April 15–19, 1974, Carnegie-Mellon Univ., Pittsburgh, Pa. (1974) p. 28

6.151   L. MOLHO: Proc. IEEE Symp. Speech Recognition, April 15–19, 1974, Carnegie-Mellon Univ., Pittsburgh, Pa., (1974) p. 68

6.152   I. KAMENY: IEEE Trans. Acoust., Speech, Signal Processing ASSP-**23**, 38 (1975)

6.153   R. A. GILLMANN: Proc. IEEE Symp. Speech Recognition, April 15–19, 1974, Carnegie-Mellon Univ., Pittsburgh, Pa. (1974) p. 74

6.154   D. E. WALKER: Proc. Third Joint Conf. on Artificial Intelligence, August 1973, Stanford Univ., Stanford, Calif. (1973) p. 208

6.155   D. E. WALKER: "Speech Understanding Research", Annual Technical Report, 3 Oct. 1972 through 31 March 1974, Stanford Research Institute, Menlo Park, Calif. (1974)

6.156   W. H. PAXTON, A. E. ROBINSON: Proc. Third Joint Conf. Artificial Intelligence, 20–23 August 1973, Stanford Univ., Stanford, Calif. (1973) p. 216

6.157   R. BECKER, F. POZA: Proc. IEEE Symp. Speech Recognition, April 15–19, 1974, Carnegie-Mellon Univ., Pittsburgh, Pa., (abstract) (1974) p. 159; the text appears attached to D. E. WALKER: "Speech Understanding Research", Annual Technical Report, 3 Oct. 1972 through 31 March 1974, Stanford Research Institute, Menlo Park, Calif. (1974)

6.158 J. W. FORGIE: Proc. IEEE Symp. Speech Recognition, April 15–19, 1974, Carnegie-Mellon Univ., Pittsburgh, Pa. (abstract) (1974) p. 27
6.159 J. W. FORGIE: "Speech Understanding Systems", Semiannual Technical Summary, 1 June 1973–30 November 1973, MIT Lincoln Laboratory, Lexington, Mass. (1974)
6.160 J. W. FORGIE: "Speech Understanding Systems", Semiannual Technical Summary, 1 December 1973–31 May 1974, MIT Lincoln Laboratory, Lexington, Mass. (1974)
6.161 J. W. FORGIE, D. E. HALL, R. A. WIESEN: J. Acoust. Soc. Am. **56**, S 27 (abstract) (1974)
6.162 D. E. HALL, J. W. FORGIE: J. Acoust. Soc. Am. **56**, S 27 (abstract) (1974)
6.163 R. A. WIESEN, J. W. FORGIE: J. Acoust. Soc. Am. **56**, S 27 (abstract) (1974)
6.164 L. GROSS: Proc. IEEE Symp. Speech Recognition, April 15–19, 1974, Carnegie-Mellon Univ., Pittsburgh, Pa. (abstract) (1974) p. 241
6.165 C. J. WEINSTEIN, S. S. MCCANDLESS, L. F. MONDSHEIN, V. W. ZUE: IEEE Trans. Acoust., Speech, Signal Processing ASSP-**23**, 54 (1975)
6.166 S. S. MCCANDLESS: IEEE Trans. Acoust., Speech, Signal Processing ASSP-**22**, 135 (1974)
6.167 M. R. SAMBUR, L. R. RABINER: Bell Sys. Tech. J. **54**, 81 (1975)
6.168 R. NEWMAN, K.-S. FU, K.-P. LI: Proc. Conf. on Speech Communication and Processing, April 24–26, 1972, Newton, Mass. (1972) p. 121

7. Recent Developments in Digital Pattern Recognition

K. S. Fu, A. Rosenfeld, J. J. Wolf

With 5 Figures

This chapter describes some highlights of the recent developments in digital pattern recognition. The topics included provide primarily an update from the first edition of the book. First, a general framework for pattern recognition is proposed. The interpretations of the three major approaches, namely, template-matching, decision-theoretic, and syntactic, in terms of the same general framework are given. Tree grammars, stochastic languages, error-correcting parsing and clustering for syntactic pattern recognition are then briefly described. Finally, recent results in picture and speech recognition such as detection and extraction of objects, representation of objects and pictures and ARPA speech understanding project are summarized.

7.1 A General Viewpoint of Pattern Recognition

Referring to Section 1.1, we can consider that the two major subproblems in pattern recognition are pattern representation and decision-making (based on a given pattern representation). The subproblem of pattern representation involves primarily the selection of representation. The subproblem of decision-making involves primarily the selection of similarity measure. For example, in the template-matching approach, patterns are represented in terms of their raw data; the decision-making process is nothing but matching the unknown input to each template, and the matching criterion (e.g., correlation) used directly reflects the similarity between the two. In the decision-theoretic approach, a pattern is represented by N features or an N-dimensional feature vector, and the decision-making process is based on a similarity measure which, in turn, is expressed in terms of a distance measure, a likelihood function or a discriminant function. However, in the syntactic approach, a pattern is represented as a string, a tree or a graph of pattern primitives and their relations, and the decision-making process is in general a parsing procedure.

Conventional parsing requires an exact match between the unknown input sentence and a sentence generated by the pattern grammar. Such a rigid requirement often limits the applicability of the syntactic approach to noise-free or artificial patterns. Recently, the concept of similarity measure between two sentences and between one sentence and a language has been developed. Parsing can be performed using a selected similarity measure (a distance measure or a likelihood function), and an exact match becomes unnecessary. Such a parsing procedure is called "error-correcting" parsing. For more detailed discussions on the recent advances in syntactic pattern recognition and application, see [7.1, 2].

A block diagram of a pattern recognition system, based on the above general point of view, is given in Fig. 7.1. Table 7.1 summarizes the major approaches in pattern recognition in terms of the general viewpoint.

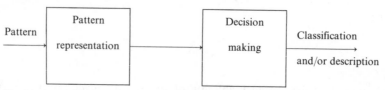

Fig. 7.1. A general pattern recognition system

Table 7.1. Classification of pattern recognition approaches

Approach	Pattern recognition	Decision-making in terms of similarity criterion
1) Template-matching	Raw data	Direct matching
2) Decision-theoretic	Feature vector	Discriminant function
		Minimum-distance
		Maximum-likelihood
		etc.
3) Syntactic	String	Parsing
	Tree	Error-correcting parsing
	Graph	Graph-matching
		Error-correcting graph matching

In the new few sections we will first introduce tree grammars and stochastic grammars for syntactic pattern recognition. Error-correcting parsing and cluster analysis of syntactic patterns (in terms of a similarity measure) are then described.

7.2 Tree Grammars for Syntactic Pattern Recognition

This section presents a brief introduction to tree grammars and their application to syntactic pattern recognition [7.3–7].

Definition 7.1. Let N^+ be the set of strictly positive integers. Let U be the universal tree domain (the free semi-group with identity element "0" generated by N^+ and a binary operation "·". Figure 7.2 represents the universal tree domain U.

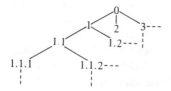

Fig. 7.2. Universal tree domain

Definition 7.2. A ranked alphabet is a pair $\langle \Sigma, r \rangle$ where Σ is a finite set of symbols and

$$r: \Sigma \rightarrow N = N^+ \cup \{0\}.$$

For $a \in \Sigma$, $r(a)$ is called the rank of a. Let $\Sigma_N = r^{-1}(n)$.

Definition 7.3. A tree over Σ (i.e., over $\langle \Sigma, r \rangle$) is a function

$$\alpha: D \rightarrow \Sigma$$

such that D is a tree domain and

$$r[\alpha(a)] = \max\{i | a \cdot i \in D\}$$

the domain of a tree α is denoted by $D(\alpha)$. Let T_Σ be the set of all trees over Σ.

Definition 7.4. Let α be a tree and "a" be a member of $D(\alpha)$. α/a, a subtree of α at a, is defined as

$$\alpha/a = \{(b, x) | (a \cdot b, x) \in \alpha\}.$$

Definition 7.5. A regular tree grammar over $\langle V_T, r \rangle$ is a 4-tuple

$$G_t = (V, r', P, S)$$

satisfying the following conditions:

    i) $\langle V, r' \rangle$ is a finite ranked alphabet with $V_T \subseteq V$ and $r'/V_T = r$. $V - V_T = V_N$, the set of nonterminals.

    ii) P is a finite set of productions of the form $\Phi \rightarrow \psi$ where Φ and ψ are trees over $\langle V, r' \rangle$.

    iii) S is a finite subset of T_V, where T_V is the set of trees over alphabet V.

Definition 7.6. $\alpha \overset{a}{\Longrightarrow} \beta$ is in G_t if and only if there exists a production $\Phi \rightarrow \psi$ in P such that Φ is a subtree of α at "a" and β is obtained by replacing the occurrence of Φ at "a" by ψ. We write $\alpha \Rightarrow \beta$ in G_t if and only if there exists $a \in D(\alpha)$ such that $\alpha \overset{a}{\Longrightarrow} \beta$.

Definition 7.7. $\alpha \overset{*}{\Longrightarrow} \beta$ is in G_t if and only if there exists $\alpha_0, \alpha_1, \ldots, \alpha_m$, $m > 0$ such that

$$\alpha = \alpha_0 \Rightarrow \alpha_1 \Rightarrow \ldots \Rightarrow \alpha_m = \beta$$

in G_t. The sequence $\alpha_0, \ldots, \alpha_m$ is called a derivative or deduction of β from α, and m is the length of the deduction.

Definition 7.8. $L(G_t) = \{\alpha \in T_{V_T} | \text{ there exists } Y \in S \text{ such that } Y \overset{*}{\Longrightarrow} \alpha \text{ in } G_t\}$ is called the (tree) language generated by G_T.

Definition 7.9. A tree grammar $G_s = (V, r, P, S)$ is expansive if and only if each production in P is of the form

$$X_0 \longrightarrow \overset{x}{\underset{X_1 \text{---} X_{r(x)}}{\bigwedge}}$$

where $x \in V_T$ and $X_0, X_1, \ldots, X_{r(x)}$ are nonterminal symbols.

Theorem 7.1. For each regular tree grammar G_t, one can effectively construct an equivalent expansive grammar G'_t i.e., $L(G'_t) = L(G_t)$ [7.3].

Example 7.1. The square object in Fig. 7.3a can be described by the tree shown in Fig. 7.3b.

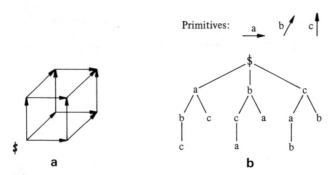

Fig. 7.3. Tree representation of a square object

Example 7.2. The tree grammar

$$G_t = (V, r, P, S),$$

where

$$V = \{S, a, b, \$, A, B\}$$
$$V_T = \{\overset{a}{\longrightarrow}, \uparrow b, \cdot \$\}$$

$$r(a) = \{2, 1, 0\}, \quad r(b) = \{2, 1, 0\}, \quad r(\$) = 2$$

and P:

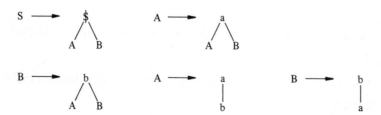

generated the patterns such as

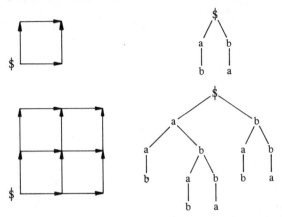

Tree automata are the recognizers (or acceptors) of regular tree languages [7.4, 5].

Definition 7.10. A tree automaton over Σ is a $(k+2)$-triple

$$M_t = (Q, f_1, ..., f_k, F),$$

where
    i) Q is a finite set of states,
    ii) for each i, $1 \leq i \leq k$, f_i is a relation on $Q^{r(\sigma_i)} \times Q$, $\sigma_i \in \Sigma$, i.e., $f_i : Q^{r(\sigma_i)} \to Q$,

and iii) $F \subseteq Q$ is a set of final states.

Definition 7.11. The response relation ϱ of a tree automaton M_t is defined as
    i) if $\sigma \in \Sigma_0$, $\varrho(\sigma) \sim X$ if and only if $f_\sigma \sim X$, i.e., $\varrho(\sigma) = f\sigma$;
    ii) if $\sigma \in \Sigma_n$, $n > 0$, $\varrho(\sigma, x_0, ..., x_{n-1}) \sim X$ if and only if there exists $x_0, ..., x_{n-1}$ such that $f\sigma(x_0, ..., x_{n-1}) \sim X$ and $\varrho(x_i) \sim X_i$, $1 \leq i \leq n$, i.e., $\varrho(\sigma, x_0, ..., x_{n-1}) = f_\sigma[\varrho(x_{n-1})]$.

Definition 7.12. $T(M_t) = \{\alpha \in T_\Sigma |$ there exists $X \in F$ such that $\varrho(\alpha) \sim X\}$ is called the set of trees accepted by M_t.

Theorem 7.2. For every regular tree grammar G_t, one can effectively construct a tree automaton M_t such that $T(M_t) = L(G_t)$ [7.4, 6].
    The construction procedure is summarized as follows:
    i) Obtain an expansive tree grammar $G_t' = (V', r, P'S)$ for the given regular tree grammar $G_t = (V, r, P, S)$ over alphabet V_T.
    ii) The equivalent (nondeterministic) tree automaton is

$$M_t = (V' - V_T, f_1, ..., f_{k'} \{S\}),$$

where $f_x(X_1, ..., X_n) \sim X_0$ if $X_0 \to x X_1, ..., X_n$ is in P'.

The tree automaton which accepts the set of trees generated by G_t in Example 7.2 is

$$M_t = (A, f_a, f_b, f, F)$$

where

$$Q = \{q_a, q_b, q, q_F\}$$
$$F = \{q_F\},$$

and f:

$$f_a = q_a \quad f_a(q, q) = q \quad f_a(q_b) = q$$
$$f_b = q_b \quad f_b(q, q) = q \quad f_b(q_a) = q$$
$$f_\$(q, q) = q_F.$$

Example 7.3. The following tree grammar can be used to generate trees representing $L - C$ networks shown in Fig. 7.4:

$$G_t = (V, r, P, S),$$

where

$$V = \{S, V_{\text{in}}, L, C, W, |\}$$
$$r(V_{\text{in}}) = 1, r(L) = \{2, 0\}, \quad r(C) = 1, \quad r(W) = 0, \quad r(\$) = 2$$

and P:

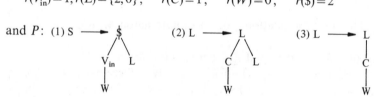

For example, after applying production (1), (2), and (3), the following tree is generated.

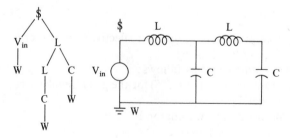

The tree automaton which accepts the set of trees generated by G_t is

$$M_t = (Q, f_{V_{\text{in}}}, f_L, f_C, f_W, f, F),$$

where

$$Q = \{q_1, q_2, q_3, q_4, q_F\}$$
$$F = \{q_F\},$$

and f:

$$f_{V_{in}}(q_1) = q_4, \quad f_L(q_3) = q_2$$
$$f_L = q_2, \quad f_L(q_2, q_3) = q_2$$
$$f_C(q_1) = q_3$$
$$f_W = q_1$$
$$f_{\$}(q_2, q_4) = q_F.$$

7.3 Syntactic Pattern Recognition Using Stochastic Languages

In some practical applications, a certain amount of uncertainty exists in the process under study. For example, due to the presence of noise and variation in the pattern measurements, segmentation error and primitive extraction error may occur, causing ambiguities in the pattern description languages. In order to describe noisy and distorted patterns under ambiguous situations, the use of stochastic languages has been suggested [7.9]. With probabilities associated with grammar rules, a stochastic grammar generates sentences with a probability distribution. The probability distribution of the sentences can be used to model the noisy situations.

A stochastic grammar is a four-tuple $G_s = (V_N, V_T, P_s, S)$ where P_s is a finite set of stochastic productions. For a stochastic context-free grammar, a production in P_s is of the form

$$A_i \xrightarrow{p_{ij}} \alpha_j, \quad A_i \in V_N, \quad \alpha_j \in (V_N \cup V_T)^*,$$

where p_{ij} is called the production probability. The probability of generating a string x, called the string probability $p(x)$, is the product of all production probabilities associated with the productions used in the generation of x. The language generated by a stochastic grammar consists of the strings generated by the grammar and their associated string probabilities.

By associating probabilities with the strings, we can impose a probabilistic structure on the language to describe noisy patterns. The probability distribution characterizing the patterns in a class can be interpreted as the probability distribution associated with the strings in a language. Thus, statistical decision rules can be applied to the classification of a pattern under ambiguous situations (for example, use the maximum-likelihood or Bayes decision rule). A block diagram of such a recognition system using maximum-likelihood decision rule is shown in Fig. 7.5. Furthermore, because of the availability of the information about production probabilities, the speed of syntactic analysis can be improved through the use of this information [7.9]. Of course, in practice, the production probabilities will have to be inferred from the observation of relatively large number of pattern samples. When the imprecision and uncertainty involving in the pattern description can be modeled by using the fuzzy set theory, the use of fuzzy languages for syntactic pattern recognition has recently been suggested [7.10].

Other approaches for the recognition of distorted or noisy patterns using syntactic methods include the use of transformational grammar [7.11, 12] and approximation [7.13], and the application of error-correcting parsing techniques.

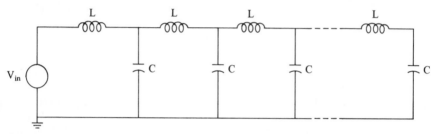

Fig. 7.4. $L-C$ network

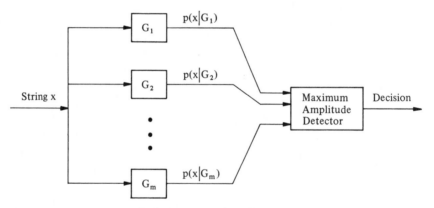

Fig. 7.5. Maximum-likelihood syntactic recognition system

7.4 Error-Correcting Parsing

In practical applications, pattern distortion and measurement noise often exist. Pattern segmentation errors and misrecognitions of primitives (and relations) and/or subpatterns will lead to erroneous or noisy sentences rejected by the grammar characterizing its class. Recently, the use of an error-correcting parser as a recognizer of noisy and distorted patterns has been proposed [7.14–18]. In the use of an error-correcting parser as a recognizer, the pattern grammar is first expanded to include all the possible errors into its productions. The original grammar is transformed into a covering grammar that generates not only the correct sentences, but also all the possible erroneous sentences. For string grammars, three types of error—substitution, deletion and insertion—are considered. Misrecognition of primitives (and relations) are regarded as substitution errors, and segmentation errors as deletion and insertion errors.

The distance between two strings is defined in terms of the minimum number of error transformations used to derive one from the other by AHO and PETERSON [7.19]. When the error transformations are defined in terms of substitution, deletion and insertion errors, the distance measurement coincides with the definition of Levenshtein metric [7.20]. For a given input string y and a given grammar G, a minimum-distance error-correcting parser[1] (MDECP) is an algorithm that searches for a sentence z in $L(G)$ such that the distance between z and y, $d(z, y)$ is the minimum among the distances between all the sentences in $L(G)$ and y. The algorithm also generates the value of $d(z, y)$ and this value is defined to be the distance between $L(G)$ and y, denoted as $d_1[L(G), y]$.

When a given grammar is a context-free grammar (CFG), its MDECP can be implemented by modifying Earley's parsing algorithm. We also extend the definition of the distance between $L(G)$ and y, $d_1[L(G), y]$, to the definition of $d_K[L(G), y]$, the average distance between y and the K sentences in $L(G)$ that are the nearest to y. The computation of $d_K[L(G), y]$ can be implemented by further modification of the algorithm of MDECP.

Definition 7.13. For two strings. $x, y \in \Sigma^*$, we can define a transformation T: $\Sigma^* \to \Sigma^*$ such that $y \in T(x)$. The following three transformations are introduced:
  1) substitution error transformation

$$\omega_1 a \omega_2 | \xrightarrow{T_S} \omega_1 b \omega_2, \quad \text{for all } a, b \in \Sigma, \quad a \neq b,$$

  2) deletion error transformation

$$\omega_1 a \omega_2 | \xrightarrow{T_D} \omega_1 \omega_2, \quad \text{for all } a \in \Sigma,$$

  3) insertion error transformation

$$\omega_1 \omega_2 | \xrightarrow{T_I} \omega_1 a \omega_2, \quad \text{for all } a \in \Sigma$$

where $\omega_1, \omega_2 \in \Sigma^*$.

Definition 7.14. The distance between two strings $x, y \in \Sigma^*$, $d^L(x, y)$, is defined as the smallest number of transformations required to derive y from x.

Example 7.4. Given a sentence $x = cbabdbb$ and a sentence $y = cbbabbdb$, then
$X = cbabdbb$

$$| \xrightarrow{T_S} cbabbbb | \xrightarrow{T_S} cbabbdb | \xrightarrow{T_I} cbbabbdb = y.$$

The minimum number of transformations required to transform x to y is three; thus, $d^L(x, y) = 3$.

---

[1] If the pattern grammar is stochastic, the maximum-likelihood and Bayes criteria can be applied [7.14, 17].

The metric defined in Definition 7.14 gives exactly the Levenshtein distance between two strings [7.20]. A weighted Levenshtein distance can be defined by assigning nonnegative numbers σ, γ, and δ to transformations T_S, T_D, and T_I, respectively. Let $x, y \in \Sigma^*$ be two strings, and let J be a sequence of transformations used to derive y from x; then the weighted Levenshtein distance between x and y, denoted as $d^w(x, y)$ is

$$d^w(x, y) = \min_j \{\sigma \cdot k_j + \gamma \cdot m_j + \delta \cdot n_j\}, \tag{7.1}$$

where k_j, m_j, and n_j are the number of substitution, deletion, and insertion error transformations, respectively, in J.

We shall propose a weighted metric that would reflect the difference of the same type of error made on different terminals. Let the weights associated with error transformations on terminal a in a string $\omega_1 a \omega_2$ where $a \in \Sigma$, ω_1 and $\omega_2 \in \Sigma^*$, be defined as follows:

1) $\omega_1 a \omega_2 |\xrightarrow{Td, S(a,b)} \omega_1 b \omega_2$ for $b \in \Sigma$, $b \neq a$, where $S(a, b)$ is the cost of substituting a for b. Let $S(a, a) = 0$.

2) $\omega_1 a \omega_2 |\xrightarrow{T_D, D(a)} \omega_1 \omega_2$ where $D(a)$ is the cost of deleting a from $\omega_1 a \omega_2$.

3) $\omega_1 a \omega_2 |\xrightarrow{T_I, I(a,b)} \omega_1 b a \omega_2$ for $b \in \Sigma$, where $I(a, b)$ is the cost of inserting b in front of a.

We further define the weight of inserting a terminal b at the end of a string x to be

4) $x |\xrightarrow{T_I, I'(b)} xb$, for $b \in \Sigma$.

Let $x, y \in \Sigma^*$ be two strings, and J be a sequence of transformations used to derive y from x. Let $|J|$ be defined as the sum of the weights associated with transformations in J; then the weighted distance between x and y, $d^W(x, y)$ is defined as

$$d^W(x, y) = \min_J \{|J|\}. \tag{7.2}$$

Let $L(G)$ be a given language and y be a given sentence; the essence of minimum-distance error-correcting parsing is to search for a sentence x in $L(G)$ that satisfies the minimum distance criterion as follows:

$$d(x, y) = \min_z \{d(z, y) | z \in L(G)\}. \tag{7.3}$$

We note that the minimum-distance correction of y is y itself if $y \in L(G)$.

We shall extend the minimum-distance ECP proposed by AHO and PETERSON [7.19] to all three types of metric, L, w, and W. In [7.19], the procedure for constructing an ECP starts with the modification of a given grammar G by adding the three types of error transformations in the form of production rules, called error productions. The grammar G is now expanded to G' such that $L(G')$ includes not only $L(G)$, but all possible sentences with the three types of errors. The parser constructed according to G' with a provision added to count the number of error productions used in a derivation is the error-correcting parser for G. For a given sentence y, the ECP will generate a parse Π which consists of the smallest number of error productions. A sentence x in $L(G)$ that satisfies the minimum-distance criterion (measured by using Levenshtein distance) can be generated from Π by eliminating error productions. With some modifications, this minimum-distance ECP can easily be extended to the three metrics proposed. We first give the algorithm of constructing an expanded grammar, in which the nonnegative numbers associated with error-productions are the weights associated with their corresponding transformations with respect to the metric used.

Algorithm 7.1. Construction of expanded grammar
  Input :   A CFG $G=(N,\Sigma,P,S)$.
  Output :   A CFG $G'=(N',\Sigma',P',S')$ where P' is a set of weighted productions.

Method :
  Step 1 $N'=N\cup\{S'\}\cup\{E_a|a\in\Sigma\}$, $\Sigma'\supseteq\Sigma$.
  Step   If $A\rightarrow\alpha_0 b_1\alpha_1 b_2\ldots b_m\alpha_m$, $m\geq0$ is a production in P such that $\alpha_i\in N^*$ and $b_i\in\Sigma$, then add $A\rightarrow\alpha_0 E_{b_1}\alpha_1 E_{b_2}\ldots E_{b_m}\alpha_m,0$ to P', where each E_{b_i} is a new non-terminal, $E_{b_i}\in N'$ and 0 is the weight associated with this production.
  Step 3   Add the following productions to P'.

Production rule	Weight					
	L	w	W (metric)			
a) $S'\rightarrow S$	0	0	0			
b) $S'\rightarrow Sa$	1	δ	$I'(a)$	for all	$a\in\Sigma'$	
c) $E_a\rightarrow a$	0	0	0	for all	$a\in\Sigma$	
d) $E_a\rightarrow b$	1	σ	$S(a,b)$	for all	$a\in\Sigma,$	$b\in\Sigma',$ and $b\neq a$
e) $E_a\rightarrow\lambda$	1	γ	$D(a)$	for all	$a\in\Sigma$	
f) $E_a\rightarrow bE_a$	1	δ	$I(a,b)$	for all	$a\in\Sigma,$	$b\in\Sigma'$

In Algorithm 7.1 the production rules added in Steps 3b, 3d, 3e, and 3f are called error productions. Each error production corresponds to one type of error transformation on a particular symbol in Σ. Therefore, the distance measured in terms of error transformations can be measured by error productions used in a derivation. The parser is a modified Earley's parsing algorithm with a provision added to accumulate the weights associated with productions used in a derivation. The algorithm is as follows.

Algorithm 7.2. Minimum-distance error-correcting parsing algorithm
  Input :   An expanded grammar $G'=(N',\Sigma',P',S')$ and an input string $y=b_1 b_2\ldots b_m$ in Σ'^*.
  Output : $I_0,I_1\ldots I_m$ the parse list for y, and $d(x,y)$ where x is the minimum-distance correction of y.

Method:

Step 1   Set $j=0$. Then add $[E \rightarrow \cdot S', 0, 0]$ to I_j.

Step 2   If $[A \rightarrow \alpha \cdot B\beta, i, \xi]$ is in I_j, and $B \rightarrow \gamma, \eta$ is a production rule in P', then add item $[B \rightarrow \cdot \gamma, j, 0]$ to I_j.

Step 3   If $[A \rightarrow \alpha \cdot, i, \xi]$ is in I_j and $[B \rightarrow \beta \cdot A\gamma, k, \xi]$ is in I_i, and if no item of the form $[B \rightarrow \beta A \cdot \gamma, k, \phi]$ can be found in I_j, then add an item $[B \rightarrow \beta A \cdot \gamma, k, \eta + \xi + \zeta)$ to I_j where ζ is the weight associated with production $A \rightarrow \alpha$. If $[B \rightarrow \beta A \cdot \gamma, k, \phi]$ is already in I_j, then replace ϕ by $\eta + \xi + \zeta$ if $\phi > \eta + \xi L \zeta$.

Step 4   If $j=m$, go to Step 6; otherwise $j=j+1$.

Step 5   For each item in I_{j-1} of the form $[A \rightarrow \alpha \cdot b_j \beta, i, \xi]$ add item $[A \rightarrow \alpha b_j \cdot \beta, i, \xi]$ to I_j; go to Step 2.

Step 6   If item $[E \rightarrow S', 0, \xi]$ is in I_m, then $d(x, y) = \xi$, where x is the minimum-distance correction of y, exit.

In Algorithm 7.2, the string x, which is the minimum-distance correction of y, can be derived from the parse of y by eliminating all the error productions. The extraction of the parse of y is the same as that described in Earley's algorithm.

We shall define the distance between a string and a given language based on any one of the three metrics as follows.

Definition 7.15. Let y be a sentence, and $L(G)$ be a given language, the distance between $L(G)$ and y, $d_K[L(G), y]$, where K is a given positive integer, is;

$$d_K[L(G), y] = \min \left\{ \sum_{i=1}^{K} \frac{1}{K} d(z_i, y) | z_i \in L(G) \right\}. \tag{7.4}$$

In particular, if $K=1$, then

$$d_1[L(G), y] = \min \{ d(z, y) | z \in L(G) \} \tag{7.5}$$

is the distance between y and its minimum-distance correction in $L(G)$.

As the distance between a string (a syntactic pattern) and a language (a set of syntactic patterns) is defined, a minimum-distance decision rule can be stated as follows: suppose that there are two classes of patterns C_1 and C_2 characterized by grammars G_1 and G_2, respectively. For a given syntactic pattern y with unknown classification, decide $y \in {c_1 \atop c_2}$ if $d[L(G_1), y] \lessgtr d[L(G_2), y]$.

The sequential parsing procedure suggested by PERSOON and FU [7.21] has been applied to the error-correcting parser to reduce the parsing time [14]. By sacrificing a small amount of error-correcting power (that is, allowing a small error in parsing), a parsing could be terminated much earlier before a complete sentence is scanned. The trade-off between the parsing time and the error committed can be easily demonstrated. In addition, error-correcting parsing for transition network grammars [7.17] and tree grammars [7.18] has also been studied. For tree grammars, five types of error—substitution, deletion, stretch, branch, and split—are considered. The original tree pattern grammar is expanded by including the five types of error transformation rule. The tree automaton constructed according to the expanded tree grammar and the minimum-distance criterion is called an error-correcting tree automaton (ECTA). When only substitution errors are considered, the structure of the tree to be analyzed remains unchanged. Such an error-correcting tree automaton is called a "structure-preserved error-correcting tree automaton" (SPECTA) [7.22]. Another approach to reduce the parsing time is the use of parallel processing [7.23].

7.5 Clustering Analysis for Syntactic Patterns

In statistical pattern recognition, a pattern is represented by a vector, called a feature vector. The similarity between two patterns can often be expressed by a distance, or more generally speaking, a metric in the feature space. Cluster analysis can be performed on a set of patterns on the basis of a selected similarity measure [7.24]. In syntactic pattern recognition a similarity measure between two syntactic patterns must include the similarity of both their structures and primitives. In Sect. 7.4, we have proposed distance measures for strings, which leads to the study of clustering analysis for syntactic patterns. The conventional clustering methods, such as the minimum spanning tree, the nearest (or K-nearest) neighbor classification rule and the method of clustering centers, can be extended to syntactic patterns.

The studies described in Section 7.5.1 are mainly on the pattern-to-pattern basis [7.24]. An input sentence (a pattern) is compared with sentences in a formed cluster, one by one, or with the representative (cluster center) of the cluster. In Section 7.5.2 we shall use the distance measure between a sentence and a language [7.25]. The proposed clustering procedure is combined with a grammatical inference procedure and an error-correcting parsing technique. The idea is to model the formed cluster by inferring a grammar, which implicitly characterizes the structural identity of the cluster. The language generated by the grammar may be larger than the set consisting of the members of the cluster, and includes some possible similar patterns due to the recursive nature of grammar. Then the distance between an input sentence (a syntactic pattern) and a language (a group of syntactic patterns) is computed by using an ECP. The recognition is based on the nearest neighbor rule.

7.5.1 Sentence-to-Sentence Clustering Algorithms

A Nearest Neighbor Classification Rule

Suppose that C_1 and C_2 are two pattern sets, represented by sentences $X_1 = \{x_1^1, x_2^1, ..., x_{n_1}^1\}$ and $X_2 = \{x_1^2, x_2^2, ..., s_{n_2}^2\}$, respectively. For an unknown syntactic pattern y, decide that y is in the same class as C_1 if

$$\min_j d(x_j^1, y) < \min_l d(x_l^2, y) \, ;$$

and y is in class C_2 if

$$\min_j d(x_j^1, y) > \min_l d(x_l^2, y). \tag{7.6}$$

In order to determine $\min_j d(x^i_j, y)$, for some i, the distances between y and every element in the set X_i have to be computed individually. The string-to-string correction algorithm proposed in [7.24] yields exactly the distance between two strings defined in Definiiton 7.14.

The nearest neighbor classification rule can be easily extended to the K-nearest neighbor rule. Let $\tilde{X}_i = \{\tilde{x}^i_1, \tilde{x}^i_2, \ldots, \tilde{x}^i_{n_i}\}$ be a reordered set of X_i such that $d(\tilde{x}^i_j, y) \leq d(\tilde{x}^i_l, y)$ if $j < l$, for all $1 \leq j$, $l \leq n_i$; then

$$\text{decide} \quad y \in \begin{smallmatrix} C_1 \\ C_2 \end{smallmatrix} \quad \text{if} \quad \sum_{j=1}^{K} \frac{1}{K} d(\tilde{x}^1_j, y) \lessgtr \sum_{j=1}^{K} \frac{1}{K} d(\tilde{x}^2_j, y). \tag{7.7}$$

We shall describe a clustering procedure in which the classification of an input pattern is based on the nearest (or K-nearest) neighbor rule.

Algorithm 7.3

    Input :   A set of samples $X = \{x_1, x_2, \ldots, x_n\}$ and a design parameter, or threshold, t.

    Output :   A partition of X into m clusters, $C_1, C_2, \ldots, C_m$.

    Method :

    Step 1   Assign to C_1, $j = 1$, $m = 1$.

    Step 2   Increase j by one. If $D = \min d(x^i_l, x_j)$ is the minimum, $1 \leq i \leq m$, and

        i) $D \leq t$, then assign x_j to C_i.

        ii) $D > t$, then initiate a new cluster for x_j, and increase m by one.

    Step 3   Repeat Step 2 until every string in X has been put in a cluster.

Note that, in Algorithm 7.3, a design parameter is required. A commonly used clustering procedure is to construct a minimum spanning tree. Each node on the minimum spanning tree represents an element in the sample set X. Then partition the tree. Actually, when the distances between all of the pairs, $d(x_i, x_j)$, x_i, $x_j \in X$, are available, the algorithm for constructing the minimum spanning tree is the same as that where X is a set of feature vectors in the statistical pattern recognition Chapter 3 and [7.26].

The Cluster Center Techniques

Let us define a β-metric for a sentence x^i_j in cluster C_i as follows:

$$\beta^i_j = \frac{1}{n_i} \sum_{l=1}^{n_i} d(x^i_j, x^i_l). \tag{7.8}$$

Then, x^i_j is the cluster center of C_i, if $\beta^i_j = \min_l \{\beta^i_l | 1 < l < n_i\}$, x^i_j is also called the representative of C_i, denoted A_i.

Algorithm 7.4

    Input :   A sample set $X = \{x_1, x_2, \ldots, x_n\}$.

    Output :   A partition of X into m clusters.

Method:

> *Step 1*   Let m elements of X, chosen at random, be the "representatives" of the m clusters. Let them be called $A_1, A_2, \ldots, A_m$.
>
> *Step 2*   For all i, $x_i \in X$ is assigned to cluster j, if $d(A_j, x_i)$ is minimum.
>
> *Step 3*   For all j, a new mean A_j is computed. A_j is the new representative of cluster j.
>
> *Step 4*   If no A_j has changed, stop. Otherwise, go to Step 2.

7.5.2 A Proposed Nearest Neighbor Syntactic Recognition Rule

With the distance between a sentence and a language defined in Section 7.4, we can construct a syntactic recognizer using the nearest (or K-nearest) neighbor rule. Suppose that we are given two classes of patterns characterized by grammar G_1 and G_2, respectively. For an unknown syntactic pattern y, decide that y is in the same class as $L(G_1)$ if

$$d[L(G_1), y] < d[L(G_2), y]$$

and decide that y is in the same class as $L(G_2)$ if

$$d[L(G_2), y] < d[L(G_1), y]. \tag{7.9}$$

The distance $d[L(G_i), y]$ can be determined by a minimum-distance ECP constructed for G_i. Consequently, a grammatical inference procedure is required to infer a grammar for each class of pattern samples. Since the parser also gives the structural description of y, the syntactic recognizer gives both the classification and description of y as its output. We shall summarize the procedure in the following algorithm.

Algorithm 7.5

> *Input:* m sets of syntactic pattern samples
>
> $$X_1 = \{x_1^1, x_2^1, \ldots, x_{n_1}^1\}, \ldots, X_m = \{x_1^m, x_2^m, \ldots, x_{n_m}^m\}$$
>
> and a pattern y with unknown classification.
>
> *Output:*   The classification and structural description of y.

Method:

> *Step 1*   Infer m grammars $G_1, G_2, \ldots, G_m$, from $X_1, X_2, \ldots, X_m$, respectively.
>
> *Step 2*   Construct minimum-distance ECP's,
>
> $$E_1, E_2, \ldots, E_m \quad \text{for} \quad G_1, G_2, \ldots, G_m, \quad \text{respectively.}$$
>
> *Step 3*   Calculate $d[L(G_k), y]$ for all $i = 1, \ldots, m$. Determine l such that
>
> $$d[L(G_l), y] = \min_k d[L(G_k), y].$$
>
> y is then classified as from class l. In the meantime, the structural description of x can be obtained from E_l.

Using the distance defined in Sect. 7.4 as a similarity measure between a syntactic pattern and a set of syntactic patterns, we can perform a cluster analysis to syntactic patterns. The procedure again involves error-correcting parsing and grammatical inference. In contrast to the nearest neighbor rule in Algorithm 7.4 which uses a supervised inference procedure, the procedure described in this section is basically nonsupervised. When the syntactic pattern samples are observed sequentially, a grammar can be easily inferred for the sample observed at each stage of the clustering procedure. We propose the following clustering procedure for syntactic patterns.

Algorithm 7.6

Input :   A set of syntactic pattern samples $X = \{x_1, x_2, \ldots, x_n\}$ where x_i is a string of terminals or primitives. A threshold t.

Output :   The assignment of x_i, $i = 1, \ldots, n$ to m clusters and the grammar $G^{(k)}$, $k = 1, \ldots, m$, characterizing each cluster.

Method:

Step 1   Input the first sample x_1; infer a grammar $G_1^{(1)}$ from x_1, $L[G_1^{(1)}] \subseteq \{x_1\}$.

Step 2   Construct an error-correcting parser $E_1^{(1)}$ for $G_1^{(1)}$.

Step 3   Input the second sample x_2; use $E_1^{(1)}$ to determine whether or not x_2 is similar to x_1 by comparing the distance between $L[G_1^{(1)}]$ and x_2, i.e., $d\{x_2, L[G_1^{(1)}]\}$, with a threshold t.

i) If $d\{x_2, L[G_1^{(1)}]\} < t$, x_1 and x_2 are put into the same cluster (Cluster 1). Infer a grammar $G_2^{(1)}$ from $\{x_1, x_2\}$.

ii) If $d\{x_2, L[G_1^{(1)}]\} \geq t$, initiate a new cluster for x_2 (Cluster 2) and infer a new grammar $G_1^{(2)}$ from x_2. In this case, there are two clusters characterized by $G_1^{(1)}$ and $G_1^{(2)}$, respectively.

Step 4   Repeat Step 2; construct error-correcting parsers for $G_2^{(1)}$ or $G_1^{(2)}$ depending upon $d\{x_2, L[G_1^{(1)}]\} < t$ or $d\{x_2, L[G_1^{(1)}]\} \geq t$, respectively.

Step 5   Repeat Step 3 for a new sample. Until all the pattern samples are observed, we have m clusters characterized by $G_{n_1}^{(1)}, G_{n_2}^{(2)}, \ldots, G_{n_m}^{(m)}$, respectively.

The parsers (non-error-correcting) constructed according to $G_{n_1}^{(1)}, G_{n_2}^{(2)}, \ldots, G_{n_m}^{(m)}$ could then form a syntactic recognizer directly for the m-class recognition problem.

The threshold t is a design parameter. It can be determined from a set of pattern samples with known classifications. For example, if we know that the sample x_i is from Class 1 characterized by $G^{(1)}$ and the sample x_j is from Class 2 characterized by $G^{(2)}$, then $t < d(x_i, x_j)$. Or, more generally speaking,

$$t < \min \{d(L[G^{(2)}], x_i), d(L[G^{(1)}], x_j)\}. \tag{7.10}$$

For m classes characterized by $G^{(1)}, G^{(2)}, \ldots, G^{(m)}$, respectively, we can choose

$$t < \min_{k,l} \{d(L[G^{(l)}], x^{(k)})\}, \quad k \neq l, \tag{7.11}$$

where $x^{(k)}$ is a pattern sample known from Class k and $L[G^{(l)}]$ is the grammar characterizing Class l $(l \neq k)$. If the above required information is not available, an appropriate value of t will have to be determined on an experimental basis until a certain stopping criterion is satisfied (for example, with a known number of clusters).

7.6 Picture Recognition

In the rapidly growing field of picture recognition, it is impractical to give a comprehensive review of developments since the original appearance of Chapter 5. We mention here only a few general references, including two new textbooks [7.27, 28] and a continuing series of bibliographies [7.29–33]. In the following sections, we briefly discuss a few specific areas, corresponding to the sections in the original chapter.

7.6.1 Properties of Regions

For a recent review of texture analysis see [7.34]. In the following paragraphs we briefly describe a number of general approaches; references on these approaches can be found in [7.34].

We can use second-order as well as first-order local property statistics as texture descriptors, by constructing co-occurrence matrices of local property values in given relative positions. If desired, we can use only selected pairs of points in constructing the matrices, e.g., pairs of extrema or pairs of above-threshold edge points, and we can use displacements that depend on the value at the point, e.g., displacements in the gradient direction. Similarly, we can use second-order gray level statistics obtained from such selected pairs of points as texture descriptors.

Rather than using a set of local properties, e.g., differences computed for a set of displacements, we can use a single property and measure it for pictures derived from the original one by a set of local operations. For example, suppose that we use a sequence of local min (or max) operations, and at each step measure the average gray level; the rate at which this decreases (or increases) is a measure of the coarseness of the high-valued (low-valued) patches in f. For a binary-valued f, the analogous idea is to shrink (or expand) the l's in f repeatedly, and at each step count the number of l's. This approach, using generalized shrinking and expanding operations, has been extensively used for texture analysis in microscopy.

A texture can be modeled as a correlated random field, e.g., as an array of independent identically distributed random variables, to which a filtering operator has been applied. This model suggests that a texture can be described by its autocorrelation and by the probability density of the original random variables; the latter can be approximated by a histogram after a "whitening" operation has been applied to decorrelate the texture. If we use the gradient or Laplacian as an approximate whitening operation, the histogram is just a histogram of difference values.

The texture descriptors considered so far are derived from local or point pair properties. We conclude by briefly discussing texture description in terms of homogeneous patches or "primitive" regions. Several types of texture models are based on such decompositions into regions. For example, textures can be generated by using a random geometric process to tessellate the plane into cells, or drop objects onto the plane, and then selecting gray levels (or gray level probability densities) for the cells or objects in accordance with some probability law.

If we can explicitly extract a reasonable set of primitives from f, we can describe the texture of f using statistics of properties of these primitives—e.g., the mean or standard deviation of their average gray level, area, perimeter, orientation (of principal axis), eccentricity, etc. Second-order statistics can also be used—i.e., we can construct matrices for pairs of values of the area (etc.) at pairs of neighboring primitives (perhaps in directions defined by each primitive's orientation). Of course, this approach depends on being able to extract a good set of primitives from f at a reasonable computational cost. A related, but much simpler, idea is to extract maximal homogeneous blocks (e.g., runs of constant gray level in various directions) from f, and describe f in terms of (first- or second-order) statistics of the block sizes (e.g., run lengths).

In general, the description of textures in terms of primitives may be hierarchical; the primitives may be composed of subprimitives, etc., or they may be arranged into groupings which in turn form larger groupings, etc. This makes it possible to define placement rules for the primitives in the form of stochastic grammars. Texture analysis can thus be carried out, in principle, by parsing with respect to a set of such grammars.

7.6.2 Detection of Objects

Template Matching

A "relaxation" approach can be used to find matches to a template that is composed of subtemplates. Initially, match merits are computed for all the subtemplates in all positions on the picture. Each of these merits is then adjusted by amounts that depend on the merits of matches to the other parts of the template in or near the proper relative positions. When this process is iterated, the merits corresponding to good matches of the entire template remain high, while all other merits become low. A general discussion of "relaxation" methods in picture processing and analysis, including references to specific uses of such methods, can be found in [7.35].

Edge Detection

A variety of local difference operators have been used for edge detection. One can take differences in two orthogonal directions, and estimate the gradient magnitude and direction by combining their responses. Three examples of this approach are the Roberts operator, based on convolving the picture with the templates

$$\begin{matrix} 0 & 1 \\ -1 & 0 \end{matrix} \quad \text{and} \quad \begin{matrix} 1 & 0 \\ 0 & -1 \end{matrix} \; ;$$

the Prewitt operator, based on convolving it with

$$
\begin{array}{ccc}
-1 & 0 & 1 \\
-1 & 0 & 1 \\
-1 & 0 & 1
\end{array}
\quad\text{and}\quad
\begin{array}{ccc}
1 & 1 & 1 \\
0 & 0 & 0 \\
-1 & -1 & -1
\end{array} ;
$$

and the Sobel operator, based on convolving with

$$
\begin{array}{ccc}
-1 & 0 & 1 \\
-2 & 0 & 2 \\
-1 & 0 & 1
\end{array}
\quad\text{and}\quad
\begin{array}{ccc}
1 & 2 & 1 \\
0 & 0 & 0 \\
-1 & -2 & -1
\end{array} .
$$

Alternatively, one can use operators in many directions and take the maximum of their responses; for example, one can use a Prewitt operator that also includes

$$
\begin{array}{ccc}
0 & 1 & 1 \\
-1 & 0 & 1 \\
-1 & -1 & 0
\end{array}
\quad\text{and}\quad
\begin{array}{ccc}
1 & 1 & 0 \\
1 & 0 & -1 \\
0 & -1 & -1
\end{array} ,
$$

or a Sobel operator that includes

$$
\begin{array}{ccc}
0 & 1 & 2 \\
-1 & 0 & 1 \\
-2 & -1 & 0
\end{array}
\quad\text{and}\quad
\begin{array}{ccc}
2 & 1 & 0 \\
1 & 0 & -1 \\
0 & -1 & -2
\end{array} ,
$$

or one can use the Kirsch operator, based on the eight templates

$$
\begin{array}{ccc}
-3 & -3 & 5 \\
-3 & 0 & 5, \\
-3 & -3 & 5
\end{array}
\quad
\begin{array}{ccc}
-3 & 5 & 5 \\
-3 & 0 & 5, \\
-3 & -3 & -3
\end{array}
\quad
\begin{array}{ccc}
5 & 5 & 5 \\
-3 & 0 & -3, \dots \\
-3 & -3 & -3
\end{array}
$$

A review of edge detection techniques can be found in [7.36].

One way of deriving useful edge detection operators is to fit a simple function to the gray levels in a neighborhood of each point, and use the gradient of that function as an estimate of the digital gradient at that point. For example, if we fit a least-squares plane to a 2-by-2 neighborhood, it turns out that the x and y partial derivatives of that plane are proportional to the differences obtained by convolving the picture with the templates

$$
\begin{array}{cc}
-1 & 1 \\
-1 & 1
\end{array}
\quad\text{and}\quad
\begin{array}{cc}
1 & 1 \\
-1 & -1
\end{array} ;
$$

while if we fit a quadric surface to a 3-by-3 neighborhood, its x and y partial derivatives are proportional to the components of the Prewitt operator.

Edges or curves having given shapes (e.g., straight, circular, etc.) can be detected by applying a coordinate transformation to the picture such that all points belonging to a particular straight line (or circle, etc.) map into a single position in the transformed space. This approach, which is known as the "Hough transform" approach, maps global features (sets of points belonging to a given locus) into local features (peaks or clusters of high values), which are often easier to detect. A review of methods of this type can be found in [7.37].

In practice, edge and curve detection operations may yield noisy responses at points that do not lie on object borders, and may fail to respond at points that do. The noisiness of the responses can be reduced by allowing responses to reinforce one another if they correspond to smooth continuations of an edge or curve. When this reinforcement process is iterated, we obtain high response values at points that lie on smooth edges or curves, and low values elsewhere. On this "relaxation" approach to edge and curve detection see [7.35].

When large pieces of edges or curves have been extracted from a picture, they can be further linked into global curves. The criteria for linking two curves into a larger curve might depend on their strengths (i.e., the average strengths of the original responses), lengths, and mutual alignment or "good continuation". Of course, if global curves of specific shapes are desired, this can also be taken into account in defining the linking criteria.

7.6.3 Object Extraction

Thresholding

A survey of threshold selection techniques can be found in [7.38]. In general, rather than classifying the picture points as object or background points in a single step, one can estimate the probability of each point's belonging to the object and background classes, and use an iterative "relaxation" process to adjust these estimates, based on the neighboring estimates [7.35].

Thresholding and edge detection can be combined in a number of ways to provide "convergent evidence" for object extraction. When a picture is thresholded, a set of borders between the above-threshold and below-threshold regions is defined. Noise edge responses can be largely eliminated by discarding all responses that do not lie on (or near) these borders. At the same time, gaps in edges can be filled by linking the edge points along the borders, using border following techniques; this makes it possible to fill large gaps without the need for extensive search. More generally, one can use a variable threshold or a set of thresholds, and link edge points that are neighbors along the borders defined over a range of thresholds. Conversely, edge detection can be used in support of object extraction by thresholding; given an above-threshold object, we can check whether its border consists largely of edge points, and reject it as a "noise object" if not.

Edge detection can also be used in a number of other ways as an aid in threshold selection. For example, a good threshold usually yields a simple thresholded picture, i.e., one containing relatively few edges. As another example, points of high edge strength tend to lie on object/background borders; thus if we eliminate such points, the gray level histogram of the remaining points should have a deeper valley between the peaks representing object and background points. Conversely, the gray level histogram of the points having high edge strength should have a single peak representing gray levels between those of objects and background, and its mean or mode should be a good threshold.

Region Growing

In thresholding, the picture is segmented by classifying its points into object and background classes. Another approach to segmentation is to partition the picture into regions, each of which is homogeneous, but such that if any two adjacent parts are merged, the result is no longer homogeneous. Good partitions can be constructed using a combination of merging and splitting processes. This approach is extensively treated in [7.39], which also deals with the use of syntactic methods in object description and recognition. For reviews of shape analysing techniques see [7.40–41].

7.6.4 Representation of Objects and Pictures

Borders

Some shape properties, such as convexity, are easy to determine from the border representation of a given object, while others, such as elongatedness, are not. There are many ways of segmenting a border or curve into parts; some of these are analogous to picture segmentation techniques, with slope playing the role of gray level. For example, the analogs of edges are "corners", i.e., points where the slope changes abruptly, or maxima of the curvature. Inflections, where the curvature changes sign, separate the curve into convex and concave parts. The mean absolute curvature is a useful measure of the curve's complexity, analogous to the mean (absolute) edge value as a texture busyness measure.

Borders can be approximated piecewise linearly, i.e., by polygons (or, analogously, using pieces of higher-order curves) in various ways. Methods of constructing and refining polygonal approximations to a border or curve are discussed in [7.39].

Given a set of successive approximations to a border, these approximations define a tree structure in which each node represents a polygon side, and the sons of a node are its immediate refinements; the sides of the coarsest polygon are the sons of the root node. If desired, we can associate with each polygon side a rectangular strip that just contains the arc; these strips define the zone in which the border might lie.

Skeletons

The "skeleton" or medial axis represents an object as a union of the maximal squares that it contains. Alternative "maximal block" representations can be defined by using maximal rectangles that are restricted in various ways as to shape, size, or position. For example, if we require them to have height 1, they become runs of object points (in which the object meets the rows of the picture); this leads to representation of the object by lists of run lengths.

Another important case is that in which we allow only squares whose sizes and positions are both powers of 2. This leads to object representation by a tree of degree 4 (a "quadtree"), constructed as follows: Let the picture size be 2^k by 2^k. The root node of the tree represents the entire picture. If the picture has all one value, we label the root node with that value and stop. Otherwise, we add four descendants to the root node, representing the four quadrants of the picture. The process is then repeated for each of these new nodes, and so on. In general, the nodes at level h (if any) represent blocks of size 2^{k-h} by 2^{k-h}, in positions whose coordinates are multiples of 2^{k-h}. If a block has constant value, its node is a leaf node; otherwise, its node has four descendants at level $h+1$, corresponding to the four quadrants of the block. The nodes at level k, if any, are all leaf nodes corresponding to single pixels. This representation was introduced by KLINGER [7.42].

When an object is approximated by maximal blocks, we can simplify it by eliminating some of the blocks, e.g., small ones. Another possibility is to use a representation based on blocks whose values are only approximately constant (e.g., have variances less than some threshold). To generalize the medial axis, we consider the set of squares centered at each point, and choose the largest one having below-threshold variance; then the picture is approximated by specifying the maximal squares of this type.

The points of the medial axis tend to lie along a set of arcs and curves. Hence we can represent an object approximately by specifying these curves (e.g., by chain codes) and defining a "radius function" along each curve. This defines a set of "generalized ribbons" whose union is the object.

7.7 Speech Recognition and Understanding

During the past five years, the field of speech recognition has been thriving, so much so that it is a breathtaking experience just trying to keep abreast of the developments. Many researchers have entered this field and have infused it with new ideas. Among the trends and events to be noted in the last half of the 1970s are the further developments in commercially available speech recognition systems, the re-entry of Bell Laboratories into the speech recognition field, the emergence of dynamic programming template matching as the dominant technique for isolated word recognition and its application to restricted continuous speech recognition, and the culmination of the ARPA speech understanding project.

In this section these topics can only be touched on briefly. For other and more complete views of the speech recognition field in the 1970s, the reader is referred to [7.43–50]. The most comprehensive book to emerge from this period is the important collection edited by LEA [7.51]. Also to be noded is the institution, beginning in 1976, of the annual IEEE International Conference on Acoustics, Speech, and Signal Processing. The printed proceedings of these conferences (available from IEEE) are valuable sources of the latest results in all fields of speech processing.

In the area of commercially available speech recognition equipment several trends can be noted. First of all, speech recognition equipment is now less expensive, due primarily to advances in integrated circuit technology. Secondly, recognizers are available with greater capability than previously, in terms of vocabulary size, vocabulary structure, speaker independence, telephone-speech capability, and restricted continuous speech recognition. Finally, not only has the range of capability increased toward the high side, but toward the low side as well. The advent of the home microcomputer system has brought with it inexpensive peripheral equipment for both speech input and output. The Heuristics, Inc., "Speechlab", selling for about $300, is a simple acoustic input interface that comes with suggested programs for isolated word recognition [7.52].

In the realm of more expensive (but generally more accurate and versatile) recognition systems, there are a number of improvements. Threshold Technology, Inc., appears to use basically the same recognition algorithm as previously, but their systems have effective recognition vocabularies up to 220 isolated words and phrases and now sell for as little as $10,000 [7.53]. Interstate Electronics, Inc., took over the Scope Electronics isolated word recognizer system and has produced several types of systems, from a single-board 40-word system selling for $1650 [7.54] to a 900-word structured-vocabulary system for $22,500 [7.55]. The systems described above are speaker-dependent, in that they require each user to "train" the set of word templates to be used for the recognition. Dialog Systems, Inc., offers a system that recognizes limited vocabularies (digits and a few command words) speaker-independently over telephone connections [7.56]. Nippon Electric Company's DP Voice Recognition System, while speaker-dependent, recognizes up to 120 words in isolation or in restricted continuous-speech applications [7.57].

In the area of very limited vocabulary speech recognition, Bell Laboratories marked its re-entry into speech recognition with projects dealing with speaker-dependent and speaker-independent recognition of isolated digits and connected digits [7. 58, 59]. Texas Instruments has also developed speaker-independent connected digit recognition [7.60], and Logicon has demonstrated very limited vocabulary connected word recognition [7.61].

Dynamic programming (DP) template matching was first used as a technique for isolated word matching by VELICHKO and ZAGORUYKO [6.28], and ITAKURA's paper [6.60] was important in bringing it to the attention of Western scientists. DP can be used for comparing two sequences of patterns (such as time sequences of short-time spectra or linear prediction coefficients) by finding a *warping function* that describes the optimum correspondence of the patterns in sequence A to those in sequence B. Since utterances of words are usually different in duration, and since speech rate affects some parts of sounds differently from others, such a *self-aligning* correspondence could be (and is) useful for comparing a parameterized utterance with previous exemplars (templates) [7.62]. DP has been shown to be particularly useful in the matching of polysyllabic words [7.63].

DP was first used in the matching of isolated words to speaker-dependent templates formed from previous single utterances, but the use of multiple templates and the application of clustering techniques to the formation of templates have been effective in speaker-independent word recognition as well [7.64, 65]. Although phonological and coarticulatory changes would at first glance to obviate template-matching techniques for recognition in continuous speech, DP template-matching techniques have been used for word spotting [7.67, 68], word verification [7.69], and limited continuous speech recognition [7.70–73]. It should be noted that the contexts in which template-matching has been applied to continuous speech are restricted; it is still a long way to the recognition of naturally spoken sentences.

DP template matching has been shown to be quite powerful in dealing with the temporal irregularities of pronunciation in isolated words and phrases and in some continuous speech situations. It is, of course, an engineering approach to speech pattern recognition (one that glosses over phonological and coarticulatory effects), not a linguistic one. More linguistically oriented speech recognition work is being done at Sperry Univac [7.51, 74, 75]. Interesting applications of syntactic pattern recognition and fuzzy logic to acoustic-phonetic recognition are being made primarily in Europe [7.76–78].

Probably the largest current effort in speech recognition is taking place at IBM. Their approach uses an acoustic processor followed by a statistical linguistic decoder, with the objective of producing standard orthography from continuous speech [7.79–81].

As noted in the first edition, the ARPA speech understanding project was an important and ambitious attempt to make a large step toward recognition and understanding of naturally spoken utterances. This project reached its planned five-year maturity in 1976, at which point four speech understanding systems were demonstrated [7.82]. One of these systems, HARPY, which was developed at Carnegie-Mellon University, met and exceeded the 1971 goals of the ARPA project (see Section 6.3.1) [7.51, 83–85]. The other three systems, Hearsay-II also from Carnegie-Mellon [6.146, 7.51, 85, 86], HWIM from Bolt Beranek and Newman, Inc. [7.51, 87], and a system from System Development Corporation [7.51, 88] had less good performance results but demonstrated many important advances in large-system speech understanding techniques. SRI International [7.51, 89, 90] also made important contributions. This brief review cannot even begin to describe or compare the ARPA systems. The reader is referred to the references cited above, to reviews of the ARPA project [7.46, 49] and to LEA's book [7.51] which contains perhaps the most comprehensive account of the entire ARPA project.

The example of the ARPA project has spurred other work in speech understanding, primarily outside the United States and primarily with more restricted task domains [7.51, 83–94]. Bell Laboratories has also described a speech understanding system that uses as input sentences composed of isolated words [7.95].

In a simple speech recognizer that always chooses among N alternatives, the vocabulary size gives a first-order description of the difficulty of the recognition task. (The phonetic similarity of the N vocabulary items is another relevant aspect, sometimes as important as the value of N itself.) With the advent of syntax-directed speech recognition systems, where only certain words in the vocabulary are possible at each point in an utterance, the value of N is no longer an adequate measure, being more relevant to the size of memory than to task difficulty. Only recently has attention been focused on the problem of characterizing the difficulty of a recognition task [7.96–98]. Until we have better measures of task difficulty, comparison of the results of different systems on different tasks (as in the ARPA project) will be impossible.

The continuing growth of the field of speech recognition is but one aspect of the recent spurt of activity in all fields of speech processing. Interesting advances have been made in the past five years in isolated word recognition, in the application of new techniques to speech recognition, and in multi-knowledge-source speech understanding systems. Fundamental problems remain, as noted in Section 6.4, but the future is still bright.

References

7.1 K.S.FU: "Recent Advances in Syntactic Pattern Recognition", Proc. Fourth International Joint Conference on Pattern Recognition, Nov. 7–10, 1978, Kyoto, Japan

7.2 K.S.FU (ed.): *Syntactic Pattern Recognition Applications* (Springer, Berlin, Heidelberg, New York 1977)

7.3 W.S.BRAINERD: Tree Generating Regular Systems. Information and Control **14**, 217–231 (1969)

7.4 J.E.DONER: Tree Acceptors and Some of Their Applications. J. Comput. System Sci. 4 (1970)

7.5 K.S.FU, B.K.BHARGAVA: Tree Systems for Syntactic Pattern Recognition. IEEE Trans. Computers C-**22**, 1087–1099 (1973)

7.6 J.W.THATCHER, J.B.WRIGHT: Generalized Finite Automata Theory with an Application to a Decision Problem of Second Order Logic. J. Math. System Theory **2** (1969)

7.7 K.S.FU: "Tree Languages and Syntactic Pattern Recognition." In: *Pattern Recognition and Artificial Intelligence*, ed. by C.H.CHEN (Academic Press, New York 1976)

7.8 J.M.BRAYER, K.S.FU: "A Note on the *k*-tail Method of Tree Grammar Interference." IEEE Trans. on Systems, Man, and Cybernetics SMC-**7**, 293–299 (1977)

7.9 K.S.FU: *Syntactic Methods in Pattern Recognition* (Academic Press, New York 1974)

7.10 R.DeMORI, P.LAFACE, M.SARDELLA: "Use of Fuzzy Algorithms for Phonetic and Phonemic Labelling of Continuous Speech", Instituto di Scienze dell'Informazione, Universita di Torino, Italy

7.11 A.K.JOSHI: "Remarks on Some Aspects of Language Structure and Their Relevance to Pattern Analysis." *Pattern Recognition*, Vol. 5, No. 4, 1973

7.12 B.K.BHARGAVA, K.S.FU: "Transformation and Inference of Tree Grammars for Syntactic Patterns Recognition", Proc. 1974 IEEE International Conference on Cybernetics and Society, October, Dallas, Texas

7.13 T.PAVLIDIS: "Syntactic Pattern Recognition on the Basis of Functional Approximation." In: *Pattern Recognition and Artificial Intelligence*, ed. by C.H.CHEN (Academic Press, New York 1976)

7.14 S.Y.LU, K.S.FU: "Stochastic Error-Correcting Syntax Analysis and Recognition of Noisy Patterns." IEEE Trans. Computers C-**26**, 1268–1276 (1977)

7.15 L.W.FUNG, K.S.FU: "Stochastic Syntactic Decoding for Pattern Classification." IEEE Trans. Computers C-**24** (1975)

7.16 M.G.THOMASON, R.C.GONZALEZ: "Error Detection and Classification in Syntactic Pattern Structures." IEEE Trans. Computers C-**24** (1975)

7.17 K.S.FU: "Error-Correcting Parsing for Syntactic Pattern Recognition." In: *Data Structure, Computer Graphics, and Pattern Recognition*, ed. by A.KLINGER et al. (Academic Press, New York 1977)

7.18 S.Y.LU, K.S.FU: "Error-Correcting Tree Automata for Syntactic Pattern Recognition." IEEE Trans. Computers C-**27** (1978)

7.19 A.V.AHO, T.G.PETERSON: "A Minimum Distance Error-Correcting Parser for Context-Free Languages." SIAM J. Computing 4 (1972)

7.20 V.I. LEVENSHTEIN: "Binary Codes Capable of Correcting Deletions, Insertions, and Reversals." Sov. Phys. Dokl. **10** (1966)

7.21 E. PERSOON, K.S. FU: "Sequential Classification of Strings Generated by SCFG's." *International Journal of Computers and Information Sciences*, Vol. **4**, Sept. 1975

7.22 S. Y. LU, K.S. FU: "Structure-Preserved Error-Correcting Tree Automata for Syntactic Pattern Recognition." Proc. 1976 IEEE Conference on Decision and Control, Dec. 1–3, Clearwater, Florida

7.23 N.S. CHANG, K.S. FU: "Parallel Parsing of Tree Languages." Proc. 1978 IEEE Computer Society Conference on Pattern Recognition and Image Processing, May 31-June 2, Chicago, Ill.

7.24 S. Y. LU, K.S. FU: "A Sentence-to-Sentence Clustering Procedure for Pattern Analysis." *IEEE Trans. on Systems, Man, and Cybernetics*, Vol. SM-8, No. 5, May 1978

7.25 K.S. FU, S. Y. LU: "A Clustering Procedure for Syntactic Patterns." *IEEE Trans. on Systems, Man, and Cybernetics*, Vol. SMC-7, No. 10, Oct. 1977, pp. 734–742

7.26 R.O. DUDA, P.E. HART: *Pattern Classification and Scene Analysis* (Wiley, New York 1972)

7.27 R.C. GONZALES, P.A. WINTZ: *Digital Image Processing* (Addison-Wesley, Reading, MA 1977)

7.28 W.K. PRATT: *Digital Image Processing* (Wiley, New York 1978)

7.29 A. Rosenfeld: Picture processing: 1974, *Computer Graphics Image Processing* **4**, 133–155 (1975)

7.30 A. ROSENFELD: Picture processing: 1975. Computer Graphics Image Processing **5**, 215–237 (1976)

7.31 A. ROSENFELD: Picture processing: 1976. Computer Graphics Image Processing **6**, 157–183 (1977)

7.32 A. ROSENFELD: Picture processing: 1977: Computer Graphics Image Processing **7**, 211–242 (1978)

7.33 A. ROSENFELD: Picture processing: 1978. Computer Graphics Image Processing **9**, 354–393 (1979)

7.34 R.M. HARALICK: Statistical and structural approaches to texture. Proc. IEEE **67**, 786–804 (1979)

7.35 A. ROSENFELD: Iterative methods in image analysis, Pattern Recognition **10**, 181–187 (1978)

7.36 L.S. DAVIS: A survey of edge detection techniques. Computer Graphics Image Processing **4**, 248–270 (1975)

7.37 S.D. SHAPIRO: Feature space transforms for curve detection. Pattern Recognition **10**, 129–143 (1978)

7.38 J.S. WESZKA: A survey of threshold selection techniques. Computer Graphics Image Processing **7**, 259–265 (1978)

7.39 T. PAVLIDIS: *Structural Pattern Recognition* (Springer, Berlin, Heidelberg, New York 1977)

7.40 T. PAVLIDIS: A review of algorithms for shape analysis. Computer Graphics Image Processing **7**, 243–258 (1978)

7.41 T. PAVLIDIS: Algorithms for shape analysis of contours and waveforms, Proc. 4th Intl. Conf. on Pattern Recognition, 1978, pp. 70–85

7.42 A. KLINGER: Data structures and pattern recognition, Proc. 1st Intl. Conf. on Pattern Recognition, 1973, pp. 497–498

7.43 G. WHITE: Computer **9**, No. 5, 40 (1976); also in [6]

7.44 T.B. Martin: Proc. IEEE **64**, 487 (1976); also in [6]

7.45 D.R. Reddy: Proc. IEEE **64**, 501 (1976); also in [6]

7.46 D.H. KLATT: J. Acoust. Soc. Am. **62**, 1345 (1977); also in [6]

7.47 R. DeMori: "Recent Advances in Automatic Speech Recognition," Proc. 4th Int. Conf. Pattern Recognition, Kyoto (1978)

7.48 N.R. DIXON, T.B. MARTIN (ed.): *Automatic Speech and Speaker Recognition* (IEEE Press, New York 1979)

7.49 W.A. LEA, J.E. SHOUP: "Review of the ARPA SUR Project and Survey of Current Technology in Speech Understanding", Final Report, Office of Naval Research, Contract No. N00014-77-C-0570, Speech Communication Research Laboratory, Los Angeles, CA (1979)

7.50 M. FERRETTI: Le Nouvel Automatisme **24**, No. 9, 39 (1979)

7.51 W.A. LEA (ed.): *Trends in Speech Recognition* (Prentice-Hall, Englewood Cliffs, NJ 1980)

7.52 H. ENEA, J. REYKJALIN: Proceedings Voice Technology for Interactive Real-Time Command/Control Systems Application, NASA-Ames Research Center, Moffett Field, CA (1977) p. 285

7.53 Technical data, Threshold 500 Voice Data Entry Terminal, Threshold Technology, Delran, NJ

7.54 Technical data, Voice Recognition Module, Interstate Electronics Corp., Anaheim, CA

7.55 Technical data, Voice Data Entry System, Interstate Electronics Corp., Anaheim, CA

7.56 S.L. MOSHIER: Speech Communication Papers Presented at the 97th Meeting of the Acoustical Society of America, Cambridge, MA (1979) p. 551

7.57 Technical data, DP Voice Recognition System, NEC America, Inc., Falls Church, VA

7.58 M.R.SAMBUR, L.R.RABINER: Bell Sys. Tech. J. **54**, 81 (1975); also in [6]

7.59 M.R.SAMBUR, L.R.RABINER: IEEE Trans. Acoust., Speech, Signal Processing ASSP-**24**, 550 (1976)

7.60 G.R.DODDINGTON, R.E.HELMS, B.M.HYDRICK: "Speaker Verification III", Texas Instruments Inc., Dallas, TX, Report RADC-TR-UI-713804-F (1976)

7.61 J.E.PORTER: "LISTEN: A System for Recognizing Connected Speech Over Small, Fixed Vocabularies, in Real Time", Logicon, Inc., San Diego, CA, Report NAVTRAEQUIPCEN 77-C-0096-1 (1978)

7.62 H.SAKOE, S.CHIBA: IEEE Trans. Acoust., Speech, Signal Processing ASSP-**26**, 43 (1978); also in [6]

7.63 G.M.WHITE, R.B.NEELY: IEEE Trans. Acoust., Speech, Signal Processing ASSP-**24**, 183 (1976); also in [6]

7.64 L.R.RABINER: IEEE Trans. Acoust., Speech, Signal Processing ASSP-**26**, 34 (1978)

7.65 L.R.RABINER, A.E.ROSENBERG, S.E.LEVINSON: IEEE Trans. Acoust., Speech, Signal Processing ASSP-**26**, 575 (1978)

7.66 L.R.RABINER, S.E.LEVINSON, A.E.ROSENBERG, J.G.WILPON: IEEE Trans. Acoust., Speech, Signal Processing ASSP-**27**, 336 (1979)

7.67 J.S.BRIDLE, M.D.BROWN: "An Experimental Automatic Word Recognition System", JSRU Research Report 1003, Joint Speech Research Unit, Great Britain (1974)

7.68 R.W.CHRISTIANSEN, C.K.RUSHWORTH: IEEE Trans. Acoust., Speech, Signal Processing ASSP-**25**, 361 (1977); also in [6]

7.69 C.COOK: Record 1976 IEEE Int. Conf. Acoust., Speech, Signal Processing, Philadelphia, PA (1976) p. 553; also in [6]

7.70 H.SAKOE: "Automatic continuous speech recognition system employing Dynamic Programming", U.S. Patent No. 4,059,725 (1976)

7.71 H.SAKOE: IEEE Trans. Acoust., Speech, Signal Processing, ASSP-**27**, 588 (1979)

7.72 J.S.BRIDLE, M.D.BROWN: "Connected Word Recognition Using Whole Word Templates", Proc. Institute of Acoustics Autumn Conf. (1979)

7.73 S.E.LEVINSON, A.E.ROSENBERG: Record 1979 IEEE Int. Conf. Acoust., Speech Signal Processing, Washington, D.C. (1979) p. 239

7.74 M.F.MEDRESS, T.E.SKINNER, D.R.KLOKER, T.C.DILLER, W.A.LEA: Record 1977 IEEE Int. Conf. Acoust. Speech, Signal Processing, Hartford, CT (1977) p. 468

7.75 M.F.MEDRESS, M.A.DERR, T.C.DILLER, D.R.KLOKER, L.L.LUTTON, H.N.OREDSON, J.F.SIEBENAND,T.E.SKINNER: Record 1979 IEEE Int. Conf. Acoust., Speech, Signal Processing, Washington, D.C. (1979) p. 599

7.76 M.BAUDRY, B.DUPEYRAT: Record 1979 IEEE Int. Conf., Acoust., Speech, Signal Processing, Washington, D.C. (1979) p. 101

7.77 R.DEMORI: In *Syntactic Pattern Recognition, Applications*, ed. by K.S.FU (Springer, Berlin, Heidelberg, New York 1977)

7.78 R.DEMORI, P.LAFACE: IEEE Trans. Pattern Analysis and Machine Intelligence PAMI-**2**, 136 (1980)

7.79 F.JELINEK: Proc. IEEE **54**, 532 (1976)

7.80 N.R.DIXON, H.F.SILVERMAN: IEEE Trans. Acoust., Speech, Signal Processing ASSP-**25**, 367 (1977)

7.81 L.R.BAHL, R.BAKIS, P.S.COHEN, A.G.COLE, F.JELINEK, B.L.LEWIS, R.L.MERCER: Record 1979 IEEE Int. Conf. Acoust., Speech, Signal Processing, Washington, D.C. (1979) p. 249

7.82 M.F.MEDRESS, F.S.COOPER, J.W.FORGIE, C.C.GREEN, D.H.KLATT, M.H.O'MALLEY, E.P.NEUBURG, A.NEWELL, D.R.REDDY, B.RITEA, J.E.SHOUP-HUMMEL, D.E.WALKER, W.A.WOODS: "Speech Understanding Systems: Report of a Study Committee", SIGART Newsletter, No. 62, 4 (1977)

7.83 B.T.LOWERRE: "The Harpy Speech Recognition System", Ph. D. dissertation, Carnegie-Mellon Univ., Pittsburgh, PA (1976)

7.84 B.T.LOWERRE: Record 1977 IEEE Int. Conf. Acoust., Speech, Signal Processing, Hartford, CT (1977) p. 788; also in [6]

7.85 CMU Computer Science Speech Group: "Speech Understanding Systems: Summary of Results of the Five-Year Research Effort at Carnegie-Mellon University", Technical Report, Carnegie-Mellon Univ., Pittsburgh, PA (1977)

7.86 L.D.ERMAN, F.HAYES-ROTH, V.R.LESSER, D.R.REDDY: "The Hearsay-II Speech Understanding System: Integrating Knowledge to Resolve Uncertainty", Computing Surveys (in press)

7.87 W.WOODS, M.BATES, G.BROWN, B.BRUCE, C.COOK, J.KLOVSTAD, J.MAKHOUL, B.NASH-WEBBER, R.SCHWARTZ, J.WOLF, V.ZUE: "Speech Understanding Systems: Final Technical Progress Report", Bolt Beranek and Newman Inc., Cambridge, MA, Report 3438 (in 5 volumes) (1976)

7.88 M.I.BERNSTEIN: "Interactive Systems Research: Final Report to the Director, Advanced Research Projects Agency", System Development Corporation, Santa Monica, CA, Report TM-5243/006/00 (1976)

7.89 D.E.WALKER (ed.): "Speech Understanding Research: Final Technical Report", Stanford Research Institute, Menlo Park, CA (1976)

7.90 D.E.WALKER (ed.): *Understanding Spoken Language* (Elsevier North-Holland, New York 1978)

7.91 S.I.NAKAGAWA: "A Machine Understanding System for Spoken Japanese Sentences", Ph. D. dissertation, Kyoto University, Kyoto (1976)

7.92 Y.NIIMI, Y.KOBAYASHI: Record 1978 IEEE Int. Conf. Acoust., Speech, Signal Processing, Tulsa, OK (1978) p. 425

7.93 J.J.MARIANI, J.S.LIENARD: "ESOPE 0: un programme de compréhension automatique de la parole procédant par prédiction-vérification aux niveaux phonétique, lexical, et syntaxique", Congrès AFCET/IRIA Reconnaissance des Formes et Traitment des Images, Paris (1978)

7.94 R.DeMORI, S.RIVOIRA, A.SERRA: Proc. 4th Int. Joint Conf. Artificial Intelligence, Tbilisi (1975) p. 468

7.95 S.E.LEVINSON, K.L.SHIPLEY: Bell Sys. Tech. J. **59**, 119 (1980)

7.96 R.G.GOODMAN: "Analysis of Languages for Man-Machine Voice Communication", Ph. D. dissertation, Stanford University, Stanford, CA (1976); also Technical Report, Carnegie-Mellon Univ., Pittsburgh, PA (1976)

7.97 M.M.SONDHI, S.E.LEVINSON: Record 1978 IEEE Int. Conf. on Acoust., Speech, Signal Processing, Tulsa, OK (1978) p. 409

7.98 F.JELINEK, R.L.MERCER, L.R.BAHL, J.K.BAKER: J. Acoust. Soc. Am **62**, Suppl. 1, S63 (Abstract) (1977)

Subject Index

T. Kohonen

Content-Adressable Memories

1980. 123 figures, 36 tables. XI, 368 pages
(Springer Series in Information Sciences, Volume 1)
ISBN 3-540-09823-2

Contents:
Associative Memory, Content Addressing, and Associative Recall. –
Content Adressing by Software. – Logic Principles of Content-
Addressable Memories. – CAM Hardware. – The CAM as a System
Part. – Content-Addressable Processors. – References. – Subject
Index.

T. Pavlidis

Structural Pattern Recognition

1977. 173 figures, 13 tables. XII, 302 pages
(Springer Series in Electrophysics, Volume 1)
ISBN 3-540-08463-0

Contents:
Mathematical Techniques for Curve Fitting. – Graphs and Grids. –
Fundamentals of Picture Segmentation. – Advanced Segmentation
Techniques. – Scene Analysis. – Analytical Description of Region
Boundaries. – Syntactic Analysis of Region Boundaries and Other
Curves. – Shape Description by Region Analysis. – Classification,
Description and Syntactic Analysis.

Syntactic Pattern Recognition, Applications

Editor: K. S. Fu
1977. 135 figures, 19 tables. XI, 270 pages
(Communication and Cybernetics, Volume 14)
ISBN 3-540-07841-X

Contents:
K. S. Fu: Introduction to Syntactic Pattern Recognition. –
S. L. Horowitz: Peak Recognition in Waveforms. – *J. E. Albus:* Electro-
cardiogram Interpretation Using a Stochastic Finite State Model. –
R. DeMori: Syntactic Recognition of Speech Patterns. – *W. W. Stallings:*
Chinese Character Recognition. – *Th. Pavlidis, H.-Y. F. Feng:* Shape
Discrimination. – *R. H. Anderson:* Two-Dimensional Mathematical
Notation. – *B. Moayer, K. S. Fu:* Fingerprint Classification. –
J. M. Brayer, P. H. Swain, K. S. Fu: Modeling of Earth Resources Satel-
ite Data. – *T. Vámos:* Industrial Objects and Machine Parts Recogni-
tion.

Picture Processing and Digital Filtering

Editor: T. S. Huang
2nd corrected and updated edition.
1979. 113 figures, 7 tables, XIII, 297 pages
(Topics in Applied Physics, Volume 6)
ISBN 3-540-09339-7

Contents:
T. S. Huang: Introduction. – *H. C. Andrews:* Two-Dimensional Trans-
forms. – *J. G. Fiasconaro:* Two-Dimensional Nonrecursive Filters. –
R. R. Read, J. L. Shanks, S. Treitel: Two-Dimensional Recursive Filter-
ing. – *B. R. Frieden:* Image Enhancement and Restoration. –
F. C. Billingsley: Noise Considerations in Digital Image Processing
Hardware. – *T. S. Huang:* Recent Advances in Picture Processing and
Digital Filtering. – Subject Index.

Springer-Verlag
Berlin
Heidelberg
New York

Digital Picture Analysis

Editor: A. Rosenfeld
1976. 114 figures, 47 tables. XIII, 351 pages
(Topics in Applied Physics, Volume 11)
ISBN 3-540-07579-8

Contents:
A. Rosenfeld: Introduction. – *R. M. Haralick:* Automatic Remote Sensor Image Processing. – *C. A. Harlow, S. J. Dwyer III, G. Lodwick:* On Radiographic Image Analysis. – *R. L. McIlwain, Jr.:* Image Processing in High Energy Physics. – *K. Preston, Jr.:* Digital Picture Analysis in Cytology. – *J. R. Ullmann:* Picture Analysis in Character Recognition.

Image Reconstruction from Projections

Implementation and Applications
Editor: G. T. Herman
1979. 120 figures, 10 tables. XII, 284 pages
(Topics in Applied Physics, Volume 32)
ISBN 3-540-09417-2

Contents:
G. T. Herman, R. M. Lewitt: Overview of Image Reconstruction from Projections. – *S. W. Roland:* Computer Implementation of Image Reconstruction Formulas. – *R. N. Bracewell:* Image Reconstruction in Radio Astronomy. – *M. D. Altschuler:* Reconstruction of the Global-Scale Three-Dimensional Solar Corona. – *T. F. Budinger, G. T. Gullberg, R. H. Huesman:* Emission Computed Tomography. – *E. H. Wood, J. H. Kinsey, R. A. Robb, B. K. Gilbert, L. D. Harris E. L. Ritman:* Applications of High Temporal Resolution Computerized Tomography to Physiology and Medicine.

The Computer in Optical Research

Methods and Applications
Editor: B. R. Frieden
1980. 92 figures, 13 tables. Approx. 400 pages
(Topics in Applied Physics, Volume 41)
ISBN 3-540-10119-5

Contents:
B. R. Frieden: Introduction. – *R. Barakat:* The Calculation of Integrals Encountered in Optical Diffraction Theory. – *B. R. Frieden:* Computational Methods of Probability and Statistics. – *A. K. Rigler, J. R. Pegis:* Optimization Methods in Optics. – *L. Mertz:* Computers and Optical Astronomy. – *W. J. Dallas:* Computer-Generated Holograms.

Computer Processing of Electron Microscope Images

Editor: P. W. Hawkes
1980. 116 figures, 2 tables. XIV, 296 pages
(Topics in Current Physics, Volume 13)
ISBN 3-540-09622-1

Contents:
P. W. Hawkes: Image Processing Based on the Linear Theory of Image Formation. – *W. O. Saxton:* Recovery of Specimen Information for Strongly Scattering Objects. – *J. E. Mellema:* Computer Reconstruction of Regular Biological Objects. – *W. Hoppe, R. Hegerl:* Three-Dimensional Structure Determination by Electron Microscopy (Nonperiodic Specimens). – *J. Frank:* The Role of Correlation Techniques in Computer Image Processing. – *R. H. Wade:* Holographic Methods in Electron Microscopy. – *M. Isaacson, M. Utlaut, D. Kopf:* Analog Computer Processing of Scanning Transmission Electron Microscope Images.

Springer-Verlag
Berlin
Heidelberg
New York